Technician Unit 10

MANAGING SYSTEMS AND PEOPLE

For assessments in 2004
and 2005

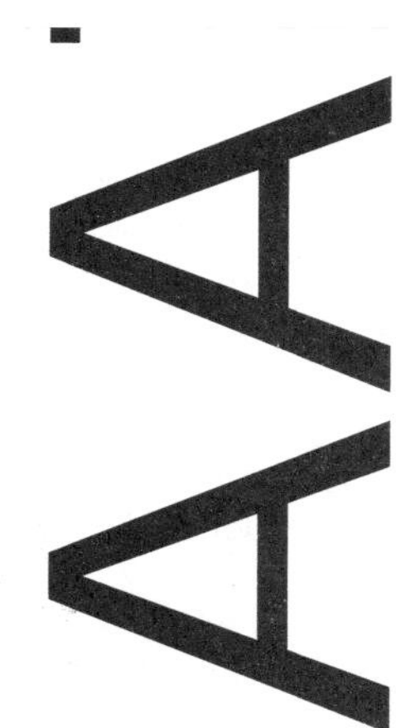

Combined Text and Kit

In this May 2004 edition

- For assessments under the AAT standards of competence
- Numerous practice activities to reinforce learning
- Layout designed to be easy on the eye – and easy to use
- Clear language and presentation
- Detailed project guidance
- The AAT's Sample Simulation
- Updated for the assessor's guidance on report preparation discussed at the 2004 AAT conference

FOR 2004 AND 2005 ASSESSMENTS

First edition June 2003
Second edition May 2004

ISBN 0 7517 1601 4 (previous edition 0 7517 1132 2)

British Library Cataloguing-in-Publication Data
A catalogue record for this book
is available from the British Library

Published by

BPP Professional Education
Aldine House, Aldine Place
London W12 8AW

www.bpp.com

Printed in Great Britain by WM Print
Frederick Street
Walsall
West Midlands
WS2 9NE

All our rights reserved. No part of this publication may be reproduced, stored in a retrieval system or transmitted, in any form or by any means, electronic, mechanical, photocopying, recording or otherwise, without the prior written permission of BPP Professional Education.

We are grateful to the Lead Body for Accounting for permission to reproduce extracts from the Standards of Competence for Accounting, and to the AAT for permission to reproduce extracts from the mapping and Guidance Notes.

©
BPP Professional Education
2004

Contents

Introduction

Introduction

How to use this Combined Interactive Text and Kit

Aims of this Combined Interactive Text and Kit

To provide the knowledge and practice to help you succeed in the assessment for Technician Unit 10 *Managing Systems and People in the Accounting Environment.*

To pass the assessments successfully you need a thorough understanding in all areas covered by the standards of competence.

To tie in with the other components of the BPP Effective Study Package to ensure you have the best possible chance of success.

Combined Interactive Text and Assessment Kit

- Parts A, B and C cover the Knowledge and Understanding and the practice activities for the skills based assessment for Unit 10 *Managing Systems and People in the Accounting Environment.* Numerous activities throughout the text help you practise what you have just learnt. Answers to Activities are in Part D.
- Part E covers the mechanics of doing the project and in writing the report. Part F contains the AAT's sample simulation.

Recommended approach to this Combined Text & Kit

This Unit is unusual in that it is assessed by a written project. This is more than just a portfolio of evidence but involves some research, analysis, conclusions and recommendations. You must write no more than 4,000 words; this might seem daunting but it should be possible.

(a) To achieve competence in Unit 10 (and all the other units), you need to be able to do **everything** specified by the standards. Study parts A to C very carefully and do not skip any of it.

(b) Learning is an **active** process. Do **all** the activities as you work through the chapters so you can be sure you really understand what you have read. There is a checklist at the end of each chapter to show which activities relate to which performance criteria. Answers to all activities are in Part D.

(c) After you have covered the learning and practice material in parts A, B and C, look at the project guidance in Part E.

(d) Should you read the **simulation material**? Doing the project by simulation should only be a last resort. It is useful reading, however, that might give you an idea as to the type of issues AAT is interested in.

This approach is only a suggestion. Your college may well adapt it to suit your needs.

Outline: what you must do

Details of what AAT requires are outlined in the introduction.

- You must do a report based on your workplace. A voluntary work assignment will do, if you are not in employment. The AAT's simulation is a last resort.
- The report must cover as many of the performance criteria as possible. Gaps that you have not covered in the report will be assessed by **documented questions** with an assessor.
- The report must be your own work. This does not stop you chatting through some of your ideas.

Quick quizzes

These include questions in formats not used by the AAT. However, these types of questions are usually very familiar to students and are used to help students adjust to otherwise unfamiliar material.

Technician qualification structure

The competence-based Education and Training Scheme of the Association of Accounting Technicians is based on an analysis of the work of accounting staff in a wide range of industries and types of organisation. The Standards of Competence for Accounting which students are expected to meet are based on this analysis.

The AAT issued new standards of competence in 2002, which take effect from 1 July 2003. This Combined Text & Kit reflects the **new standards.**

The Standards identify the key purpose of the accounting occupation, which is to operate, maintain and improve systems to record, plan, monitor and report on the financial activities of an organisation, and a number of key roles of the occupation. Each key role is subdivided into units of competence, which are further divided into elements of competences. By successfully completing assessments in specified units of competence, students can gain qualifications at NVQ/SVQ levels 2, 3 and 4, which correspond to the AAT Foundation, Intermediate and Technician stages of competence respectively.

Whether you are competent in a Unit is demonstrated by means of:

- *Either* an Exam Based Assessment (set and marked by AAT assessors)
- *Or* a Skills Based Assessment (where competence is judged by an Approved Assessment Centre to whom responsibility for this is devolved)
- Or *both* Exam *and* Skills Based Assessment

Below we set out the overall structure of the Technician stage, indicating how competence in each Unit is assessed. In the next section there is more detail about the Skills Based Assessment for Unit 10.

Accounting N/SVQ Level 4

Group 1 Core Units – All units are mandatory

Unit 8	**Contributing to the Management of Performance and the Enhancement of Value**	Element 8.1	Collect, analyse and disseminate information about costs
		Element 8.2	Make recommendations and make recommendations to enhance value
Unit 9	**Contributing to the Planning and Control of Resources**	Element 9.1	Prepare forecasts of income and expenditure
		Element 9.2	Product draft budget proposals
		Element 9.3	Monitor the performance of responsibility centres against budgets
Unit 10	**Managing Systems and People in the Accounting Environment**	Element 10.1	Manage people within the accounting environment
		Element 10.2	Identify opportunities for improving the effectiveness of an accounting systems
Unit 22	**Contribute to the Maintenance of a Healthy, Safe and Productive Working Environment**	Element 22.1	Contribute to the maintenance of a healthy, safe and productive working environment
		Element 22.2	Monitor and maintain an effective and efficient working environment

Level 4, continued

Group 2 Optional Units – Choose **one** of the following **four** units

Unit 11 Drafting Financial Statements (Accounting Practice, Industry and Commerce)	Element 11.1 Draft limited company financial statements Element 11.2 Interpret limited company financial statements
Unit 12 Drafting Financial Statements (Central Government)	Element 12.1 Draft Central Government financial statements Element 12.2 Interpret Central Government financial statements
Unit 13 Drafting Financial Statements (Local Government)	Element 13.1 Draft Local Authority financial statements Element 13.2 Interpret Local Authority financial statements
Unit 14 Contribute to the Maintenance of a Healthy, Safe and Productive Working Environment	Element 14.1 Draft NHS accounting statements and returns Element 14.2 Interpret NHS accounting statements and returns

Group 3 Optional Units – Choose **two** of the following **four** units

Unit 15 Operating a Cash Management and Credit Control System	Element 15.1 Monitor and control cash receipts and payments Element 15.2 Manage cash balances Element 15.3 Grant credit Element 15.4 Monitor and control the collection of debts
Unit 17 Implementing Auditing Procedures	Element 17.1 Contribute to the planning of an audit assignment Element 17.2 Contribute to the conduct of an audit assignment Element 17.3 Prepare related draft reports
Unit 18 Preparing Business Taxation Computations	Element 18.1 Prepare capital allowances computations Element 18.2 Compute assessable business income Element 18.3 Prepare capital gains computations Element 18.4 Prepare corporation tax computations
Unit 19 Preparing personal tax computations	Element 19.1 Calculate income from employment Element 19.2 Calculate property and investment income Element 19.3 Prepare income tax computations Element 19.4 Prepare capital gains tax computations

Unit 10 Standards of competence

The structure of the Standards for Unit 10

The Unit commences with a statement of the **knowledge and understanding** which underpin competence in the Unit's elements.

The Unit of Competence is then divided into **elements of competence** describing activities which the individual should be able to perform.

Each element includes:

(a) A set of **performance criteria.** This defines what constitutes competent performance.

(b) A **range statement.** This defines the situations, contexts, methods etc in which competence should be displayed.

(c) **Evidence requirements.** These state that competence must be demonstrated consistently, over an appropriate time scale with evidence of performance being provided from the appropriate sources.

(d) **Sources of evidence.** In Unit 10, evidence requirements are closely linked to the assessment strategy. You are required to write a 4,000 word report based on an accounting system.

The elements of competence for Unit 10 *Managing Systems and People in the Accounting Environment* are set out below. Knowledge and understanding required for the unit as a whole are listed first, followed by the performance criteria and range statements for each element. Knowledge and understanding and performance criteria are cross-referenced below to chapters in this Unit 10 *Managing Systems and People in the Accounting Environment* Combined Text and Kit.

Unit 10 Managing Systems and People in the Accounting Environment

Unit Commentary

This unit is about your role as a manager in the accounting environment, whether you are a line manager or are managing a particular function or project.

The first element requires you to show that you co-ordinate work activities effectively within the accounting environment. This includes setting realistic objectives, targets and deadlines and managing people in such a way that these can be met. You also need to show that you prepare contingency plans to cover a variety of problems that can reduce the likelihood of meeting objectives, targets and deadlines.

The second element is about identifying weaknesses in an accounting system and making recommendations to rectify these. This requires you to make recommendations to rectify weaknesses and consider the impact that these would have on the organisation; to update the system to comply, for example, with legislative changes, and to subsequently check that the post-change output is now correct.

Elements contained within this unit are:

Element 10.1 Manage people within the accounting environment

Element 10.2 Identify opportunities to improve the effectiveness of an accounting system

Knowledge and understanding

Performance criteria		Chapters in this Text
To perform this unit effectively you will need to know and understand:		
The business environment		
1	The range of external regulations affecting accounting practice (Element 10.2)	2
2	Common types of fraud (Element 10.2)	9
3	The implications of fraud (Element 10.2)	9
Management Techniques		
4	Methods for scheduling and planning work (Element 10.1)	5, 6
5	Techniques for managing your own time effectively (Element 10.1)	6
6	Methods of measuring cost-effectiveness (Element 10.2)	10
7	Methods of detecting fraud within accounting systems (Element 10.2)	9
8	Techniques for influencing and negotiating with decision-makers and controllers of resources (Element 10.1)	5
Management Principles and Theory		
9	Principles of supervision and delegation (Element 10.1)	3, 6
10	Principles of fostering effective working relationships, building teams and motivating staff (Element 10.1)	3, 4
The Organisation		
11	How the accounting systems of an organisation are affected by its organisational structure, its Management Information Systems, its administrative systems and procedures and the nature of its business transactions (Elements 10.1 & 10.2)	12, 8
12	The overview of the organisation's business and its critical external relationships (customers/clients, suppliers, etc.) (Elements 10.1 & 10.2)	1
13	The purpose, structure and organisation of the accounting function and its relationships with other functions within the organisation (Element 10.2)	2
14	Who controls the supply of resources (equipment, materials, information and people) within the organisation (Element 10.1)	2, 5

BPP note

The Knowledge and Understanding for this Unit are comprehensively covered in Parts A, B and C of this Text.

Element 10.1 Managing people in the accounting environment

Performance criteria		**Chapters in this Text**
In order to perform this element successfully you need to:		
10.1.A	Plan work activities to make the optimum use of resources and to ensure that work is completed within agreed timescales	5, 6
10.1.B	Review the competence of individuals undertaking work activities and arrange the necessary training	3, 4
10.1.C	Prepare, in collaboration with management, **contingency plans** to meet possible emergencies	7
10.1.D	Communicate work methods and schedules to colleagues in ways that help them to understand what is expected of them	3, 5, 6
10.1.E	Monitor work activities sufficiently closely to ensure that quality standards are being met	8
10.1.F	Co-ordinate work activities effectively and in accordance with work plans and contingency plans	2, 5, 6
10.1.G	Encourage colleagues to report to you promptly any problems and queries that are beyond their authority or expertise to resolve, and resolve these where they are within your authority and expertise	1, 2, 3, 6, 7
10.1.H	Refer problems and queries to the appropriate person where resolution is beyond your authority or expertise	1, 2, 3, 6, 7

Range statement

Performance in this element relates to the following contexts:

Contingency plans allowing for:

- Fully functioning computer system not being available
- Staff absence
- Changes in work patterns and demands

Element 10.2 Identify opportunities to improve the effectiveness of an accounting system

Performance criteria		**Chapters in this Text**
In order to perform this element successfully you need to:		
10.2.A	Identify **weaknesses** and potential for improvements to the accounting system and consider their impact on the operation of the organisation	8, 9, 10
10.2.B	Identify potential areas of fraud arising from control avoidance within the accounting system and grade the risk	9
10.2.C	Review methods of operating regularly in respect of their cost-effectiveness, reliability and speed	10
10.2.D	Make **recommendations** to the appropriate person in a clear, easily understood format	8, 9, 10
10.2.E	Ensure **recommendations** are supported by a clear rationale which includes an explanation of any assumption made	8, 9, 10
10.2.F	Update the system in accordance with **changes** that affect the way the system should operate and check that your update is producing the required results	8, 9

Range statement

Performance in this element relates to the following contexts:

Weaknesses:

- Potential for errors
- Exposure to possible fraud

Accounting system:

- Manual
- Computerised

Recommendations:

- Oral
- Written

Changes affecting systems:

- External regulations
- Organisational policies and procedures

Assessment strategy

This unit is assessed by means of a **project plus assessor questioning** and **employer testimony**.

The project takes the form of a report to management that analyses the management accounting system and the skills of the people working within it. It should identify how both might be enhanced to improve their effectiveness. In producing this report students will need to prove competence in the co-ordination of work activities and the identification and trading of fraud in that system. Students may be able to identify weaknesses and make recommendations for improvement. All changes made must be monitored and reviewed for their effectiveness.

The total length of the project (excluding appendices) should not exceed 4,000 words. An appropriate manager should attest to the originality, authenticity and quality of the project report. The project should be based on an actual management accounting style, or part-system, within the student's workplace in the present or recent past. For students not in relevant employment, an unpaid placement such as a voluntary organisation or charity, club or society or a college department may be suitable. Alternatively (if no work placement is available/the student is not in employment) an AAT simulation in the form of a case study should be used as the basis of the project.

The Approved Assessment Centre's role

The AAC should undertake the following steps:

- make an initial assessment of the project idea
- use one-to-one sessions to advise and support the student
- encourage workplace mentors to participate (testimony etc)
- ensure the project is the student's original work
- use formative assessments and action plans to guide the student
- undertake summative assessment against performance criteria, range statements and knowledge and understanding
- sign off each performance criterion
- conduct a final assessment interview with documented questioning

The student's role:

The student should ensure that the project's format is such that it:

- covers all performance criteria, range statements and knowledge and understanding
- covers the objectives set out in the Terms of Reference of the project
- is well laid out, easy to read and includes an executive summary
- uses report form style with appropriate language
- shows clear progression from one idea to the next
- cross-refers the main text to any appendices
- uses diagrams and flow charts appropriately
- starts each section on a fresh page

Note

The simulation will place students in a simulated work place role play situation, where they will be given a range of tasks to undertake. The simulation will aim to cover as many of the Performance Criteria and as much of the Underpinning Knowledge and Understanding as is considered to be feasible for the scenario.

Where all of the listed Performance Criteria and underpinning Knowledge and Understanding have **not** been addressed sufficiently by the simulation, documented assessor questioning **must** be employed to address any gaps.

All Performance Criteria and Underpinning Knowledge and Understanding must be evidenced.

PART A

Managing people in the accounting environment

chapter 1

Your organisation

Contents

Range statement

10.2 Changes affecting systems

- External regulations
- Organisational polices and procedures

Knowledge and understanding

11 How the accounting systems of an organisation are affected by its organisational structure, its Management Information Systems, its administrative systems and procedures and the nature of its business transactions (Elements 10.1 & 10.2)

12 The overview of the organisation's business and its critical external relationships (customers/clients, suppliers etc) (Elements 10.1 & 10.2)

1 Introduction

What do we need to get anything done? How would you get complex tasks, involving lots of people, done at all? And how can you ensure that the work is done to the right standard and achieves the right results?

Organisations are a 'solution' to the 'problem' of how we can get **people** to work together towards common **goals**, adhering to common **standards**.

Characteristics	Car manufacturer	Army
A group of people gathered together for a purpose	People work in different divisions, making different cars	Soldiers are in different regiments, and there is a chain of command from the top to the bottom
Common goals	Sell cars, make money	Defend the country, defeat the enemy, international peace keeping
Results and standards: performance is monitored against the goals and changed if necessary to ensure the goals are accomplished	Costs and quality are reviewed and controlled. Standards are constantly improved	Strict disciplinary procedures, training
Boundary: the organisation is distinct from its environment	Physical: factory gates Social: employment status	Physical: barracks Social: different rules for soldiers, civilians

2 Organisations

2.1 Characteristics

An organisation is an arrangement of **people**, pursuing common **goals**, achieving results and standards of performance. Here are some characteristics.

- Organisations pursue **goals**.
- Most organisations obtain **inputs** (eg materials), and **process** them into **outputs** (eg for others to buy) in order to achieve the goals.
- Within the organisation different people do different things, and might **specialise** in one activity.
- Organisations contain formal, documented **systems and procedures** which enable them to control what they do.
- Organisations are preoccupied with **performance**, and meeting or improving their standards. Achieving **quality targets** is an example of performance. Achieving **profit targets** is also an example.

2.2 How organisations differ

Here are some possible differences between organisations.

Factor	Example
Ownership (public vs private)	Private sector: owned by private owners/shareholders. Public sector: owned by the government
Control	By the owners themselves, by people working on their behalf, or indirectly by government-sponsored regulators
Activity (ie what they do)	Manufacturing, healthcare
Profit or non-profit **orientation**	Business exists to make a profit. The army, on the other hand, is not profit orientated
Legal status	Limited company, partnership, sole trader or plc
Size	Size can be measured in many ways, for example number of staff, number of branches, sales revenue each year, number of customers and market share
Sources of **finance**	Borrowing, government funding, share issues
Technology	High use of technology (eg computer firms) vs low use (eg corner shop)

2.3 Organisations and their goals

We mentioned in Section 1 that an organisation has goals. It has many different types of goals.

2.3.1 Mission

At the very top is an organisation's mission. This is useful to know, for the simple reason that, in your **project**, the mission is a good way of describing what your organisation does.

Example

Mission outlines why an organisation exists. You may find it in the latest Report and Accounts or other documentation.

The following statement was taken from an annual report of two organisations.

The **Guinness Group:** Guinness plc is one of the world's leading drinks companies, producing and marketing an unrivalled portfolio of international best-selling brands, such as Johnnie Walker, Bell's and Dewar's Scotch whiskies, Gordon's and Tanqueray gins, and Guinness stout itself – the world's most distinctive beer. The strategy is to focus resources on the development of the Group's alcoholic drinks businesses. The objectives are to provide superior long-term financial returns for shareholders, to create a working environment in which people can perform to their fullest potential and to be recognised as one of the world's leading consumer brand development companies.

The British Film Institute. The BFI's stated mission is 'to develop greater understanding and appreciation of film, television and the moving image'.

2.3.2 Goals and objectives

In practice, people often use the words **goals**, **aims** and **objectives** interchangeably. But remember that some goals fulfil SMART criteria, and others do not, even though they are still meaningful. SMART criteria are outlined below.

Characteristics	Example
Objectives are SMART	Objective: reduce expenditure on stationery by 5% in the next 12 months
Specific	Refers to a defined item of expenditure
Measurable	5% is measurable
Attainable	We can assume this is no too completely unrealistic: perhaps lower prices can be negotiated
Realistic	5% may or may not be realistic. A cut of 75% may not be realistic.
Time-bounded	eg over the next 12 months

Objectives can be used in three ways.

- Reference points, directing people's work
- Yardsticks, to measure performance
- Motivators

Objectives and goals often appear in a hierarchy, as in the diagram below.

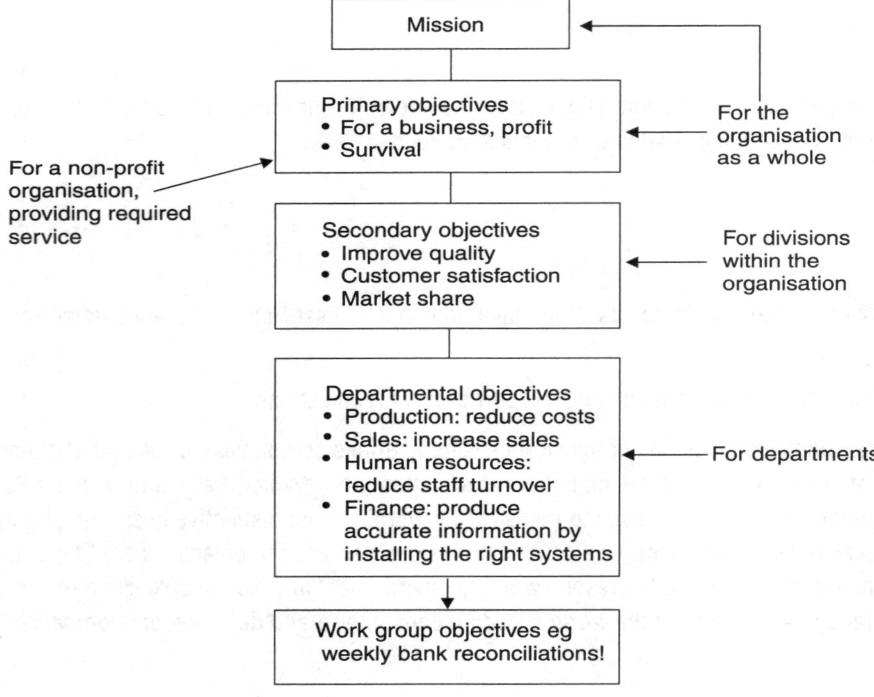

Primary and financial objectives might include profit or shareholder value. **Secondary objectives** can include:

- Improved **quality** of a product or service
- Gaining a **share of the market** for a product (for example, to sell 30% of all 'x's bought in the country in a year).

Finally objectives are achieved over different time scales. A year might be an objective for market share. A month might be an objective for installing a new system.

Example

Let us take the example of a holiday firm.

Organisational goal	**Survive and profit in the leisure industry**
Sales dept goal	Achieve an average of 10% year-on-year growth in holiday sales
High Street office sales target	Achieve £X total sales turnover in the first quarter of the current year
Accounts department goal	Reduce amount spent on bank charges by 50% (eg by better cash management)

Activity 1.1

Tasks

(a) What are four ways of classifying and distinguishing organisations?
(b) How may the size of an organisation be measured?

Note down what type of organisation you work for. How big is it?

Activity 1.2

Tasks

Long-term and short-term objectives are relative to the context. List some long-term and short-term objectives for your accounts department. Try to dream up a 'mission statement' for it, too.

In your project, if you make recommendations, you will need to consider the timescale for implementing them. If it involves training staff, how long do you think this would take? Change rarely happens overnight.

3 Finding your place: organisation structure and the organisation chart

3.1 Activities in the organisation

Within a typical organisation, there are many different types of activity.

- **Purchasing materials** and components
- Carrying out **operations** on purchased materials and components, to make them into something
- **Accounting and record keeping**
- **Research and development** of new products or technologies
- Taking **orders** from customers
- **Planning** and implementing marketing strategies to obtain new customers
- **Employing** people and paying them
- **Co-ordinating** all the above to ensure the organisation reaches its goals

In many organisations large numbers of people are involved in these tasks.

The large numbers of staff and the variety of activities mean that people have to be grouped together in some way. This grouping together is called **organisation structure**.

3.2 What is organisation structure?

Organisation structure is a framework of formal work relationships between people in an organisation. It serves several purposes.

- It **links individuals** in an established network of relationships so that authority, responsibility and communications can be controlled.
- It **allocates the tasks** required to fulfil the objectives of the organisation to suitable individuals or groups.
- It gives each individual or group the **authority** required to perform the allocated tasks, while **controlling** their use of resources.
- It **co-ordinates** the objectives and activities of separate units, so that overall aims are achieved without gaps or overlaps in the flow of work.
- It facilitates the **flow of work**, information and other resources through the organisation.

Activity 1.3

Jason, Mark, Gary and Robbie set up in business together as repairers of musical instruments – specialising in guitars and drums. They are a bit uncertain as to how they should run the business, but when they discuss it in the pub, they decide that attention needs to be paid to three major areas: taking orders from customers, doing the repairs (of course) and checking the quality of the repairs before notifying the customers.

Task

Suggest three ways in which they could structure their business.

Most organisations of any size are split into **departments**. They can be illustrated on the organisation chart.

3.3 Organisation charts and their limitations

The **organisation chart** is an aid to designing, expressing and understanding the shape and structure of an organisation. The chart is a traditional way of setting out in pictures **the various relationships between individuals and groups** in an organisation in terms of their functions, responsibilities and the bounds of their authority.

(a) The parts, or **departments**, into which the organisation is divided and how they relate to each other formally
(b) Formal **communication and reporting channels**
(c) **Structure**: how many management levels there are
(d) **People**: The people each manager is **responsible** (and accountable) for, and *to*.

The most common is the **vertical organisation chart**.

Vertical

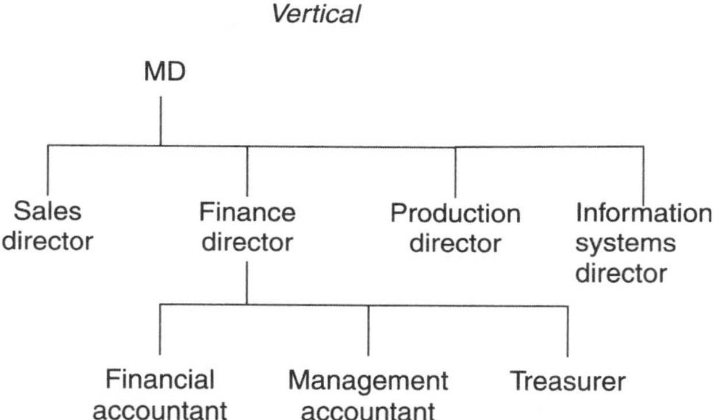

You can see from the 'family tree'-like chart that the organisation divides its work into different **areas**, **groups** and **levels.** Departmentation occurs 'below' the Managing Director's level. So the lines and levels do tell us about relationships: how many people have authority and over how many others, how they pass on authority to others, who is responsible for decisions and so on.

You will also have realised that the **accounting function** has its own structure. We shall look at this in Chapter 2. For now we are getting an overview of the organisation as a whole.

Limitations of organisation charts

Any organisation chart, of course, only gives an **impression** of how the organisation is run – what actually happens may be very different.

- They are a **static** model, whereas an **organisation is dynamic**, continually changing.
- They show only the **formal and not the informal structure** of communications across departments and ranks and the 'networks' of contacts and friends.
- They do not tell you what each person **actually** does, or **how well** he/she does it.
- They do not show relationships and information flows between departments

3.4 Different organisation structures

3.4.1 Functional structure

The firm is organised into departments containing people who do the **same type of work** (eg sales, accounting, production).

Departmentation by function allows the division of work into **specialist areas**, for example, all the finance staff are grouped into one department. The main functions in a **manufacturing** company might be production, sales, purchasing, finance and human resources.

Specialisation can be continued, dividing these into functional sub-departments, for example, the finance department may be split into purchase ledger, sales ledger, payroll and so on.

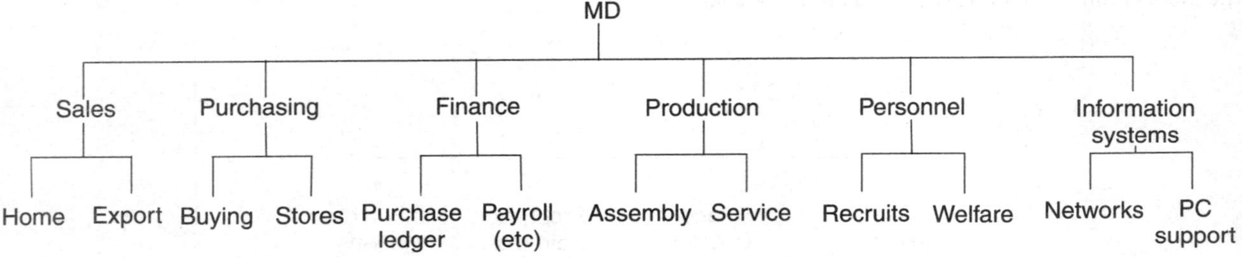

3.4.2 Geographical or territorial structure

Activities are organised on an **area basis** (eg South East England, Scotland), with some activities retained at head office. This means, for example, that account staff will be split and will report to a regional manager, responsible for all the activities in a region.

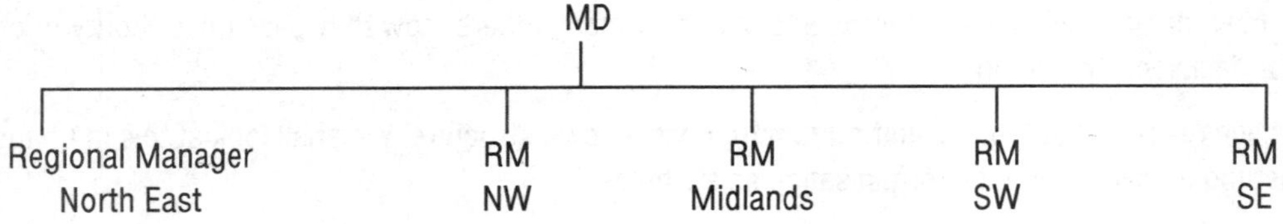

3.4.3 Product– or brand-based structure

Most companies have a mix of products. Department or divisional product managers may thus be given responsibility for a product, line or brand of products. For example for a printing firm:

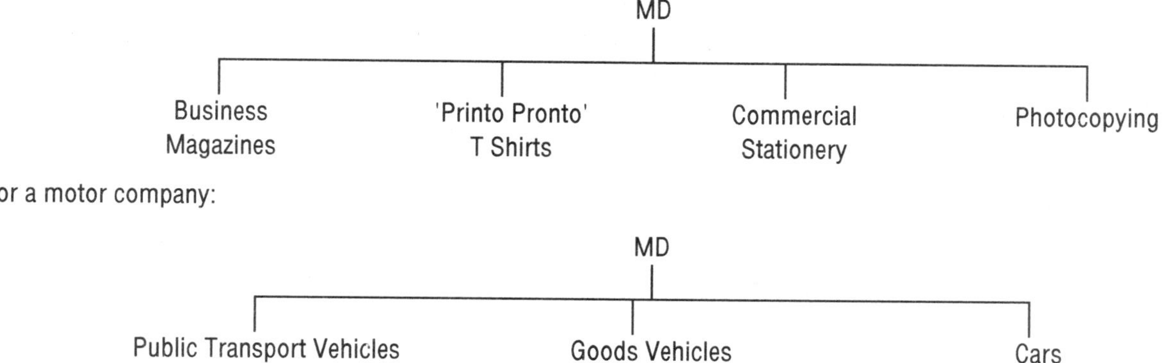

3.4.4 Customer or market segment

The organisation is organised around **groups of customers** (eg 'business customers' and 'domestic customers').

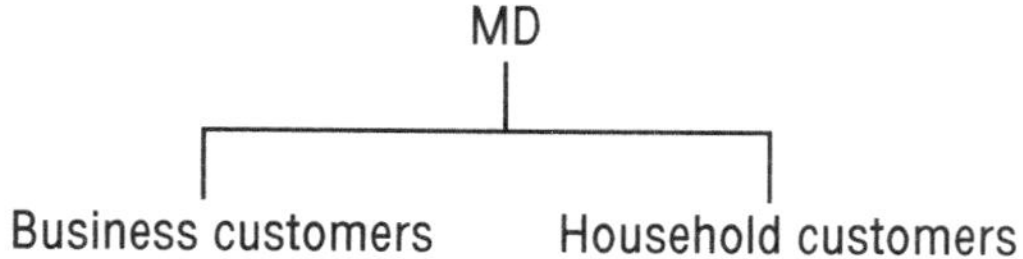

3.4.5 Structure throughout the organisation: hybrids

Most firms do not stick to one of these types of departmentation. They mix and match. For example, sales staff are usually organised by regions. Within product departments, functional areas such as manufacturing and distribution, still operate.

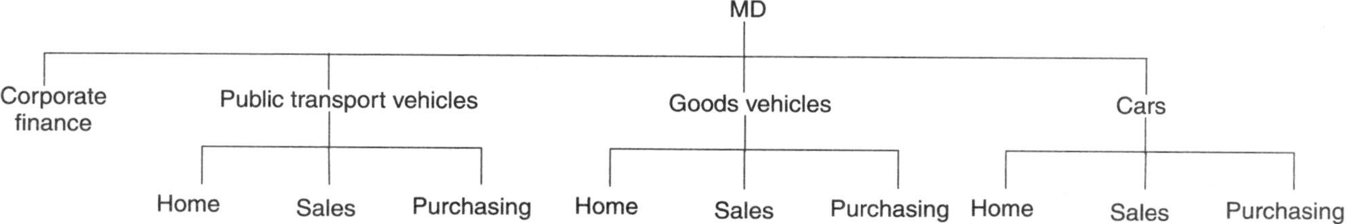

3.4.6 Matrix structures

Organisation structures – and the charts that depict them – can become very complicated! Another development you need to be aware of is a matrix or project structure. This is where a person might report to two bosses, for example a functional boss and a regional boss.

3.4.7 Decentralisation

Whatever the organisation structure, an important feature of the way it is managed is the degree of decentralisation in force. Decentralisation is about power to make decisions. If all decisions are made at Head Office or by the Managing Director, the organisation is centralised. This is good for control and standardisation and consistency of policy.

Decentralisation of decision-making is a sign of an organisation that wishes to respond rapidly to new developments and make full use of its managers' abilities. It gives good experience to managers at all levels and enhances their job satisfaction. It also tends to lead to new ideas and ways of doing things.

3.4.8 Other changes

Some organisations are doing away with strict lines of authority. Instead the organisation is managed in teams.

Activity 1.4

Q plc is a business which is divided into three product divisions. Each of these divisions has been operating from different sites and relatively old-fashioned buildings. It has become possible to acquire an eminently suitable site cheaply, to which Q plc intends to move all the divisions. It has been decided to take the opportunity to reorganise on a functional basis.

At present, the following activities take place in the divisions:

Division A	*Division B*	*Division C*
Purchasing	Purchasing	Commercial (ie sales, finance and administration)
Stamping	Machining	Stamping
Machining	Wiring	Wiring
Wiring	Drilling	Drilling
Drilling	Painting	Painting
Commercial (ie sales, finance and administration)	Assembly	Assembly
	Sales	
	Finance	

Tasks

(a) Draw an organisation chart showing the revised functional structure for Q plc.

(b) Suggest reasons why the decision to switch from a product organisation structure to a functional organisation structure might have been taken.

(c) Suggest what impact this might have on the accounting function.

4 Critical external relationships

4.1 The environment

There are various ways in which the **environment** is related to an organisation or, indeed, a department.

Issue	Example	Accounts dept
Resources	The organisation brings in resources such as raw materials from outside suppliers; employees are often recruited from outside.	• Qualified people
Opportunities and threats	The organisation **can exploit opportunities** (for example, for a company, new markets, or for a hospital, new medical discoveries). The organisation **must respond to threats** in order to survive (for example, for a company, competitors' actions, restrictive government laws, political unrest).	• New system • Risk of fraud
Outputs	The organisation processes the resources it gets from the environment, and produces **outputs** to the environment such as finished goods, payment to employees, tax payments to the government).	• Reports

The organisation is also influenced by **stakeholders**.

4.2 Stakeholders, interest and pressure groups

A **stakeholder** is a person, group or organisation with an **interest** in what the organisation does. Stakeholders have different objectives and so make different demands over what the organisation does.

There are three broad types of stakeholder.

- Internal stakeholders (employees, management)
- Connected stakeholders (investors, shareholders, customers, suppliers, financiers)
- External stakeholders (the community, government, pressure groups)

4.2.1 Employees and management

Both employees and management have an interest in a business because it employs and pays them.

4.2.2 Investors/shareholders

A business organisation exists to provide a return to shareholders – but in practice there are many different kinds of shareholders.

Shareholder type	Comments
Institutional investors	These generally invest money on behalf of other people (eg pension funds).
Venture capital firms	These provide capital to risky or new businesses. They expect to recover their investment – with profit – once the firm is established.
Private investors	Most private individuals invest via institutional investors, but many people own shares.
Employees and managers	Some firms run schemes enabling employees to acquire shares, perhaps at a reduced 'option' price.

4.2.3 Lenders and bankers

Finance can be provided for the long term and the short term.

	Providers of long term finance. As well as profit, they are interested in security.	**Providers of short term finance**
Banks	**Banks** lend long-term so that borrowers can acquire long term assets.	**Banks** provide overdraft finance, and so have an intimate knowledge of the cash flows of the business.
Other	Bond holders. **Bonds** are financial instruments promising the **bondholder** a fixed rate of interest. Bond holders can be individuals of institutions. **Shareholders** own the company.	**Factors**: These will 'buy' a company's debts for a fee in order to collect them. **Lease companies**: These enable firms to buy expensive items of equipment. (These can also be long term.)

Many companies do not always choose the right type of finance. Ideally, a long-term investment should be matched by long-term finance, but many smaller businesses often rely on bank overdrafts. In some cases, it might better for a company to have a bank loan, repayable in instalments, than an overdraft.

Such lenders are mainly concerned with the **security** of their loan and their **income**.

4.2.4 Suppliers

Suppliers are stakeholders because the organisation is their customer.

- A long-term relationship
- Preference over other suppliers
- A sufficient volume of business: in other words, plenty of work
- Payment on time

4.2.5 Customers

Businesses have to **satisfy customers** to generate a return. Customers want three things.

- The products and services offered to live up to expectations
- Fair treatment
- Easy redress of any grievances, complaints or replacements for any defective items

4.2.6 Regulatory bodies

Regulatory bodies are government-sponsored organisations set up to regulate particular industries.

The **Financial Reporting Council** deals with accounting standards

For **privatised utilities**, regulators are Ofgem, Ofwat, Ofcom and ORR. They are not primarily consumer protection organisations, but they do have extensive control over pricing and competition policy.

The main **consumer protection** body is the **Office of Fair Trading** which has four roles.

- Promote competition
- Encourage the adoption of codes of practice
- Curb anti-competitive practices
- Issue licences under the Consumer Credit Act

Other bodies include

- **Ombudsmen**, paid for by representatives of an industry to adjudicate between customers and suppliers in cases of dispute (eg the Banking Ombudsman)
- The **Financial Services Authority** is currently taking over most of the **regulatory roles** in the world of financial services

Interest groups

There are voluntary associations of people interested in a particular cause. For example, the **Consumers Association** influences government policy on consumer protection issues.

You may have also come across other **pressure groups**. Some companies report on their 'environmental' performance and give statistics relevant to pollution and recycling in their annual report and accounts. This in part is in response to pressure from groups for them to be socially responsible.

4.2.7 Government

The government shapes the environment of organisations in many ways.

Factor	Example
Personnel	Minimum wage, discrimination, job security, working hours, redundancy payments
Operations	Health and safety at work, product safety standards, working hours
Marketing	Sending unsolicited goods, dangerous packaging, misleading advertising, weights and measures
Environmental issues	Products or operations which are damaging to health, or pollute water, air or land
Finance (eg taxation)	Organisations *collect* tax for the government (PAYE and VAT) and *pay* tax to the government (corporation tax). There are also legal requirements to produce financial information (for example, annual returns, annual report and accounts).
Economic policy	Interest rates. Joining the euro zone. Negotiating free trade agreements

Activity 1.5

Task

(a) Give some examples of organisational objectives.
(b) What is a corporate mission?
(c) What do you understand by the term 'hierarchy of objectives'?
(d) Briefly explain the ways in which an organisation affects or is affected by its environment.

Activity 1.6

Task

How might you, as a supervisor of an accounts section, be involved in the critical external relationships of an organisation?

Key learning points

- ☑ Organisations can be classified and distinguished in a variety of ways (eg size, activity).
- ☑ **Organisation structure** is shaped by **divisions of labour, authority and relationships**.
- ☑ Many organisations have a **formal organisation structure**.
- ☑ As a business grows, **tasks have to be divided up.** Departmentation may be functional, geographical, product-based, and so on.
- ☑ **Organisation charts** can be a useful aid to designing, describing and understanding the shape and structure of an organisation.
- ☑ Organisations have **goals**. These are arranged in a hierarchy with the **corporate mission** at the top and department or section **objectives** at the bottom. SMART goals are quantified and time-bounded.
- ☑ **Many factors influence the way an organisation works**: not only its own objectives, but also its environment and the objectives of its stakeholders.
- ☑ **Critical external relationships** include investors, customers, suppliers and the government.

Quick quiz

1. Why are organisations useful?
2. List some of the different activities in a typical business organisation.
3. What is the purpose of organisation structure?
4. What is functional structure?
5. What is 'mission'?
6. What is a SMART objective?
7. What is a stakeholder?
8. List four types of shareholder.
9. What are banks concerned with?
10. What are customers concerned with?

Answers to quick quiz

1. They achieve more than people do individually.
2. Purchasing, operations, marketing, management, selling
3. To group people together on a useful basis
4. People who do similar jobs are grouped together.
5. The organisation's basic purpose
6. Specific, measurable, accountable, realistic, time-bounded
7. A person, group or organisation with an interest in what the organisation does
8. Institutions, employees, venture capitalists, individuals
9. Security and income
10. Quality, delivery, the product

Activity checklist

This checklist shows which performance criteria, range statement or knowledge and understanding point is covered by each activity in this chapter. Tick off each activity as you complete it.

Activity		
1.1	☐	This activity deals with Knowledge and Understanding point 12: The overview of the organisation's business and its critical external relationships (customers/clients, suppliers, etc) (Elements 10.1 & 10.2)
1.2	☐	This activity deals with Knowledge and Understanding point 11: How the accounting systems of an organisation are affected by its organisational structure, its Management Information Systems, its administrative systems and procedures and the nature of its business transactions (Elements 10.1 & 10.2)
1.3	☐	This activity deals with Knowledge and Understanding point 11: How the accounting systems of an organisation are affected by its organisational structure, its Management Information Systems, its administrative systems and procedures and the nature of its business transactions (Elements 10.1 & 10.2)
1.4	☐	This activity deals with Knowledge and Understanding point 11: How the accounting systems of an organisation are affected by its organisational structure, its Management Information Systems, its administrative systems and procedures and the nature of its business transactions (Elements 10.1 & 10.2) and Range Statement (Changes affecting systems).
1.5	☐	This activity deals with Knowledge and Understanding points 11: How the accounting systems of an organisation are affected by its organisational structure, its Management Information Systems, its administrative systems and procedures and the nature of its business transactions (Elements 10.1 & 10.2) and 12: The overview of the organisation's business and its critical external relationships (customers/clients, suppliers, etc) (Elements 10.1 & 10.2)
1.6	☐	This activity deals with Knowledge and Understanding point 12: The overview of the organisation's business and its critical external relationships (customers/clients, suppliers, etc) (Elements 10.1 & 10.2)

chapter 2

The accounting function

Contents

Performance criteria

10.1.F Co-ordinate work activities effectively and in accordance with work plans and contingency plans.

10.1.G Encourage colleagues to report to you promptly any problems and queries that are beyond their authority or expertise to resolve, and resolve these where they are within your authority and expertise.

10.1.H Refer problems and queries to the appropriate person where resolution is beyond your authority or expertise

Range statement

10.2 Changes affecting systems: external regulations, organisational polices and procedures

Knowledge and understanding

1 The range of external regulations affecting accounting practice (Element 10.2)

11 How the accounting systems of an organisation are affected by its organisational structure, its Management Information Systems, its administrative systems and procedures and the nature of its business transactions (Elements 10.1 & 10.2)

13 The purpose, structure and organisation of the accounting function and its relationships with other functions within the organisation (Element 10.2)

14 Who controls the supply of resources (equipment, materials, information and people) within the organisation (Element 10.1)

1 Introduction

In Chapter 1 we described how the tasks in the organisation could be divided up. The accounts department is one of several departments in the organisation. How should the accounts department itself be structured? How can we be sure it is playing its role? In some organisations, accounting personnel will be dispersed over a number of different divisions, in others they will be centralised. The role of the accounting function will stay the same, even though it can be organised in different ways.

2 The role of the accounting function

In Chapter 1, we asked you to develop a mission for the accounting function. In Activity 1.2 we identified that the **purpose of the accounting function** is 'to ensure the business's transactions are recorded and processed completely accurately and securely, and that relevant information is given to management'.

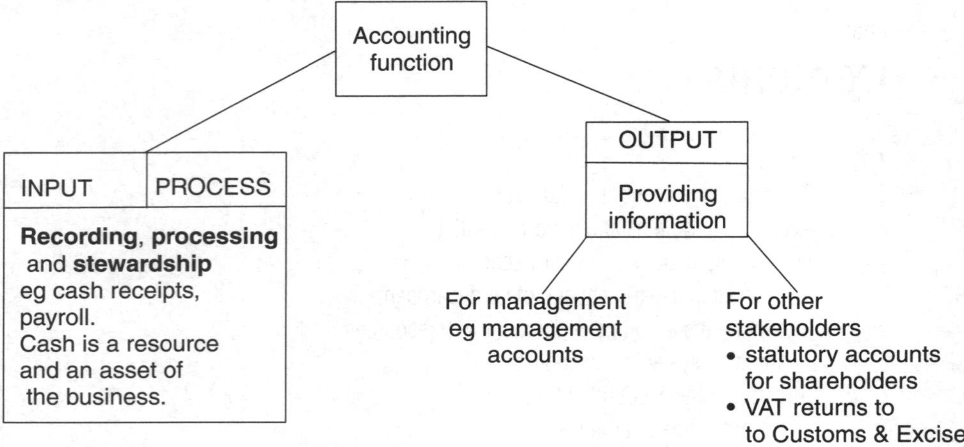

Bear in mind that external regulations affect both these functions

- **Recording and processing**. VAT records must be maintained. Payroll must follow PAYE procedures. Company law requires that accounting records must be maintained.
- Providing **information** – there are strict rules for the presentation of information to shareholders.

If you keep in mind the purpose of the accounting function you will be able to determine the objectives of the project. Keeping the 'big picture' in mind will help you develop the objectives of your project.

2.1 Recording, processing and stewardship

Handling the financial operations aspects of running an organisation involves.

- Handling receipts and payments – ie managing the **cash flows** of the business
- Acting as a collection and reporting agency for the **government** (payroll, VAT)
- Receiving and checking invoices from **suppliers**
- Sending out invoices to **credit customers** and chasing up late payers; keeping a record of debts
- **Borrowing** money and repaying loans
- Keeping the financial position of the organisation – cash flows, gearing and debt – in good order
- Through **internal controls**, preventing errors or fraud, and safeguarding the assets of the business

2.2 Providing information

Providing information (and advice if required) to the managers of other departments helps them do their work better. **Performance reports** enable managers and others to judge how well the organisation is doing.

Type of information	Comments
Planning information	For instance, information for budgets is often provided by accountants.
Control information	This helps other managers to identify problem areas and take control decisions. Budgetary control variance reports are an example of this.
Information to make one-off decisions	Sometimes, a decision has to be taken by management, and some knowledge about the financial consequences of each choice needs to be available. Accountants can provide such information (eg information about the costs and likely cash benefits of capital expenditure proposals).

2.3 Importance of the accounts department

The accounts department is crucial to the organisation.

- If it provides the wrong information, managers will make bad decisions
- It if confuses the data, important transactions might slip through the net, and fraud may result
- There is a legal duty to ensure that accounting records are in good order

3 Accounting systems and the organisation

3.1 Factors affecting accounting systems

An organisation's accounting **systems** as well as the department are affected by the nature of its business transactions and the sort of business it is.

Factor	Example
Size	A **small business** like a greengrocer will have a simple, accounting system, where the main accounting record will probably be the till roll. A **large retail business**, such as a chain of supermarkets, will have elaborate accounting systems covering a large number of product ranges and sites.
Type of organisation	A **service business** might need to record the time employees take on particular jobs. Accounting on a **job or client basis** might also be a feature of service businesses. A **public sector organisation**, such as a government department, may be more concerned with the **monitoring of expenditure** against performance targets than recording revenue. A **manufacturing company** will account both for unit sales and revenue, but needs to keep **track of costs** for decision-making purposes and so forth.
Organisation structure	In a business managed by **area**, accounts will be prepared on an area basis by area staff. In a **functional organisation**, the accounts staff are in a separate self-contained department of their own.
External regulations	Accounting work has to comply with a wide range of regulations, including law such as the Companies Act. As a result, it tends to be rather formalised and procedural in order to make sure that nothing is overlooked.
Internal regulations	Organisations often lay down their accounting rules and procedures in writing, and this may form part of an **organisation manual** or **procedures manual**. Some organisations aim to achieve external verification of their quality procedures.

3.2 Organisation structure

Some organisations are spread over many different **countries** or areas. Here is how the accounting function will be specifically affected.

Difference	Comment
Different currencies	**Recording information**. Customers might want to pay in local currency, but the business might have to pay for imported supplies in a different currency. **Reporting information**. If you wanted to compare the performance of a Belgian subsidiary company with that, say, of a subsidiary in Uruguay, you may have to convert the results to a single currency such as the Euro.

Difference	Comment
Different legal and accounting requirements	In some countries, the state regulates the keeping of accounts, down to minute detail. In the UK, on the other hand, companies can prepare accounts as they wish, subject to the Companies Act, and financial reporting standards.
Different ways of doing business	The emphasis of the accountant's job differs from country to country. In a country in which payments are made by cash, management of debtors is likely to take up far less time and effort than in a country where extended credit periods are the norm.
Different economic conditions	Some countries have very high rates of inflation; this can affect accounting practice.

If your company operates on an **area basis**, you will probably find that the accounting information, such as monthly management accounts, is structured by area. In other words reports for regions are aggregated together to build up a picture of the performance of the whole company. In a functional organisation structure, however, you would separately analyse costs and revenues for each function department.

3.3 Product-division structure

When an organisation has a product-based structure, accounting information must be grouped in a particular way to highlight revenue earned and costs incurred by a particular product. It is possible, then, that the product divisional basis will affect the **account coding system** of the company.

(a) **Revenue.** Recording accounting information relating to revenue is usually easy. Each product has a price, and it is relatively simple to record unit sales. Invoices may be analysed by product group.

(b) **Costs.** Some costs, such as materials, can be traced to individual products. Overheads are more difficult to deal with.

Cost information is not just a feature of a product-division structured organisation, as this information is necessary for decision making in **any** organisation. There will still be some areas (eg research and development) which are shared by all divisions, and it might not be easy to allocate these common costs.

Activity 2.1

Task

Draft some brief notes on how **functional** departmentation could affect accounting information in an organisation managed on this basis.

4 External regulations and their impact

The Knowledge and Understanding for Unit 10 states that you should know about the **range of external regulations affecting accounting practice**.

4.1 Financial accounting regulations

For an **unincorporated business**, any form of accounting information is adequate if it gives the owner(s) of the business a basis for planning and control, and satisfies the requirements, of external users such as the Inland Revenue. Limited companies are more closely regulated. The **regulations on accounts** come from a number of sources.

Regulations	
Company law: the UK government is reviewing companies legislation	Limited companies are required by law to publish **financial statements annually** for distribution to their shareholders. • A copy of these accounts must be lodged with the Registrar of Companies and is available for inspection by any member of the public. • The published accounts should show a 'true and fair view'. This is a complex concept which you will learn about elsewhere. • The Companies Act also contains set formats for company accounts and states what information must be disclosed.
Non-statutory regulations: See Unit 11 for example	The **Financial Reporting Council** (FRC) is independent of the accountancy profession and draws its membership from a wide spectrum of accounts preparers and users. Its chairman is appointed by the Government. The FRC guides the standard setting process. The **Accounting Standards Board** (ASB) is responsible for the issue of **Financial Reporting Standards** (FRSs). Prior to publication, the ASB circulates its proposals in the form of a financial reporting exposure draft (inevitably referred to as a FRED) and invites comments. Some **Statements of Standard Accounting Practice** (SSAPs) issued by the ASB's predecessor are still in force. • FRSs lay down prescribed accounting treatments in areas where a variety of approaches might be taken. • The aim is to ensure that users can compare the accounts of different companies. The **Urgent Issues Task Force** (UITF) is an offshoot of the ASB. Its role is to assist the ASB in areas where an accounting standard or Companies Act provision already exists, but where unsatisfactory or conflicting interpretations have developed. As its name suggests, the UITF is designed to act quickly.
International accounting standards	The International Accounting Standards Committee (IASC) attempts to co-ordinate the development of international accounting standards. It includes representatives from many countries throughout the world. The UK and other countries in the EU are committed to adopting international accounting by 2005. You many need to be aware of these before this time. The introduction of IASs has implications for the accounting function. A good idea for a project, perhaps.
The Stock Exchange regulations	The Stock Exchange is a market for stocks and shares, and a company whose securities are traded in this market is known as a 'quoted' or 'listed' company. Such a company commits itself to certain procedures and standards, including matters concerning the disclosure of accounting information, which are more extensive than the disclosure requirements of the Companies Acts. Directors of a company are required to certify that there are internal controls in place: This directly affects your work.

4.2 Auditing regulations

Company legislation also requires that the accounts of a limited company must be **audited**. An **audit** may be defined as an 'independent examination of, and expression of opinion on, the financial statements of an enterprise'.

In practice, a limited company must engage a firm of chartered or chartered certified accountants to examine its accounting records and its financial statements in order to form an opinion as to whether the accounts present a 'true and fair view' and comply with the Companies Act. At the conclusion of their audit work, the auditors issue a report addressed to the owners of the company (its **members** or **shareholders**) which is published as part of the accounts. Audit work is governed by Auditing Standards which are issued by the Auditing Practices Board.

You are **required by law** to provide auditors with any information that they need to do their job.

4.3 Taxation regulations

Taxation regulations will affect the work of the accounts department of any organisation that runs a PAYE system or is registered for VAT.

(a) A substantial amount of **payroll work** consists of keeping records (P11s) and submitting returns (P11D, P14, P35 and so on) to the Inland Revenue and the DSS. You probably learnt all about this at Foundation stage.

(b) **VAT returns** must be submitted at regular intervals and can also involve considerable administrative effort.

Regulations such as these have a significant impact on the **timing** of accounting work, since returns are required every month for payroll and (usually) every three months for VAT, and the **information must be ready in time** to comply with these requirements.

4.4 Other external influences

Cost and management accounting is not subject to any statutory rules. There may, however, be circumstances in which outsiders can influence the **timing** of the production of management information, and its **format**, or affect the procedures adopted in the accounts department.

Influence	Effect
Investors	People who have invested in the business are entitled to know how well it is doing, at least annually.
Banks	Banks often make it a condition of their loan that they be supplied with regular monthly management accounts, or cash flow projections.
Suppliers	They insist on having their bills paid on time, especially if they are larger than the organisation they are supplying and the organisation is dependent upon them. This may disrupt the normal operating cycles of the purchases section.
Customers	Can also sometimes have an impact on the operation of an accounting system. Tesco, for example, have encouraged many of their small suppliers to install sophisticated *electronic data interchange systems.*
Benchmarking	Some industries have standard formats for management reports so that companies can be compared anonymously under a scheme of inter-firm comparison or benchmarking.
Privatised utilities	Former public sector bodies like British Gas have their costs and revenues closely scrutinised by their regulators.
Management	Managers may want information to be provided in specific ways.

Activity 2.2

Task

Review the accounting information produced by your department. Identify all the different users, internal and external. How have they influenced the information presented?

5 The accounts department and other departments

5.1 Scope of activities

In section 2 we showed how the roles of the accounting function involved providing information and processing transactions.

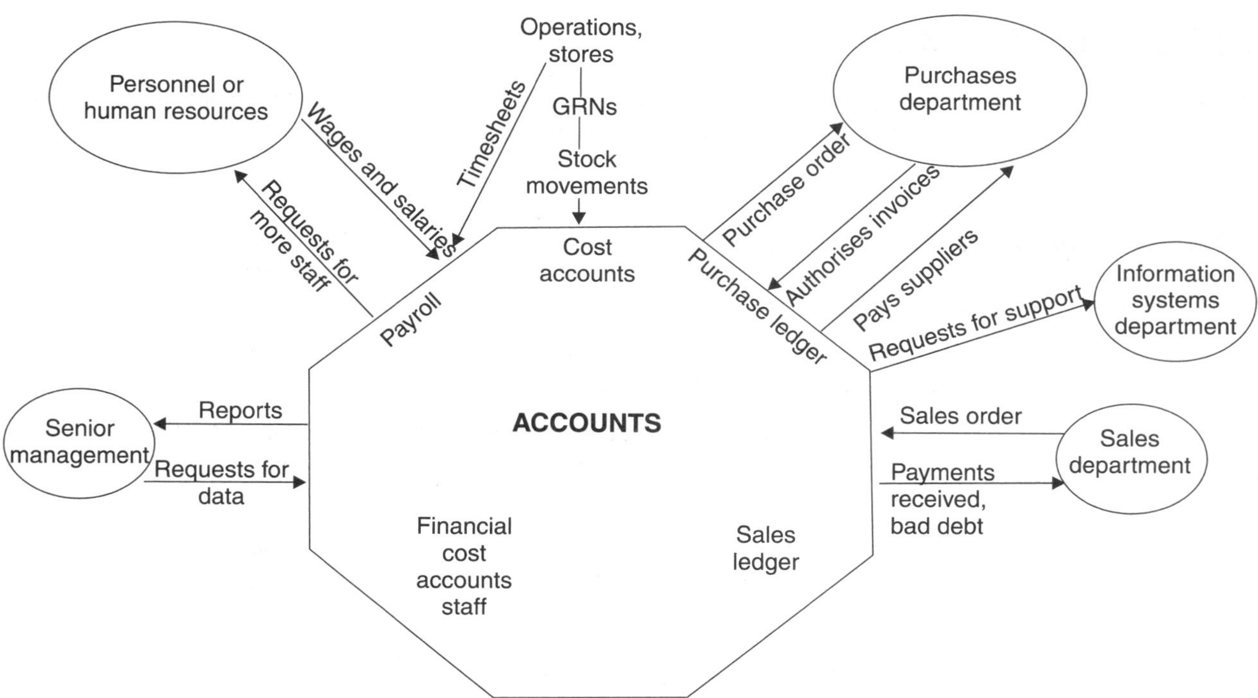

The diagram above shows some of the complexity of the **accounts department's relationships** with other departments.

5.2 Processing transactions

Some relationships deal with **processing transactions**. In each case, **input information** from **other departments** is necessary to carry out the accounting activity. For example, before an **invoice** for raw material supplies is paid, the accounting department will need to check the details of the invoice against the **purchase order form** (co-ordination with the **purchasing department**) and the **goods received note** (co-ordination with the **stores department**).

Department	Accounts section	Relationship
Purchases dept (PD)	Purchase ledger (PL) Cashier (C)	PD advises PL of purchase orders PD indicates valid invoices C informs PD and PL of payment
Personnel dept	Payroll	Personnel gives details of wage rates, starters and leavers, to payroll
Sales dept (SD) **Credit control (CC)**	Sales ledger (SL)	SD advises SL of sales order SL might give CC information about overdue debts SL might give details about debtors ageing
Operations, stock control	Cost accounting staff	Operations might give details of movements of stock, so that the accounts staff can value stock.
Senior management	Financial accounting and cost accounting staff	The accounts department produces management information for decision making and control

5.3 Providing information

We have only briefly alluded to the variety of reports that may be needed here. Some reports are routine – for example monthly management accounts. Others are requests for ad hoc information.

5.4 Requesting help

On the diagrams, two of the arrows show the accounts department itself making requests.

- For example, in a company with a separate **information systems** department, the accounts department will have to contact information systems personnel for support and/or equipment.
- Similarly, in some companies, all **recruitment** is managed by the **human resources department**.

Moreover, the other departments can influence how the accounts department functions.

Activity 2.3

The Modern Company is concerned to provide the best possible working conditions for its staff. Each department has one or two representatives on a staff liaison committee that meets regularly to consider matters of common interest regarding working conditions, social activities and so on. the house committee is managed by the Human Resources department.

The HR department is now reporting that there is a keen interest by most, but not all, staff, in requesting the management to consider the introduction of 'flexitime', whereby staff attendance hours are flexible within given times and a minimum number of hours worked each month.

You are the representative from the accounts and wages section and the HR director for your department has asked you to help her to consider the implications of this request.

Tasks

(a) Prepare briefing notes of how you envisage this flexitime might be organised.
(b) Discuss what control systems you might wish to introduce.
(c) Explain how you think you might communicate your initial proposals to all staff.

6 Supplying the accounts department with resources

In the previous section, we identified the need for the accounts department. Although the accounts department is very important, it does not make and sell products or services, the activities that drive the profit of the business. It does, however, need a **supply of resources**.

6.1 Budgeting for the accounting function

Like all other items of expenditure, a **budget** will be prepared for the accounting function.

In a functionally organised company, the head of the finance function should have a fairly good idea as to the people, equipment, materials and people that are needed to provide the accounting service.

In organisations structured in a different way, the resources allocated to he accounting will depend on who is the decision maker. However, the keeping of suitable financial resources, and the maintenance of internal controls is a legal and financial necessity, and a minimum level of resources is likely to be required.

The Knowledge and Understanding for this unit identifies four key issues: 'Who controls the supply of resources – equipment, material, information and people – within the organisation? The answer to this question varies from organisation to organisation.

An important assessment of resources required is a **needs analysis**. What does the department need to fulfil its role? You may work in superbly modern, fully-equipped, user-friendly offices. On the other hand, you may not. Practical matters like this are not trivial; they can have a profound influence on the way work is performed and its efficiency.

	Example	Control/responsibility
Materials and equipment	IT equipment Office supplies (eg stationery) Materials for production	**Depends**: there many be an IT budget, but it may need to be passed through the IT department. **Depends**: may be delegated to individual departments, or may be the responsibility of the **purchases department** to buy in bulk. There may be a central purchasing department.
Information • Some is likely to be sensitive and some is not • Different departments many maintain their own information systems	Sales data General information Financial data	**Depends** – sales personnel to keep data about customers, but must adhere to the Data Protection Act. The information systems department may have a role in disseminating information (eg setting up a corporate intranet). The accounts department, is a major provider of information.
People	• Temporary staff • Permanent recruits	The number of people is influenced by the work of the department. In terms of actual recruitment, this **procedure** may determine how these needs are satisfied. This will vary from organisation to organisation. Finally, in a large organisation, you may have to deal with a trade union, and the agreements made between unions and management.

6.2 Premises, location of accounting staff

Issues affecting location are as follows.

Issue	Comment
By **post**	The location of the accounts receivable group and cashier's section dealing with receipts is unlikely to be significant if most payments arrive by post.
'Over the counter'	In order to account for the receipts as soon as possible, and to minimise the movement of cash before it is banked, it might be appropriate to have an accounts receivable section in a location where customers can come to pay in person. Some large organisations make these arrangements: for example, customers can pay a gas bill or electricity bill at their local gas or electricity showroom.
Telephone	More and more firms are taking orders over the phone by obtaining credit card details. These are frequently managed in *call centres*, which do not have to be in any particular location as long as telecommunications links are suitable. The accounts department may instead have to deal with *Mastercard* or *Visa*.
Geography	There might be several accounts receivable groups and cashiers' offices **around the country**.
Paperwork	Even with computerisation of accounting records, financial accounting work involves passing large amounts of paper between sections for checking – for example, goods received notes, purchase orders and suppliers' invoices.
Information	Information providers should not be remote from the managers for whom the information is intended.
Treasury managers	Might need to be close to the London money markets.
Management	**Managers** should ideally have an office close to their staff. Supervisors should preferably be in the same room as their staff.
Environment	Accountants, like other office workers, will work better in a good office environment. Issues include light, heat, security, health and safety and sufficient space for storing accounting records.

Activity 2.4

The TAA Group is a manufacturing organisation with several factories and distribution centres. Over the years office accommodation of differing standards has been added to each site as required and in some cases existing buildings close to a location have been leased. The opportunity has now arisen for land to be acquired adjacent to the main factory. This would be sufficient for the building of an office block to accommodate all selling and administrative departments for the group.

Tasks

(a) Outline the case for locating all the accounting functions for the group centrally in this new building.

(b) Draft guidelines to determine the location and layout of the space allocated to the accounting staff

6.3 Equipment and supplies

You will need to ensure **adequate supplies** for the smooth, efficient and secure functioning of the accounts department.

Item	Comment
Stationery	Accounts departments typically use pre-printed stationery (eg invoices and cheques) and internal forms.
Seating	Bad furniture can cause health problems and make it hard to work.
Filing	Trays and filing cabinets ensure that material is properly sorted.
Safes	Cash and confidential information need to be locked away. Some departments have sophisticated entry-code systems for this purpose.
Calculators/adding machines	Not everything can be computerised, although some of the tasks of adding machines can be taken over by a spreadsheet. A basic adding machine produces a tally roll able to record and provide an audit trail of each calculation as it is done.
Communications	Most offices have internal phones and fax machines. Some have direct lines, some are accessed via a switchboard. **E-mail** will be set up in most networked systems.
Computers	Many accounts staff use networked PCs or PCs connected to a specialised system.

7 Information systems and coding

You should already be familiar with computers from your earlier studies and quite probably also from your personal work experience, and so only a few comments on accountancy and computers are appropriate here. IT options available to management are increasingly varied.

7.1 Hardware

Most **small** accounting sections to have one or several office PCs for processing sales ledger, purchase ledger, nominal ledger, payroll and cash book transactions. **Increasingly, PCs are linked to each other in a network**, so that the computers can exchange data. These **networks** provide greater flexibility for data processing and can improve the quality of the information service provided to management. The network may have a **file server** which provides additional services such as e-mail and database storage, for users of the network.

In terms of hardware, **mainframes** are used for **very large volumes** of transaction processing and as **enterprise servers**. Their advantages are supposed to be greater **reliability**, **functionality** and **security** than networked systems. Most small to medium sized businesses use networked PCs.

Batch processing remains possible, of course. In some supermarkets, for example, bar code data is read to a storage medium, and the file is updated at the day's end.

7.2 Software

Software is the generic term for computer programs. In addition to **accounts software** an accounts department needs a variety of standard software packages, including **word processing**, **spreadsheets**, e-mail software and communications. Microsoft Office, including Word, Excel and Outlook, is widely used. There are a number of versions of the underpinning Windows Operating Systems.

The software used will depend on the size of the accounts department and the volume of processing.

- Some large organisations, such as banks, have **bespoke** software packages written especially for them.
- Other firms will be able to use **off-the-shelf** packages, such as Sage.

7.3 Files and applications

An application is a program developed to work on a particular task, for example processing sales information. Some firms have separate applications for different types of data or processing tasks. For example, the **payroll system** may be entirely separate from stock control – indeed, there is no reason why they should be connected.

In other systems, different applications are **integrated**. In other words, they are linked closely and share common files.

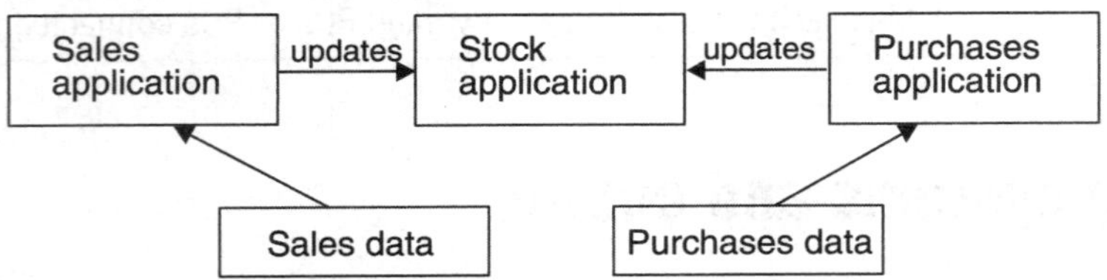

Advantages of integrated processing

(a) Each part of the system can be used **separately**, or in a **combination** of the parts, or as a **total** system.

(b) A transaction item only has to be **entered once** to update all parts of the system. **Duplication of effort** is avoided, and so is the need to store the same data in several different places (**data redundancy**).

(c) Integration of data means that all departments in a company are using the same information and inter-departmental disagreements based on differences about facts can be avoided.

(d) **Managers** throughout the organisation should have access to fully **up-to-date information** drawn from sources right across the organisation, not just from one source. This ought to improve the breadth of vision and quality of management decisions.

(e) Integration will require **standardisation** and better defined and documented system design. For example it should bring about standard ways of naming files and of constructing spreadsheets.

In other systems, **a database approach** is used in which all the data is coded and held on one file which can be accessed easily.

7.3.1 Levels of information

It is quite common for an organisation to have a number of systems. The nominal/main ledger may be quite separate from the big transactions processing systems, and the task of the accounts department may be to try to prepare meaningful aggregated data from a number of different, perhaps conflicting, systems.

This is why issues such as coding are important.

Transactons	Comment
Recording transactions	**Transactions processing systems**, or data processing systems, are the lowest level in an organisation's use of information systems. They are used for **routine tasks** in which data items or transactions must be processed so that operations can continue. Handling sales orders, purchase orders, payroll items and stock records are typical examples.
Initiating transactions	In some cases, the system may make a purchase order automatically.
Producing reports and information for management	Transactions processing systems provide the raw material which is often used more extensively by **management information systems** or **decision support systems** to produce **management information**.

A **management information system (MIS)** is a system to **convert data** from internal and external sources into **information** and to communicate that information, in an appropriate form, to **managers** at all levels in all functions to enable them to make timely and effective decisions for planning, directing and controlling the activities for which they are responsible.

An MIS is good at analysing and summarising **regular formal information** gleaned from normal commercial data. For example, an MIS could provide managers with information relating to sales.

- Gross profit margins of particular products
- Success in particular markets
- Credit control information (aged debtors and payments against old balances)

Remember that good management reports will not create information overload. **Management by exception** depends on reports that highlight unusual or unexpected events. This focuses scarce management time on the things that need attention. MIS may be less efficient at presenting information which is relatively **unpredictable**, or **informal**, or unstructured. So, for example, an MIS could not provide information relating to the sudden emergence of a new competitor into the market.

7.4 Codes

Whenever a transaction arises, it must be recorded. **Codes** are used because they can **identify** items more concisely and precisely than written descriptions, and so help to **classify** the items into groups for recording data.

- **Classification** is 'the arrangement of items in logical groups, having regard to their nature (subjective classification) or purpose (objective classification)'.

- A **code** is defined as 'a system of symbols designed to be applied to a classified set of items, to give a brief accurate reference, facilitating entry, collation and analysis.'

Codes are, arguably, the heart of transaction processing, and the integrity of the information derived from it.

Example

Suppose that an organisation spends £500 sending one of its trainee accountants on a training course. The transaction can be classified in two ways.

(a) The **nature** of the transaction is that it is an **administrative expense**, so it could be coded in a way that linked it to Accounts department overheads; this would be a **subjective classification**.

(b) The **purpose** of the transaction is to provide training. **Objective classification** would therefore require it to be coded as a **training expense**.

In a combined financial and cost accounting system, the transaction might be given a composite code, one to identify it as a **training expense** and the other as an **administration cost centre expense** – for example code 224.316.

7.4.1 Accounting codes

(a) The **sales ledger** consists of the various individual accounts for each credit sale **customer**. Each customer is allocated an account, and an account is identified by a unique customer account number (a code number) as well as by name and address. Adding new accounts to the sales ledger is a regular accounting practice.

(b) The **purchase ledger** is organised in a similar way to the sales ledger.

(c) The **nominal, or general ledger** summarises the financial affairs of a business. It contains details of assets, liabilities and capital, income and expenditure, and hence profit and loss. It consists of a large number of different accounts, each account having its own purpose, name and identity code. Here is an example.

Grouping

Fixed assets	*Code*
Land and buildings at cost	101
Plant and machinery at cost	102
Motor vehicles at cost	103
Fixtures and fittings at cost	104

and so on. (Current assets might start at Code 201 for stock.)Every accounting transaction must be identifiable as belonging to a particular classification, so that it can be recorded correctly.

(d) **Cost accounts** are used to make records of the cost of producing goods or providing a service, with an analysis where appropriate of the costs of individual products, jobs, batches, services or departments.

A **cost centre** is a location, person or item of equipment (or group of these) for which costs may be ascertained and used for control purposes. Every cost centre will have its own unique **cost code** for recording the expense item. **Cost centres** could be established for functional costs, with a number of cost centres for each type of functional cost. For example, administration costs might have a range of cost

centres, coded 2000 to 2999. Accounts department costs within this group of administration costs might have cost centres coded 2100 to 2199.

(e) **Shared costs** (for example rent, rates, electricity or gas bills) may require cost centres of their own, in order to be directly allocated. Shared cost items may be charged to separate, individual cost centres, or they may be grouped into a larger cost centre (for example factory occupancy costs, for rents, rates, heating, lighting, building repairs, cleaning and maintenance of a particular factory).

Charging costs to a cost centre involves identifying the correct cost centre and allocating the cost to it by means of the cost code. Cost centres, therefore, provide a basis for further analysis of actual costs, and a means of building up estimated costs in **budgeting**.

Some items of cost may be charged directly to a **cost unit**. A cost unit is a unit of product (a single item, or a batch, or a job or contract, or a notional unit of output such as a standard hour or similar time unit), in relation to which costs may be ascertained or expressed. Each unit (for example a job) will be given its own unique code or number, so that direct costs can be charged to it in a system of cost accounts.

7.4.2 Good coding systems

Good coding systems have the following features.

- Ease of use and communication
- Potential for expansion
- Flexibility: small changes in item classification can be incorporated without major changes to the coding system itself.
- A unique reference code for key items, such as customer account number, supplier account number, stock code number or employee number
- Universality: every recorded item can be suitably coded.
- Simplicity.
- The likelihood of errors going undetected should be minimised.
- No duplication.
- A readily available index or reference book of codes.
- Existing codes should be reviewed regularly and out-of-date codes removed.
- Code numbers should be issued from a single, central point. Different people should not be allowed to add new codes to the existing list independently.

7.4.3 Types of coding systems

Various coding systems (or combinations of them) may be used when designing codes.

Sequence codes. No attempt is made to **classify** the item to be coded. It is simply given the next available number in a rising sequence. New items can only be inserted at the end of the list; thus the codes for similar items may be very different.

For example:

1 = saucepans
2 = kettles
3 = pianos
4 = dusters

Sequence codes are rarely used when a large number of items are involved.

Block codes provide a different sequence for each differing group of items. For example for a particular firm, customers may be divided up according to area:

South East Code numbers 10,000 – 19,999
South West Code numbers 20,000 – 29,999
Wales Code numbers 30,000 – 39,999
and so on

The code is sequential within each block.

Significant digit codes incorporate some digits which are part of the description of the item being coded. An example is:

5000 Electric light bulbs
5025 25 watt
5040 40 watt
5060 60 watt
5100 100 watt
and so on

Faceted

Where the digits in a code are intended to follow a pattern or structure, but the code numbers themselves are of no significance, the term **faceted code** is sometimes used in preference to significant digit codes. For example, in a costing system, we might have a three-figure code.

Digit	*Code*	*Meaning*
First	1	Material cost
	2	Labour cost
	3	Expense
Second	1	Direct production cost
	2	Indirect production cost
	3	Marketing cost
	4	Administration cost
Third	1	Variable cost
	2	Fixed cost
	3	Mixed cost

Code 211 would then indicate a variable direct labour production cost.

Mnemonic codes help people to recognise the meaning of the code more easily. A mnemonic code uses letters that give some clue to the meaning of the code, for example area codes might be N, S, E, W, SW etc, or clothes sizes S (small), M (medium), L (large). The first letters of a UK postcode are mnemonic (eg BS = Bristol; YO = York) but the remainder of the code is not.

8 Structuring the accounting function

8.1 Sections in the accounts department

In UK companies, the head of the accounting management structure is usually the **finance director**. The finance (or financial) director has a seat on the **board of directors** and is responsible for routine accounting matters and also for broad financial policy matters. In many larger companies the finance director has one or more deputies.

	Comments
Some responsibilities of the **Financial Controller**	• Routine accounting • Providing accounting reports for other departments • Cashiers' duties and cash control
Management accounting is such an important function that a **Management Accountant** is often appointed with status equal to the financial controller and separate responsibilities.	• Cost accounting • Budgets and budgetary control • Financial management of projects
A very large organisation might have a **Treasurer** in charge of treasury work.	• Raising funds by borrowing • Investing surplus funds on the money market or other investment markets • Cash flow control.

Bear in mind, of course, that just like organisations as a whole, departments can be structured in different ways, and this is true at each level of the hierarchy.

- Cost and management accounting, for example, may be organised with a separate team for each product.
- Financial accounting may be done on a country by country basis, to reflect different legal requirements. You might want to make recommendations for change.

An organisation is shown in the diagram on the next page. This organisation is typical of a functional organisation structure, where people are grouped together by the type of work they do.

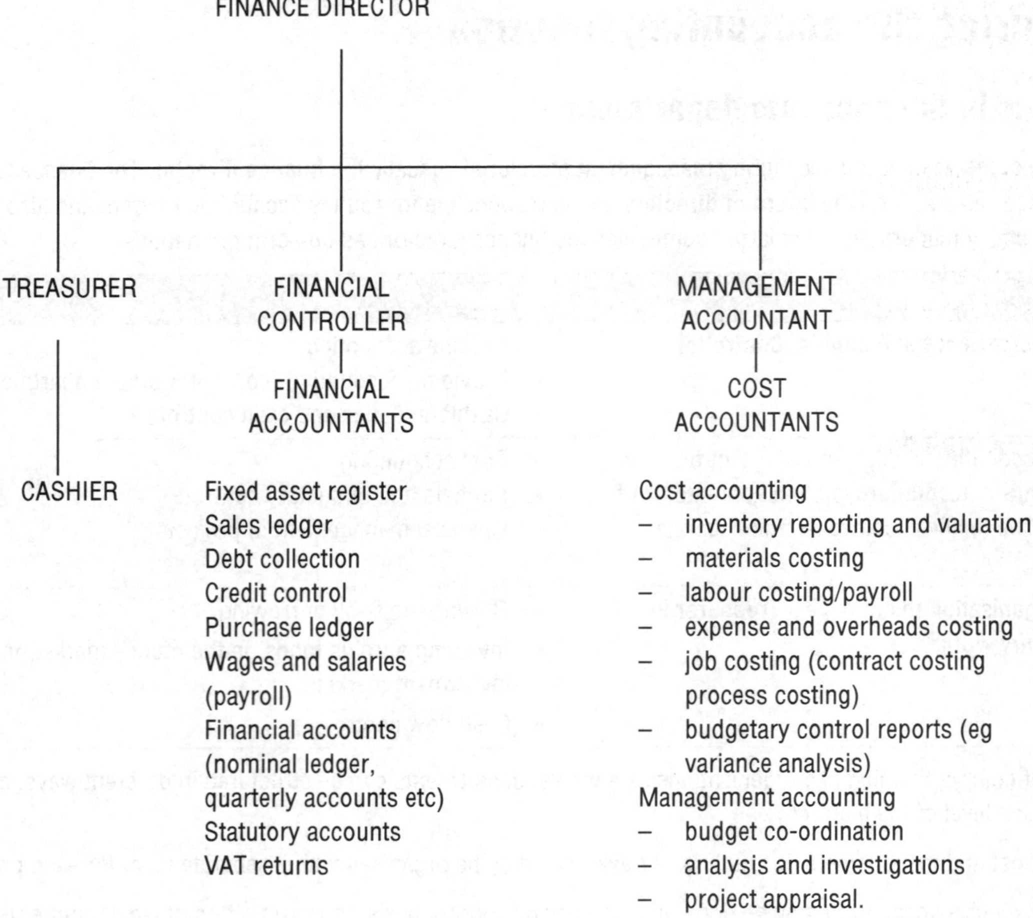

8.2 The structure of a section

Taking just one section of a large accounts department, here is a possible structure.

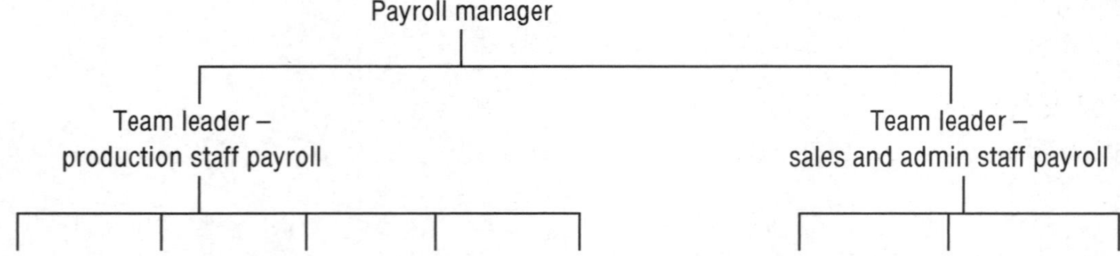

(a) In this example we are envisaging a business which has a large number of weekly paid production staff. The five **assistants** would be carrying out tasks like extracting information from production records about normal time, overtime, piecework rates and so on.

(b) On the sales and administration side the employees are monthly paid and there are fewer of them. Only three assistants are needed to deal with timesheets, bonuses and so forth.

(c) There may be significant differences between jobs that look as if they are fairly similar on the organisation chart. For this reason you may find that individual jobs are described more fully in the **job descriptions** for the people involved.

8.3 Job descriptions for accounting staff

The work of the section is ultimately analysed into individual jobs. A **job description** attempts to describe the contents of the job and work performed, the responsibilities involved, skill and training required, working conditions (if appropriate – this is more likely to mean location), relationships with other jobs and personal requirements of the job, including skill, experience and social aptitudes.

8.3.1 Purpose of job description

Purpose	Comment
Organisational	The job description defines the job's place in the organisational structure.
Recruitment	The job description provides information for identifying the sort of person needed (person specification).
Legal	The job description provides the basis for a contract of employment.
Performance	Performance objectives can be set around the job description.
Operational	Job descriptions clarify what people are expected to do, thereby avoiding confusion and conflict.

8.3.2 Contents of a job description

(a) **Job title** (eg Assistant Financial Controller). This indicates the function/department in which the job is performed, and the level of job within that function.

(b) **Reporting to** (eg the Assistant Financial controller reports to the Financial Controller), in other words the person's immediate supervisor

(c) **Subordinates** directly reporting to the job holders

(d) **Overall purpose** of the job, distinguishing it from other jobs

(e) **Principal accountabilities or main tasks**

   (i) Group the main activities into a number of broad areas.

   (ii) Define each activity as a statement of accountability: what the job holder is expected to achieve (eg **tests** new system to ensure they meet agreed systems specifications).

(f) The current movement towards multi-skilled teams means that **flexibility** is sometimes expected.

(g) Required **competences**.

Activity 2.5

Broadside Retail Services of Leeds has a vacancy for an assistant accountant. The post is located in the financial accounting section of the company's large finance department which, among other things, is responsible for the preparation of interim and published accounts and the maintenance of the computerised nominal ledger records from which these accounts are compiled. The person appointed to the post is responsible for updating these records and this entails the supervision of a number of clerks. For these reasons the Chief Accountant is seeking to recruit a qualified accounting technician.

Tasks

(a) Prepare a draft of an appropriate advertisement for the post and indicate what you consider would be the most appropriate media of communication to prospective applicants.

(b) Specify the types of information that you consider should be incorporated in the job description of the post.

Here is a job description in outline.

JOB DESCRIPTION

1 Job title: Accounts Assistant

2 Department: Payroll – Production Staff

3 Responsible to: Supervisor, Production Staff Payroll

4 Age range: over 18 (no upper limit)

5 Supervises work of: N/A

6 Has regular co-operative contact with: Production department supervisors and clerical staff; fellow accounts assistants

7 Main duties/responsibilities: Calculating wages due to production staff and statutory and other deductions. Analysing labour costs for management information purposes

8 Location: Head office, accounts department

9 Employment conditions: Salary: £12,000 per annum
Hours: 9 am – 5 pm (1 hour for lunch)
Holidays: 4 weeks per annum

Prepared by: Sue James, Production Staff Payroll Supervisor **Date**: 20 November 200X

8.3.3 Preparing job descriptions

Job descriptions might be prepared by any of the following people.

(a) **The job holder's manager or supervisor.** The manager should have a good understanding of the job, and how it fits into the work of the section or department as a whole. However, managers might not know the job in detail, and it might be easy to confuse the job itself with the current holder of the job.

(b) **The job holder** knows the job best, but he does not have the advantage of the manager's overview.

(c) **A specialist in preparing job descriptions.** A specialist has the advantage of being experienced in preparing job descriptions, and in being detached from the job (and so less likely to make subjective judgements). However, he will lack a detailed knowledge of the work, and must rely on others to obtain the information he requires.

(d) **A committee**. A committee of job analysts has the advantage of limiting personal bias, but it is likely to be cumbersome.

If you are preparing job descriptions for your project, you are restricted to options (a) or (b). Probably the most useful approach is to prepare job descriptions yourself initially and then allow the current job-holders to comment. There is clearly a problem to be sorted out if you do not agree with your staff about what their jobs involve!

8.3.4 Competences

A more recent approach to job design is the development and outlining of **competences**.

A person's **competence** is 'a capacity that leads to behaviour that meets the job demands within the parameters of the organisational environment and that, in turn, brings about desired results'. A competence embodies the ability to transfer skills and knowledge to new situations. This is the approach of the **AAT scheme**.

Different sorts of competences

(a) **Behavioural/personal** competences: underlying personal characteristics people bring to work (eg interpersonal skills); personal characteristics and behaviour for successful performance, for example, 'ability to relate well to others'. Most jobs require people to be good communicators.

(b) **Work-based/occupational competences** refer to 'expectations of workplace performance and the outputs and standards people in specific roles are expected to obtain'. They cover what people have to do to achieve the results of the job.

(c) **Generic competences** can apply to all people in an occupation.

Some lists of competences confuse:

- Areas of **work** at which people are competent
- Underlying **aspects of behaviour**

In the UK, the competences for many organisations are described by national standards as a benchmark of what people in certain positions are expected to be able to do.

8.4 Separate internal audit department

Many organisations have an **internal audit department**. This functions as an internal financial control. One of its responsibilities is to prevent fraud and error. For this reason it should be separate from the **finance department** and the chief internal auditor should report to the audit committee of the board of directors, bypassing the Financial Director.

9 Office procedures in outline

It would take too long to list all the clerical work procedures in accounting. However, the following list of clerical activities in the accounting department might act as a basis for a more detailed checklist of the procedures carried out in your own department.

Financial accounting procedures

- **Recording transactions** in a **book of prime entry** (a day book) or the **journal** (or the equivalent in a computer system)
- Recording **receipts and payments** in the cash book, with analysis columns to indicate the nature of the receipt or payment
- Keeping a **petty cash book** and using the imprest system
- Making **bank reconciliation** statements, to reconcile the cash book with bank statements
- **Posting transactions** from books of prime entry, for example to the nominal/main ledger, to individual supplier or customer accounts.
- Preparing the **payroll** for wage-earning and salary-earning staff
- Keeping an **asset register**
- **Collecting debts**: issuing monthly statements and reminders: recording bad debts
- Checking and approving the **credit-worthiness** of credit customers
- Conducting an annual **stocktake**

Cost accounting procedures

- Recording **expenditures** (and revenues) according to a **cost** (or revenue) classification – as a direct cost or as a charge to a cost centre
- **Pricing** materials issued from stores
- Recording and costing **labour times**
- Allocating, apportioning and absorbing **overheads**
- Preparing **statements** of costs such as unit costs, job costs and contract costs
- Preparing **budgets**
- Preparing and distributing **performance reports** and variance statements

Much of this work is done on a routine basis. For example, bank reconciliations might be prepared each day, management accounts each month and so forth. The **cycle of operations** describes the routine tasks of the section and how they fit into each other. For example, bank reconciliations are generally prepared before the balance sheet cash figure can be determined at the month end.

Activity 2.6

All the accounting tasks for your organisation are carried out in the one open-plan office accommodating about twenty staff. Although most customers pay by cheque through the mail, occasionally some customers call in to the office to settle their accounts by cash. Only the Finance Director has his own private office. Whenever he can he takes a wide interest in the work of his staff and tries to provide a broad experience for AAT trainees.

He is now proposing that you concentrate more on management accounting duties and relinquish your current cash handling responsibilities. Specifically these are:

Task 1 Receipt of cash and cheques from customers and subsequent payment into the bank.
Task 2 Full control of petty cash (about 10-15 payments per week).

In discussing this proposal with you, the Finance Director suggests someone in the office to take over the tasks. You consider her to be eminently suitable. To help her you both eventually decide that you will make a note of the procedures for reference. It is also suggested that this could be the pilot for the preparation of a procedures manual for the office.

Tasks

(a) Prepare a draft outline for incorporation into a procedure manual of task 1, that is, receipts of cash and cheques and subsequent payment into the bank.

(b) Briefly discuss the control activities that you would stress to your colleague to be aware of when dealing with task 2, that is, petty cash procedures.

Key learning points

- ☑ An organisation's **accounting systems** are affected by the nature of its business transactions and the sort of business it is.
- ☑ Accounting work can be seen as a mixture of the financial aspects of **running an organisation** and **providing information** and advice to other departments.
- ☑ Accounting work is affected by **external regulations** relating to financial accounting, company law, auditing, tax and other influences on the business.
- ☑ The **structure** of accounting departments and the sections within them can be as varied as the structure of organisations as a whole.
- ☑ It is possible that there may be **separate sections** for different types of accounting work.
- ☑ Detailed responsibilities of individuals may be set out in **job descriptions**.
- ☑ The **physical environment** in which work is done can have a profound influence on the way the work is done.
- ☑ The choice of **equipment**, both mundane items such as stationery and more sophisticated items such as computers, influence the effectiveness of the accounts department.

Quick quiz

1. What impact will size, organisation structure and geography have on the organisation of the accounting function?
2. What difference is there between information and operational work for accountants in terms of relationships with other parts of the organisation?
3. Why should *any* external regulations affect accounting practice?
4. Briefly, what impact does company law have on accounting systems?
5. How could the Urgent Issues Task Force affect the work of an accounts department?
6. Besides the government and the accountancy bodies, who else has an influence on accounting practices, and in what way?
7. Do any external regulations affect cost and management accounting practice?
8. List ten sections that there might be in an accounts department.
9. If job descriptions are useful why do many organisations not bother to prepare them?
10. Briefly, what matters need to be considered relating to the location of parts of the accounting department?
11. What problems could arise for an accounting section if office equipment is not properly managed?

Answers to quick quiz

1. A **small** business will have a simple accounting system, whereas a **large** business will have elaborate accounting systems of some technological complexity covering a large number of product ranges and sites. The **structure** of the organisation will determine the way in which accounting information is aggregated, summarised and reported. There are a number of ways in which the accounting function will be affected by **geography**: different currencies, different legal standards and requirements for recording accounting information, different ways of doing business might mean that the emphasis of the accountant's job differs from country to country.
2. Operations work for the most part involves **obtaining** input information from other departments for processing by the accounts department. Information work involves the **output** of information to other departments, although it may also be necessary to obtain extra input information from those departments first.
3. Some organisations are very little affected by external regulations, except for their tax affairs. However, one of the prices that a limited company pays for its limited liability is that its dealings are open to public scrutiny: it has to lodge a copy of its financial statements with the Registrar of Companies so that they are available for inspection by the public. Accounting regulations and standards are meant to ensure that what is published in this way is understandable by the public.
4. The Companies Act contains set formats for company accounts and lists of what information must be disclosed. In normal circumstances, company accounts should adhere to these requirements in every detail, and the accounting system should be set up in such a way that it can provide the information needed. The Companies Act requires companies (generally meaning you and your department) to provide auditors with any information that they need to do their job.

5 The role of the Urgent Issues Task Force is to assist the Accounting Standards Board in areas where an accounting standard or Companies Act provision already exists, but where unsatisfactory or conflicting interpretations have developed. If the UITF issued a ruling on a matter and your company happened to be one of those that had adopted an accounting practice that was contrary to this ruling, your company's approach would have to be changed. This might require all sorts of re-analysis of data and so on. UITF rulings generally only apply to large companies listed on the Stock Exchange.

6 Depending on the organisation, influential parties may include the International Accounting Standards Committee (IASC), the Stock Exchange, people who have invested in the business, such as banks, and sometimes suppliers or customers. Each of these may be able to influence what information has to be made available, in what way, and at what time intervals.

7 Generally, no. However there may be a standard way of accounting for something in certain industries. Also, former public sector bodies like British Gas have their costing methods very closely scrutinised by government watchdogs, because they still at present have a monopoly which could otherwise be abused.

8 There are endless possible answers to this question. Here are some suggestions (we only asked for ten).

Analysis and investigations section
Budget co-ordination section
Budgetary control section
Cost reports section
Credit control section
Debt collection section
Expense and overheads costing section
Financial accounts section
Fixed asset register section
Inventory reporting and valuation section
Job costing/contract costing section
Labour costing section
Management accounting section
Materials costing section
Nominal ledger, section
Payroll section
Process costing section
Project appraisal section
Purchase ledger section
Sales ledger section
Statutory accounts section
Treasurers section
VAT section

9 Job descriptions are useful for job evaluation, in the recruitment of staff, in helping new employees to understand the scope and functions of their job; in helping the organisation's managers to recognise weaknesses in the organisation structure, in identifying training needs and for work study when surveys of current practice are conducted.

However, job descriptions are not **essential** for any of these tasks, and they are not the only way of doing them. They take time to prepare, and have to be kept up-to-date, and so demand time and effort. Some jobs, particularly general management jobs, are very difficult to describe because they entail responding to whatever situation may happen to arise.

10 The location of accounting staff within an organisation is often of some significance.

(a) When an organisation has a lot of cash transactions the location decision is important. In order to account for the receipts as soon as possible, and to minimise the movement of cash before it is banked, it might be appropriate to have an accounts receivable section in a location where customers can come to pay in person.

(b) The location of different sections of accounting staff in relation to each other will be a factor to consider in deciding office layout. It will usually be convenient to locate some sections close together, to minimise the transfer of paper and to make the checking of queries (and audit work) quicker and simpler.

(c) Much accounting work, especially cost and management accounting, is concerned with providing information to others. A close rapport ought to exist between accountants who provide the information and the managers they serve, and locating them close together is one very useful way of improving this rapport.

(d) Managers should ideally have an office close to their staff. Supervisors should preferably be in the same room as their staff.

11 Here are some suggestions. You may have thought of others from practical experience.

(a) Running out of forms or other stationery may hold up work, or lead to vital controls being neglected.

(b) If workspace is inadequate, or becomes so because of untidiness or neglect it is more than likely that documents will be lost and time will be wasted searching for them or doing work twice.

(c) Lack of proper storage facilities is again likely to lead to difficulties in locating documents and wasted time. Problems of confidentiality may occur. There is also the danger of theft.

(d) Sharing telephones between several people that frequently need to use the telephone or be contactable by telephone is inefficient. Queues to use photocopiers or fax machines, or machines that are always breaking down also waste time. For more expensive items of equipment, of course, there is a cost-benefit calculation to be done: does the cost of wasted time exceed the cost of an extra machine? If, say, a computer printer is idle for long periods and much in demand at other times this is a case for rescheduling workloads, not for buying new equipment.

Activity checklist

This checklist shows which performance criteria, range statement or knowledge and understanding point is covered by each activity in this chapter. Tick off each activity as you complete it.

Activity		
2.1	☐	This activity deals with Knowledge and Understanding point 13: The purpose, structure and organisation of the accounting function and its relationships with other functions within the organisation (Element 10.2)
2.2	☐	This activity deals with Knowledge and Understanding point 1: The range of external regulations affecting accounting practice (Element 10.2)
2.3	☐	This activity deals with Knowledge and Understanding point 13: The purpose, structure and organisation of the accounting function and its relationships with other functions within the organisation (Element 10.2) and 14: Who controls the supply of resources (equipment, materials, information and people) within the organisation (Element 10.1) and Performance Criteria 10.1.H: Refer problems and queries to the appropriate person where resolution is beyond your authority and expertise and 10.2.D: Make recommendations to the appropriate person in a clear, easily understood format and 10.2.E: Ensure recommendations are supported by a clear rationale which includes an explanation of any assumption made.
2.4	☐	This activity deals with Knowledge and Understanding point 14: Who controls the supply of resources (equipment, materials, information and people) within the organisation (Element 10.1) and Performance Criteria 10.2.D: Make recommendations to the appropriate person in a clear, easily understood format and 10.2.E: Ensure recommendations are supported by a clear rationale which includes an explanation of any assumption made.
2.5	☐	This activity deals with Knowledge and Understanding point 14: Who controls the supply of resources (equipment, materials, information and people) within the organisation (Element 10.1) and Performance Criteria 10.2.D: Make recommendations to the appropriate person in a clear, easily understood format and 10.2.E: Ensure recommendations are supported by a clear rationale which includes an explanation of any assumption made.
2.6	☐	This activity deals with Knowledge and Understanding point 13: The purpose, structure and organisation of the accounting function and its relationships with other functions within the organisation (Element 10.2)

chapter 3

Managing the team

Contents

Performance criteria

10.1.B Review the competence of individuals undertaking work activities and arrange the necessary training

10.1.D Communicate work methods and schedules to colleagues in ways that help them to understand what is expected of them

10.1.G Encourage colleagues to report to you promptly any problems and queries that are beyond their authority or expertise to resolve, and resolve these where they are within your authority and expertise

10.1.H Refer problems and queries to the appropriate person where resolution is beyond your authority or expertise

Knowledge and understanding

9 Principles of supervision and delegation (Element 10.1)

10 Principles of fostering effective working relationships, building teams and motivating staff (Element 10.1)

1 Introduction

In the previous chapter, we covered how the department is organised. Now we shall cover how to manage the people in it.

In an organisation, managerial work has a purpose: directing the organisation's activities in order to carry out the mission. Your managerial or supervisory job is not simply to follow procedures blindly. You should be looking actively for ways in which your role and department can better satisfy the objectives of the organisation.

You may have some control over determining how things are managed. For example, perhaps you feel there are too many people reporting to one person. One way of dealing with this may be to appoint section leaders. For example, if there are three people looking after cash, say, one person could be asked to look after that mini-section. You would have one person reporting to you rather than three – even though you have increased the number of management levels.

If your changes go beyond the established way of doing things – eg go against the culture – you will need to justify them. However, relatively simple issues such as **motivation** can be an area for improvement. (Although you are unlikely to be able to determine pay levels, you can enrich people's jobs in other ways.)

Remember, if you are not a manager yourself, you can still observe your boss or other managers in the organisation.

2 Managers: what they are for and what they do

Management can be defined as 'getting things done through other people'.

2.1 What managers should do

Possible **management** tasks based on the views of a number of theorists are outlined below.

Task	Comment
Planning for the future	Selecting **objectives** and the designing the strategies and procedures for achieving them.
Organising the work	Establishing a **structure of tasks** to be performed to achieve the goals, **grouping these tasks into jobs** for individuals, creating **groups of jobs** within departments, **delegating authority** to carry out the jobs and providing **systems of information**. In other words, determining what activities are necessary to achieve the objectives of the business, then dividing the work and assigning this to different people.
Commanding and directing	Giving **instructions** to subordinates to carry out tasks.
Co-ordinating and communicating	**Harmonising** the activities of individuals and groups within the organisation, reconciling differences of **priority**. The manager must communicate within the organisation and with outsiders.
Controlling and measuring	**Measuring** the activities of individuals and groups, to ensure that their **performance is in accordance with plans**. Targets are achieved, objectives are met and orders are carried out in conformity with procedures.

Task	Comment
Leading and motivating	A leader does not just tell people what to do. A leader is able to inspire and develop people.
Staffing	Making sure there are enough people with the right skills.

Activity 3.1

Tasks

Using the list above, indicate under which of the five headings the activities below fall.

1 Ensuring that the sales department does not exceed its budget.
2 Deciding which products will form the main thrust of advertising during the next financial year.
3 Ensuring that new working practices are followed.
4 Ensuring that the sales department liases with production on delivery dates.
5 Changing work schedules to reduce idle time.

Here are some more modern perspectives.

Task	Comment
Diagnosing problems	• **Identify the symptoms** in the situation (eg low productivity, high labour turnover). • **Diagnose the disease** or cause of the trouble. • **Decide how it might be dealt with** by developing a strategy for better health. • **Start the treatment.**
Coaching and support	• **Supporting operations** and helping them become efficient. • Providing **counselling** and advice. • Bringing the **organisation's resources** to bear on problems identified by.
Innovating	Many organisations innovate. **Innovation** can occur in new product design, production, marketing, service delivery, organisation structure and culture. People should be able to **communicate their insights** to others in the organisation, creating a pool of knowledge from which the **whole** organisation can draw. Creativity does not only reside in individuals, but in groups.

2.2 What managers actually do

Henry Mintzberg suggests that in their daily working lives, managers fulfil three **types** of managerial role. This classification was based on observations of senior managers, rather than junior management. Even so, you can **observe** managers at all levels enacting all these **roles** at different times.

Role category	Role	Comment
Interpersonal, from formal authority and position	**Figurehead** (or ceremonial)	A large part of a Chief Executive's time is spent representing the company, both outside it and within. Not all that relevant to accounts supervisors.
	Leader	Hiring, firing and training staff, motivating employees, and reconciling individual needs with the requirements of the organisation or department.
	Liaison	Making contacts outside the vertical chain of command. Some managers spend up to half their meeting time with their peers rather than with their subordinates.
Informational Managers have: Access to all their staff Many external contracts	**Monitor**	The manager **monitors** the environment, and receives information from subordinates, superiors and colleagues in other departments. Much of this information is of an informal nature.
	Spokesperson	The manager provides information within and outside the organisation.
	Disseminator	The manager **disseminates** this information to subordinates and others.
Decisional The manager's formal authority and access to information mean that no one else is in a position to take decisions relating to the work of the department as a whole.	**Entrepreneur**	A manager initiates projects to improve the department or to help it react to a changed environment. This is relevant to the project.
	Disturbance handler	A manager has to respond to pressures, taking decisions in unusual or unexpected situations.
	Resource allocator	A manager allocates scarce resources and authorises decisions taken by subordinates.
	Negotiator	Both inside and outside the organisation takes up a great deal of management time.

The manager needs to wear the right 'hat' for each task and situation. A manager will wear some hats more than others.

- Senior officials, for example, are more likely to be called upon to at as figureheads than team leaders.
- Supervisors are more concerned with resource allocation and disturbance handling.

Activity 3.2

The *Telegraph Magazine* asked a cinema manager: 'What do you actually do? The answer was as follows.

'Everything, apart from being the projectionist and cleaning the lavatories. My office is also the ticket office. If there is a big queue at the confectionery kiosk, I'll help serve and I'll usher people to their seat if we're really busy. Sometimes I go into the cinema before a show and tell the audience about any special events, such as a director coming to give a talk.

'I get in around lunchtime, deal with messages and ensure that the lights and heating are working. I write orders for posters and publicity pictures, popcorn and ice creams and cope with the correspondence for the 2,000 members on our mailing list. I'll brief the projectionist, ushers and kiosk staff and at about 1.45pm the first matinee customers arrive. Our afternoon audience is mainly elderly people and they take some time to settle, so I'll help them to their seats and only start the film when everyone is comfortable. In the evening, more ushers and bar staff arrive and I'll brief them about the programme, seating and timing. While the film is on, I'm selling tickets for the other screen, counting the takings and planning tomorrow. If I get a moment I try to grab something to eat.'

Task

Which of Mintzberg's roles does this manager take on in his average day?

2.3 Some principles of management and supervision

Traditionally 'the principles of supervision' and 'delegation' include the following principles.

Principle	Comment
Division of work (specialisation of tasks)	Specialisation allows an individual to build up an expertise and thereby be more productive. In manufacturing, there is a trend towards **multi-skilling**.
Authority and responsibility	A supervisor's **official** authority derives from his or her rank or office. **Authority is the right to issue orders**. With authority goes **responsibility** for exercising it. Responsibility means being accountable for the way authority is exercised.
Discipline	**Discipline** is the enforcement of **standards of behaviour**. Managers and supervisors should set a good example.
Remuneration	The rewards given to employees should be fair, satisfying both employer and employee alike. Rewards mean more than financial rewards.
Scalar chain	The scalar chain is the term used to describe the organisation's management hierarchy, ie the chain of superiors from lowest to highest rank.
Fairness	Everybody must be judged on their performance. This means not rewarding the under-achievers, as well as rewarding the achievers.
Initiative	This is one of the most important ideas in modern management thinking: it is essential to encourage and develop this capacity in staff to the full.
Team spirit	Building up a team spirit takes considerable talent: to co-ordinate efforts, encourage enthusiasm and avoid inter-personal conflict.

3 The management hierarchy

Organisational structure shows how tasks are differentiated and distributed. Management structure is an aspect of this. It shows the distribution of authority and responsibility.

3.1 Chain of command

The **scalar chain** or **chain of command** is the organisation's formal management hierarchy, that is the chain of superiors from lowest to highest rank. **Formal communication runs up and down the lines of authority**, eg E to D to C to B to A in the diagram below. If communication between different branches of the chain is necessary (eg D to H) the use of a 'gang plank' of horizontal communication saves time.

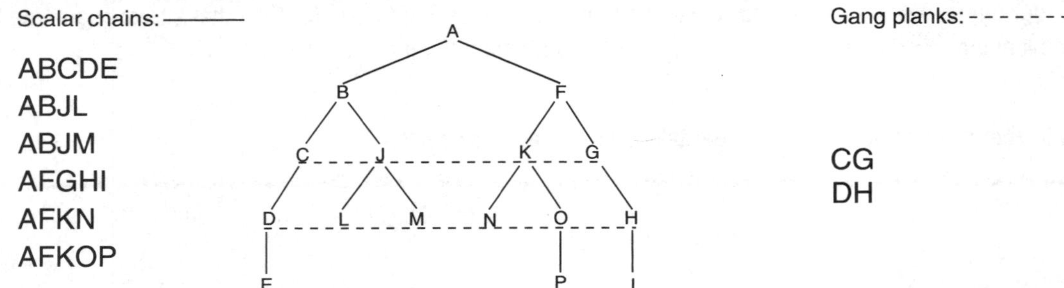

The length of the chains of command is influenced by five things.

- Work practices
- Size of the organisation
- Products and services (type, range, complexity)
- Geographical dispersion
- Controls

An organisation has many such scalar chains of authority and command, but all of them originate at the **topmost management authority** which in a company is the **board of directors**. Managers at **different levels in the hierarchy are all links** in a chain of command.

How many links should there be?

(a) Short chains of command: few links from top to bottom

- Information – good or bad – can, in theory, flow quickly up and down, without going through too many levels.
- Junior managers can influence and obtain insight into senior management decisions.

(b) Long chains of command provide a satisfying career structure and reduce **span of control** which we will now discuss.

3.2 Span of control: how many people report to you directly?

Span of control is the number of staff immediately responsible to a particular manager or supervisor.

In the diagram under Paragraph 3.1, C has a span of control of 1 (because D is the only person directly reporting to C) and J has a span of control of 2. B also has a span of control of 2. When an organisation tends to have narrow spans of control, it follows that it has more managers and layers of management than one that has wide spans of control. As a result, an organisation with narrow spans will be **tall**, while one with wide spans will be **flat**.

Currently the fashion is for flat organisations with few layers, and with responsibility delegated to teams.

The number of subordinates and tasks over which a manager has supervisory responsibilities should be restricted to what is physically and mentally possible.

Width of span	Key issues
Narrow (ie few direct reports)	• Tight **control** and close supervision and co-ordination of subordinates activities. • **Time** to think and plan; managers are not burdened with too many day to day problems. • **Reduced delegation**; a manager can do more of his work himself. • **Better communication** with subordinates, who are sufficiently small in number to allow this to occur.
Wide (many people)	• **Greater decision-making authority** for subordinates. • **Lower supervisory costs**. • Less control, but perhaps **greater motivation** though job satisfaction.

Influence on span of control

- The nature of the manager's work load. As a supervisor you will have to deal with technical accounting issues yourself as well as delegate them to your staff. You need time for this and this may mean you cannot have too many people reporting to you.
- Where subordinates are located (eg other offices).
- Subordinates' work: if subordinates do the same simple job a wide span is possible.
- The nature of problems that a supervisor might have to help subordinates with.
- The degree of interaction between subordinates (with close interaction, a wider span of control should be possible).
- The competence and abilities of both team leaders and team members.
- Whether close group cohesion is desirable. Small groups will be more cohesive, with a better sense of team work. This would call for narrow spans of control.
- The amount of help that supervisors receive from other departments (such as the personnel department or the production planning department).

3.3 Project and matrix management

A golden rule of older management theory is that one person should have one boss. However, in many modern organisations this is impractical.

A project, such as the development of a new product, for example, may be **inter-disciplinary**, and require the contributions of an engineer, a marketing person and a production expert, who would each be appointed to the team from their separate departments, whilst still retaining membership and status within their own departments. Someone from the finance department may also be taken on board, to manage the costs.

Matrix organisations are permanent arrangements, in which two (or more) lines of authority overlap. For example, a section leader in a regional accounts department might have to report both to a **financial controller** at head office and to a **regional general manager**, so that functional and geographic organisation run at the same time.

Advantages

- Greater flexibility and co-operation from everyone involved
- Co-ordination between business functions at local level

Disadvantages

- Dual authority threatens a conflict between managers.
- One individual with two or more bosses is more likely to suffer stress at work.

Activity 3.3

Six months ago Dawn Reeves, your friend in another section of the accounts department, was promoted to a first line supervisory position. She undertook her new duties enthusiastically and the performance of her section has improved. Dawn, however, is not as happy as she used to be when she was an ordinary member of the section. 'I'm not sure I'm the type to be a supervisor,' she confided to you recently. 'There seems to be so much to do, but not a lot of it is what I call proper work.' This seems to be an ideal opportunity to talk to Dawn about 'managerial roles'.

Tasks

(a) Note what you would say to Dawn about managerial roles in general. Try to draw your answer from your *own* experience (and *observation* of others) rather than merely listing the roles outlined in this text.

(b) List the key roles which Dawn should play in her current job.

4 Supervisors and what they do

4.1 Where do supervisors fit in?

The diagram in Paragraph 3.1 in this chapter showed a pyramid, with A at the apex and others below. This suggests that there are different **levels** of management. A **finance department** in an organisation might be headed by the finance director (at A), supported by a chief **financial accountant** (B) and chief **management accountant** (F). C, J, K and G are lower down in the hierarchy; they might be assistant accountants.

The **supervisor is the lowest level of management**. 'A **supervisor** is a person selected by middle management to take charge of a group of people, or special task, to ensure that work is carried out satisfactorily ... the job is largely reactive dealing with situations as they arise, allocating and reporting back to higher management.' (Savedra and Hawthorn).

4.2 Features of supervision

(a) A **supervisor** is usually a 'front-line' manager, dealing with the levels of the organisation where the bread-and-butter work is done. The supervisor's **subordinates are non-managerial employees**.

(b) A supervisor does not spend all his or her time on the managerial aspects of his job. A supervisor does **technical/operational work**.

(c) The supervisor monitors and controls work by means of **day-to-day, frequent and detailed information:** higher levels of management plan and control using longer-term, less frequent and less detailed information.

(d) The **managerial aspects and responsibilities of a supervisor's job are often ill-defined**, and have no precise targets to measure achievement against.

4.3 What do supervisors do?

As a supervisor's job is a junior management job, the tasks of supervision can be listed under similar headings to the tasks of management. Use this as a checklist for your own position.

Comments	Your role	
Planning	• Planning **work** so as to **meet work targets** or schedules set by more senior management • Planning work **methods and procedures** • Preparing **budgets** for the section • Planning **staff training** and staff development	
Organising and overseeing the work of others	• **Ordering** materials and equipment • Authorising overtime • **Allocating work and equipment** to staff • Monitoring **performance standards** for staff • Deciding **job priorities**	
Controlling: making sure the work is done properly	• Keeping **records** of time worked, time spent on each job, time spent idle • **Disciplining** staff (for late arrival at work and so on) • Ensuring that the **quality of work** is sustained to the required levels • Ensuring that **safety standards** are maintained • **Co-ordinating** the work of the section with the work of other sections • Ensuring that **work targets are achieved**, and explaining the cause to senior management of any failure to achieve these targets	
Motivating employees, and dealing with others	• Dealing with **staff problems** • **Reporting to a senior manager** • Dealing with **customers** • Helping staff to **understand** the organisation's goals and targets • **Training staff**, and identifying the need for more training	
Communicating	• **Telling employees about plans, targets and work schedules** • **Telling managers** about the work that has been done, and the attitudes of staff to the work and work conditions • **Filling in reports** (for example absentee reports for the personnel department, on appraisal forms) • **Collecting information** and distributing it to the other persons interested in it.	
'Doing'	• Doing technical operations work • Standing in for a senior manager when he or she is on holiday or otherwise absent • Giving advice to others to help solve problems	

Activity 3.4

Tasks

Look at the job of the supervisor (or similar position) in your office (your own job, if you are in such a position).

(a) Identify the (i) managerial and (ii) technical aspects of the job, and list as many as you can think of the duties they entail.

(b) Get hold of a copy of the **job description** of a supervisory job (or have a look at one in the organisation manual). Does it bear any relation to the list you compiled yourself? Is it a realistic description of the actual work of the supervisor? Is the supervisory part of the job well-defined (as compared with the technical part)? Are there targets or standards, and training requirements?

(c) Consider your own experience of promotion to a supervisory post (or ask your supervisor). What preparation, training, coaching, and/or advice was given by the manager for this first step into managerial work – or was it sink or swim?

5 Interpersonal relationships

5.1 Interpersonal behaviour and roles

Interpersonal behaviour is behaviour between people. It includes two way processes such as communicating, delegating, negotiating, resolving conflict, persuading, selling, using and responding to authority, as well as a person's manner with other people. Desirable interpersonal behaviour includes:

- **Perceiving** other people
- **Listening to** and **understanding** other people
- **Behaving** in a way which builds on this understanding
- Being **sensitive** to the impression one gives, in the light of the roles one is expected to play

Many people behave in any situation according to the **roles** they are expected to perform, and the **role** tends to influence the type of interpersonal relationships that people have.

A role is a 'part' you play in relation to other people in a situation. For example, your role as a parent entitles you to exercise authority but your role in the workplace may not involve authority. A role is more than just a job. A certain type of behaviour is expected from your role.

Activity 3.5

Managers could exert a powerful influence over team members if they could establish themselves as role models.

Task

What kind of example could they set that might be helpful for the team members and for the organisation?

5.2 Interpersonal skills

We **need Interpersonal skills** in order to do three things.

- Understand and manage the roles, relationships, attitudes and perceptions operating in any situation in which two or more people are involved
- Communicate clearly and effectively
- Achieve our aims from an interpersonal encounter (ideally, allowing the other parties to emerge satisfied too)

Interpersonal skills may include the ability to:

- Interpret other people's **body language** (and to control your own, to reinforce the message you want to give)
- Identify what **roles** you and others are in, as these roles interact with each other
- **Listen** attentively and actively to people
- **'Read between the lines'** of a message, by recognising where attitudes, bias, or deliberate ambiguity are distorting the real message being given
- Put **others at their ease**, to persuade, to smooth over difficult situations – ie diplomacy
- Use **communication media** effectively: to speak articulately, write legibly and in an appropriate vocabulary, or draw diagrams where required
- Communicate and show **enthusiasm** – ie leadership or inspiration

The above list does not cover everything. There are many types of skill brought into play in encounters between people, especially if their purpose is not just informing but persuading, disciplining, dealing with problems or sharing emotions.

6 Individuals at work

6.1 Personality

In order to identify, describe and explain the differences between people, we use the concept of **personality**. We use this word every day. Some organisations use sophisticated tests to analyse personality.

Personality descries how an individual thinks, feels and believes in response to other people and the environment. (We sometimes refer to people as having an outgoing personality.)

Self and self-image

Personality **develops** from experience whereby the individual interacts with his or her environment and other people.

(a) **Self-image.** People tend to behave, and expect to be treated, in accordance with their self-image but this self-image may not be accurate. Some people have low self-esteem and a manager may have to build their confidence. It may be harder to deal with people whose view of their abilities is higher than their actual performance.

(b) **Personality development.** People have different goals as they age.

6.2 Personality and work behaviour

An individual can be 'compatible' in three ways.

Compatibility	Comments
With the task	Different personality types suit different types of work. A person who appears unsociable and inhibited will find sales work, involving a lot of social interactions, intensely stressful – and will probably not be very good at it.
With the systems and management culture of the organisation	Some people hate to be controlled, but others accept and even exploit their place in the hierarchy.
With other personalities in the team	**Personality clashes** are a prime source of conflict at work at all levels.

What should you do if people are 'incompatible'?

	Comments
Restore compatibility	Give people different jobs more suited to their personality type or change management style to suit the personalities of the team.
Achieve a compromise	Individuals should be encouraged to **understand the nature** of their differences. Others have the right to be themselves (within the demands of the team). It may be necessary for some to **change their behaviour** if necessary.
Remove the incompatible personality	In the last resort, obstinately difficult or disruptive people may simply have to be weeded out of the team.

It is worth bearing in mind that there is the potential for interpersonal conflict at all levels in the organisation.

Activity 3.6

Tasks

Look at the following list and number the qualities in priority order. 1 is very important, 2 is quite important, 3 is unimportant.

(a) Good appearance
(b) Ability to do the job
(c) Ability to answer questions clearly
(d) A pleasant speaking voice
(e) Being objective
(f) A pleasant personality
(g) The ability to reason
(h) Being interested in further training
(i) Being used to working in a team
(j) Being a good listener

6.3 Perception

The ability to assess the personality of others – with very little information – is an essential part of social behaviour, enabling individuals to interact with each other effectively.

The way in which we perceive other people is obviously going to be crucial to how we will relate to them and communicate with them in any context. There are two important forms of bias in the perception of other people that tend to operate in any situation.

	Comment
The halo effect	**First impressions,** based on immediately obvious characteristics like dress, manner or facial expression, colour later perceptions of other features of those people, whether to positive or negative effect.
Stereotyping	We group together people who share certain characteristics, and then attribute traits to the group as a whole, assuming that all members of the group are the same in all characteristics. The grouping may be done according to nationality, occupation, social position, age, sex or physical characteristics.

Activity 3.7

In general terms, organisations will make certain generalised assumptions about the personalities of the individuals they wish to employ. They may have an idea of the character traits or types that are considered desirable in whatever business they are in, or in whatever role the individual is to fill. You only have to look in job advertisements to see the recurrence of the desired characteristics: extrovert, steady, lively, responsible, hard working and so on.

However, research has not been able to show a significant correlation between personality (on the basis of test results) and performance.

(a) The extrovert may be active, cheerful, social and not averse to risk – but may also be unreliable, easily bored, irresponsible and fickle.

(b) Neurotics tend to be depressive, anxious, obsessive and emotional, and take too many days off sick – but they may also be conscientious, highly disciplined and they do not fret under authority. Moreover, the ability to display and share emotion can be a healthy and desirable quality.

Which of these would *you* rather have working in your section?

One of the commonest mistakes that managers make is to want to 'clone' themselves: to assume that what motivates them is (or should be) what motivates everybody else or, worse, to assume that anybody whose approach and attitude to work is not the same as their own is 'wrong' or inappropriate.

7 How are people motivated?

In Chapter 1 we saw that an **organisation has goals**, which can only be achieved by the efforts of the people who work in the organisation. **Individual people also have their own goals** in life, and these may not be consistent with those of the organisation. A major consideration for supervisors and management is the problem of motivating the employees to work in such a way that the organisation achieves its goals.

Activity 3.8

What factors in yourself or your organisation motivate you to:

(a) Turn up to work at all?
(b) Do an average day's work?
(c) 'Bust a gut' on a task or for a boss?

The words **motives** and **motivation** are commonly used in at least three ways.

- **Motives** are **goals or outcomes** that have become desirable for a particular individual. We say that money, power or friendship are **motives** for doing something.
- Motivation is the **mental process of choosing desired outcomes**, deciding how to go about them and **setting in motion** the required behaviour. ('I want the job so I must apply for it'.)
- **Other people try to motivate us** to behave in the ways they wish. **Motivation** in this sense usually applies to the attempts of organisations to motivate their staff to do a better job.

7.1 Maslow's hierarchy of needs

Maslow described motivation in terms of a hierarchy of needs, as in the diagram below, and put forward certain propositions. He said that all people have a set of four needs and are motivated to satisfy theses needs in a **particular order**. The bottom need on the hierarchy in the diagram following must be satisfied first, and so on.

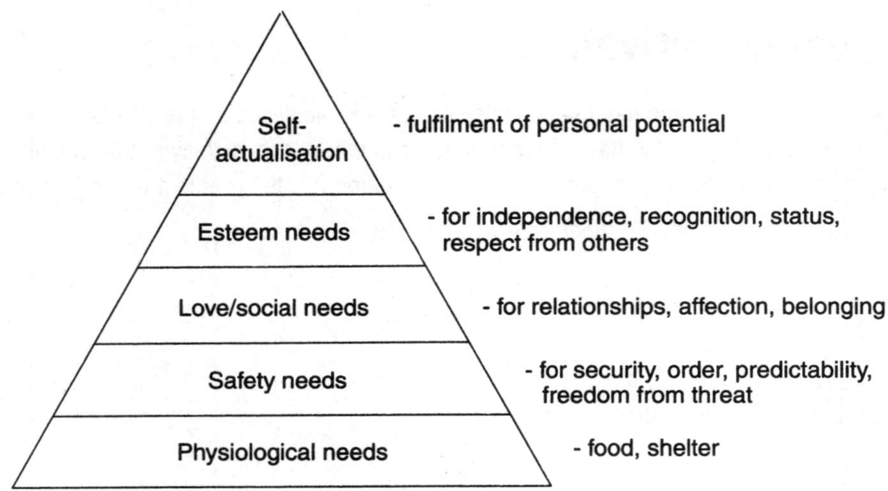

A **need which has been satisfied no longer motivates** an individual's behaviour to do better.

Activity 3.9

Task

Decide which of Maslow's categories of need the following fit into. The theory does not cover work as such, hence two 'non-work' examples.

(a) Receiving praise from your manager
(b) Birthday party for a colleague
(c) An artist forgetting to eat
(d) The first cup of tea of the day
(e) A pay increase
(f) Joining a local drama group
(g) Being awarded the 'employee of the year' award

Problems with Maslow's hierarchy

- Someone's behaviour may be in response to **several needs**. Work, after all, can either satisfy or thwart the satisfaction of a number of needs.
- The **same need may cause different behaviour** in different individuals.
- Some people are prepared to put off satisfying some needs into the future.

7.2 Herzberg

Herzberg's two-factor theory identified **hygiene factors** and **motivator factors**.

Factors	Comments
Hygiene factors are based on a **need to avoid unpleasantness**	If inadequate, they cause **dissatisfaction** with work. Unpleasantness demotivates: pleasantness is a steady state. Hygiene factors (the conditions of work) include: • Company policy and administration • Interpersonal relations • Salary • Working conditions • The quality of supervision • Job security
Motivator factors are based on a **need for personal growth**	They actively create job satisfaction and are effective in motivating an individual to superior performance and effort. These factors are: • Status (this may be a hygiene factor too) • Challenging work • Advancement • Achievement • Gaining recognition • Growth in the job • Responsibility

A lack of motivators at work will encourage employees to concentrate on bad hygiene factors (such as to demand more pay). Stemming from his fundamental division of motivator and hygiene factors, *Herzberg* encouraged managers to **change the job** itself (the type of work done, the nature of tasks, levels of responsibility) rather than conditions of work. This is particularly important if you have little say over pay, or if there are few opportunities for promotion.

7.3 Expectancy theory –Vroom

Vroom suggested that people will decide how much they are going to put into their work, according to two factors.

(a) **Valence:** the value that they place on the outcome for themselves (whether the positive value of a reward, or the negative value of a punishment)

(b) **Expectancy:** the strength of their expectation that behaving in a certain way will in fact bring out the desired outcome.

Expectancy × Valence = Force of motivation.

Put more simply, if you **believe** that if you work hard to get promoted, but then find that you do not get promoted you will be less highly motivated to work hard in future.

7.4 Targets: goal theory

Goal theory suggests that people respond to goals and targets. Some goals are difficult, others are easy. some goals are of a general nature ('do your best'); others are specific ('I want that report by 10am Thursday morning').

- **Difficult goals lead to better performance** than easy goals, so long as they have been *accepted* by the person trying to achieve them.

- **Specific goals lead to higher performance** than general 'do your best' goals perhaps because it is easy to focus on something precise.

- **Knowledge of results (feedback) is essential** if the full performance benefits of setting difficult and specific goals are to be achieved.

What are *your* goals at work?

8 Improving motivation

Ways of increasing the motivation of staff include

- **Pay and incentive schemes**
- The **job itself** and changes to it.
- **Participation by subordinates in decision-making**

8.1 The role of rewards

People can be rewarded in different ways.

- **Extrinsic rewards** are separate from (or external to) the job itself, and dependent on the decisions of others (that is, also external to the control of the workers themselves). Pay, benefits, cash and non-cash incentives and working conditions are examples of extrinsic rewards.

- **Intrinsic rewards** are those which arise from the performance of the work itself. They are therefore psychological rather than material and relate to the concept of job satisfaction. Intrinsic rewards include the satisfaction that comes from completing a piece of work, the status that certain jobs convey, and the feeling of achievement that comes from doing a difficult job well.

8.2 Pay

Pay satisfies several of the needs in Maslow's hierarchy. Not only does it indirectly provide food and shelter, it can be a **mark of status and esteem.** Pay can be used as a motivator, for example, performance-related pay, bonuses and so on. However:

- Many people are motivated by **other needs** in Maslow's hierarchy, and look for intrinsic rewards.

- **Satisfaction** with pay is often connected with notions of what is **fair in relation to what other people** in the organisation are earning.

- **Performance-related pay schemes have not been very successful in practice**. Some evidence suggests that if people are assessed and rewarded as individuals they are less likely to co-operate or help fellow team members.

It is quite likely that you have **no control at all over the pay of the staff** you supervise, so we shall not explore this topic further, except to remind you that you can reward people by saying 'thank you' and praising them, as well as with money.

8.3 The job as motivator

The job itself can be a motivator, or it can be a cause of dissatisfaction. This is where you might have some influence.

8.3.1 Job design

Job design is the incorporation of the tasks the organisation needs to be done into a job for one person. Job design can influence motivation by giving wider **responsibility**. You will have seen an example of a job description in Chapter 2.

Job specialisation tends to reduce breadth of responsibility.

- How many **different tasks** are contained in the job and how broad and narrow are these tasks?
- To what extent **does the worker have control over the work**?

8.3.2 Job simplification and specialisation

Job simplification means that a task is divided into many different narrow activities and a job only covers a small number of these activities. In an accounting context, it may be that someone has the sole responsibility for inputting sales orders, and that this is all they do.

Advantages of job simplification

Advantage	Comment
Little training	A job is divided up into the smallest number of sequential tasks possible. Each task is so simple and straightforward that it can be learned with very little training.
Replacement	If labour turnover is high, this does not matter because unskilled replacements can be found and trained to do the work in a very short time.
Flexibility	Since the skill required is low, workers can be shifted from one task to another very easily. The production flow will therefore be unaffected by absenteeism.
Control	If tasks are closely defined and standard times set for their completion, production is easier to predict and control.
Quality	Standardisation of work into simple tasks means that quality is easier to predict. There is less scope for doing a task badly, in theory at least.

Disadvantages of job simplification

Comments	
Boring	The work is **monotonous** and makes employees tired, bored and dissatisfied.
Ineffective	**People work better** when their work is **variable**.
Understanding	An individual doing a simple task has no **sense of contributing to the organisation's end product** or service. This can have a bad effect on customer service.
Knowledge	Excessive specialisation **isolates** the individual in his or her work and inhibits not only social contacts with 'work mates', but knowledge generation.
Inattention	In practice, excessive job simplification leads to **lower quality, through inattention**.

Herzberg suggest three ways of improving job design, to make jobs more interesting to the employee, and hopefully to improve performance. This relates to **intrinsic rewards.**

- Job enrichment
- Job enlargement
- Job rotation

8.3.3 Job enrichment and delegation

Job enrichment is planned, deliberate action to build greater responsibility, breadth and challenge of work into a job.

- Give the job holder **decision-making capabilities of a 'higher' order**. What is, mundane detail at a high level can represent significant job interest at a lower level.
- Give the **employee greater freedom** to decide how the job should be done.
- Encourage employees **to participate** in the planning decisions of their superiors.
- Give the employee regular **feedback**.

Job enrichment alone will not **automatically** or immediately make employees more **productive**, but it will benefit the firm in the less visible costs of morale, climate and working relationships.

Job enrichment is one justification for **delegation**. If you delegate a task, you get someone else to do it for you, even though you are, yourself, ultimately responsible for the work to be done. Delegating is a way of managing your **own** workload – we shall cover time management in a later chapter – as well as job enrichment.

As a manager, you may have to encourage your team members to delegate their own work.

8.3.4 Job enlargement

Job enlargement is the attempt to widen jobs by increasing the number of operations in which a job holder is involved.

Reducing the number of repetitions of the same work should reduce the dullness of a job. Job enlargement is therefore a **'horizontal' extension** of an individual's work, whereas job enrichment is a 'vertical' extension.

(a) Just giving an employee tasks which span a larger part of the total production work should **reduce boredom**.

(b) Enlarged jobs can provide a **challenge and incentive**. A trusted employee might be given added responsibilities, such as **checking the quality of output**. Employees who are responsible for their own work quality might easily see a challenging responsibility in such a job. Another possibility is **on the job training** of new recruits.

(c) Enlarged jobs might also be regarded as **'status' jobs** within the department, and as stepping stones towards promotion.

8.3.5 Job rotation

Job rotation might take two forms.

(a) Someone might be **transferred to another job** to offer a new interest and challenge.

(b) **Job rotation can be used as a form of training**. Trainees might be expected to learn a bit about a number of different jobs, by spending six months or one year in each job before being moved on. The employee is regarded as a trainee rather than as an experienced person holding down a demanding job.

8.3.6 Job optimisation

A **well designed job** should therefore provide the individual with several advantages.

- **Scope** for individuals to set their own work standards and targets
- **Control** over the pace and methods of working
- **Variety** by allowing for inter-locking tasks to be done by the same person
- **Voice**: a chance to add comments about the design of the product, or the job
- **Feedback** of information about performance to the individual

8.4 Participation and empowerment

Many people want more interesting work and to have a say in decision-making. These expectations support the movement towards greater **participation** at work. The methods of achieving increased involvement have largely crystallised into two main streams.

(a) **Immediate participation** is used to refer to the involvement of employees in the **day-to-day** decisions of their work group. **Empowerment** often relates to teams. Teams manager their own work.

(b) **Distant participation** refers to the process of including company employees at the top levels of the organisation which deal with long-term policy issues including investment and employment. Major firms in the EU are required to have **works councils**.

Participation can involve employees and make them feel committed to their task, given the following conditions (5 Cs).

Condition	Comment
Certainty	Participation should be genuine.
Consistency	Efforts to establish participation should be made consistently over a long period.
Clarity	The purpose of participation is made quite clear.
Capacity	The individual has the ability and information to participate effectively.
Commitment	The manager believes in participation.

However, remember that some people do **not** want extra responsibility at work and are happiest performing predictable, undemanding tasks.

8.5 Conclusions on motivation

Individuals **vary in the kind of needs** they have and the satisfactions they want. Managers may be able to improve staff motivation and performance by studying these needs and providing opportunities for staff to fulfil them through their work.

Some general principles might help you in the project.

- A **clear meaning and purpose** in relation to the objectives of the organisation
- Being as **self-contained as possible**, so that the employee will be doing a 'complete' job
- **Opportunities for making decisions** or participating in decisions which affect work and targets (eg in deciding the methods for doing work)
- **Regular feedback** of information to the employee about his performance
- **Avoidance of monotony and repetitiveness**.

You may consider that changing the way employers are motivated is not really your role. But you can affect intrinsic rewards by giving people interesting work and recognition.

Activity 3.10

Harriet has just been appointed to take charge of part of a management accounting department concerned with processing information from the operating division of a large company.

Based on her previous experience she has determined that the running costs of the department are too high, due to absenteeism, lateness, low productivity and time spent in correcting errors.

Investigation of the design of the jobs in the department reveals that each employee is trained in a task which is made as simple as possible. The equipment used is maintained by a service department. Strict discipline ensures that clerks do not carry on conversations during working hours, and that tasks are performed in exactly the order and method laid down.

Harriet has decided that performance can be improved by changing the job design.

Harriet's superiors approve the changes, the correct training is provided and that resistance by the staff to change is properly overcome.

Tasks

(a) Describe six changes which might achieve improved job satisfaction;
(b) Explain four problems which may make it difficult to change the design of such jobs.

9 Working in teams

Organisations enable the activities and skills of the people within them to be combined so that the output of the whole is greater than the sum of the parts. This is relevant **within** organisations, too, especially large organisations. A team is more than just a collection of individuals – it has a specific purpose and even a sense of an identity, and in a work context it has a task to perform.

9.1 Groups and teams

A **group** is 'any collection of people who perceive themselves to be a group'. A group of individuals share a common sense of identity and belonging.

What do group's have?	Comments
A sense of identity	There are acknowledged boundaries to the group which define it.
Loyalty to the group	Acceptance within the group is generally expressed through acceptance of the 'norms' of behaviour and attitude that bind the group together and exclude others from it.
Purpose and leadership	Most groups have an express purpose, whatever field they are in: most will, spontaneously or formally, choose individuals or sub-groups to lead them towards the fulfilment of those goals.

In a workplace there are two types of group.

- A **primary working group** is the immediate social environment of the individual worker, in other words, the people he/she works with most of the time.
- A **team** is a **formal group** used for particular objectives in the work place. Although many people enjoy working in teams, their popularity in the work place arises because of their **effectiveness in fulfilling the organisation's work**.

9.2 Teams

A **team** is a 'small number of people with complementary skills who are committed to a **common purpose**, performance **goals** and approach, for which they hold themselves basically accountable'.

9.2.1 Team roles

Teams can fulfil a variety of roles in an organisation.

Type of role	Comments
Organising work	• A tem combines skills of different individuals. • Teams can co-ordinate their work to suit their members.
Control	• Fear of letting down the team or breaking its unwritten rules can be powerful motivator. • Teams can be used to resolve conflict.
Knowledge generation	• Teams can generate ideas.
Decision-making	• Decisions can be evaluated from more than one viewpoint. • Teams can be set up to investigate new developments.

9.2.2 Teamworking

Teamworking allows work to be shared among a number of individuals, so it is done faster than by individuals working alone, but without people losing sight of their whole tasks or having to co-ordinate their efforts through lengthy channels of communication.

A team may be called together temporarily, to achieve specific task objectives (**project team**), or may be more or less permanent, with responsibilities for a particular product, product group or stage of the production process (a **product or process team**). There are two basic approaches to the organisation of team work; **multi-skilled teams** and **multi-disciplinary teams**.

9.2.3 Multi disciplinary teams

Multi-disciplinary teams bring together individuals with **different skills and specialisms**, so that their skills, experience and knowledge can be **pooled** or exchanged. A member of the accounts department might belong to such a team.

9.2.4 Multi skilled teams

A **multi-skilled team** brings together a number of multi-skilled individuals who can perform **any of the** team tasks. These tasks can then be shared out in a more flexible way between group members, according to who is available and best placed to do a given job at the time it is required. In an accounts department, someone may be able to do the sales ledger, post the cash book and so on. Multi-skilling will help deal with peaks and troughs of work.

Activity 3.11

Task

Before reading on, list five types of people that you would want to have on a project team, involved (say) in organising an end-of-year party at your office.

9.2.5 Membership of the team

Belbin drew up a list of the most effective character mix in a team. This involves eight necessary roles which should ideally be balanced and evenly spread in the team. An effective group will have all these roles represented; one person may play more then one role.

Member	Role
Co-ordinator	Presides and co-ordinates; balanced, disciplined, good at working through others.
Shaper	Highly strung, dominant, extrovert, passionate about the task itself, a spur to action.
Plant	Individualistic, but intellectually dominant and imaginative; source of ideas and proposals.
Monitor-evaluator	Analytically (rather than creatively) intelligent; dissects ideas, spots flaws; possibly aloof, tactless – but necessary.
Resource-investigator	Popular, sociable, extrovert, relaxed; source of new contacts; responds to challenge.
Implementer	Practical organiser; scheduling, planning; trustworthy and efficient, but not excited by unproven ideas.
Team worker	Most concerned with team maintenance – supportive, understanding, diplomatic; popular but uncompetitive – contribution noticed only in absence.
Finisher	Chivvies the team to meet deadlines, attend to details; urgency and follow-through important, though not always popular.

The **specialist** joins the team to offer expert advice when needed.

Effective teams therefore need a mix of people who have two main abilities.

- Getting things done
- Getting along with other people

Analysing the functioning of a team

You may have an opportunity to analyse a team you work with.

(a) Assess who (if anybody) is performing each of Belbin's **team roles**. Which is the team's plant? co-ordinator? monitor-evaluator? and so on.

(b) Analyse the frequency and type of individual members' contributions to group discussions and interactions. This is a relatively simple framework, which can revolutionise the way you behave in groups – as well as your understanding of the dynamics of a given team.

9.3 Team development

You probably have had experience of being put into a group of people you do not know. Many teams are set up in this way and it takes some time for the team to become effective. Four stages in this development were identified by *Tuckman.*

	Comments
Step 1. Forming	The team is just coming together, and may still be seen as a collection of individuals. Each member wishes to impress his or her personality on the group. The individuals will be trying to find out about each other, and about the aims and norms of the team. There will at this stage probably be **awareness about introducing new ideas**. The **objectives** being pursued may as yet be unclear and a leader may not yet have emerged.
Step 2. Storming	This frequently involves more or less open **conflict** between team members. There may be **changes** agreed in the original objectives, procedures and norms established for the group. If the team is developing successfully this may be a fruitful phase as more realistic targets are set and **trust** between the group members increases.
Step 3. Norming	A period of **settling down**: there will be agreements about work sharing, individual requirements and expectations of output. Norms and procedures may evolve which enable methodical working to be introduced and maintained.
Step 4. Performing	The team sets to work to execute its task. The difficulties of growth and development no longer hinder the group's objectives.

Two further stages may be added. **Dorming** occurs once a team has been performing for while. It becomes complacent and may lose interest in the task (being more concerned with the happiness of team members). **Mourning/adjoining** occurs when a team breaks up once its task has been completed.

Some teams are temporary; others are permanent and may exist in the performing and dorming stages.

Activity 3.12

Task

Read the following statements and decide to which category they belong (forming, storming, norming, performing).

(a) Two of the group arguing as to whose idea is best
(b) Desired outputs being achieved
(c) Shy member of group not participating
(d) Activities being allocated

Team leaders must consider these issues.

Issues	Comments
Team identity	Get people to see themselves as part of this group
Team solidarity	Encourage loyalty so that members put in extra effort for the sake of the team
Shared objectives	Encourage the team to commit itself to shared work objectives and to co-operate willingly and effectively in achieving them.

9.4 Effective teams

Some teams work more effectively than others, for a variety of reasons, and we can identify ways of evaluating whether a team is effective. Here are some examples.

Factor	Effective team	Ineffective team
Labour turnover (people are always changing jobs)	Low	High
Accident rate	Low	High
Absenteeism (people not turning up for work)	Low	High
Quality of output	High	Low
Commitment to targets and organisational goals	High	Low
Understanding of individual roles	High	Low
Communication between team members	Free and open	Mistrust
Interest in work decisions	Active	Passive acceptance
Opinions	Consensus	Imposed solutions
Job satisfaction	High	Low

Activity 3.13

Neville is in charge of a group of twelve people involved in complex work. The group has been working together amicably and successfully for a considerable time. Its members value Neville's leadership and the back-up given him by Olivia. She is very keen on getting the job done and is good at encouraging the others when there are problems.

Much of the success of the group has been due to Peter, who is very creative at problem solving, and Rosalinde who has an encyclopaedic knowledge of sources of supply and information. Quentin is particularly reliable and efficient; he has reduce the scheduling of the team's work to a fine art. Sheila is invaluable at sorting out disagreements and keeping everyone cheerful. The remaining members of the group also have roles which are acceptable to themselves and to the others.

Recently Olivia resigned for family reasons. Because the workload has been increasing, Neville recruited four new people to the group. Neville now finds that various members of the group complain to him about what they are expected to do, and about other people's failings. Peter and Rosalinde have been unusually helpful to Neville but have had several serious arguments between themselves and with others, usually about priorities.

Task

Relate your answer to the theories of team working.

(a) Analyse the situation before and after the changes
(b) Recommend how Neville should proceed.

10 Leading the team

Leadership is the process of influencing others to work *willingly* towards a goal, and to the best of their capabilities. The essence of leadership is *followership:* it is the willingness of people to follow that makes a person a leader.

Leadership comes about in a number of different ways.

- A manager is **appointed** to a position of authority within the organisation. He relies mainly on the authority of that position.
- Some leaders (for example in politics or in trade unions) might be **elected**.
- Other leaders might **emerge** through their personal drive and social skills. Unofficial spokesmen for groups of people are leaders of this style.

10.1 Theories of leadership: superman?

Early writers believed that leaders were 'born, not made'. Studies on leadership concentrated on the personal **traits**, (eg intelligence, initiative, self assurance) of existing and past leadership figures. However, the trait approach does not take account of the individuality of the **subordinates** and other factors in the **leadership situation**.

10.2 Leadership styles: the Ashridge model

Some work on leadership has concentrated on what leaders do and how they do it. The research unit at Ashridge Management College identified four styles of leadership: tells, sells, consults, joins.

Style	Characteristics
Tells (autocratic)	The manager makes all the decisions, and issues instructions which must be obeyed without question.
Sells (persuasive)	The manager still makes all the decisions, but believes that subordinates have to be motivated to accept them in order to carry the out properly.
Consults	The manager confers with subordinates and takes their views into account, but has the final say.
Joins (democratic)	Leader and followers make the decision on the basis of consensus.

(a) The studies found, in an ideal world, team members preferred the **consults** style of leadership. Those managed in that way had the most favourable attitude to work, but managers were most commonly thought to be exercising the **tells** or **sells** style.

(b) In practice, consistency was far more important. The least favourable attitudes were found amongst those team members who were **unable to perceive a consistent style** of leadership in their team leader.

It may however be appropriate to vary the style of leadership according to the prevailing circumstances. This is called a **contingency approach** and reflects the view that there is a variety a single best solutions to a given type of problem. Many managers will, for instance, use a **consults** style for preference, but will use a **tells** style for dealing with a sudden crisis, such as an epidemic of flu in the department.

Activity 3.14

Ruth Parker is 42 years old, married, with two children aged 13 and 9. She returned to work on a part time basis two years ago. As her manager you have offered her, and she has accepted, promotion (on a full time basis) to what will be her first managerial position.

She will be in charge of a well established team of six (all in their mid-twenties) who carry out a processing function which is basically routine work but which does give rise to some (often complex) problems. Their work requires accuracy and occasionally there are high volumes, particularly during holiday periods.

As a parent, Ruth has a lot of managerial experience. She is good at solving problems by making decisions swiftly and implementing them efficiently. She rarely feels the need to consult with other people.

Her predecessor as head of the section believed in allowing people to develop themselves through implementing their own solutions. He accustomed the section to operating with a minimum of managerial interference.

The labour turnover in the section is very low.

Tasks

(a) Identify and explain the difficulties in Ruth's choice of managerial style
(b) Suggest how Ruth should approach her choice of managerial style.

10.3 Practical application

Most theories provide some useful pointers but they cannot be applied uncritically.

(a) A manager's personality may not suit certain kinds of leadership style: some managers find it hard to order people around. Others find it hard to delegate.

(b) The **demands** of the **task**, **technology**, organisation **culture** and **other managers constrain** the manager in the range of 'styles' and leadership behaviours open to him.

(c) **Consistency is important** to subordinates. A manager who tries to practise a flexible approach to leadership may be see as unreliable or untrustworthy, and hence difficult to work with.

11 Communication in the organisation

11.1 Communication processes in the organisation

In any organisation, the communication of information is necessary for four purposes.

(a) **Management decision-making**

(b) **Interdepartmental co-ordination**. All the interdependent systems for purchasing, production, marketing and administration must co-operate in accomplishing the organisation's aims.

(c) **Individual motivation and effectiveness**. People must know what they have to do and why.

(d) **Control**. Results must be reported for comparison with targets.

11.2 Direction of communication

Communication goes in many different directions

(a) **Vertical** up and down the scalar chain (from superior to subordinate and back).

(b) **Horizontal or lateral** between people of the same level, in the same section or department, or in different sections or departments. Sometimes this is most efficient.

(c) **Diagonal** interdepartmental communication by people of different levels. This may relate to the work that is being done. For example, the sales director may ask someone in the accounts department to run a report on a particular customer.

11.3 Barriers to communication

General faults in the communication process occur in any situation. These are:

- **Distortion** or omission of information by the sender.
- **Misunderstanding** due to lack of clarity.
- **Non-verbal signs** (gesture, posture, facial expression) contradicting the verbal message, so that its meaning is in doubt.
- **Overload** – a person being given too much information to digest in the time available.
- **People** hearing **only what they want** to hear in a message.
- **Differences** in social, racial or educational **background**, compounded by age and personality differences, creating barriers to understanding and co-operation.

11.4 Improving the communications system

Establishing better communication links in all directions can improve communication

- **Standing instructions** should be recorded in easily accessible manuals which are kept fully up-to-date.
- Management **decisions** should be sent to all people affected by them, preferably in writing or via e-mail.
- Regular **staff meetings**, may be appropriate.
- **A house journal** may be helpful.
- **Appraisal schemes** give opportunities for detailed discussion of a worker's progress, prospects and potential.
- Use **new technology** such as e-mail – but not so as to overload everybody in messages of no importance.
- **Redundancy of method.** For example, issuing a message in more than one form (eg by word of mouth at a meeting, confirmed later in minutes)
- **Reporting by exception** should operate to prevent **information overload** on managers.
- **Train** managers who do not express themselves clearly and concisely. Necessary jargon should be taught in some degree to people new to the organisation or unfamiliar with the terminology of the specialists.

We cover particular communications skills for supervisors in Chapter 6.

Key learning points

- ☑ Managers **forecast** and **plan**, **organise**, **motivate** and **command**, **co-ordinate**, **control** and **measure**. Communication is essential for all of this.
- ☑ A **supervisor is a junior manager** who gets more actively involved in the actual work of his or her section than more senior managers.
- ☑ Particularly important principles of management are **authority** and **responsibility**, **discipline**, **scalar chains**, fairness, initiative and team spirit.
- ☑ The nature of a supervisor's job is affected by the chains of command in the organisation and the span of control.
- ☑ **Matrix organisation** structures challenge classical ideas of one person, one boss.
- ☑ People are different so there **is no foolproof set of golden rules** to follow that will enable you to deal successfully with everybody at all times.
- ☑ There are various theories about what motivates people. Maslow identifies a **hierarchy of needs** that must be fulfilled; Herzberg distinguishes between what causes dissatisfaction and what encourages superior effort; others have introduced the factor of people's expectations into the equation; **goal theory** is the important modern approach.
- ☑ Various methods of increasing motivation have been suggested, such as empowerment (job enrichment, job enlargement and job rotation), rewards and participation.
- ☑ Most work is done in **teams**. This raises issues of **team development and effectiveness**. The effectiveness of a team depends upon the personalities of individual members, the nature of their task, and the environment in which they do it, motivation, leadership, the processes and procedures involved in the task, and how far high productivity coincides with individual satisfaction.
- ☑ A variety of **leadership styles** can be identified: dictatorial, autocratic, consultative, democratic.
- ☑ The essence of leadership is **followership**.
- ☑ **Communication** is important for the supervisor so that staff know what is expected of them and managers are informed of what is going on.

Quick quiz

1 What does a manager do?

2 What is meant by 'organising'?

3 List some of the characteristics of the work of a supervisor.

4 One of the most important tasks of a supervisor is communication. What might this involve?

5 What is horizontal communication?

6 Would you agree that managers and supervisors should have an intimate knowledge of the work that their staff are doing at all times?

7 What is a chain of command?

8 What is a span of control?

9 What influences the width of a manager's span of control?

10 What are the characteristics of organisation culture?

11 What is the halo effect?

12 What is the link between personality and performance at work?

13 What is motivation?

14 What did Maslow mean by 'esteem needs', 'social needs' and 'self-actualisation' needs? Where do these needs come in Maslow's hierarchy?

15 Distinguish between what Herzberg called 'hygiene factors' and 'motivator factors'.

16 What are the three fundamental elements of goal theory?

17 What is the difference between job enrichment and job enlargement?

18 What conditions are necessary in order for participation to be an effective motivator?

19 List four stages of group development.

20 List four leadership styles.

Answers to quick quiz

1 Writers have identified a number of elements of management including the following.

- Formulating policy
- Forecasting and planning
- Organising
- Motivating
- Controlling and measuring
- Communicating
- Staffing
- Leading

2 Organising means determining what activities are necessary to achieve the objectives of the business and then dividing the work and assigning it to different groups and individuals.

3 A supervisor is a 'front line' manager, dealing directly with people who do the work. Supervisors do not spend all their time managing other people. Much of their time will be spent doing operational work. However, a supervisor *is* responsible for getting things done: supervisory work is really management work, but at a lower level in the organisation than that of managers.

4 (a) Telling employees about plans, targets and work schedules.
(b) Telling managers about the work that has been done.
(c) Filling in reports (eg absentee reports for the personnel department, job appraisal forms).
(d) Collecting information and distributing it to the other persons interested in it.

5 Horizontal communication takes place when people at the same management level in different departments communicate with each other directly.

6 The answer depends partly upon the precise work involved and the nature of the management post. In general the job of the manager or supervisor is to co-ordinate, control, provide information, motivate, and so on rather than to interfere in the detailed operations: in other words, to do whatever is necessary to **enable** others to do the work. The manager or supervisor **may** do some of the detailed work, too, but this is in his or her role as the operative for some of the team's work, it is not part of managing the team.

7 A chain of command in an organisation is a line of authority from the top of the management hierarchy down to employees at the very bottom.

8 The span of control is the number of subordinates responsible to each superior. In other words, if a manager has five subordinates, the span of control is five.

9 The extent of a manager's span of control is determined by the following factors.

(a) The amount of non-supervisory work in his or her workload.

(b) The geographical dispersion of the subordinates.

(c) Whether subordinates' work is all of a similar nature (wide span possible) or diversified.

(d) The nature of problems that a supervisor might have to help subordinates with.

(e) The degree of interaction between subordinates (with close interaction, a wider span of control should be possible).

(f) The competence and abilities of both management and subordinates.

(g) Whether close group cohesion is desirable. Small groups will be more cohesive, with a better sense of team work. This would call for narrow spans of control.

(h) The amount of help that supervisors receive from staff functions (such as the personnel department or the production planning department).

10 **Culture** in an organisation is the sum total of the beliefs, knowledge, attitudes of mind and customs to which people are exposed. The culture will consist of the **basic, underlying assumptions** which guide the behaviour of the individuals and groups in the organisation, for example customer orientation, or belief in quality; **overt beliefs** expressed by the organisation and its members, which may emerge as sayings like 'the customer is always right', or in jokes and stories about past successes; and **visible artefacts –** the style of the offices or other premises, dress rules and the degree of informality between superiors and subordinates.

11 The halo effect is a term used to describe the way that our first judgements about people – based on immediately obvious characteristics like dress, manner or facial expression – affect our later perception of other features of those people, whether to positive or negative effect. Information subsequently gathered that does not agree with the first assessment tends to be filtered out.

12 Research into this question has not been able to show any significant correlation between personality on the basis of test results and performance. The important point is that managers and supervisors must realise and accept that different people will behave in different ways.

13 Depending on the context, the words motivation may mean: **goals**, that have become desirable for a particular individual; the **mental process** of choosing desired outcomes, deciding how to go about them; **assessing** whether the likelihood of success warrants the amount of effort that will be necessary and setting in motion the required behaviours; or the **social process** by which the behaviour of an individual is influenced by others.

14 **Esteem needs** are needs for status, recognition, respect and appreciation, the desire to excel. **Social needs** are needs for friendship, affection and acceptance. **Self-actualisation needs** are needs for individuals to realise their full potential and for self-development. Social needs come above safety and physiological needs, but below esteem needs and self-actualisation needs.

15 Hygiene factors are essentially preventative. They prevent or minimise dissatisfaction but do not give satisfaction, in the same way that sanitation minimises threats to health, but does not cure disease. Motivator factors create job satisfaction and are effective in motivating an individual to superior performance and effort.

16 Goal theory suggests the following.

(a) **Difficult** goals lead to higher performance than easy goals, so long as they have been *accepted* by the person trying to achieve them.

(b) **Specific** goals lead to higher performance than general 'do your best' goals. Specific goals seem to create a precise intention, which in turn helps the person to shape their behaviour with precision.

(c) Knowledge of results (**feedback**) is essential if the full performance benefits of setting difficult and specific goals are to be achieved.

17 Job **enlargement** is the attempt to widen jobs by increasing the number of operations in which a job holder is involved. Job **enrichment** is planned, deliberate action to build greater responsibility, depth and challenge of work into a job.

18 Participation may be effective if the following conditions are satisfied.

(a) If it is **genuine**. It is very easy for a manager to pretend to invite participation from staff but end up issuing orders.

(b) If efforts to establish participation are **consistent,** that is, continuous, energetic and long-lived.

(c) If the **purpose** of the participation is made clear. If employees are consulted to make a **decision**, their views should carry the decision. If, however, they are consulted for advice, their views need not necessarily be accepted.

(d) If the individuals have the **abilities and the information** to join in decision-making effectively.

(e) If the individuals **want** to participate. Some people expect and want authoritarian management and fear responsibility.

19 The four stages are as follows.

(a) During the **forming** stage the group is just coming together, and may still be seen as a collection of individuals.

(b) The second stage is called **storming** because it frequently involves more or less open conflict between group members.

(c) The third stage (**norming**) is a period of settling down.

(d) The fourth stage is **performing**. At this stage the group sets to work to execute its task. This stage marks the point where the difficulties of growth and development no longer hinder the group's objectives.

20 The research unit at Ashridge Management College identified four styles: tells, sells, consults, joins.

Activity checklist

This checklist shows which performance criteria, range statement or knowledge and understanding point is covered by each activity in this chapter. Tick off each activity as you complete it.

Activity		
3.1	☐	This activity deals with Knowledge & Understanding point 9: Principles of supervision and delegation (Element 10.1)
3.2	☐	This activity deals with Knowledge & Understanding point 9: Principles of supervision and delegation (Element 10.1)
3.3	☐	This activity deals with Performance Criterion 10.1.D: Communicate work methods and schedules to colleagues in ways that help them to understand what is expected of them and Knowledge & Understanding point 9: Principles of supervision and delegation (Element 10.1)
3.4	☐	This activity deals with Knowledge & Understanding point 9: Principles of supervision and delegation (Element 10.1)
3.5	☐	This activity deals with Knowledge & Understanding point 10: Principles of fostering effective working relationships, building teams and motivating staff and Performance Criterion 10.1.D Communicate work methods and schedules to colleagues in ways that help them to understand what is expected of them
3.6	☐	This activity deals with Knowledge & Understanding points 9: Principles of supervision and delegation (Element 10.1) and 10: Principles of fostering effective working relationships, building teams and motivating staff (Element 10.1)
3.7	☐	This activity deals with Knowledge & Understanding point 9: Principles of supervision and delegation (Element 10.1)
3.8	☐	This activity deals with Knowledge & Understanding point 9: Principles of supervision and delegation (Element 10.1)
3.9	☐	This activity deals with Knowledge & Understanding point 9: Principles of supervision and delegation (Element 10.1)
3.10	☐	This activity deals with Knowledge & Understanding points 9: Principles of supervision and delegation (Element 10.1) and 10: Principles of fostering effective working relationships, building teams and motivating staff (Element 10.1)
3.11	☐	This activity deals with Knowledge & Understanding points 9: Principles of supervision and delegation (Element 10.1) and 10: Principles of fostering effective working relationships, building teams and motivating staff (Element 10.1)
3.12	☐	This activity deals with Knowledge & Understanding points 9: Principles of supervision and delegation (Element 10.1) and 10: Principles of fostering effective working relationships, building teams and motivating staff (Element 10.1)

3.13	☐	This activity deals with Knowledge & Understanding point 9: Principles of supervision and delegation (Element 10.1) and 10: Principles of fostering effective working relationships, building teams and motivating staff (Element 10.1) and Performance Criterion 10.2.E: Ensure recommendations are supported by a clear rationale which includes an explanation of any assumptions made.
3.14	☐	This activity deals with Knowledge & Understanding point 9: Principles of supervision and delegation (Element 10.1) and 10: Principles of fostering effective working relationships, building teams and motivating staff (Element 10.1) and Performance Criteria 10.1.D Communicate work methods and schedules to colleagues in ways that help them to understand what is expected of them and 10.2.E: Ensure recommendations are supported by a clear rationale which includes an explanation of any assumptions made.

chapter 4

Developing the team

Contents

Performance criterion

10.1.B Review the competence of individuals undertaking work activities and arrange the necessary training

Range statement

Changes affecting systems: organisational policies and procedures

Knowledge and understanding

10 Principles of fostering effective working relationships, building teams and motivating staff (Element 10.1)

1 Introduction

One of the management functions is to control and improve performance. The appraisal system is an important way of doing this. You may have appraised other people or you may have been appraised yourself. Firms use appraisals in many different ways, but chiefly it is to align performance with the company's goals.

This chapter deals with appraisal and training together because they are both essential parts of a system of staff development and performance management.

2 Appraisal and performance management

2.1 Performance management: set objectives for the future

Performance management is an approach which aims 'to get better results from the organisations, teams and individuals by measuring and managing performance within agreed frameworks of objectives and competence requirements, assessing and improving performance'. Performance management is part of the control system of the organisation.

2.2 Appraisal: review past performance to establish the current position.

Whilst performance management as a whole is forward looking, the process of **appraisal** is designed to review an **individual's performance** over the past period, with a view to identifying any deficiencies and improving it in the future. Appraisals might involve some form filling. They generally involve a discussion.

2.2.1 Objectives of appraisals

- Establishing what **the individual has to do** in a job in order that the objectives for the section or department are realised
- Establishing the **key or main results** which the individual will be expected to achieve in the course of his or her work over a period of time
- **Comparing the individual's level of performance against a standard**, to provide a basis for remuneration above the basic pay rate
- Identifying the individual's **training and development needs** in the light of actual **performance**
- Identifying **potential candidates for promotion**
- Identifying **areas for improvement**
- Establishing an **inventory of actual and potential performance** within the undertaking to provide a basis for manpower planning
- Monitoring the undertaking's **initial selection procedures** against the subsequent performance of recruits, relative to the organisation's expectations
- **Improving communication** about work tasks between different levels in the hierarchy

2.2.2 The need for appraisal

Managers and supervisors may obtain **random impressions** of subordinates' performance (perhaps from their more noticeable successes and failures), but rarely form a coherent, complete and objective picture. However a more formal system is needed.

(a) They may have a fair idea of their subordinates' shortcomings – but may not have devoted time and attention to the matter of **improvement and development**.

(b) Judgements are **easy to make**, but **less easy to justify** in detail, in writing, or to the subject's face.

(c) **Different assessors** may be applying a **different set of criteria**, and varying standards of objectivity and judgement. This undermines the value of appraisal for comparison, as well as its credibility in the eyes of the appraisees.

(d) Unless stimulated to do so, managers rarely give their subordinates adequate **feedback** on their performance.

Activity 4.1

Task

List four disadvantages to the individual of not having an appraisal system.

2.2.3 Three basic problems for appraisers

Appraisal is not easy for the organisation, if it is done **properly**.

(a) **Desired traits and standards** against which individuals can be consistently and objectively assessed, must be formulated and understood.

(b) **Appraisals must be recorded**. Managers should be encouraged to utilise a standard and understood framework, but still allowed to express what they consider important, and without too much form-filling.

(c) **The appraiser and appraisee must be brought together**, so that both contribute to the assessment and plans for improvement and/or development.

2.3 Appraisal as an opportunity

An appraisal is an opportunity for supervisors and the people who report to them to focus on the work. It is also an opportunity for change. If the organisation has to do new tasks, and requires new competences, the appraisal process is when these can be formally introduced.

3 The process of appraisal and follow up

3.1 A typical appraisal system

Step 1. **Identification of criteria** for assessment, perhaps based on job analysis, performance standards, required **competences** and so on. Personality is strictly speaking not relevant, but can become so if it affects the appraisees performance or the performance of others.

Step 2. The preparation by the subordinate's manager or, increasingly often, the appraisee of an **appraisal report.** In some systems both the appraisee and appraiser prepare a report. These reports are then compared.

Step 3. An **appraisal interview,** for an exchange of views about the appraisal report, targets for improvement, solutions to problems and so on.

Step 4. **Review of the assessment** by the assessor's own superior, so that the appraisee does not feel subject to one person's prejudices. Formal appeals may be allowed, if necessary to establish the fairness of the procedure.

Step 5. The preparation and implementation of action plans to achieve improvements and changes agreed.

Step 6. **Follow-up**: monitoring the progress of the action plan.

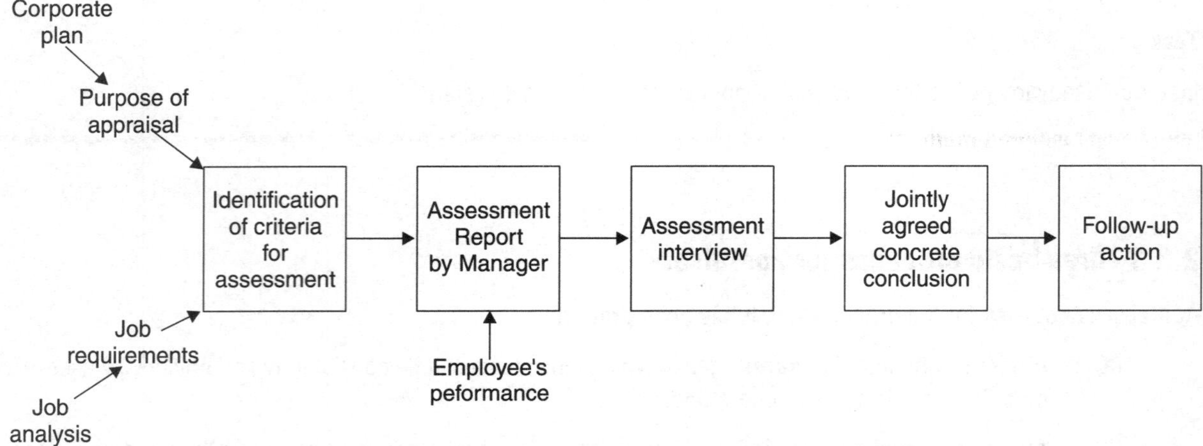

Activity 4.2

Task

Identify specific competences which may be relevant to some jobs of your choice.

3.2 Techniques of appraisal

During the appraisal a number of techniques can be used

Appraisal techniques	Description
Overall assessment	The manager writes in narrative form his judgements about the appraisee. There will be no guaranteed consistency of the criteria and areas of assessment, however, and managers may not be able to convey clear, effective judgements in writing.
Guided assessment	Assessors are required to comment on a number of specified characteristics and performance elements, with guidelines as to how terms such as **application**, **integrity** and **adaptability** are to be interpreted in the work context. This is more precise, but still rather vague.
Grading	Grading adds a comparative frame of reference to the general guidelines, whereby managers are asked to select one of a number of levels or degrees to which the individual in question displays the given characteristic. These are also known as **rating scales**. Numerical values may be added to ratings to give rating scores. Alternatively a less precise **graphic scale** may be used to indicate general position on a plus/minus scale. **Factor: job knowledge** High ___√___ Average ________ Low
Behavioural incident methods.	These concentrate on **employee behaviour**, which is measured against typical behaviour in each job, as defined by common **critical incidents** of successful and unsuccessful job behaviour reported by managers.
Results-orientated schemes	This reviews performance against specific targets and standards of performance **agreed in advance by manager and subordinates together.** The advantages of this are as follows. (i) Subordinates are more involved in appraisal because they are able to evaluate their success or progress in achieving specific, jointly-agreed targets. (ii) The manager is therefore relieved, to an extent, of a critic's role, and becomes a counsellor. (iii) Learning and motivation theories suggest that clear and known targets are important in modifying and determining behaviour. The effectiveness of the scheme will still, however, depend on the **targets set** (are they clearly defined? realistic?) and the **commitment** of both parties to make it work.

Activity 4.3

Task

What sort of appraisal systems are suggested by the following examples?

(a) Every year, your boss arranges to have a meeting and a quick chat as to how you are doing. 'You've had a good year' she says. 'Let's hope that the next year will be good next year'. And that's it.

(b) A firm of auditors assess the performance of their staff in four categories: technical ability, relationships with clients, relationships with other members of the audit team, and professional attitude. On each of these criteria staff are marked from A (= excellent) to E (= poor).

(c) A firm of insurance brokers assesses the performance of its staff by the number of clients they have visited and the number of policies sold.

3.3 The appraisal interview

The process of the interview is given below. This is from the appraiser's perspective.

Step 1. **Prepare**

- Plan and place, time and environment
- Review employee's history
- Consult other managers – let employee prepare
- Prepare report. Review employee's self-appraisal

Step 2. **Interview**

- Listen to employee. Discuss, don't argue
- Encourage employee to talk, identify problems and solutions
- Be fair
- Gain employee commitment
- Agree plan of action
- Summarise to check understanding

Step 3. **Complete appraisal report**, if not already prepared

Step 4. **Follow up**

- Take action as agreed
- Monitor progress
- Keep employee informed

3.4 Interview and counselling

The report may be shown to the appraisee and thus form a basis for discussion. Three types of approach to the appraisal interview are discussed below.

	Comments
The tell and sell method	The manager tells the subordinate how he/she has been assessed, and then tries to 'sell' (gain acceptance of) the evaluation and the improvement plan. This requires unusual human relations skills in order to convey constructive criticism in an acceptable manner, and to motivate the appraisee to alter his/her behaviour.
The tell and listen method	The manager tells the subordinate how he/she has been assessed, and then invites the appraisee to respond. The manager therefore no longer dominates the interview throughout, and there is greater opportunity for **counselling** as opposed to pure **direction**. The employee is **encouraged to participate** in the assessment and the working out of improvement targets and methods.
The problem-solving approach	The manager abandons the role of critic altogether, and becomes a helper. The discussion is centred not on the assessment, but on the employee's **work problems**. The employee is encouraged to think solutions through, and to make a commitment to the recognised need for personal improvement.

Activity 4.4

What approach was taken at your last appraisal interview? Could it have been better?

3.5 Problems in appraisal

Even the most objective and systematic appraisal scheme is subject to problems.

- **Defensiveness on the part of the subordinate,** who may believe that criticism may mean a low bonus or pay rise, or lost promotion opportunity.
- **Defensiveness on the part of the team leader**, who cannot reconcile the role of judge and critic with the human relations aspect of interviewing and management.
- The team leader might show **conscious or unconscious bias** in the appraisal or may be influenced by rapport (or lack of it) with the interviewee.
- The manager and subordinate may both be **reluctant to devote time and attention to appraisal.**
- The organisational culture may simply **not take appraisal seriously.**
- The team **leader's** performance is not at issue, whereas this could be important in the team member's effectiveness.

Activity 4.5

This activity shows some of the problems of operating appraisal schemes in practice.

It is time for Pauline Radway's annual performance appraisal and Steve Taylor, her manager, has sought your advice on two problem areas which he has identified as 'motivation' and 'the organisation's systems'.

The appraisal system has a six point rating scale:

1	Excellent	4	Acceptable
2	Outstanding	5	Room for improvement
3	Competent	6	Unacceptable

The annual pay increase is determined, in part, by the overall rating of the employee.

Pauline was recruited into Steve's section 18 months ago. She took about five months to learn the job and achieve competence. Accordingly, at last year's appraisal she and Steve agreed that an overall rating of '4' was appropriate.

Over the next six months Pauline worked hard and well and in effect developed her job so she was able to accept more responsibility and expand her range of activities into areas which were both interesting and demanding.

During the last six months the section has been 'rationalised' and the workforce has been reduced (although the workload has increased). Steve is under pressure to contain costs – particularly in the area of salary increases.

Steve now has to rely on Pauline performing her enriched job which, taking the past six months as a whole and given the increased pressure, she performs 'satisfactorily' rather than 'outstandingly'; there are aspects of her performance in this enriched job which she could improve.

When Steve met Pauline to agree the time for the appraisal interview she said – only half jokingly – 'I warn you, I'm looking forward to a respectable pay rise this year.

Task

(a) Outline the problems for Steve that arise from the above scenario:

(i) in relation to Pauline's feelings;
(ii) in relation to the organisation's systems.

(b) Suggest how Steve should proceed.

3.6 Follow-up

After the appraisal interview, the manager may complete the report, with an overall assessment, assessment of potential and the jointly-reached conclusion of the interview, with **recommendations for follow-up action**. The manager should then discuss the report with the counter-signing manager (usually his or her own superior), resolving any problems that have arisen in making the appraisal or report, and agreeing on action to be taken. The report form may then go to the management development adviser, training officer or other relevant people as appropriate for follow-up.

Follow-up procedures

- **Informing appraisees of the results** of the appraisal, if this has not been central to the review interview
- **Carrying out agreed actions** on training, promotion and so on
- **Monitoring the appraisee's progress** and checking that he/she has carried out agreed actions or improvements
- Taking necessary steps to **help the appraisee to attain improvement objectives**, by guidance, providing feedback, upgrading equipment, altering work methods or whatever

Activity 4.6

What would happen without follow-up?

4 Development and the role of training

4.1 Training and development

Development is a 'wider' approach to fulfilling an individual's potential than training. Development may include training, but may also include a range of learning experiences whereby:

(a) Employees gain work experience of increasing challenge and responsibility, which will enable them to other more senior jobs in due course of time.

(b) Employees are given guidance, support and counselling to help them to formulate personal and career development goals.

(c) Employees are given suitable education and training to develop their skills and knowledge.

(d) Employees are facilitated in planning their future and identifying opportunities open to them in the organisation.

Approaches to development include the following.

Approach	Comment
Management development	'An attempt to improve managerial effectiveness through a planned and deliberate learning process' (Mumford). This may include the development of management/ leadership skills (or competences), management education (such as MBA programmes) and planned experience of different functions, positions and work settings, in preparation for increasing managerial responsibility,.
Career development	Individuals plan career paths. The trend for delayered organisation has reduced opportunities for upward progression: opportunities may be planned for sideways/ lateral transfers, secondments to project groups, short external secondments and so on, to offer new opportunities.

Approach	Comment
Professional development	Professional bodies offer structured programmes of continuing professional development (CPD). The aim is to ensure that professional standards are maintained and enhanced through educational, development and training self-managed by the individual. A CPD approach is based on the belief that a professional qualification should be the basis for a career lifetime of development *and* adherence to a professional code of ethics and standards.
Personal development	Businesses are increasingly offering employees wider-ranging development opportunities, rather than focusing on skills required in the current job. Personal development creates more rounded, competent employees who may contribute more innovatively and flexibly to the organisation's future needs. It may also help to foster employee job satisfaction, commitment and loyalty.

4.2 Personal development plans

Increasingly, employees are supposed to manage their own development. They might be asked to set up **personal development plans**, whereby they set targets – in consultation with management – and propose a number of activities to achieve them.

There is an important distinction to be made between training and development. Perhaps the easiest way to grasp the difference is to see training as immediately practical and connected to job performance. On the other hand, development may have no immediate practical application but tends, over time, to enable a person to deal with wider problems.

In the rest of this chapter, try to distinguish when we are talking about training, when about development and when about both.

A **personal development plan** is a 'clear developmental action plan for an individual which incorporates a wide set of developmental opportunities including formal training.'

4.2.1 Purposes of a personal development plan

- Improving performance in the existing job
- Developing **skills** for future career moves within and outside the organisation.

Skills are: what the individual needs to be able to do if results are to be achieved. Skills are built up progressively by repeated training. They may be manual, intellectual or mental, perceptual or social.

4.2.2 Preparing a personal development plan involves these steps

Step 1. **Analysis** of the current position. You could do a personal SWOT (strengths, weaknesses, opportunities, threats) analysis. The supervisor can have an input into this by categorising the skills use of the employee on a grid as follows, in a **skills analysis**.

		Performance	
		High	**Low**
Liking of skills	**High**	***Like and do well***	***Like but don't do well***
	Low	***Dislike but do well***	***Dislike and don't do well***

The aim is to try to incorporate more of the employees' interests into their actual roles.

Step 2. **Set goals to cover performance in the existing job**, future changes in the current role, moving elsewhere in the organisations, developing specialist expertise. Naturally, such goals should have the characteristic, as far as possible of SMART objectives (ie specific, measurable, attainable, realistic and time-bounded).

Step 3. **Draw up action plan** to achieve the goals, covering the developmental activities listed above.

Activity 4.7

Task

Note down key experiences which have developed your capacity and confidence at work, and the skills you are able to bring to your employer (or indeed a new employer!)

4.3 Training and the organisation

Organisations are supposed to benefit from training

Benefit	Comment
Planning minimises costs	Ad hoc courses can increase cost and fail to address real training needs.
Lower costs and increased productivity	Some people suggest that higher levels of training explain the higher productivity of German as opposed to many British manufacturers
Better health and safety practices	EU health and safety directives require a certain level of training. Employees can take employers to court if accidents occur or if unhealthy work practices persist.
Less need for detailed supervision	If people are trained they can get on with the job, and managers can concentrate on other things. Training is an aspect of **empowerment**.
Flexibility	Training ensures that people have the **variety** of skills needed – multi-skilling is only possible if people are properly trained.
Recruitment and succession planning	Training and development attracts new recruits and ensures that the organisation has a supply of suitable managerial and technical staff to take over when people retire.
Change management	Training helps organisations manage change by letting people know why the change is happening and giving them the skills to cope with it.
Corporate culture	• Training programmes can be used to build the corporate culture or to direct it in certain ways, by indicating that certain **values** are espoused. • Training programmes can **build relationships** between staff and managers in different areas of the business
Motivation	Training programmes can increase commitment to the organisation's goals

However, the training must be the right kind for it to be effective. Some managers are worried that employees who are trained will find it easier to leave the company.

4.4 Training and the individual

For the individual employee, the benefits of training and development are more clear-cut, and few refuse it if it is offered especially if it ties in with personal development.

Benefit	Comment
Enhances portfolio of skills and competences	Even if not specifically related to the current job, training can be useful in other contexts, and the employee becomes more attractive to employers and more promotable
Psychological benefits	The trainee might feel reassured that he/she is of continuing value to the organisation
Social benefit	People's social needs can be met by training courses – they can also develop networks of contacts
The job	Training can help people do their job better, thereby increasing job satisfaction

5 The training process

5.1 The training process in outline

In order to ensure that training meets the real needs of the organisation, large firms adopt a planned approach to training. This has the following steps.

Step 1. (a) Identify and define the **organisation's skills requirements**. It may be the case that recruitment is a better solution to a problem than training for some skills

(b) Identify the individual's learning requirements for example, as a result of appraisal

(c) See where there is an overlap between organisational needs and individual needs.

Step 2. **Define the learning required** – in other words, specify the knowledge, skills or competences that have to be acquired. For technical training, this is not difficult: for example all finance department staff would have to become conversant with a new accounting system.

Step 3. **Establish training objectives** – what must be learnt and what trainees must be able to do after the training exercise

Step 4. **Plan training programmes** – training and development can be planned in a number of ways, employing a number of techniques, as we shall learn about in Section 3. (Also, people have different approaches to learning, which have to be considered.) This covers:

- Who provides the training
- Where the training takes place
- Divisions of responsibilities between trainers, line managers or team leaders and the individual personally.

Step 5. **Implement the training**

Step 6. **Evaluate** the training: has it been successful in achieving learning objectives?

Step 7. Go back to Step 2 if more training is needed.

Activity 4.8

Task

Draw up a training plan for introducing a new employee into your department. Repeat this exercise after you have completed this chapter to see if your chosen approach has changed.

5.2 Training needs

Training needs analysis covers three issues.

Current state	Desired state
Organisation's current results	Desired results, standards
Existing knowledge and skill	Knowledge and skill needed
Individual performance	Required standards

The difference between the two columns is the **training gap**. Training programmes are designed to improve individual performance, thereby improving the performance of the organisation.

5.3 Setting training objectives

The **training manager** will have to make an initial investigation into the problem of the gap between job or competence **requirements** and current **performance**.

If training would improve work performance, training **objectives** can then be defined. They should be clear, specific and related to observable, measurable targets, ideally detailing three aspects.

(a) Behaviour – what the trainee should be able to do
(b) Standard – to what level of performance
(c) Environment – under what conditions (so that the performance level is realistic)

Example

'At the end of the course the trainee should be able to describe … or identify … or distinguish x from y … or calculate … or assemble …' and so on. It is insufficient to define the objectives of **training** as 'to give trainees a grounding in …' or 'to encourage trainees in a better appreciation of …': this offers no target achievement which can be quantifiably measured. However, the aims of **development** will be less specific.

Training objectives link the identification of training needs with the content, methods and technology of training. Some examples of translating training needs into learning objectives are given by *Torrington and Hall*.

Training needs	Learning objectives
To know more about the Data Protection Act	The employee will be able to answer four out of every five queries about the Data Protection Act without having to search for details.
To establish a better rapport with customers	The employee will immediately attend to a customer unless already engaged with another customers. The employee will greet each customer using the customer's name where known. The employee will apologise to every customer who has had to wait to be attended to.
To assemble clocks more quickly	The employee will be able to assemble each clock correctly within thirty minutes.

Having identified training needs and objectives, the manager will have to decide on the best way to approach training: there are a number of types and techniques of training, which we will discuss below.

6 Methods of development and training

6.1 Incorporating training needs into an individual development programme

Any scheme of training should incorporate these general features:

(a) **Establish learning targets**. The areas to be learnt should be identified, and specific, realistic goals (eg completion dates, performance standards) stated by agreement with the trainee.

(b) **Plan a systematic learning and development programme.** This will ensure regular progress, appropriate stages for consolidation and practice.

(c) **Identify opportunities for broadening the trainee's knowledge and experience**, for example, by involvement in new projects, placement on inter-departmental committees, suggesting new contacts, or simply extending the job, adding more tasks, greater responsibility etc.

(d) **Take into account the strengths and limitations of the trainee** in learning, and take advantage of learning opportunities that suit the trainee's ability, preferred style and goals.

(e) **Exchange feedback**. The coach will want to know how the trainee sees his or her progress and future. He or she will also need performance information in order to monitor the trainee's progress, adjust the learning programme if necessary, identify further needs which may emerge and plan future development for the trainee.

6.2 Formal training

Formal training covers the following types.

	Comments
Internal courses	Run by the organisation's training department or external suppliers.
Types of course	• **Day release**: the employee works in the organisation and on one day per week attends a local college or training centre for theoretical learning. • **Distance learning, evening classes and correspondence courses**, make demands on the individual's time outside work. This is commonly used, for example, in accountancy training. • **Revision courses** are often used for examinations of professional bodies. • **Block release** courses may involve four weeks at a college or training centre followed by a period back at work. • **Sandwich courses** usually involve six months at college then six months at work, in rotation, for two or three years. • A **sponsored full-time course** at a university may last for one or two years

	Comments
Computer-based training	Interactive training via PC. The typing program, Mavis Beacon, is a good example.
Techniques	• Lectures • Seminars, in which participation is encouraged • Simulation. For example, you may have been sent on an audit training course.

Disadvantages of formal training include:

(a) An individual will not benefit from formal training unless he or she **wants to learn**. The individual's superior may need to provide encouragement in this respect.

(b) If the **subject matter** of the training course does not **relate to an individual's job**, the learning may quickly be forgotten.

(c) Individuals may not be able to carry over what they have learned to their own particular job.

6.3 On the job training

Some companies only train people when they start work. An employee will be 'looked' after by another member of staff but will do 'real work'.

6.3.1 Successful on the job training

(a) The assignments should have a **specific purpose** from which the trainee can learn and gain experience.

(b) The organisation must **tolerate any mistakes** which the trainee makes. Mistakes are an inevitable part of on the job learning.

(c) The work should **not be too complex**.

6.3.2 Methods of on the job training

(a) **Demonstration/instruction:** show the trainee how to do the job and let them get on with it. It should combine **telling** a person what to do and **showing** them how, using appropriate media. The trainee imitates the instructor, and asks questions.

(b) **Coaching:** the trainee is put under the guidance of an experienced employee who shows the trainee how to do the job.

(c) **Job rotation:** the trainee is given several jobs in succession, to gain experience of a wide range of activities. (Even experienced managers may rotate their jobs, to gain wider experience; this philosophy of job education is commonly applied in the Civil Service, where an employee may expect to move on to another job after a few years.)

(d) **Temporary promotion:** an individual is promoted into his/her superior's position whilst the superior is absent due to illness. This gives the individual a chance to experience the demands of a more senior position.

(e) **'Assistant to' positions:** a junior manager with good potential may be appointed as assistant to the managing director or another executive director. In this way, the individual gains experience of how the organisation is managed at the top.

(f) **Action learning:** a group of managers are brought together to solve a real problem with the help of an advisor who exposes the management process that actually happens.

(g) **Committees:** trainees might be included in the membership of committees, in order to obtain an understanding of inter-departmental relationships.

(h) **Project work**. work on a project with other people can expose the trainee to other parts of the organisation.

Activity 4.9

Task

Suggest a suitable training method for each of the following situations.

(a) A worker is transferred onto a new machine and needs to learn its operation.

(b) An accounts clerk wishes to work towards becoming qualified with the relevant professional body.

(c) An organisation decides that its supervisors would benefit from ideas on participative management and democratic leadership.

(d) A new member of staff is about to join the organisation.

6.3.3 Mentoring

Mentoring is the use of specially trained individuals to provide guidance and advice which will help develop the careers of those allocate to them. A person's line manager should not be his or her mentor.

Mentors can assist in several ways.

- Drawing up personal development plans
- Advice with administrative problems people face in their new jobs
- Help in tackling projects, by pointing people in the right direction

6.4 Induction training

On the first day, a manager or personnel officer should welcome the new recruit. He/she should then introduce the new recruit to the person who will be their **immediate supervisor.**

The immediate supervisor should commence the **process of induction**.

Step 1. Pinpoint the areas that the recruit will have to learn about in order to **start the job**. Some things (such as detailed technical knowledge) may be identified as areas for later study or training.

Step 2. Explain first of all the nature of the job, and the goals of each task, both of the recruit's job and of the department as a whole.

Step 3. Explain about hours of work, and stress the importance of time-keeping. If flexitime is operated, the supervisor should explain how it works.

Step 4. Explain the structure of the department: to whom the recruit will report, to whom he/she can go with complaints or queries and so on.

Step 5. Introduce the recruit to the people in the office. One particular colleague may be assigned to the recruit as a **mentor**, to teach the basics and answer routine queries.

Step 6. Plan and implement an appropriate **training programmes** for whatever technical or practical knowledge is required. Again, the programme should have a clear schedule and set of goals so that the recruit has a sense of purpose, and so that the programme can be efficiently organised to fit in with the activities of the department.

Step 7. Coach and/or train the recruit; and check regularly on their progress, as demonstrated by performance, as reported by the recruit's mentor, and as perceived by the recruit him or herself.

After three months, six months or one year the performance of a new recruit should be formally appraised and discussed with them. Indeed, when the process of induction has been finished, a recruit should continue to receive periodic appraisals, just like every other employee in the organisation.

6.5 Learning

There are different learning theories which explain and describe how people learn. How people learn is very relevant to how they can be trained.

Learning styles

The way in which people learn best will differ according to the type of person. That is, there are **learning styles** which suit different individuals. *Honey and Mumford* have drawn up a popular classification of four learning styles.

Theorists

Theorists seek to understand **underlying concepts** and to take an intellectual, 'hands-off' approach based on logical argument. They prefer training to be:

- Programmed and structured.
- Designed to allow time for analysis.
- Provided by teachers who share his/her preference for concepts and analysis.

Theorists find learning difficult if they have a teacher with a different style (particularly an activist style); material which skims over basic principles; and a programme which is hurried and unstructured.

Reflectors

- **Observe** phenomena, **think** about them and then **choose** how to act.
- Need to work at their own pace
- Find learning difficult if forced into a hurried programme with little notice or information.
- Produce carefully thought-out conclusions after research and reflection
- Tend to be fairly slow, non-participative (unless to ask questions) and cautious.

Activists

- Deal with practical, active problems and who **do not have much patience with theory**.
- Require training based on **hands-on experience**.
- **Excited by participation** and pressure, such as making presentations and new projects.
- Flexible and optimistic, but tend to rush at something without due preparation, take risks and then get bored.

Pragmatists

- Only like to study if they can see its direct link to practical problems – they are not interested in theory for its own sake.
- Good at learning new techniques in on-the-job training which they see as useful improvements.
- Aim is to implement action plans and/or do the task better.
- May discard as being impractical good ideas which only require some development.

The implications for management are that people react to problem situations in different ways and that, in particular, training methods should be tailored to the preferred style of trainees where possible. Moreover, training interventions should ideally be designed to accommodate the preferences of all four styles. This can often be overlooked especially as the majority of training staff are activists.

Activity 4.10

With reference to the four learning styles drawn up by Honey and Mumford, which of these styles do you think most closely resembles your own? What implications has this got for the way you learn?

Key learning points

- ☑ Appraisal is part of the system of **performance management.**
- ☑ The main difference in emphasis is that **appraisals are backward looking**, whereas performance management as a whole looks to the future.
- ☑ Appraisal can be used to reward but also to **identify potential**.
- ☑ Three basic problems are defining **what** is to be appraised, **recording** assessments, and **getting the appraiser and appraisee together**.
- ☑ Normally a report is written – but both manager and appraisee can contribute to the process, hence the value of self-appraisal.
- ☑ Problems with appraisal are its implementation in practice and the fact that it ignores, by and large, the context of performance.
- ☑ In order to achieve its goals, an organisation requires a **skilled workforce**. This is partly achieved by training.
- ☑ The main purpose of training and development is to **raise competence and therefore performance standards**. It is also concerned with **personal development**, helping and motivating employees to fulfil their potential.
- ☑ A thorough analysis of **training needs** should be carried out as part of a systematic approach to training, to ensure that training programmes meet organisational and individual requirements. Once training needs have been identified, they should be translated into **training objectives**.
- ☑ Individuals can incorporate training and development objectives into a **personal development plan**.
- ☑ There are different schools of thought as to how people learn. Different people have different learning styles.
- ☑ There are a variety of training methods. These include:
  - Formal education and training
  - On-the-job training

Quick quiz

1 What are the purposes of appraisal?

2 What bases or criteria of assessment might an appraisal system use?

3 What is a results-oriented approach to appraisal?

4 What follow-up should there be after an appraisal?

5 What kinds of criticism might be levelled at appraisal schemes by a manager who thought they were a waste of time?

6 What is the difference between performance appraisal and performance management?

7 List examples of development opportunities within organisations.

8 List how training can contribute to:

   (a) Organisational effectiveness
   (b) Individual effectiveness and motivation

9 Define the term 'training need'.

10 How should training objectives be expressed?

11 What does learning theory tell us about the design of training programmes?

12 List the four learning styles put forward by Honey and Mumford.

13 List the available methods of on-the-job training.

14 What is the supervisor's role in training?

Answers to quick quiz

1. Identifying performance levels, improvements needed and promotion prospects; deciding on rewards; assessing team work and encouraging communication between manager and employee.
2. Job analysis, job description, plans, targets and standards
3. Performance is assessed against specific mutually agreed targets and standards.
4. Appraisees should be informed of the results, agreed activity should be taken, progress should be monitored and whatever resources or changes are needed should be provided or implemented.
5. The manager may say that he has better things to do with his time, that appraisals have no relevance to the job and there is no reliable follow-up action, and that they involve too much paperwork.
6. Appraisal **on its own** is a backward-looking performance review. But it is a vital input into performance management, which is forward-looking.
7. Career planning, job rotation, deputising, on-the-job training, counselling, guidance, education and training
8. (a) Increased efficiency and productivity; reduced costs, supervisory problems and accidents; improved quality, motivation and morale

   (b) Demonstrates individual value, enhances security, enhances skills portfolio, motivates, helps develop networks and contacts
9. The required level of competence minus the present level of competence.
10. Actively – for example, 'after completing this chapter you should understand how to design and evaluate training programmes'.
11. The trainee should be motivated to learn, there should be clear objectives and timely feedback. Positive and negative reinforcement should be used carefully, to encourage active participation where possible.
12. Theorist, reflector, activist and pragmatist
13. Induction, job rotation, temporary promotion, 'assistant to' positions, project or committee work
14. Identifying training needs of the department or section, identifying the skills of the individual employee, and deficiencies in performance; providing or supervising on-the-job training (eg coaching); providing feedback on an individual's performance.

Activity checklist

This checklist shows which performance criteria, range statement or knowledge and understanding point is covered by each activity in this chapter. Tick off each activity as you complete it.

Activity		
4.1	☐	This activity deals with Knowledge & Understanding point 10: Principles of fostering effective working relationships, building teams and motivating staff (Element 10.1)
4.2	☐	This activity deals with Performance Criterion 10.1.B: Review the competence of individuals undertaking work activities and arrange the necessary training
4.3	☐	This activity deals with Knowledge & Understanding point 10: Principles of fostering effective working relationships, building teams and motivating staff (Element 10.1)
4.4	☐	This activity deals with Performance Criterion 10.1.B: Review the competence of individuals undertaking work activities and arrange the necessary training
4.5	☐	This activity deals with Performance Criterion 10.1.B :Review the competence of individuals undertaking work activities and arrange the necessary training
4.6	☐	This activity deals with Performance Criterion 10.1.B: Review the competence of individuals undertaking work activities and arrange the necessary training
4.7	☐	This activity deals with Performance Criterion 10.1.B: Review the competence of individuals undertaking work activities and arrange the necessary training
4.8	☐	This activity deals with Knowledge & Understanding point 10: Principles of fostering effective working relationships, building teams and motivating staff (Element 10.1)
4.9	☐	This activity deals with Knowledge & Understanding point 10: Principles of fostering effective working relationships, building teams and motivating staff (Element 10.1)
4.10	☐	This activity deals with Knowledge & Understanding point 10: Principles of fostering effective working relationships, building teams and motivating staff (Element 10.1)

PART B

Managing work activities in the accounting environment

chapter 5

Making plans and making decisions

Contents

Performance criteria

10.1.A Plan work activities to make the optimum use of resources and to ensure that work is completed within agreed timescales

10.1.D Communicate work methods and schedules to colleagues in ways that help them to understand what is expected of them

10.1.F Co-ordinate work activities effectively and in accordance with work plans and contingency plans

Knowledge and understanding

4 Methods for scheduling and planning work (Element 10.1)

8 Techniques for influencing and negotiating with decision-makers and controllers of resources (Element 10.1)

14 Who controls the supply of resources in the organisation (equipment, materials, information and people) within the organisation (Element 10.1)

1 Introduction

In Chapter 1, we saw that organisations have goals they want to achieve. They make plans as to how to achieve their goals.

This planning process occurs throughout the organisation, from the top to the bottom.

A company might have an objective to increase revenues by developing and selling a new products. This requires resources to be obtained and work to be scheduled (eg the production department needs to allocate labour and machine time). At departmental level, you may have to plan the work of your staff.

In your project, planning is relevant for a number of reasons.

(a) **You will have to plan the project itself**. Evidence that you have done so and can go forwards meeting some of the performance criteria

(b) The plans that you make for your own staff are relevant to their work

(c) If you do not manage anyone yourself, or plan for them, you can still use documentation used by others. What plans are made by your manager, for example?

A 'recommendation' is almost a decision – it just has not been implemented.

When obtaining scarce resources (internally), authorisation to spend money, or external suppliers, that you will need negotiation skills within the organisation.

2 Planning

2.1 Planning and control

Because organisations have goals they want to achieve, they need to direct their activities by:

- Deciding **what** they want to achieve: setting **objectives**
- Deciding **how and when** to do it and who is to do it: **planning**
- **Checking** that they do achieve what they want, by **monitoring** what has been achieved and **comparing** it with the plan
- Taking action to **correct any deviation**: **controlling**

The overall framework for this is a system of **planning and control**. Where there is a deviation from standard, a decision has to be made as to whether to adjust the plans or the standard, or whether it is the performance itself that needs correction.

Control system

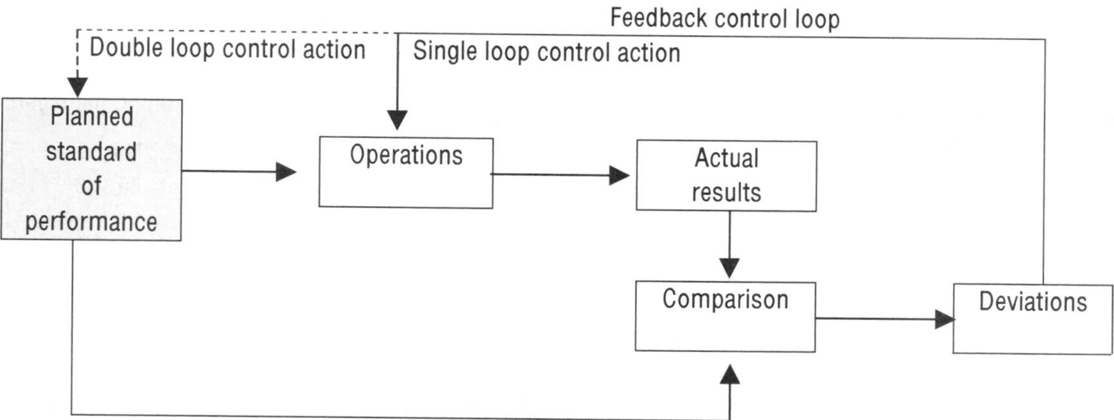

Example

The **Barings debacle** occurred when securities trader Nick Leeson, in charge of Barings Bank's Singapore office, ran up losses of £830m. A report severely criticised the management of Barings Bank for **failing to control their operations properly**.

(a) Mr Leeson apparently was given job responsibilities which made it easy for him to cover his tracks. In other words, there was poor segregation of duties.

(b) Senior managers apparently did not understand the business, failed to define who was responsible and failed to monitor the situation adequately.

We will look more closely at control in Chapter 8.

3 Types of plan

We have already discussed **mission** and **objectives** for the organisation as a whole, but there are other types of **plan** you need to know about as they indicate the direction in which your department is going. and the standards it must adhere to.

3.1 Strategies

Strategies follow on from the determination of long-term goals and objectives. Strategies are plans of activity (mainly long-term) and plans for the allocation of resources which will achieve the organisation's goals and objectives. For example, the **computerisation of an accounts department** is a **strategy** to help **achieve** the **objective** of a more efficient accounts department.

3.2 Policies

These are general statements that provide guidelines for management decision-making. Here are some examples.

- Offer five year guarantees on all products sold and give money back to customers with valid complaints.
- Promote managers from within the organisation, wherever possible, instead of recruiting managers to senior positions from outside.
- Insist that all accounts personnel obtain a qualification

3.3 Budgets

A **budget** is a formal statement of expected results **set out in money values**.

- The budget indicates what **resources will be allocated** to each department or activity in order to carry out the planned activities, for example how much money the accounts department will be allowed to spend.
- The budget gives detailed objectives for departments.
- Budgets are numerical statements and, as such, tend to **ignore qualitative aspects** of planning and achievement.
- Budgets are used to **control** activities. For example, if your section is spending a lot more in terms of overtime than budgeted the difference from budget would encourage an investigation.

3.4 Programmes

A **programme** is a co-ordinated group of plans for the achievement of a particular objective. It has a clear, separate identity within the organisation and its planning structure.

Activity 5.1

Dial-a-DVD Limited offers home delivery DVD rental service to subscribers. From a catalogue, subscribers choose which video they would like. They phone Dial-a-DVD Limited. The DVD is delivered by a despatch rider, who calls at several homes in an area. The Chairman, Rajiv Bharat, says: 'I hope to expand the business. I've discovered a market segment for those who'll pay extra for art movie videos. I've had to knock the marketing and production directors' heads together to develop a plan for building a distribution system for this market. We charge £2 per video per 24 hours including delivery'.

Task

Identify the type of plan used in this situation.

3.5 Procedures

A **procedure** is a logical sequence of required actions for performing a certain task. **Procedures** exist at all levels of management (even a board of directors will have procedures for the conduct of board meetings) but procedures become more numerous, onerous and extensive lower down in an organisation's hierarchy.

3.6 Rules

A **rule** is a specific, definite course of action that **must** be taken in a given situation. Unlike a procedure, a rule does not set out the **sequence** of events. The following are **rules** but not procedures.

- Employees in department X are allowed ten minutes exactly at the end of their shift for clearing up and cleaning their work-bench.
- Employees with access to a telephone must not use the telephone for personal calls.

Advantages of rules and procedures

Advantage	Description
Reduction of inter-personal tension	They take away from subordinates the feeling that their superiors, in issuing orders, hold power over them.
Efficiency	Procedures prescribe an efficient way of getting a job done.
Certainty	They remove the need to exercise discretion in routine tasks.
Simplicity	Staff will find jobs easier to do when they are familiar with established procedures.
Standardisation of work	Prescribed procedures ensure that a task of a certain type will be done in the same way throughout the organisation.
Continuity	The work will be done the same way even when a different person starts in a job or takes over from the previous holder.
Documentation	A **written record** of required procedures can be kept in a procedures manual. People unfamiliar with how a job should be done can learn quickly and easily by referring to the manual.
Reduction of inter-departmental friction	For example, work done by the warehousing department of a factory will affect the work of the sales force, delivery and distribution department and production department. Established procedures limit disputes between departments about who should do what, and when, and how.

Problems with rules and procedures

Problem	Description
Close supervision increases tension	Employees learn what is the **minimum** level of behaviour expected from them and tend to work at this minimum level of behaviour. This creates a requirement for close supervision which may increase tension within the work group.
Red tape	Too many rules and procedures can reduce the efficiency with which business is conducted. Keeping them up to date is difficult and time consuming.
Conflict	Occasionally, **overlapping areas of authority** might lengthen the time it takes to get things done.
Conformism	**Individual initiative may be stifled** which may hamper the best possible service.
Can't cope with the unusual	Procedures cannot cope with the **unexpected** or exceptional case.
Bad design	Procedures may be too complicated, or difficult to understand, or may have unexpected consequences. Many procedures, especially when form filling is considered, collect information which is not really needed.

Activity 5.2

Albert Spencer is the owner of ten retail mini-markets spread over a radius of 25 miles from his home town. He employs a manager at each location who, in addition to other duties, is required to carry out simple clerical procedures. These cover both the routine administration of the branch and the provision of data for processing at Spencer's head office. Typical tasks include such things as the certification of hours worked by staff, paying in cash receipts daily to the bank and stock administration.

At a meeting of Mr Spencer and his managers, several expressed concern that despite verbal instructions they were not certain of just how, and when, they should complete the records. It was eventually agreed that a member of the head office accounting staff should prepare a simple procedures manual to be issued to all managers.

Tasks

(a) Outline and describe the contents you would expect to be included in such a manual.

(b) Recommend the presentation and layout for the manual.

(c) State the advantages for the *control* of the business that you would expect to be gained by the introduction of such a manual?

3.7 Quality standards and ISO 9000

Many departments, especially those which process transactions, may have targets that they want to achieve.

- A manufacturing department may wish to ensure that there are few defects in goods made
- A sales department may set targets for how many times a phone rings before it is answered
- An accounts department may have targets for the sped of processing transactions and to ensure error rates are minimal.

ISO 9000 certification is a standard of quality assurance. This is only awarded after **audit and inspection of a company's operations**. In order to gain registration, a company must **obtain independent verification that its quality system meets standards**.

A company that gains registration has a certificate testifying that it is operating to a structure of **written polices and procedures** which are designed to ensure that it can consistently deliver a product or service to meet customer requirements.

The standard does not address the quality of individual goods and service, but aims to ensure that quality management systems of a suitable standard are in place. The British Standards Institution states that the standard 'sets out how you can establish, document and maintain an effective quality system which will demonstrated to your customers that you are committed to quality and are able to satisfy their quality needs'.

Documentation, record keeping and adherence to procedures are very important in such a system.

We will return to quality standards in Chapter 10.

3.8 Action plans

An action plan is what it says: it is a plan of actins to be done to achieve a required objectives. For example, if you have been asked to implement a new computer system, you will set out sequence of steps.

3.9 Schedules

There are programmes of work for individuals and teams to do, with details of tasks and timescales. The important thing to realise is that many types of planning instruments are relevant to the work of your organisation and department.

4 Steps in planning for a section

Different parts of the organisation may have different approaches to planning. **Steps in planning** for improvements in an **accounts section** might be as follows:

Step 1. Identify the **purpose of the section** and of each job within it, by consultation with superiors and the wider corporate plan (to ensure that the job's aim contributes to the section's aim, which contributes to the branch's aim, which contributes to the area division's aim and so on)

Step 2. Identify the **section's key results** (objectives which **must** be achieved if the section is to fulfil its aims) and **key tasks** (those things that **must** be done on time and to the required standard if the key results are to be

achieved). Another term for this process is 'prioritising' – ie considering tasks in the order of their importance for the objective concerned.

Step 3. **Develop performance standards** ie indicators that the job is being done 'well' and contributing to the fulfilment of objectives. Effective standards usually relate to specific targets for cost, time taken, quantity and quality of output, or all of them together, ie X staff should process Y items per hour, under normal conditions, with an error rate of no more than 1%.

Step 4. Set **short-term objectives** for key tasks, so that progress towards longer-term goals can be monitored at suitable intervals for control action to be taken.

Step 5. Identify or forecast the future **resource needs**. Do you need more staff?

Step 6. On an operational work planning level, **organise and schedule** tasks, and **allocate** them to people within appropriate timescales so that the flow of work within and through the section is smooth and continuous as far as possible.

Step 7. **Communicate the plan** to staff so that they know what they have to do and why.

Step 8. **Monitoring and control**. Control information should answer certain specific questions.

- Whether short-term goals are being met, and performance is therefore on target to meet its objectives
- Whether performance standards are being maintained
- The extent of any shortfall or deviation
- What needs to be done to correct the activity or adjust the plans and standards themselves.

Activity 5.3

Task

Identify a plan which you prepared or for which you were consulted, or which determines your work. Did it follow the features identified above?

5 Making and communicating decisions

5.1 Types of decision

Planning and control involve frequent decisions. Planning requires you to decide what to do in the first place and control requires you to decide what control action (if any) is necessary to keep to the planned course. There are different types of decision.

Type of decision	Comment
Routine planning decisions	Typically, budgeting and scheduling. You will almost certainly be involved.
Short-run problem decisions	Decisions of a non-recurring nature. For example, a manager might have to deal with a staff problem.
Investment or disinvestment decisions	For example, should an item of equipment be purchased? Should a department be shut down? Decisions of this nature often have long-term consequences, and are taken at a fairly senior level.
Longer-range decisions	Decisions made once and reviewed infrequently, but which are intended to solve a continuing solution to a continuing or recurring problem. For example, you may decide to institute a new procedures in response to a problem or confusion.
Control decisions	Decisions about what to do when performance is disappointing and below expectations.

5.2 Types of problems

Decisions are needed to **resolve problems**, when there is a **choice** about what to do. Problems vary, not just according to what they are about, but to other factors described in the table below.

Factor	Comments
Difficulty	Some problems are difficult to resolve, and call for: • Careful judgement • A lot of thought • Technical skill or experience on the part of the manager
Frequency	**Problems which recur regularly** can be dealt with in a **routine or standardised way,** with the help of **regulations and procedures.** Here are some examples. • If a member of staff is continually late for work, a disciplinary code of practice should be available to give guidance to the employee's supervisor about what steps to take • If a supplier is late with a delivery, there should be procedures in the purchasing department for chasing up the delivery Problems of a **non-recurring and non-foreseeable nature** cannot easily be provided for in a book of regulations and procedures, and a **higher decision-making ability** is usually needed from managers to deal with them.
Quantifiability	**Quantifiable problems** are those in which numerical values can be given to the inputs and likely outcome of each decision option. Many problems are, at best, only partly quantifiable.

	Comments
Consequences	The outcome of a decision might be measured in several ways. • Money terms – revenue, costs, profits • Units of output or work – number of items produced or sold, hours of work • Productivity or efficiency – units of work produced per unit of input resource employed, such as 'invoices processed per hour of accounts assistant's time'. • Impact on customers or competitors
Responsibility	Decisions can only be made by people who have the authority to do so. Expenditure authorisation limits are an example of this.

You are asked to show evidence that you can refer issues to the right person. Recognising the significance of a problem can help you know when to pass it upwards.

5.3 Stages in making a decision

So, having recognised a problem, how do you go abut making a decision.

Step 1. **Recognise the problem**. The decision maker needs to be informed of a problem in the first place. This is sometimes referred to as the **decision trigger**.

Step 2. **Define the problem**. Consider a head office accounts department that is constantly late in generating management accounting data.

(a) The failure to meet deadlines would be the *trigger*. Further information would be needed to identify where the problems were occurring. A regional office may not product information in the right format, and so lots of data has to be rekeyed by hand.

(b) The problem can therefore be defined.

Step 3. **Identify possible courses of action**. Regions may be required to submit data correctly

Step 4. **Make the decision**. The decision is made after evaluating the alternatives. More people? New systems?

Step 5. **Communicate the decision**. Regional departments are informed what they need to do (and given resources and training)

Step 6. **Implement the decision**. Implementation may need substantial planning and review. Information is needed to ensure that implementation is going according to plan. Introducing new software is an example.

Step 7. **Monitor the effects of the decision**. For example, if you have introduced new procedures, you need to check they are having the desired effect.

6 Negotiating for resources

6.1 What is a negotiation?

A negotiation is a special kind of interpersonal interaction between two or more people or organisations. Alan Fowler *(Negotiation Skills and Strategies)* defines a **negotiation** as: 'a process of interaction by which two or more parties who consider they need to be jointly involved in an outcome, but who initially have different objectives seek by the use of argument and persuasion to resolve their differences in order to achieve a mutually acceptable solution'.

6.2 Examples of negotiations

(a) **Employers and trade unions** negotiate over a **pay and productivity agreement**. Both have an interest in reaching the settlement. The employer wants to avoid industrial action; the employees want to keep their jobs.

(b) A negotiation between **solicitors** on behalf of their clients to avoid **litigation** for example, for unfair dismissal.

(c) Negotiation between a **salesperson and purchasing personnel** in a company. The customer wants, or perhaps can be persuaded to want, a product that conforms with a number of needs. The salesperson wishes to make a sale at a profit. An example would be the purchase of stationery or IT equipment or a new computer system.

(d) Negotiations between the **management of a company and its auditors** cover the accounting treatment of certain items if these were disputed, the audit report and last, but not least, the fee.

(e) Negotiation between **specialists in the company** and **line managers**. Specialists (eg human resource managers) may wish to impose certain solutions on what only **they** see as problems. For example, the personnel director might want to try out a new pay and remuneration system. The line manager may not share this perspective.

(f) Negotiation between **different departments** (for scarce resources). For example, you may have to negotiate with the IT department.

(g) Negotiations between **team leaders** and **team members**, for example, on overtime working. Such negotiations can be formal or informal.

(h) Negotiations at **budget formation**. For 'overhead' departments, such as the accounts department, a budget in terms of staff and resources is likely to be set annually, in terms of how many staff are needed, IT systems requirements and so on. These will be determined by what the department is expected to do.

6.3 Stages of negotiation

The stages below describe a complex negotiation, for example with a new supplier.

Step 1. **Preparation**

The preparation stage involves considering a number of questions.

(a) **What are the real issues?**

(b) **Who should be involved?** Exclusion of some people could be taken to be an insult, whereas inclusion is a recognition of someone's power or right to be there.

(c) **Weigh up the strengths** of each party to the negotiation in terms of authority, determination, ability to influence the outcome, and strength of argument.

(d) **Determine the objectives** of a negotiation.

- The **ideal outcome** (either the best possible in an ideal world, or the best achievable within the bounds of practicality).
- The expected outcome.
- The **minimum acceptable outcome**, below which it would be better not to have entered negotiation at all.

(e) Assess the case of the other side before the negotiation begins.

- **What outcomes are the other participants looking for?**
- **What evidence of fact and logic can they marshal to their cause?**
- **Is there a hidden agenda?**

(f) Look for WIN:WIN
In some cases, both sides can WIN from a negotiation, and this is the best outcome. For example, employees might get a pay rise (WIN) in return for more flexible ways of working (WIN). But WIN:WIN is not the only outcome. In some negotiations, one party must lose.

(g) **Set the context of meeting**

- **Style or tone**: is the negotiation **collaborative** (win/win) or **aggressive** (win/lose)?
- **Who to involve?** Many negotiations involve teams. One should act as **leader**, being constructive and positive. Another should take a tougher line. The third listens.
- **Pace and timing** can affect the outcome.
- **Location** can influence confidence and attitudes.
- **Seating and refreshments**.
- **Documentation**.

Step 2. **Setting the agenda** is important, as this establishes the subject matter well in advance.

Step 3. **Negotiate**. During the negotiation, while remembering the **objective is to come to an agreement**:

(a) Concessions should not be made lightly (so the opposition's case should be probed and weakened).

(b) Every opportunity should be taken to **build** up your own position.

(c) Expose flaws in the opposition's argument eg it is better to ask questions which undermine assertions than flatly deny those assertions.

(d) Strengthen your own case

- **Identifying possible sanctions** (eg strike, job losses) and reminding your opponents of them. Threats do not work, but occasional reminders do.
- Introduce **new issues** (eg by packaging a number of topics)
- Attach **conditions to concessions** (provided that the condition is introduced before the concession)
- Use emotion (only effective if sincere, and used consciously).

(e) The **search for common ground** (real or imagined) is a better way of **reaching an agreement** than adversarial point-scoring.

- **Listen**. The importance of listening, and asking questions to assess both the content of what is being said and the tone in which it is said.
- **Read between the lines.**
- **Highlight the benefits of your proposals** to the opposition. Common interests include: the success of the business, morale, job security, avoidance of third-party intervention and reputation

Step 4. **Move towards an agreement**

(a) **Periodic summaries** of what has been agreed are useful progress markers. They provide a way of ensuring that all sides have understood what has gone on.

(b) **Hypothetical suggestions** introduce proposals without creating a strong commitment.

(c) The other side should be **helped to move** (by not gloating, by under-playing the benefits to your side).

(d) **Avoid loss of face** for yourself and the other party.

(e) **Constructive compromise** involves: retreating on minor issues in the **cause** of greater ones and agreeing on minor issues, as a **precedent** for agreeing on major ones.

Step 5. Striking the deal (or closing the sale) is the 'point of no return'.

(a) Close the deal at the right time, when there is a good morale in the meeting and when it is also clear that no further concessions are available.

(b) **Last minute deadlocks** can be broken by:

- Linking agreement now to a future benefit.
- A stated willingness to review the matter at a future date.
- Pointing out, quietly, the consequences of not reaching agreement.
- A full explanation as to why no further concessions are available.

(c) **Ensure all points have been included** (eg dates of implementation, definition of terms) in the agreement.

(d) The leader should make a **final summary**, obtain verbal agreement, and ensure it is in writing as soon as possible.

(e) **Avoid fudging issues** (ie using a form of words to gloss over important differences). This leads to confrontation later.

Activity 5.4

The Managing Director and Finance Director of Towering Visions plc are preparing for a negotiation with the General Employees Association about the latter's pay claim. The General Employees Association has been recognised as a 'model union' by some companies. It has pioneered no-strike deals, flexible working, and is favourably disposed to the introduction of advanced work practices, new technology and so forth. The Financial Director has told the Managing Director that it is unlikely that the company will meet its profit targets this year, but that a cut in the wage bill of 1% would do the trick. 'After all, it's only 1% – the union has been co-operative: it has always put the good of the company first'. This idea is presented to the union leader, whose jaw drops in astonishment. This is not the expected response.

Task

State what you think has gone wrong.

Key learning points

- ☑ **Planning** involves decisions about **what** to do, **how** to do it, **when** to do it and **who** is to do it. Managers and supervisors are sometimes reluctant to plan.
- ☑ **Plans come in various forms**: objectives, strategies, programmes, budgets, policy statements, procedures and regulations.
- ☑ **Decision making** is central to both planning and control. Decisions are based both on facts and on judgement. Because problems vary in nature (eg short-term/long-term; easy/complex; quantifiable/qualitative) so too does the task of decision making.
- ☑ Decision making is a **sequence**: identify the problem, analyse it, generate alternative courses of action, make the decision, communicate, implement and monitor the decision.
- ☑ Planning sometimes requires the acquisition of resources. In many organisations, these may have to be achieved by **negotiation**. There are many types of negotiation, from relatively informal chats to major procurement exercises or annual wage bargaining with unions.

Quick quiz

1 Explain briefly what is meant by each of the following terms.

(a) Objective
(b) Strategy
(c) Programme
(d) Budget
(e) Policy
(f) Procedure
(g) Regulation

2 What are the steps in planning for your section?

3 Should plans be rigidly adhered to?

4 What are the disadvantages of procedures?

5 What type of information might be needed for monitoring and control?

6 What are five categories of decision?

7 How can decisions be made about problems which occur regularly?

8 Describe the decision sequence.

Answers to quick quiz

1 These terms are not always used in the same way in by different organisations.

(a) **Objective** is a term that is generally used about planning for the organisation as a whole. In this sense it is a goal towards which all the organisation's activities should be aimed, for example to earn a profit, or provide a certain service. Objectives might also be identified for **individual departments**.

(b) **Strategies** follow on from the determination of long-term goals and objectives. Strategies are plans of activity (mainly long-term) and plans for the allocation of resources which will achieve the organisation's objectives.

(c) **Programmes** are co-ordinated groups of plans (objectives, policies, procedures, budgets) for the achievement of a particular objective. An example is an expansion programme.

(d) The **budget** is a formal statement of expected results set out in **numerical** terms, and summarised in money values (and sometimes in physical quantities). It is a plan for carrying out certain activities within a given period of time, indicating how many resources will be allocated to each department or activity in order to carry out the planned activities. The budget is usually prepared on an organisation-wide basis, so that all the activities of the organisation are co-ordinated within a single plan.

(e) **Policies** are general statements which provide guidelines for management decision making. A company's policies might include, for example, to offer 5-year guarantees on all products sold and that employees in the purchasing department should decline gifts from suppliers.

(f) **Procedures** are a logical sequence of required actions for performing a certain task. They exist at all levels of management but they become more numerous, onerous and extensive lower down in an organisation's hierarchy. Prescribed procedures ensure that a task of a certain type will be done in the same way throughout the organisation and reduce the likelihood of inter-departmental friction.

(g) A **regulation** (or rule) is a specific, definite course of action that must be taken in a given situation. Unlike a procedure, it does not set out the sequence of events. Regulations allow no deviations or exceptions, unlike policies, which are general guidelines allowing the exercise of some discretion by the manager or supervisor.

2 The steps in planning are as follows.

- Identify purpose or objective of an activity or your section
- Identify key results and key tasks
- List performance standards
- Set short term objectives
- Forecast resource requirements
- Organise and schedule tasks
- Communicate the plan
- Implement and monitor the plan

3 Once formulated plans should be adhered to if controllable circumstances permit, but because the future is uncertain, plans should be changed to meet unforeseen circumstances.

4 People do not use their initiative. They cannot cope with the unexpected. They can waste time.

5 Information for monitoring makes it possible to compare output to standards. It should be biased towards numerical measurements such as quantities and money values, though there is an important place for realistic qualitative assessment also.

6 (a) Routine planning decisions; typically, budgeting and scheduling

(b) Short-run problem decisions typically of a non-recurring nature, such as dealing with a staff problem

(c) Investment or disinvestment decisions. For example, should an item of equipment be purchased?

(d) Longer-range decisions; decisions made once and reviewed infrequently, but which are intended to provide a continuing solution to a continuing or recurring problem.

(e) Control decisions; decisions about what to do when performance is disappointing and below expectation.

7 Problems which recur regularly can be dealt with in a routine and standardised way, perhaps with the help of regulations and procedures. The decision about how to resolve the problem is made once and applied consistently.

8 The sequence is as follows. You might list some of these elements in a different order.

- Identify and specify the problem.
- Analyse the problem.
- Appraise available resources.
- List and evaluate possible solutions.
- Select the optimum solution.
- Draw up an action plan to implement the solution.
- Carry out the decision required.
- Re-check that planned benefits actually accrue.

Activity checklist

This checklist shows which performance criteria, range statement or knowledge and understanding point is covered by each activity in this chapter. Tick off each activity as you complete it.

Activity		
5.1	☐	This activity deals with Performance Criteria point 10.1.A: Plan work activities to make the optimum use of resources and to ensure that work is completed within agreed timescales and Knowledge and Understanding point 4: Methods of scheduling and planning work (Element 10.1).
5.2	☐	This activity deals with Performance Criteria point 10.1.A: Plan work activities to make the optimum use of resources and to ensure that work is completed within agreed timescales, 10.1.D: Communicate work methods and schedules to colleagues in ways that help them to understand what is expected of them, 10.1.F: Co-ordinate work activities effectively and in accordance with work plans and contingency plans and Knowledge and Understanding point 4: Methods of scheduling and planning work (Element 10.1).
5.3	☐	This activity deals with Performance Criteria point 10.1.A: Plan work activities to make the optimum use of resources and to ensure that work is completed within agreed timescales.
5.4	☐	This activity deals with Knowledge & Understanding point 8: Techniques for influencing and negotiating with decision makers and controllers of resources (Element 10.1) and 14: Who controls the supply of resources (equipment, materials, information and people) within the organisation (Element 10.1).

chapter 6

chapter 6

Co-ordinating work

Contents

Performance criteria

10.1.A Plan work activities to make the optimum use of resources and to ensure that work is completed within agreed timescales

10.1.D Communicate work methods and schedules to colleagues in ways that help them to understand what is expected of them

10.1.F Co-ordinate work activities effectively and in accordance with work plans and contingency plans

10.1 G Encourage colleagues to report to you promptly any problems and queries that are beyond their authority or expertise to resolve, and resolve these where they are within your authority and expertise

10.1.H Refer problems and queries to the appropriate person where resolution is beyond your authority or expertise

Knowledge and understanding

4 Methods for scheduling and planning work (Element 10.1)

5 Techniques for managing your own time effectively (Element 10.1)

9 Principles of supervision and delegation (Element 10.1)

1 Introduction

The previous chapter covered planning in general terms, the sort of plans you may observe and indeed help create. Also, we discussed some of the interpersonal skills needed to obtain resources from other departments.

In this chapter, we focus far more closely on planning in your section. If you are a section leader, then you will have some freedom to determine who does what, and when, in your department.

Again, there is a lot of information here that could be relevant to your project.

(a) You can observe how, and how well, the work of your department is planned even though you may not do the planning yourself.

(b) You may have to plan work of others. This is evidence that you have achieved the Performance Criteria as to who is responsible for what.

(c) Failure to delegate, or lack of clarity can be weakness in an accounting system.

2 Allocating tasks and delegating responsibility

2.1 Authority, responsibility and delegation

Before we can discuss how supervisors and managers go about planning their work we must identify a key issue for work planning and how it relates to organisation structure.

Firstly, some necessary definitions:

- **Power** is the **ability** to do something, or to get others to do it.
- **Authority** is the **right** to do something, or to get others to do it.
- **Accountability** is the **liability** of a person to be called to account for the exercise of delegated authority.
- **Responsibility** is the obligation to do something, or to get others to do it.
- **Delegation** is the process whereby a superior gives a subordinate authority over a defined area which falls within the scope of the superior's own authority. The superior remains responsible and accountable for the results of the tasks and decisions which have been delegated.

Here is how it works.

(a) A **manager** is usually given **authority** from above, by virtue of holding a position in the **organisation hierarchy**. On the other hand, an **elected team leader**, for example, is given authority from below.

(b) Authority is passed down the organisation structure, by **delegation**.

(c) The delegated authority of a manager over a subordinate in a direct line down the chain of command is sometimes called **line authority**.

(d) **Responsibility** is also delegated down the organisation. A person has **responsibility** if he or she has been given a task and has to ensure that it gets done: a responsibility is an obligation for which one is **accountable**.

2.2 Responsibility without authority

In many organisations, responsibility and authority are **unclear** or **shifting**.

Condition	Comments
Unclear	When the organisation is doing something new or in a different way, its existing rules and procedures may be out of date or unable to cope with the new development. Various people may try to build empires. The managers may not have designed the organisation very well.
Shifting	In large organisations there may be real conflict between different departments; or the organisation may, as it adapts to its environment, need to change.

Authority and responsibility should be comparable. Authority without accountability leads to irresponsible actions. Responsibility without authority is an impossible burden.

Activity 6.1

You have just joined a small accounts department. The Financial Controller keeps a very close eye on expenditure and, being prudent, believes that nothing should be spent that is not strictly necessary. She has recently gone on a three week holiday to Venezuela. You have been told that you need to prepare management accounts, and for this you have to obtain information from the payroll department in two weeks time. This is standard procedure. However, there are two problems. One of the other people in your department has gone sick, and a temporary replacement will be needed very shortly. The personnel department say: 'We need a staff requisition from the Financial Controller before we can get in a temp. Sorry, you'll just have to cancel your weekend'. The payroll department is happy to give you the information you need – except directors' salaries, essential for the accounts to be truly accurate.

Task

State the underlying cause of the problem.

2.3 Delegation

Delegation can only occur if the manager initially possesses the **authority** to delegate; a subordinate cannot be given authority to make decisions unless it would otherwise be the manager's **right** to make those decisions personally. Delegation is not abdication. A manager might delegate authority and responsibility for all his or her department's functions. The subordinates would then to responsible to the manager **but the manager would still be fully accountable** to his or her own superior for the department's work.

Managers and supervisors **must** delegate some authority for practical reasons.

- There are **physical and mental limitations** to the work load of any individual or group.
- Managers and supervisors are free to **concentrate on the aspects of the work** (such as planning), which only **they** are supposed to do.
- The **increasing size and complexity** of some organisations means tasks have to be delegated to specialist experts,

However, by delegating authority to assistants, the superior takes on two extra tasks.

- Monitoring assistants' performance
- Co-ordinating the efforts of different assistants.

Delegation implies confidence in the subordinate's competence. The greater the **competence**, the greater the scope for delegation and the lower the need for supervision. Competence depends upon training and experience and it is therefore appropriate for the manager to provide both.

2.3.1 The process of delegation

It helps to think of the process as a number of steps.

Step 1. **Formally** assign tasks to the assistant, who should formally agree to do them.

Step 2. **Allocate resources and authority** to the assistant to enable him or her to carry out the delegated tasks.

Step 3. **Specify the expected performance** levels of the assistant, keeping in mind the assistant's level of expertise.

Step 4. **Maintain contact** with the assistant to review the progress made and to make constructive criticism. **Feedback** is essential for control, and also as part of the learning process.

Remember that **ultimate accountability for the task remains with the supervisor**: if it is not well done it is at least partly the fault of poor delegation, and it is still the supervisor's responsibility to get it re-done.

2.3.2 Problems of delegation

Many **managers and supervisors** are **reluctant to delegate** and attempt to deal with many routine matters themselves in addition to their other duties.

(a) **Low confidence and trust** in the abilities of their staff: the suspicion that 'if you want it done well, you have to do it yourself'. This is self-defeating.

(b) The burden of **accountability for the mistakes of subordinates**, aggravated by (a) above.

(c) A **desire to stay in touch** with the department or team – both in terms of workload and staff – particularly if the manager does not feel at home in a management role, or misses aspects of the more junior job.

(d) **Feeling threatened.** An unwillingness to admit that assistants have developed to the extent that they could perform some of the supervisor's duties.

(e) **Unwillingness to accept** that a job can be done as well in a different way.

2.3.3 Overcoming the reluctance of managers to delegate

(a) **Train the subordinates** so that they are capable of handling delegated authority in a responsible way. If assistants are of the right 'quality', supervisors will be prepared to trust them more.

(b) Have a system of **open communications**, in which the supervisor and assistants freely interchange ideas and information. If the assistant is given all the information needed to do the job, and if the supervisor is aware of what the assistant is doing the assistant will make better-informed decisions and the supervisor will have greater confidence.

(c) **Ensure that a system of control is established**. Supervisors are reluctant to delegate authority because they retain absolute accountability for the performance of their assistants. If an efficient control system is in operation, the dangers of relinquishing authority and control to assistants are significantly lessened.

2.3.4 When to delegate work

When deciding when to delegate, a manager will have to consider certain issues.

- Is the **acceptance** of the work by staff required?
- Is the **quality** of the work most important, and acceptance less so? Some technical financial decisions may be of this type, and should be retained by the supervisor.
- Is the **expertise or experience** of assistants relevant or **necessary** to the task, and will it enhance the quality of the work?
- Can **trust** be placed in the competence and reliability of the assistants?

Activity 6.2

You are the manager of an accounts section of your organisation and have stopped to talk to one of the junior staff in the office to see what progress he is making. He complains bitterly that he is not learning anything. He gets only routine work to do and it is the same routine. He has not even been given the chance to swap jobs with someone else. You have picked up the same message from others in the office. You discuss the situation with the recently appointed supervisor. She appears to be very busy and harassed. When confronted with your observations she says that she is fed up with the job. She is worked off her feet, comes early, goes late, takes work home and gets criticised behind her back by incompetent clerks.

Task

(a) State what the underlying nature of the problem is.
(b) What reasons can you give for the underlying problem.

What has gone wrong?

2.3.5 Empowerment

Empowerment and delegation are related. **Empowerment** means making workers (and particularly work teams) responsible for achieving, and even setting work targets, with the freedom to make decisions about how they are to be achieved. **Empowerment** goes in hand in hand with three other trends in office life.

- **Delayering** or a cut in the number of levels (and managers) in the chain of command, since responsibility previously held by middle managers is, in effect, being given to operational workers. This cuts cost and improves communication.
- **Flexibility**, since giving responsibility to the people closest to the products and customer encourages responsiveness – and cutting out layers of communication, decision-making and reporting speeds up the process.
- **New technology**, since there are more 'knowledge workers'. Better information systems also remove the mystique and power of managers as possessors of knowledge and information in the organisation.

Reasons for empowerment are stated below:

> 'The people lower down the organisation possess the knowledge of what is going wrong with a process but lack the authority to make changes. Those further up the structure have the authority to make changes, but lack the profound knowledge required to identify the right solutions. The only solution is to change the culture of the organisation so that everyone can become involved in the process of improvement and work together to make the changes.' (*Max Hand*)

2.3.6 Impact of empowerment on organisation structure

The change in organisation structure and culture as a result of empowerment can be shown in the diagrams below.

Traditional hierarchical structure: fulfilling management requirements

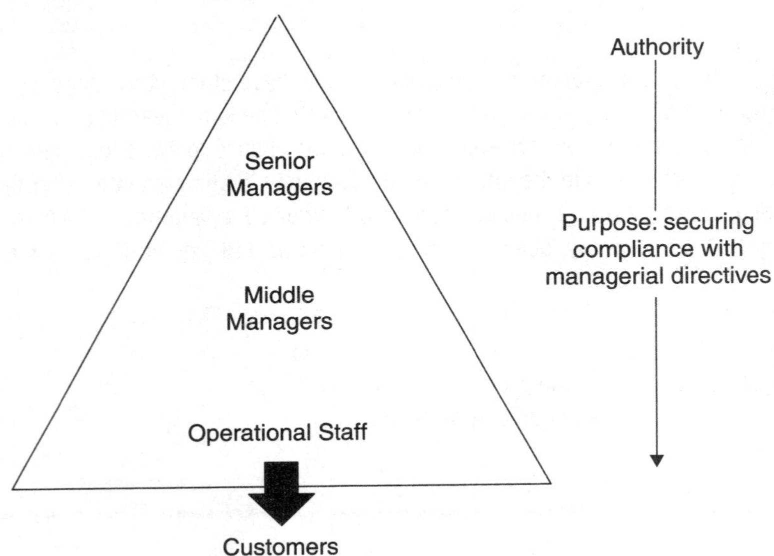

Empowerment structure: supporting workers in serving the customer

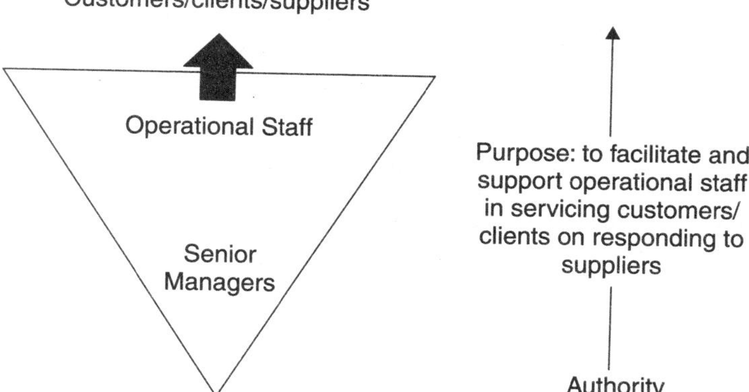

In practice, empowerment has meant different things to different people.

3 Communicating requirements

If you are delegating and allocating tasks, as well as supervising a team, you need to ensure that the communications processes are effective.

3.1 The work of departments

Larger businesses are likely to have proper plans for the organisation and for every unit in it, so that objectives of sections and departments contribute properly to organisational objectives and everybody knows what they are supposed to be doing in relation to everybody else.

No matter how the functional duties are divided in the organisation structure, they must be clear to managers and employees alike. A **departmental job description**, like the individual equivalent, sets out an outline of general aims and duties. This has several desirable effects.

- Individuals recognise the **general aim** of the work of the department and their section of it, and how they relate to it.
- Departmental managers recognise their **sphere of authority**.
- **Specialist work, training and recruitment requirements** can be highlighted in the description of various types of activities.
- **Systems and procedures** can be established, maintained and reviewed on the basis of fulfilling the general aim and specific duties of the section.
- **Duplication of work can be spotted** between and within departments; specialisation, and centralisation of functions are two ways of ensuring that several people are not spending time and money doing the same or similar work in isolation from each other.

3.2 Manuals and intranets

An organisation may have a manual to set out the structure of the organisation and the jobs within it: job descriptions, responsibilities, functions, details of duties and activities, and how all these activities relate to each other. Because the organisation is likely to change, the manual will need to be adaptable – perhaps a loose-leaf system – and regularly reviewed.

Many firms are putting general data about the organisation and the department within an **intranet** for all staff to access. This uses internet technology, but within the company only.

3.3 How to communicate well

Rules of good communication

This applies to your project as well as your communications at work.

	Comments
Clarify what you want to say.	You need to ensure that the right messages get across
Be clear why you are communicating.	Communication may be intended to establish and disseminate the goals of the organisation, to develop plans, to monitor and control the performance of subordinates, to obtain essential information or for many other purposes. The purpose of the communication may affect the way in which the message should be conveyed.
Understand the physical and human context.	For example, should the message be conveyed orally or in writing? Should the message be delivered publicly or in private conversation with an individual? For a written message, is a formal memorandum or a jotted note more appropriate? What is the normal practice of the organisation in conveying particular types of information?
Get your facts right.	People will not trust if you do not. If you have to make assumptions, then state them.
Consider the content and the overtones of the message.	The content may be distorted by non-verbal factors, such as tone of voice, facial expressions, the choice of words and phrases in a written communication.
Communicate something that is valued by, the receiver.	Have you been copied in on e-mails that are of no relevance to you?
Communication requires follow-up.	Has the message been understood? Has action been taken as a result?
Communicate messages that are of short-run and long-run impoxrtance.	People need to know things in advance.
Actions must be congruent with communications.	Don't say one thing and so another.
Be a good listener.	Understanding other people's viewpoints is an important element in communicating effectively.

3.4 Communication difficulties at work

Here are some particular problems in communication at work.

Problem	Comment
Status (of the sender and receiver of information).	• A senior manager's words are listened to closely and a colleague's perhaps discounted. • A subordinate might mistrust his or her superior and might look for 'hidden meanings' in a message.
Jargon	People from different job or specialist backgrounds (such as accountants and personnel managers) can have difficulty in talking to one another.
Suspicion	People discount information from those they do not respect.
Priorities	People or departments have different priorities or perspectives so that one person places more or less emphasis on a situation than another.
Selective reporting	Subordinates may give superiors incorrect or incomplete information (eg to protect a colleague, to avoid 'bothering' the superior); a senior manager may only be able to handle edited information because he does not have time to sift through details.
Timing	Information which has **no immediate** use tends to be forgotten.
Opportunity	Opportunities for people to say what they think may be lacking.
Conflict	Where there is conflict between individuals or departments, communications will be withdrawn and information withheld.
Personal differences	Such as age, educational/social background or personality mean that people have different views as to what is important or different ways of expressing. sometimes views may be discounted because of who they are, not what they say.
Culture	• **Secrecy.** Information might be given on a need-to-know basis, rather than be considered as a potential resource for everyone to use. • **Can't handle bad news.** The culture of some organisations may prevent the communication of certain messages. Organisations with a 'can-do' philosophy may not want to hear that certain tasks are impossible.

3.5 General skills in sending messages

Here is what you should do when sending a message.

- **Select and organise your material:** marshalling your thoughts and constructing your sentences and arguments
- **Judge the effect of your message** on the particular recipient in the particular situation
- **Choose appropriate language and media**
- **Adapt your communication style** accordingly: putting people at their ease, smoothing over difficulties, or being comforting/challenging/informal/formal as the situation and relationship demand

- **Use non-verbal signals** to reinforce (or at least not to undermine) your spoken message
- **Seek and interpret feedback**

The skills needed in different types of communication can be contrasted below.

Oral	Written	Visual/non verbal
Clear pronunciation	Correct spelling	Understanding and control over 'body language' and facial expressions
Suitable vocabulary	Suitable vocabulary	Drawing ability
Clear message	Correct grammar	
Fluency	Suitable style	
Expressive delivery		

3.6 Skills in receiving messages

Here is what you should do when **receiving** a message.

- **Reading** attentively and actively: making sure you understand the content, looking up unfamiliar words and doubtful facts if necessary; evaluating the information given: is it logical? correct? objective?
- **Extracting relevant information** from the message, and filtering out inessentials
- **Listening** attentively and actively; concentrating on the message – not on what you are going to say next, or other matters; questioning and evaluating what you are hearing
- **Interpreting the message's underlying meaning**, if any, and evaluating your own reactions: are your reading into the message more or less than what is really there?
- **Asking questions** in a way that will elicit the information you wish to obtain – this is, using **open** questions
- **Interpreting non-verbal signals**, and how they confirm or contradict the spoken message
- **Giving helpful feedback**, if the medium is inappropriate (eg a bad telephone line) or the message is unclear or insufficient

3.7 Informal communication channels

The formal pattern of communication in an organisation is always supplemented by an informal one, driven perhaps by rumours or gossip, which is sometimes referred to as the **grapevine**. Informal communication is speculative and sometimes inaccurate, but it is also 'hotter' and more current

3.8 Communication in writing

We cover written communication in detail when we discuss reports in Chapter 15.

3.9 Communicating orally

You may sometimes have to make recommendations in person. Sometimes, this will be in the form of a conversation with your boss, for example, or a negotiation. In other cases you may have to give an oral presentation, outlining a case.

Some guidance on oral presentation now follows.

3.9.1 Advantages or oral presentations

Oral presentation requires a **tighter editing** of material than in a written report (After all, listeners cannot glance back to earlier notes.) It is also the case that, in a given time, **less information** an be conveyed orally than in a written document.

The presentation can be **tailored precisely** to the audience, with the presenter increasing or decreasing speed as appropriate.

It is sometimes **easier to explain** items orally, with the use of suitable graphic assistance.

A lecture an be '**interactive**' in the way that a report is not. In other words the presenter can be asked to say things in 'another way'.

3.9.2 Skills in successful oral presentation

(a) **Speak clearly**. Mumbling can make it hard to be heard, and impede the message.

(b) The **material must be mastered** before the lecture. There is little point in simply reading of cards.

(c) Make **eye-contact** with the listeners.

(d) Complex points should be **covered more than once** in different ways.

(e) **Objections should be anticipated** ('if you're wondering why X = Y, I'll come to that in a few moments'), otherwise listeners will be distracted.

(f) **Understand the other party's point of view**. In a selling situation this means:

- Not just extolling the virtues of a product.
- Detailing how exactly it will satisfy the customer's needs.

(g) **Never underestimate the effect of your own personal style** on the audience. Although 'good listeners' will make an effort to listen to what you have to say, much of what you say will be judged by your appearance and posture.

(h) **Questions and comments** from the audience, even hostile ones, **are better than silence**. They are feedback information. They might indicate that your message has failed to get across.

(i) Persuasion sometimes can involve **rephrasing your case** in the language of the other party.

3.9.3 Use of visual aids

(a) PCs can be used in the presentation. Microsoft **Powerpoint** enables slide shows, standard formats and so on.

(b) **Overhead projectors** (eg for graphs, diagrams). Slides can be prepared for these, or alternatively they can be used as a sort of 'blackboard' (eg to write the process of a calculation).

(c) **Videos** can be used to support a presentation. These allow visual information from outside sites to be brought into the hall, interviews with third parties to be presented and so forth.

(d) Flipcharts can be used for diagrams, lists etc.

Activity 6.3

After returning from the monthly management meeting, your Finance Director calls a meeting of the senior accounting staff. She is concerned that her colleagues in the other functional areas are not receiving the most efficient service from the accounting departments. The most repeated comment in the management meeting was 'You accountants do not seem able to communicate properly'. To consider this criticism it is agreed to hold a workshop session to re-evaluate the approaches of the various sections. Although the session will be expected to be wide ranging it was recognised that some form of structure for this meeting should be prepared. To assist her in leading this session the Financial Director has now asked you to prepare the appropriate notes, and also to obtain further information from other departments.

Task

(a) Outline the likely points which you anticipate may be raised by the other departments.
(b) Prepare a plan of the possible remedies which may be explored by your department in relation to these points.

4 Planning work

4.1 Efficiency

Whenever people work, they are using up resources, and resources cost money. Resources are:

- Their own time
- The time of colleagues, bosses and subordinates
- Materials
- Equipment, such as telephones, typewriters and computers
- Other items which cost money – such as electricity
- Cash

Efficient working means that resources are used wisely, with minimal waste in order to achieve the aims of the department.

4.2 Work planning

Work planning, as the term implies, means planning how work should be done: establishing work methods and practices to ensure that predetermined objectives are **efficiently** met at all levels. There are several activities which use work planning as a basis.

- Scheduling and allocating of **routine** tasks
- Handling of **high priority** tasks and deadlines
- **Adapting to changes** and unexpected demands; that is, being prepared for emergencies, as far as possible
- **Setting standards** for working, against which performance can be measured
- **Co-ordination** of individual and combined efforts

4.2.1 The resources at the supervisor's disposal

(a) **Human resources.** A supervisor can deploy staff to do different tasks at different times.

(b) **Material resources.** Some management or supervisory posts give the person responsibility for the use of machinery.

(c) **Financial resources.** Discretion in financial matters varies according to the level in the management hierarchy. Normally the supervisor would be set a budget and be expected to work within it.

4.2.2 Steps in work planning

To plan the work of the department, you can follow the steps below.

Step 1. **Task sequencing or prioritisation** (ie considering tasks in order of importance for the objective concerned), or at least assessing where the resources are most usefully spent.

Step 2. **Scheduling or timetabling tasks**, and allocating them to different individuals within appropriate time scales (for example, there will be continuous routine work, and arrangement for priority work with short-term deadlines).

Step 3. **Establishing checks and controls** to ensure that priority deadlines are being met and routine tasks are achieving their objectives.

Step 4. **Contingency plans for unscheduled events.** Nothing goes exactly according to plan, and one feature of good planning is to make arrangements for what should be done if a major upset were to occur, for instance if the company's main computer were to break down, or if the major supplier of key raw materials were to become insolvent.

Step 5. **Co-ordinating the efforts of individuals**

Step 6. **Reviewing and controlling performance**

Some jobs are entirely routine, and can be performed one step at a time, but for most people, some kind of planning and judgement will be required.

4.2.3 Assessing where resources are most usefully allocated

If managers or supervisors are simply given targets, they will be responsible for allocating resources effectively.

(a) **Different routes** may exist to achieve the same objective (eg to increase total profits, sell more, or cut costs).

(b) There may be **competing areas,** where total resources are limited.

Pareto analysis. Pareto, an economist, demonstrated that 80% of the nation's wealth was held by 20% of the population. This 80:20 rules has many other applications. For example, 20% of customers may generate 80% of turnover. This means that the manager will be able to concentrate scarce resources on the crucial 20%; and devise policies and procedures for the remaining 80%.

4.2.4 Priorities

Some work is **essential** and has to be done fairly **promptly**: other work can wait a bit if necessary. For example, sending out invoices might be an essential daily task, whereas filing office copies of invoices can usually wait a few days. Essential work has a higher priority than other work.

A piece of work will be **high priority** in the following cases.

- If it has to be completed by a **certain time**
- If other **tasks depend** on it
- If other **people depend** on it. An item being given low priority by one individual or department may hold up the activities of others for whom the processing of the item is high priority.
- If it is **important**. There may be a clash of priorities between two urgent tasks, in which case relative consequences should be considered: if an important decision or action rests on a task (eg a report for senior management, or correction of an error in a large customer order) that task should take precedence over, say, the preparation of notes for a meeting, or processing a smaller order.

Routine priorities, or regular peak times such as monthly issue of account statements and yearly tax returns, can be **planned ahead of time**, and other tasks postponed or redistributed around them.

Non-routine priorities occur when **unexpected demands** are made. Thus planning of work should cover routine scheduled peaks and **contingency plans** for unscheduled peaks and emergencies.

4.2.5 Timescales

In practice planning for individuals, sections, departments and organisations may be long-term, medium-term or short-term.

- **Long-range planning** will have to be more general (to allow for change), concerned with objectives and strategy.
- **Medium-term planning** will cover the development of systems and the development of resources to carry out the strategy, for example through training.
- **Short-term planning** will cover the precise details of how resources, including work time, will be used.

Different organisations and functions will have different ideas about what is long or short term.

A section of a department is unlikely to plan to such long time scales. The end of next year is perhaps the furthest that you, as a supervisor, will have to look ahead. Your **planning periods** may be as follows.

	Comments
The organisation's **financial year**	This is relevant for preparation of final accounts, stock counts and so on.
Other **reporting periods**	VAT returns may have to be prepared quarterly. The company may have its own timescales for preparing management information.
The **calendar year**	It is common to have a wall planner on which you can record details of your team members' holidays (staff availability), absences through training, the dates of the annual and interim visits from the auditors, seasonal peaks and troughs in workload, and so on.
The next **operating cycle** for your section	• In a **sales ledger** section, statements sent out at the end of the month may mark the end of one cycle and the beginning of another. • A **payroll department** might have a weekly cycle, ending on a Thursday, say, and a monthly cycle, ending on the 26th of each month. • A **costing section** may be dependent upon production cycles, because information about the costs involved in producing a batch of a product becomes available at the end of the process, every three working days, say.
The **next week** and the **next day** are planning periods	We shall say more about this when we discuss personal time management at the end of this chapter.

4.3 Deadlines

A **deadline** is the end of the longest span of time which may be allotted to a task: in other words, the last acceptable date for completion.

Setting deadlines (or having them set for you) may seem easy, but remember that to achieve a deadline, some things will have to be ready an appropriate time beforehand. No employee or group in an organisation is working in isolation. For example, a machine operator on the shop floor cannot start work until he gets the job card telling him what to do and the materials to do it with: this should create a deadline for people in the production planning department to get the job card prepared, and then a deadline for people in the stores department to get the materials into the production room.

Failure to meet deadlines has a 'knock-on' effect on other parts of the organisation, and on other tasks within an individual's duties. If you are late with one task (updating the nominal ledger), you will be late or rushed with the one depending on it (preparing a trial balance).

4.4 Work allocation

Here are some rules of thumb about work allocation.

- **Allocate specialist tasks to specialists.**
- **Some tasks can only be done by one person**, who should not be given tasks which others can do as well. Skills are a scarce resource.
- Some unattractive jobs may have to be done by **rota**.
- **Plan ahead for peak periods** – staff may need to do more than the normal.
- Be **sensitive to people's experience and feelings** about the job they do.
- People's efforts must be co-ordinated.

Activity 6.4

Usha has 6 jobs to get completed and she has made a list of them.

	Time
Tidy office	30 mins
Filing	1½ hours
Job A	1 day
Job B	½ day
Job C	2 days
Job D	1 week

What further information do you need to enable you to suggest to Usha what order these jobs should be done in?

5 Scheduling activities

5.1 Work planning

Work planning may be divided into three stages.

- Allocating **work** to **people** (or machines)
- Determining the **order** in which activities are performed
- Determining the **times** for each activity

In practice, the term **scheduling** is often used to describe all of these stages, but it may also be used for the time planning aspect in particular.

5.1.1 Who does things?

The allocation of work to teams or individuals will depend upon a number of factors.

- The **precise skills** required to do a job (and who has the skills)
- The other work already allocated to people with the appropriate skills or available to be allocated
- The demand for commonly used facilities which may form **bottlenecks**.

Example

In a firm of accountants the most complex audit tasks will be allocated to the experienced and qualified auditing staff, while checking invoices will be done by trainees. Most jobs may require the use of an accounts preparation package: if there are only five terminals, only five jobs can be in progress at any one time.

5.1.2 What order do you do them in?

Sequencing provides a list of necessary activities in the **order** in which they must be completed. The priorities will depend on the circumstances and perhaps upon a declared customer service commitment ('we will make you a new pair of glasses in one hour', for example). Here is a list of possible criteria for deciding what order to do tasks in.

Example	Comment
Arrival time (first come, first served)	Serving members of the public in a bank is a typical example.
Least slack time	Find the time when the job is due to be finished and take away the amount of time it will take to finish it. This gives you the slack time. The job with the least slack time is done first.
Most nearly finished	This gets small distractions out of the way.
Shortest job first	Then next shortest, and so on. Once again this gets those niggling little things out of the way.
Longest job first	Then next longest, and so on. This ensures that the worst jobs are not continually put off.

Activity 6.5

Choose a task or event that needs planning. On your own or in a group:

(a) Make a checklist.
(b) Re-arrange items in order of priority and time sequence.
(c) Estimate the time for each activity and schedule it, working back from a deadline.
(d) Prepare an action sheet.
(e) Draw a chart with columns for time units, and rows for activities.
(f) Decide what items may have to be 'brought forward' later and how.

5.1.3 Scheduling

Scheduling is where priorities and deadlines are planned and controlled. A schedule establishes a timetable for a logical sequence of tasks, leading up to completion date.

- All involved in a task must be given adequate **notice** of work schedules.
- The schedules themselves should allow a **realistic time allocation** for each task.
- Allowance will have to be made for **unexpected events** in the intervening time, and the timetable regularly revised.

A number of activities may have to be undertaken in sequence, with some depending on, or taking priority over others.

(a) **Activity scheduling** provides **a list of necessary activities** in the order in which they must be completed. You might use this to plan each day's work, or to set up standard procedures for jobs which you undertake regularly.

(b) **Time scheduling** adds to this **the time scale for each activity**, and is useful for setting deadlines for tasks. The time for each step is estimated; the total time for the task can then be calculated, allowing for some steps which may be undertaken simultaneously by different people or departments.

5.2 Work programmes and other aids to planning

From activity and time schedules, detailed **work programmes** can be designed for jobs which are carried out over a period of time. Some tasks will have to be started well before the deadline, others may be commenced immediately before, others will be done on the day itself. **Organising a meeting**, for example, may include:

Step 1. Booking accommodation two months before.
Step 2. Retrieving relevant files one week before.
Step 3. Preparing and circulating an agenda 2-3 days before.
Step 4. Checking conference room layout the day before.
Step 5. Taking minutes on the day.

The same applies to stock ordering in advance of production (based on a schedule of known delivery times), preparing correspondence in advance of posting and so on.

Once time scales are known and final deadlines set, it is possible to produce control documents such as **job cards, route cards** and **action sheets**. Here is an example of an action sheet.

	Activity	*Days before*	*Date*	*Begun*	*Completed*
1	Request file	6	3.9		
2	Draft report	5	4.9		
3	Type report	3	6.9		
4	Approve report	1	8.9		
5	Signature	1	8.9		
6	Internal messenger	same day	9.9		

Longer-term schedules may be shown conveniently on charts, pegboards or year planners. These can be used to show lengths of time and the relationships between various tasks or timetabled events, as illustrated below.

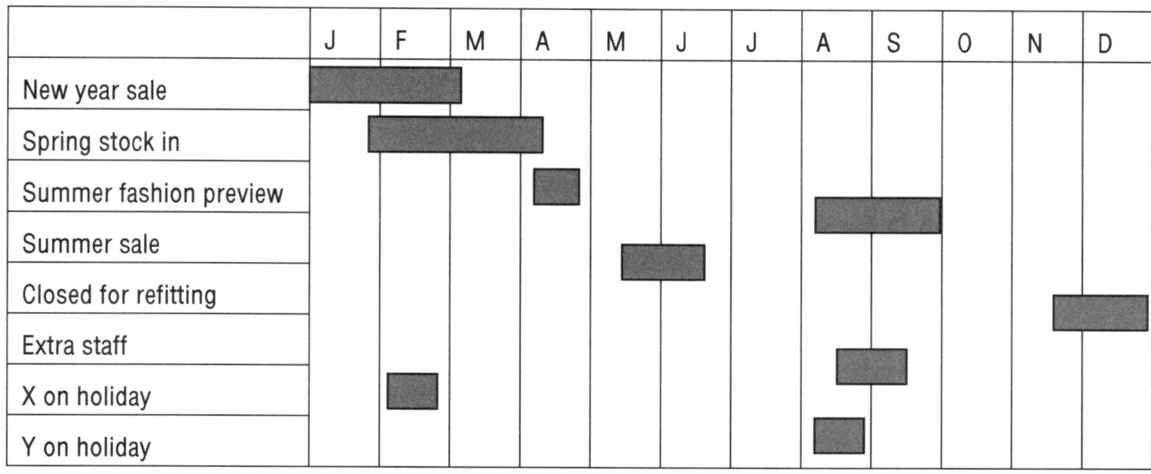

5.2.1 Gantt charts

Another well-known and widely used form of progressing chart is the Gantt chart. On the Gantt chart a division of space represents both an amount of time and an amount of work to be done in that time. Lines drawn horizontally through the space show the relation of the amount of work actually done in the time to the amount of work scheduled, on a proportional or percentage basis. It shows the relationship between time spent and work done, and what has happened and when. It indicates future action required, so that records charted in this way become dynamic.

Example

The information below about planned work and actual progress is set out in a Gantt chart, to show you what it looks like.

Day	*Work Daily schedule*	*Work Cumulative Schedule*	*Work done in the day*	*Cumulative work done*	*Cumulative position as % of a day in front or % of a day behind*
Mon	100	100	75	75	-25%
Tues	125	225	100	175	-40%
Wed	150	375	150	325	-33%
Thu	150	525	180	505	-13%
Fri	150	675	75	580	-63%

The Gantt chart shows the daily schedule, the work actually accomplished each day plus the cumulative schedule and the cumulative work done. The numbers represent hours of time.

(a) Daily schedule and work actually done each day

	Monday	Tuesday	Wednesday	Thursday	Friday
Scheduled work	100	125	150	150	150
Work done	75	100	150	180	75

(b) Cumulative schedule and cumulative accomplishment

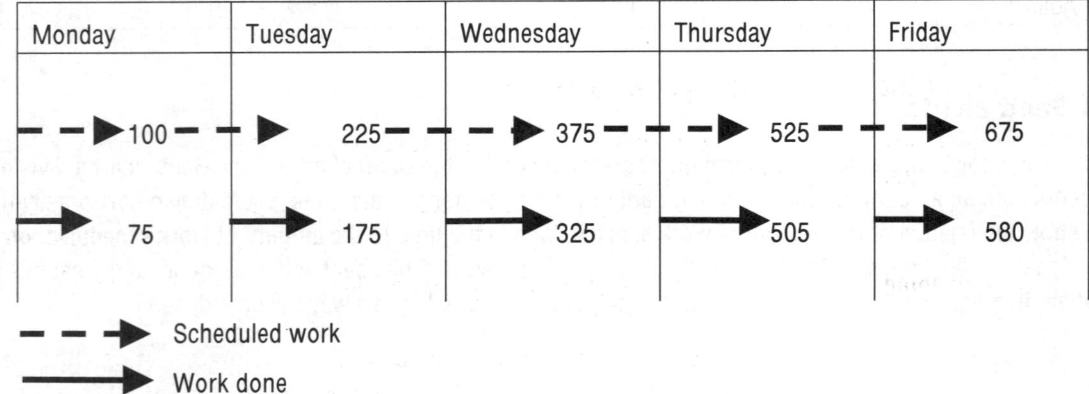

Another form of scheduling for larger projects is **network analysis**. This is a topic for other Units and it is of limited use for day to day work, so we shall not explore it here.

5.2.2 Microsoft Outlook and other types of software

You can use Microsoft Outlook to set up meetings, to allocate time and to find out when other people are busy. It will not assist you in project **planning** but can make **administration** much more easy.

5.3 Projects

The difference between project planning and other parts of planning is that a **project is not a repetitive activity**. That said, it encapsulates on a smaller scale many issues of planning and management, including the details of resource allocation.

5.3.1 Characteristics of projects

- Specific start and end points
- Well-defined objectives
- The project endeavour is unique
- The project is usually limited in terms of funds and time available
- A project cuts across many organisational and functional boundaries

5.3.2 Examples of projects

Project	Comment
Site management, construction	For example, redecorating the floor of a building. This may require temporary office accommodation for some staff.
Manufacturing	The manufacture of an oil rig, involves co-ordinating a large number of separate activities. This will cease when the rig is finished.
Management	Installing new information system. For example, if your firm is changing its accounting software, then it will have to plan how the work of the department will carry on whilst the new software is installed and tested.

'The job of **project management** is to foresee as many dangers as possible, and to plan, organise and control activities so that they are avoided.'

5.3.3 The role of the project manager or supervisor

The project manager has resources of time, money and staff. These have to be co-ordinated effectively. The supervisor's project management duties are summarised below.

Duty	Comment
Outline project planning	• Developing project targets such as overall costs or timescale needed (eg project should take 20 weeks). • Dividing the project into activities (eg analysis, programming, testing), and placing these activities into the right sequence, this is often a complicated task if overlapping. • Developing a framework for the procedures and structures, manage the project (eg decide, in principle, to have weekly team meetings, performance reviews etc).
Detailed planning	Identifying the tasks, resource requirements, network analysis for scheduling.
Teambuilding	The project manager has to create an effective team.
Communication	The project manager must let superiors know what is going on, and ensure that members of the project team are properly briefed.
Co-ordinating project activities	Between the project team and users, and other external parties (eg suppliers of hardware and software).
Monitoring and control	The project manager should estimate the causes for each departure from the standard, and take corrective measures.
Problem-resolution	Even with the best planning, unforeseen problems may arise, and it falls upon the project manager to sort them out, or to delegate the responsibility for so doing to a subordinate.
Quality control	This is a problematic issue, as there is often a short-sighted trade-off between quality and getting the project out on time.

6 Managing your time

6.1 Why is time important?

Time is a resource (you are being paid for it) and is something which you have to be able to **manage effectively**. Some people are better at this than others. If you are good at managing time, you will achieve four good results.

- Your boss will be happy as you will complete the tasks assigned to you efficiently and effectively
- You will work less overtime, as you will not be wasting time.
- You will avoid stress caused by poor time management.
- You will manage your staff better.

6.2 Monitoring your use of time

You cannot make more effective use of your time **until you know how you currently spend your time**. Do not rely on your memory at the end of the day! Keep a note not only of *how* you spent your time, but also on how effectively you think it was spent. If it was a meeting how valuable was it to you? (or to others?). How much is your work interrupted, by whom and why? Try and establish a true picture of where your time is actually going.

So, produce a **breakdown** of the way you spend each day in a typical week.

(a) The proportion of your time spent:

Activity	%	*Activity*	%
• In meetings?		• With subordinates?	
• On the phone?		• With superiors?	
• Travelling? (to and from work/during work)		• With colleagues?	
• Waiting?		• Socialising at work?	
• With customers?		• Doing routine administration?	

(b) What is the typical breakdown of your time between:

- Work
- Home
- You (eg private study. Leisure)

(c) What proportion of your time was spent in ways which were:

- Important to you?
- Important to others?
- Easily delegated to others?

This will help you to:

- help others undertake a similar analysis
- identify activities which should be reviewed as they are of little value to you or others
- identify activities which can be delegated to others
- identify areas where time is not being used effectively and could be better organised.

6.3 Time management

The **principles of good time management** are listed below and then we deal with them in more detail.

- Goals
- Plans
- Lists
- Priorities
- Concentration
- Urgency

6.3.1 Goals

You might think that your goal at work is to supervise a section of an accounts department and to see that whatever tasks are required get done efficiently. This is fine as an overall description of what you do, but it is not *specific* enough to help you to do it. Nor is there any way of telling whether you have done it or not. As discussed in Chapter 1, to be useful, goals need to be SMART:

Characteristic	Comment
Specific, attainable, realistic	In work terms you could probably set specific goals by reference to your job description: 'prepare and despatch invoices for all goods sold'; 'issue monthly statements'; 'monitor slow paying customers' and so on.
Measurable, time-bounded	If you say 'My goal is to see that invoices are issued and despatched for all goods sold *on the day of sale*' you have a very clear and specific idea of what it is that you and your section have to achieve and whether you are achieving it or not. The same applies to personal goals. 'I'd like a promotion' is just a wish; 'I aim to be promoted to head of the payroll department by the end of next year' gives you something to aim at. How realistic and attainable is it?

6.3.2 Plans

You must make plans that set out in detail how you intend to achieve your goals: the timescale, the deadlines, the tasks involved, the people to see or write to, the resources required, how one plan fits in with (or conflicts with) another and so on.

Example

Here is a sales ledger section supervisor's plan of how to prepare a list of bad and doubtful debtors for the purposes of the year-end accounts.

BAD AND DOUBTFUL DEBTORS

Action

(a) Obtain aged debtors listing as at 31 March 1995

(b) Identify all debts unpaid for over 60 days

(c) Send out special payment requests to these debtors

(d) Prepare list of amount of debts identified in (b)

(e) Investigate all debts over £5,000 by reviewing correspondence files, telephoning the debtor, discussing with sales staff, obtaining third party information if possible

(f) In the light of (e) prepare list distinguishing bad and doubtful debtors in format requested by auditors

(g) Discuss with managers whether immediate legal action should be taken to recover any of the debts

(h) Review position at 30 April in the light of cash received in the month. Amend bad and doubtful debtors lists as appropriate

Timescale

The work should be completed over the next three weeks

Deadline

The final list and backing documentation should be ready in time for the auditors' visit commencing on 5 May

6.3.3 Lists

You should work from a list of things to do all the time. If you don't do this already, try this approach once and you will be hooked. What's more, your daily productivity will shoot up.

	Comments
Plan the whole of the coming week in advance	Do this when you are free from the pressures and distractions of actually being at work. You will be more able to see the whole picture.
Make a list every day before you start work	Do this the night before, so long as you don't forget to take your list into work with you the next day.
On the day itself refuse to do anything that is not on your list	This does not mean that you can ignore something more urgent. It means that every new task that arises has to be **added** to your list.
Every time you finish something on your list, cross it off	This is the really satisfying part of making lists!
At the end of the day take all the items that are still on the list and transfer them to your list for the next day	Don't skip this part and just staple today's unfinished list to tomorrow's unstarted one. The physical act of writing tasks down on paper is an important part of the process. They will not be channelled through your mind if you just look at them.
Do not rely on your memory	You are not just creating a memory-jogger: you should be able to see at a glance **all** the things you have to do so that you can get them into perspective.

6.3.4 Priorities

Now you can set priorities on your list. Look over the list and decide which tasks are the most important – what is the most valuable use of your time at that very moment.

6.3.5 Concentration: one thing at a time

Work on **one thing at a time until it is finished.**

If a task cannot be completely finished in one session, complete everything that it is in your power to complete at that time and use a **follow-up system** to make sure that it is not forgotten in the future. **Correspondence,** in particular, will involve varying periods of delay between question and answer, action and response.

Make sure that everything that you need is **available before you start work**. If something is not, put it on your **list**.

Before you start a task **clear away everything from your desk** that you do not need for that particular task.

(a) Once tidy working becomes a habit, it will take no time at all, because your desk will always be either clear or have on it only the things you are using at that precise moment.

(b) By removing distractions, you will help yourself to concentrate.

In accounts work it is not always easy to have a tidy desk. You may have to use large A3-sized computer print-out folders. The office furniture in most offices is not really designed for this. This does not, however, alter the basic

principle of tidy working. (And anyway, there may be a solution: would it be possible to print out reports in a smaller font size or on thinner paper to make physical handling easier?)

6.3.6 Urgency: do it now!

Do not put off large, difficult or unpleasant tasks. If you put it off, today's routine will be tomorrow's emergency: worse, ***today's* emergency will be even more of an emergency tomorrow**. Do it now!

6.4 How to do it: some hints and tips

(a) Plan each day

(b) **Produce a longer-term plan**. A longer term plan can also help you cope with more complicated jobs, by breaking them down into a number of stages. In addition long-term planning helps you anticipate busy periods so that backlogs of routine work are cleared during quieter times.

(c) Assess whether your time could be used more economically, eg by **delegation**, or re-prioritising.

(d) **The ACIB method of in-tray management**. When a piece of paper comes into your in-tray or you get a work-related e-mail, you should not simply look at it and put it back! Instead, you should:

- **A**ct on the item immediately, or
- **C**o-opt someone else to act on it, or
- **I**nput a time to your diary, when you will deal with it, or
- **B**in it; if you're sure it is worthless, or delete it if it is an e-mail.

(e) The **half open door**. Do not be available to everyone at all times.

- Be **unavailable**. (Use call-diverting facilities on your telephone).
- Set up **'surgery hours'** during which – and *only* during which – your door is open to visitors
- Determine which **people** are urgent or important
- Arrange **regular meetings** with people you have to deal with frequently
- Stay in **control of interruptions**, (by asking people to come back later)
- **Do not allow people to by-pass the hierarchy**. Most people should deal with your staff first of all

(f) **Stay in control of the telephone**. The telephone can be a major barrier to good time management, by being a source of constant interruption.

(g) **Don't be a slave to e-mail**. If you cannot stop yourself responding, then switch it off.

(h) **Appointments with yourself**. If you need to spend time alone (eg making plans, reviewing progress) treat this as if it were a meeting. Make a time for it in your diary, and stick to it.

(i) **Work to schedules and use checklists.**

(j) **Organise work in batches,** with relevant files to hand to save time turning from one job to another.

(k) Keep a **list of 'five-minute' jobs** which can be completed whilst waiting for a meeting or phone call.

(l) **Take advantage of work patterns**, for instance by telephoning people when they are likely to be available.

(m) **Follow up tasks – see them through**.

Activity 6.6

About nine months ago, Andrew Barret was appointed an assistant manager in a large finance department where you are also an assistant manager. Recently he approached you for some guidance because he feels he is not performing as well as he should.

He says that his boss has criticised him because his work is not of sufficiently high quality and his wife criticises him because of the amount of work which he takes home. He is, however, happy with the relationships he has built up with the team who work for him.

You have done some preliminary investigation which reveals that:

(a) Andrew apparently delegates well and there is little scope for the delegation of further aspects of his job.

(b) He has built up his good relationship with his team by encouraging them to bring him their work problems as they arise. He is often willing to devote considerable time to the solutions of these problems.

(c) His job description states only that he is required to manage the work and people of his section.

(d) His boss sets him performance standards which concentrate on the qualitative aspects of tasks. In these standards his boss asks Andrew to produce excellent work.

Task

What suggestions would you make to Andrew to help him to improve his time management and his job performance? Give reasons for your suggestions.

Key learning points

- ☑ **Authority** is the right to do something. Managers are given authority to take certain decisions.
- ☑ **Delegation** is an important management skill and the principles must be clearly understood. Some managers are often reluctant to accept this.
- ☑ **Delegation** means that authority to do a task is given to someone lower down the hierarchy, although the overall responsibility for the task remains with the manager doing the delegating.
- ☑ **Communication** is essential to get a job done but the process is often faulty. Managers and supervisors should be aware of the possible pitfalls and follow the rules of good communication.
- ☑ **Work planning** involves establishing priorities, scheduling tasks and establishing checks and controls to ensure that the work gets done.
- ☑ There are a variety of **scheduling methods**, ranging from simple lists to full-scale network analysis.
- ☑ **Time management** has six principles: goals, plans, lists, priorities, concentration and urgency.

Quick quiz

1. Briefly describe the matters to be taken into account when considering work allocation.
2. Why must supervisors delegate?
3. List the four stages of the process of delegation.
4. What are the principles of delegation?
5. List five matters that should be considered when deciding whether or not to delegate a piece of work.
6. What are the ten principles of good communication?
7. What are the basic steps in work planning?
8. When should a piece of work be regarded as high priority?
9. Distinguish between scheduled and unscheduled peaks, giving examples.
10. What are the likely planning periods for a section supervisor in an accounts department?
11. Why is it important to meet deadlines?
12. What is shown on a Gantt chart?
13. Briefly explain some principles of good time management.

Answers to quick quiz

1. Problems of work allocation
   (i) Menial tasks such as filing and document copying may not justify the attention of a dedicated employee, but they still need to be done.
   (ii) If duties need to be redistributed during peak periods, are staff sufficiently flexible to be able to do the required tasks?
   (iii) Status and staff attitudes must be considered.
   (iv) Planning must recognise that junior employees may desire and expect challenges and greater responsibility, and may leave if bored and frustrated.
   (v) Individual abilities and temperaments differ: some staff like routine work, for example, but crack under pressure, and vice versa. Work should be allocated to the best person for the job, but this may not be immediately obvious.
2. Supervisors must delegate some authority because there are physical and mental limitations to the work load of any individual; because the supervisor needs to be free to concentrate on the more important aspects of the work (such as planning), which only he or she is competent (and paid) to do; and because the larger and more complex an organisation is the greater the need for specialisation.
3. The four stages of delegating to an assistant are as follows.

(i) The expected performance levels of the assistant should be clearly specified and fully understood and accepted by the assistant.

(ii) Tasks should be assigned to the assistant, and the assistant should agree to do them.

(iii) Resources should be allocated to the assistant to enable him or her to carry out the delegated tasks at the expected level of performance, and authority should be delegated to enable the assistant to do this job.

(iv) The assistant should be made **responsible** for results obtained. However, ultimate **accountability** for the task remains with the supervisor: if it is not well done it is at least partly the fault of poor delegation, and it is still the supervisor's responsibility to get it re-done.

4 Principles of delegation

(i) There should be a proper balance: a manager who is not held accountable for any of his authority or power may well exercise his authority in a capricious way; a manager who is held accountable for aspects of performance which he has no power or authority to control is in an impossible position.

(ii) The assistant should not have to refer decisions back up to the supervisor for ratification provided that they are within the assistant's scope of delegated authority.

(iii) There must be no doubts about the boundaries of authority because where doubts exist, decision making will be weak, confused and possibly contradictory.

(iv) If the functions, activities and authority of each department and the ways in which departments are meant to interact and co-operate are clear, individuals with authority in each department will more easily be able to contribute to the achievement of the organisation's goals.

5 When considering instances in which he or she should or should not delegate, the supervisor will have to consider the following issues.

(i) Whether the **acceptance** of staff is required for morale, relationships, ease of implementation of the decision and so on. They will accept something more readily if they have a large say in how it is done.

(ii) Whether the **quality** of the decision is more important than its acceptance. Many technical financial decisions may be of this type, and should be retained by the supervisor if he or she alone has the knowledge and experience to make them.

(iii) Whether, on the other hand, the expertise or experience of **assistants** will enhance the quality of the decision. If a manager is required to perform a task which is not within his or her own specialised knowledge or experience, he or she should delegate to the appropriate person.

(iv) Whether trust can be placed in the competence and reliability of the assistants. The manager should not delegate if there are **genuine** grounds for lack of confidence in the team. In this case, there are other problems to solve first.

(v) Whether the decision requires tact and confidentiality (for example disciplinary action), or, on the other hand, maximum exposure and assimilation by employees.

6 **Ten principles of good communication**

(i) Clarify ideas before attempting to communicate.

(ii) Examine the purpose of communication, which may affect the way in which the message should be conveyed.

(iii) Understand the physical and human environment when communicating; for example, whether the message is conveyed orally or in writing, or publicly or in private and so on.

(iv) In planning communication, consult with others to obtain their support as well as the facts.

(v) Consider the content and the overtones of the message. The content may be distorted by non-verbal factors.

(vi) Whenever possible, communicate something that helps, or is valued by, the receiver. Seek a favourable reaction.

(vii) Communication, to be effective, requires follow-up.

(viii) Communicate messages that are of short-run and long-run importance.

(ix) Actions must be congruent with communications. Staff will not act in accordance with communications unless they see that their supervisor is doing so himself.

(x) Be a good listener. Understanding other people's viewpoints is an important element in communicating effectively.

7 **Basic steps in work planning**

(i) Establishment of priorities

(ii) Scheduling or timetabling tasks, and allocating them to different individuals within appropriate time scales

(iii) Establishing checks and controls to ensure that priority deadlines are being met and routine tasks are achieving their objectives

(iv) Setting up contingency plans for unscheduled events

8 A piece of work will be high priority in the following circumstances.

(i) If it has to be completed by a certain time. The closer the deadline, the more urgent the work will be.

(ii) If other tasks depend on it.

(iii) If other people depend on it.

(iv) If it is important, considering the relative consequences, for example the correction of an error in a large customer order as opposed to processing a smaller order.

9 A peak is a time when an organisation is at its busiest, for example, for retailers at Christmas. A *scheduled* peak is one that can be anticipated with certainty so that, say, extra staff can be employed or work re-scheduled for these times. Unscheduled peaks arise when unexpected events, which cannot be planned for, occur. Examples may include equipment breakdown, staff illness, and environmental factors (suppliers going into insolvency, unanticipated action by competitors).

10 An accounts department section supervisor's planning periods are likely to be as follows.

(i) The organisation's financial year

(ii) The calendar year, if it is not the same as the organisation's financial year

(iii) The next operating cycle for the section. For example a costing section may be dependent upon, say, three-day production cycles, because information becomes available for processing at the end of each (three-day) production run.

(iv) The next week and the next day, for personal and sectional time management purposes.

11 Deadlines are important because failure to meet them has a knock-on effect on other parts of the organisation, and on other tasks within an individual's duties. If you are late with one task (updating the nominal ledger), you will be late or rushed with the one depending on it (preparing a trial balance).

12 A Gantt chart is a form of progress chart. On a Gantt chart a division of space represents both an amount of **time** and an amount of **work** to be done in that time. Lines drawn horizontally through the space show the relation of the amount of work actually **done** in the time to the amount of work **scheduled**. It therefore indicates whether future action is required to catch up with the schedule.

13 (a) Goals help to focus the mind on what it is that supposed to be achieved. If a person has no idea what it is he is supposed to accomplish, or only a vague idea, all the time in the world will not be long enough to get it done. To be useful, goals need to be **specific** ('do a bank reconciliation', not 'implement controls over the management of pecuniary resources'), and **measurable**, so that the person with the goal can see how far he has gone towards achieving it.

(b) Plans should be made that set out in detail how goals are to be achieved: the timescale, the deadlines, the tasks involved, the people to see or write to, the resources required, how one plan fits in with (or conflicts with) another and so on.

(c) A list of things to do should be compiled daily, and worked from and adhered to all the time.

(d) The items on the list should be allocated priorities as appropriate and the tasks done in that order.

(e) One thing at a time should be worked on until it is finished (or cannot be progressed any further for reasons outside your control).

(f) Tasks should be tackled with a sense of urgency.

Activity checklist

This checklist shows which performance criteria, range statement or knowledge and understanding point is covered by each activity in this chapter. Tick off each activity as you complete it.

Activity

Activity		
6.1	☐	This activity deals with Knowledge and Understanding point 9: Principles of supervision and delegation (Element 10.1) and Performance Criterion 10.1.H: Refer problems and queries to the appropriate person where resolution is beyond your authority or expertise.
6.2	☐	This activity deals with Knowledge and Understanding point 9: Principles of supervision and delegation (Element 10.1) and Performance Criterion 10.1.G: Encourage colleagues to report to you promptly any problems and queries that are beyond their authority or expertise to resolve, and resolve these where they are within your authority and expertise.
6.3	☐	This activity deals with Knowledge and Understanding point 4: Methods for scheduling and planning work (Element 10.1) and Performance Criteria 10.1.A: Plan work activities to make the optimum use of resources and to ensure that work is completed within agreed timescales, and 10.1.D: Communicate work methods and schedules to colleagues in ways that help them to understand what is expected of them.
6.4	☐	This activity deals with Performance Criteria 10.1.A: Plan work activities to make the optimum use of resources and to ensure that work is completed within agreed timescales, and 10.1.D: Communicate work methods and schedules to colleagues in ways that help them to understand what is expected of them.
6.5	☐	This activity deals with Performance Criteria 10.1.A: Plan work activities to make the optimum use of resources and to ensure that work is completed within agreed timescales, and 10.1 F: Co-ordinate work activities effectively and in accordance with work plans and contingency plans
6.6	☐	This activity deals with Knowledge and Understanding point 5: Techniques for managing your own time effectively (Element 10.1).

chapter 7

Problems and contingencies

Contents

Performance criteria

10.1.C Prepare, in collaboration with management, contingency plans to meet possible emergencies

10.1.G Encourage colleagues to report to you promptly any problems and queries that are beyond their authority or expertise to resolve, and resolve these when they are within your authority and expertise

10.1.H Refer problems and queries to the appropriate person where resolution is beyond your authority or expertise

Range statement

Performance in this element relates to the following contexts:

Contingency plans allowing for:

- Fully functioning computer system not being available
- Staff absence
- Changes in work patterns and demands

1 Introduction

No matter how good a supervisor you are problems will sometimes arise, because you can never have total control over people and circumstances. The Performance Criteria for Unit 10 recognise this. Your Unit 10 report can include 'case histories of how contingencies, crises, problems were handled' and explain what you learnt from the experience.

Contingency planning is carried out at a number of levels. Arguably, ensuring that computer files are backed up is a form of contingency planning – they are backed up 'in case' something happens to the original.

Contingency plans feature in the Unit. If our section does not have contingency plans for staff absence, say, then one of your recommendations could be that this important work is done.

2 Contingency plans

2.1 What can go wrong?

Here are some suggestions of things that can go wrong. These are of varying degrees of importance.

	Comments
Computer problems	• Fire, floods or explosions destroying data files and equipment • A computer virus completely destroying a data or program file • For new systems or parts of systems, software bugs not discovered at the design or parallel running stages • Accidental damage to telecommunications links (eg if builders cut a cable)
Procedural difficulties	• Data input errors, such as posting invoices or crediting cash receipts to the wrong accounts, posting the wrong amounts, making single entries, and so on • Processing errors, for example closing down the ledgers and running the month-end program before all the month's data has been input or using incorrect opening balances • Other accounting errors, due to uncertainty about how to treat certain items, or about how the system is supposed to work
Staff problems	• Insufficient staff, due to sickness, strikes and so on • The departure or temporary absence of key personnel • Disciplinary problems • Conflict between individuals or between supervisor and those supervised
Sudden changes in operating conditions	• The failure or takeover of a **competitor**, causing a sudden increase in demand and therefore transactions • The bankruptcy of a major **supplier** • A takeover by a **new senior management** with different reporting requirements • A **new tax** affecting all transactions

2.2 Contingency plans and controls

After reading the chapter on internal controls you may be thinking that some of the above problems should not arise in the first place if proper controls are in place. To justify setting up a control, **the risk of the problem arising must be great enough to outweigh the cost,** in terms of time and resources, of operating the control. If it is not, the organisation will run the risk, but it must remain aware that there *is* a risk, and have a plan ready to deal with the problem in the unlikely event that it does arise.

A contingency plan sets out what needs to be done to restore normality after something has gone wrong. The plan has some essential features.

- **Standby procedures** so that some operations can be performed while normal services are disrupted
- **Recovery procedures** once the cause of the problem has been addressed
- The **personnel management policies** to ensure that (a) and (b) above are implemented properly

2.3 How do you prepare a contingency plan?

2.3.1 Identify risks

You cannot prepare a contingency plan without first being aware that the contingency exists. **Risk identification** should be a continuous process, so that new risks and changes affecting existing risks may be identified quickly and dealt with appropriately, before they can cause unacceptable losses.

(a) **Keep abreast of all the events affecting the work of the accounts department** at present and in the future and anticipating problems that could occur. It helps, though, if there are good two-way communications between your section and everybody else that it deals with in the organisation and if you take a keen interest in new developments in your organisation and in its business environment.

(b) **Speak to people** who have been in the organisation longer than you have, and have encountered problems in the past.

(c) **Speak to your staff**, who may be aware of problems starting to become crises long before you are.

(d) **Speak to others outside your organisation** who may have encountered problems that could equally well be faced by your section. Sharing experiences in class will be fruitful, as will chatting to friends in similar jobs.

(e) **Encounter the problem itself and dealing with it**. This is almost certainly the commonest way in practice. It means that a contingency plan should have been in place, but wasn't! In the light of this **experience** a contingency plan is formed after the event to ensure that mistakes that were made in dealing with it the first time do not happen again.

2.3.2 Decide action

Once the problem has been identified the next step is to decide what to do. A distinction is sometimes made between the **emergency plan** and the **recovery plan**.

(a) The **emergency plan** should be designed to ensure that action at the time of the event is swift and decisive. Everyone should know where to go, what to do, when to do it and when to stop.

(b) The **recovery plan** comes into play once the initial crisis is dealt with and is intended to make sure that the business gets back on its feet as soon as possible.

2.3.3 Prepare contingency plans

You should consider the issues below.

(a) **Define responsibilities**. Somebody should be designated to take control in a crisis. This individual can then delegate specific tasks or responsibilities to other designated personnel.

(b) **Priorities** must be **established in advance**. Section heads may have a distorted view of the organisation's overall needs or be self-interested so priorities need to be **agreed with more senior management.**

(c) **Up-to-date information.** How, for example, do you turn *off* the sprinklers once a fire is extinguished? If you don't know you will have a flood as well! All the information that will need to be available during and after the event should be gathered in advance. This will include names and addresses of staff, details of equipment maintenance firms and so on.

(d) **Communication with staff**. The problems of disaster can be made worse by poor communications between members of staff.

(e) **Public relations**. If the disaster has a public impact, the recovery team may come under pressure from the public or from the media. If your organisation has a PR department all enquiries should be referred to them. The best way for you to deal with the media is to tell them nothing at all.

(f) **Heath and safety**. Many contingencies involve threats to health and safety and these may continue during the recovery phase. Do not compromise on dealing with risks to health and safety.

(g) **Practice**. Unless the plan has been tested there is no guarantee that it will work.

2.4 Crisis management

Example

A few days after sending out the July statements to her company's customers, Claudia, the head of the sales ledger section began to receive phone calls querying the amounts shown. Over the succeeding days a flood of complaints was received and it was clear that the problem was a serious one, affecting a large proportion of the company's many debtors.

Claudia's investigations revealed that each of the customers affected had had at least one false invoice added to their account. This appeared to be the work of one of the invoicing assistants who had resigned the previous week after being passed over for promotion. After further investigation it transpired that all documentary evidence that would have enabled the company to identify the extent of the problem quickly (original orders, the false invoices themselves, etc) had disappeared. The invoicing assistant responsible had not left a forwarding address or contact number and had long since moved away from the address shown in the company's records. He was thought to be abroad on holiday.

To deal with the emergency Claudia took the following emergency and recovery action.

Step 1. All complaints were put straight through to her.

Step 2. She wrote to all of the company's debtors asking them to ignore the July statements.

Step 3. The extent of the problem was isolated by establishing that the statements issued at the end of June had been correct.

Step 4. All cash received from debtors since the beginning of August was posted to a carefully documented suspense account (rather than allowing attempts to be made to match it against open items shown on debtors' accounts).

Step 5. Two employees were appointed to carry out the task of matching up despatches during July (as shown in warehouse records) to invoices, to determine which were genuine and which were not. (The arrangement of relevant information in the systems used by the company was such that this was an extremely laborious and painstaking operation.)

Step 6. Recovery procedures were implemented. Once the spurious invoices had all been identified they were cleared off the system, the cash received was credited to accounts and new statements were issued, with further apologies and assurances. Customers who had actually paid the false invoices were sent cash refunds and letters of apology.

We have not described this case in full detail, but there are clearly lessons to be learnt from it. Some **general principles** could be established for dealing with emergencies of this type.

(a) **Customer care** is vitally important and supervisors should take personal charge of problems affecting more than, say, 3 customers simultaneously as this would indicate a system fault.

(b) Customers should receive a clear and reasonably open **notification** of the nature of the problem.

(c) The **PR department** should be informed (not mentioned here).

(d) Problems of this type should be reported to higher management up to a suitable level – probably director, or in a large organisation, the general manager of the site.

The case illustrates a general lack of control, and so the department would be unlikely to possess a contingency plan for fraud. You may like to make your own list before continuing: these are just suggestions.

(a) The guilty invoicing assistant's bitterness towards the organisation was not recognised at all until after the event.

(b) The perpetrator managed to override a number of controls. These would need to be strengthened if possible.

(c) There was no way of identifying which invoicing assistant was responsible for posting which invoices. An enhancement to the system is required in the longer term, and in the meantime more careful records should be kept regarding the allocation of work.

(d) Links between sales order processing information and the despatch system need to be strengthened.

(e) Employee records were not being kept up to date.

(f) No monitoring procedures seem to have been operating on the section's work.

We have now established the basic principles of dealing with contingencies. In the remainder of this chapter we are going to concentrate on two areas in particular – computer problems and people problems.

Activity 7.1

Samdip is the supervisor of a small section of 10 staff, including himself. In July, which is the section's busiest time of the year, one of his staff is on honeymoon for three weeks, two are injured in a car accident and are not expected to be back at work for the foreseeable future and one has resigned to work for a competitor.

Identify the problems for Samdip's section and discuss possible ways of dealing with them.

3 Contingency plans for staff absences

3.1 Absence cover

Absence cover can affect a department in many ways.

Type of absence	Comment
Short term For example • Sickness, • Compassionate leave	This can be disruptive at busy periods, especially as this type of absence is hard to predict. A **short-term** contingency plan could involve: • Rescheduling the work • Delaying the work, if it is not critical • Allocating the work to someone else – not able (ie trained)to do it • Delaying other, less essential work • Obtaining help from other departments • Outsourcing or obtaining temporary staff • Requiring staff to work overtime
Long-term absence For example • Pregnancy • Parental leave	This is known in advance. You may be asked to recruit a temporary replacement for 'maternity cover'. It is quite common for people to be employed on six-month contracts. Do you need a separate contingency plan for this?
Holidays	As a supervisor you should have some discretion over when people take holidays. This should be part of your normal planning and scheduling. Clear organisational policies should make this easier. For example, you have the right to expect notice and you can insist that no more than a maximum number of people can be off on holiday at the same time.
Major disruption	This is covered in more detail below.

3.2 Major disruption requiring a contingency plan

Example

Here a firm has become aware that most of its staff will be affected if a series of threatened public transport strikes goes ahead. An outline plan is drawn up showing how different sections of the business will be affected.

Action	Example	Consequence	
		Sales section	*Payroll section*
Identify contingency	Disruption to public transport	All staff have difficulty getting to work	All staff have difficulty getting to work
Draw up emergency plan	Operate whatever level of service is necessary to minimise the (financial) loss to the business	Take orders: this requires a skeleton staff of 3 persons to man the telephones	No service need be provided: salaries paid monthly by BACS; no weekly paid staff
Draw up recovery plan	Restore operations to normal	Process backlog of orders	Clear backlog due to lost time

Once it is confirmed that the strikes are going ahead the plans are fleshed out. Here is the emergency plan.

Emergency plan

Aim

To operate as normally as possible depending upon the number of staff available. The priority is to ensure that sufficient staff are available to take a typical day's orders: the minimum staffing requirement is the section supervisor or assistant supervisor plus two others with appropriate experience.

Action

(a) The section supervisor should make whatever arrangements are necessary to ensure that she can be on site at 9 am. If a taxi or hotel accommodation are needed the company will pay for this.

(b) Any staff who are likely to have difficulties in getting to work on time should call in with an estimate of when, if at all, they expect to arrive. Staff who do not call in will be assumed to be taking a day's holiday. Staff who notify the company that they are unable to get to work will be paid, but they should clearly understand that their full co-operation will be expected in implementing recovery procedures.

(c) The section supervisor will be responsible for making whatever arrangements are necessary to ensure that the sales telephones are manned. This may mean securing the assistance of staff from other sections, or failing this, authorising or arranging for transport for staff members at the company's expense. The appended list [not shown in this text] gives addresses and telephone numbers of all staff with appropriate skills and the approximate distance of their homes from head office.

(d) **Customer care**. Staff should understand that some customers may become angry or frustrated if there are delays and should make apologies as appropriate. Customers placing orders should be told that there may be a slight delay in processing their order because the disruption to public transport means that only a skeleton staff is operating. Customers should be asked whether they wish their order to be treated as urgent, once normal services are resumed. A note of all urgent orders should be passed to the section supervisor or assistant supervisor.

Appendix

This would contain information such as names and addresses of staff, taxi firms and hotels, and a brief guide to sales section procedures in case inexperienced or 'rusty' staff have to be used.

Activity 7.2

Task

Now prepare the recovery plan.

3.3 Changes in work patterns and demands

Some changes in work patterns and demands can be predicted and planned for – some cannot.

Example	Comment
Seasonal increase in transactions	This can be predicted, and competent managers will have arranged the recourse n advance – 'resources' can include temporary staff, or, if contractually provided, compulsory overtime.
New products	Again, if new products increase the number of transactions, then this ought to have been predicted.
Queries	Mounting queries (eg customers querying invoices) can cause the whole department to grind to a halt. A contingency plan might involve focusing on priorities and 'quarantining' the queries.
General increase in workload	This requires an increase in resources either or people or new systems – not really a contingency.
Reduction in workload	Measures such as an overtime ban, voluntary redundancy, or encouraging part time work, can be considered.

4 Computer contingencies

The range statement for this unit identifies a contingency that 'fully functioning computer systems' are not available. The contingency plans in response to this will depend in part on the cause of the malfunction, how long it lasts, and its seriousness. A firm's procedures and systems should be robust enough to avoid the impact of any disaster.

4.1 Loss of data

One of the worst things that could happen in a computerised accounts section is the loss of all the up-to-date data on a **current file** or the **loss of a program**.

(a) Files can be physically **lost** (for example, if the hardware is damaged, or the disks or CD-ROMs on which the file is held are damaged).

(b) A file can become **corrupted** when it is written and so include false data. Some errors might occur with the software.

An important set of procedural controls is therefore to enable a data or program is recreated if the original is lost or corrupted. To recreate a master file, it is possible to go back to earlier generations of the file.

4.2 Back-up and stand-by facilities

Loss of data can be minimised by having **back up.**

Many organisations ensure that a **minimum of two copies** is always held in addition to the original data. The reason for holding two back-up copies is simple. If the original data is lost, the back-up becomes the only version in existence and is no longer a back-up. It is now the master.

A different approach will be used with PCs and smaller network servers. One technique is to make backups daily using a set of **weekly** media, one for each working day in the week. These are thus re-used once each week.

Back-up media

(a) In **networked systems**, copies can be backed up on to the hard disk drive of a PC as well as on to the **file server** as suggested above. The file server may itself be backed up.

(b) Backing up a **hard disk on to a tape** is quicker and more convenient, although the user has to go to the expense of buying a tape streamer unit. (**File server data** can be backed up every day in this way.)

(c) CD-ROM. Many computer systems have a **CD-ROM drive**. CD-ROMs can store a huge amount of data in a small space. Zip drives can also be used.

Back-up copies should be stored in a different place from the original file and preferably in a fire-proof safe.

4.3 Investigate the cause

The backing-up of data is a critical requirement for systems security. However, data on a back-up file will not itself be entirely secure unless some additional measures are used. If there is a **hardware fault** which causes data loss or corruption the fault must be diagnosed and corrected before the correct data is put at risk in the system.

The back-up data should also be **isolated from the operations staff** so that it is not too readily available. Back-up data which is easily available could be used before system errors have been fully corrected and may then become corrupted too.

4.4 Stand-by hardware facilities

In some cases, stronger measures are needed.

Hardware duplication will permit a system to function in case of breakdown. The provision of **back-up computers** tends to be quite costly, particularly where these systems have no other function.

(a) Many organisations will use many PCs and so protection against system faults can be provided by **shifting operations** to one of the working PCs still functioning.

(b) Where an organisation has only a **single system** to rely on, this ready recourse to a backup facility is unavailable. In these instances one response would be to negotiate a **maintenance contract** which provides for backup facilities.

(c) **Computer bureaux** can agree to make their own systems available in the event of an emergency. Such an arrangement has to be specified in advance, as there might be other demands on a bureau's resources.

(d) Co-operating with **other organisations** in the locality, through a mutual aid agreement, may be a way of pooling resources. However, these other organisations themselves might not, in the event, be able to spare the computer time.

(e) **Contingency centres** (specially set up computer rooms only used for the purpose) are rare and expensive, and the disaster-stricken organisation may pay large amounts in hardware rental. Also, the organisation's staff would have to be familiar with the hardware so equipped. As with a bureau, membership of such a scheme limits system developments in house to those compatible with the backup facility.

4.5 Other security measures to guard against contingencies

With the vast quantities of computers and computer material the risks of data corruption have increased.

4.5.1 Unauthorised access: passwords and user profiles

Email, **intranets** and the **Internet** means that computer systems are increasingly connected over telecommunications lines. These are rarely completely secure, and an expert **hacker** can easily enter the system.

A **password** is a unique code a person uses to enter the system. A **user profile** in a networked system only allows certain people access to particular files, but does not involve a password.

(a) **User profiles** can prevent people accessing the **system at all** without a password.

(b) User profiles allow a person access to a system, but with **restrictions** to the files that can be used.

- Computer files marked 'restricted access' might only be accessed by a few people with appropriate profiles. This is very important for database or network systems.
- Data and software will be classified according to the **sensitivity and confidentiality** of data.

(c) Records can be kept of access to files, so that a 'trail' can be left of unauthorised attempts at entry.

Passwords ought to be effective in keeping out unauthorised users, but they are by no means foolproof. For a password system to be effective, passwords should be:

- Changed regularly
- Difficult to guess
- Confidential
- Hidden

4.5.2 Viruses

A virus is a computer program that infects a computer system and replicates itself within it, much in the same way as a human being catches a cold. Some viruses can destroy data and files; other just display messages. The best way to deal with viruses is to **avoid infection** in the first place.

It is difficult for the typical user to identify the presence of a virus.

(a) **Anti-virus software** is capable of detecting and eradicating a vast number of viruses before they do any damage. Upgrades are released regularly to deal with new viruses.

(b) Organisations must guard against the introduction of unauthorised software to their systems. Many viruses have been spread on **pirated versions** of popular computer games or possibly the Internet.

(c) **Check any disk received from the outside is virus-free** before the data on the disk is downloaded.

(d) Any flaws in a widely used program should be rectified as soon as they come to light.

(e) **Do not open email attachments**, unless you are sure of the source. Many organisations have strict policies on this issue.

4.5.3 Network security

When data are transmitted over a network or a telecommunications line (especially the Internet) there are numerous security dangers.

(a) Corruptions such as viruses on a single computer **can spread through the network** to all of the organisation's computers.

(b) Unless care is exercised, it is **easy to overwrite somebody else's data**.

(c) **Disaffected employees** have much greater potential to do deliberate damage to valuable corporate data or systems because the network could give them access to parts of the system that they are not really authorised to use.

(d) If the organisation is linked to an external network, persons outside the company (**hackers**) may be able to get into the company's internal network, either to steal data or to damage the system. Intranets can have **firewalls** (which disable part of the telecoms technology) to prevent unwelcome intrusions into company systems, but a determined hacker may well be able to bypass even these.

(e) Employees may download **inaccurate information** or imperfect or virus-ridden software from an external network. For example 'beta' (free trial) versions of forthcoming new editions of many major packages are often available on the Internet, but the whole point about a beta version is that it is not fully tested and may contain bugs that could disrupt an entire system.

(f) Information transmitted from one part of an organisation to another may be **intercepted**. Data can by encrypted in an attempt to make it unintelligible to eavesdroppers, but there is not yet any entirely satisfactory method of doing this.

(g) The **communications link** itself may break down or distort data.

4.5.4 Data transmission

One of the big problems in transmitting data down a public or private telephone wire is the possibility of distortion or loss of the message. There needs to be some way for a computer to:

(a) Detect whether there are **errors in data transmission** (eg loss of data, or data arriving out of sequence.

(b) Take steps **to recover the lost data**, even if this is simply to notify the computer or terminal operator to telephone the sender of the message that the whole data package will have to be re-transmitted. However, a more sophisticated system can identify the corrupted or lost data more specifically, and request re-transmission of only the lost or distorted parts.

(c) Both of these functions are provided by the TCP/IP communication protocols which are now widely used on networks.

Activity 7.3

Every so often, the media report the existence of a new virus, that might be spread by e-mail, that can do significant damage. Simply opening an e-mail will run the virus, and might even forward it to all the addresses in a person's address book.

(a) Next time this happens, note down carefully **all** the steps your organisation has taken to deal with this contingency.

(b) What would you do if you suspected an e-mail you had been sent contained a virus?

Key learning points

☑ Many problems can arise in an accounts section and they will be dealt with more effectively if they are anticipated and planned for.

☑ Contingency planning entails identifying the risks and drawing up an **emergency plan** and a **recovery plan**. Ideally, the data would be secure and contingency plans will only be operational.

☑ One of the biggest dangers is the loss or corruption of **computer data**. Back-up procedures are vital.

☑ There may be **contingency plans** for **staff absence**. Some types of staff absence can be planned for well in advance and can be incorporated in the normal planning procedures. Resources can be obtained from elsewhere or changes can be made to the short schedule, but it often helps to know who in advance is able to do a task.

Quick quiz

1 What is a contingency plan?

2 List problems that might arise in an accounts department.

3 What is the link between contingency plans and controls?

4 How can risks be identified?

5 What is the difference between an emergency plan and a recovery plan?

6 What provisions may be included in a contingency plan?

7 In what way may a disaster be beneficial to an organisation and its staff?

8 How can a master file be recreated?

9 If a back-up copy of data is taken, is the data then secure? (Several points should be made in your answer.)

10 What problems arise in making provisions for the breakdown of computer hardware? (Again, there are several points you can make.)

11 What are passwords used for?

Answers to quick quiz

1 A contingency plan sets out what needs to be done to restore normality after something has gone wrong. It provides for: standby procedures so that some operations can be performed while normal services are disrupted; recovery procedures once the cause of the problem has been addressed; and appropriate personnel management policies to allow standby and recovery procedures to be implemented properly.

2 Here are some examples

- Computer problems
- Procedural difficulties
- Staff problems
- Sudden changes in operating conditions
- Fraud

3 To justify setting up a control to avoid a problem, the risk of the problem arising must be great enough to outweigh the cost, in terms of time and resources, of operating the control. If it is not, the organisation will run the risk, but it must remain aware that there *is* a risk, and have a contingency plan ready to deal with the problem in the unlikely event that it does arise.

4 Means of identifying risks

(a) Keeping abreast of all relevant events at present and in the future and anticipating problems that could occur. This is very difficult in practice.

(b) Speaking to experienced people in the organisation who may have encountered problems in the past.

(c) Speaking to staff, whose more direct involvement in operations may mean that they have early warning of problems.

(d) Speaking to people outside the organisation who may have encountered problems that could equally well affect your section. Some consultants advise on risks for a living, and insurance companies also specialise in this area.

(e) Encountering the problem itself and dealing with it.

5 The emergency plan is intended to ensure that action **at the time of** the event is swift and decisive. The recovery plan comes into play once the initial crisis is dealt with. It is intended to make sure that the business gets back on its feet as soon as possible.

6 A contingency plan will include provisions for each of the following.

(a) **Definition of responsibilities**: someone should take control and delegate specific tasks or responsibilities to other designated personnel.

(b) **Priorities**. Some tasks are more important than others and these must be established and agreed with senior management in advance.

(c) **Information**. All the information that will need to be available during and after the event should be gathered in advance, kept up to date and circulated to anyone who might need it.

(d) **Communication with staff**. Everyone should be made aware of the problems that are possible and how they can be controlled.

(e) **Public relations**. Refer to the PR department. Say nothing to the media.

(f) **Practice**. If a full scale test is not possible, simulations should be as realistic as possible and should be taken seriously by all involved. The results of any testing should be monitored so that amendments can be made to the plan as necessary.

7 A disaster may be beneficial if it is used as a **learning** experience, and action is taken to ensure that the same mistakes are not made twice. All too often this is not the case, however.

8 To recreate a master file it is necessary to keep copies of earlier generations of the master file and transactions files. Lost or unrecorded data processing has to be done again from the original input sources, and so these too must be kept.

9 The data is more secure than if no copy is taken, but there are still potential problems.

(a) The data is not really secure if it is the **only** other copy: if the original data is lost the single back-up becomes the only version in existence.

(b) It is not secure if it is stored on the same site as the original, or somewhere else where it is liable to get damaged.

(c) If there is a hardware fault which causes data loss or corruption the fault must be diagnosed and corrected before the correct data is put at risk in the system. The usefulness of data on back-up would be entirely negated if it were fed mindlessly into a faulty system.

(d) The back-up data may also be at risk if it is too readily available to operations staff. Back-up data which is easily available could be used before system errors have been fully corrected and may then become corrupted too.

For all of these reasons it is better to keep **two** back-up copies.

10 The provision of back-up hardware tends to be quite costly, particularly where these systems have no other function. Arrangements with computer bureaux have to be specified in advance, as there might be other demands on a bureau's resources.

Pooling resources with other organisations may be a way of obtaining stand-by facilities, but these other organisations themselves might not, in the event, be able to spare the computer time. If the damage was caused by a local power surge or a terrorist attack, for example, all of the organisations might be equally badly affected.

Contingency centres (specially set up computer rooms only used for the purpose) are rare and expensive, and in any case the organisation's staff would have to be familiar with the hardware so equipped.

In addition, membership of any such scheme limits system developments in house to those compatible with the backup facility.

11 Passwords are used to deny access to the system entirely and to restrict access to particular files.

Activity checklist

This checklist shows which performance criteria, range statement or knowledge and understanding point is covered by each activity in this chapter. Tick off each activity as you complete it.

Activity		
7.1	☐	This activity deals with Range statement: Staff absence, changes in work patterns, and Performance Criteria 10.1.G: Encourage colleagues to report to you promptly any problems and queries that are beyond their authority or expertise to resolve, and resolve these where they are within your authority and expertise and Performance Criteria 10.1.C: Prepare, in collaboration with management, contingency plans to meet possible emergencies .
7.2	☐	This activity deals with Range statement: Fully functioning computer system not being available and Performance Criteria 10.1.G: Encourage colleagues to report to you promptly any problems and queries that are beyond their authority or expertise to resolve, and resolve these where they are within your authority and expertise and Performance Criteria 10.1.C: Prepare, in collaboration with management, contingency plans to meet possible emergencies.
7.3	☐	This activity deals with Range statement: Fully functioning computer system not being available and Performance Criteria 10.1.H: Refer problems and queries to the appropriate person where resolution is beyond your authority or expertise.

PART C

Reviewing and improving accounting systems and procedures

chapter 8

Control in the organisation

Contents

Performance criteria

10.2.A Identify weaknesses and potential for improvements to the accounting system and consider their impact on the operation of the organisation.

10.2.D Make recommendations to the appropriate person in a clear, easily understood format

10.2.E Ensure recommendations are supported by a clear rationale which includes an explanation of any assumption made.

10.2.F Update the system in accordance with changes that affect the way the system should operate and check that your update is producing the required results.

Range statement

- Potential for errors

Knowledge and understanding

11 How the accounting systems of an organisation are affected by its organisational structure, its Management Information Systems, its administrative systems and procedures and the nature of its business transactions (Elements 10.1 & 10.2)

1 Introduction

In this section of the book we focus on some of the particular procedures within the accounting section. **Control** is a management function which ensures that plans are followed and objectives are achieved. In this section, we are going to describe **formalised systems** of control, although the principles also apply to more informal and one-off control measures – for example, a supervisor coaching a team member who is not performing to standard.

Accounting controls are not the **only** controls in an organisation, but they are an important part of the control system. Accounting controls have two main focuses, which go back to the purpose of the accounting function discussed in Chapter 2.

- **Integrity of the data**, in other words avoidance of mis-statement of assets and liabilities, income and expenditure.
- **Safety of the assets**: the accounts department deals in money. Fraud occupies a smaller space in the current standards than before. Even so, one of the Performance Criteria in Element 1.2 is directly related to fraud.

You might identify two types of failures in how control systems work.

- The control system and control procedures are badly designed.
- The control system is largely over-ridden or ignored.

Not all organisations have an **internal auditor** or an **internal audit** department (the smaller the organisation the less likely such a role is to be cost-effective). However, all organisations can have problems with internal control, and there ought to be **somebody** who periodically reviews the effectiveness of the organisation's operations. If the system in your organisation is less well developed, not everything will be relevant to your current job. As usual, though, you should take note of anything you read that could be useful in your job.

2 Control in the organisation

There are two uses of the word 'control'.

- The **action**, to **control**, means to check or to regulate, or to give directions, so as to ensure that action is taken to achieve a goal or target, or to conform to expectations.
- The **thing**, **a control**, describes a device or technique for putting control into practice. This is what we are principally with concerned here.

2.1 Managers and supervisors as controllers

The management function of **control** comprises the measurement of **results** and **correction of activities**. This is to ensure that the goals of the organisation, or planning targets, are achieved and to point out departures from plans in order to rectify them. In short, control is making sure that the **right things** get done **properly**.

2.2 Plans and standards

We shall have seen earlier **plans** state what should be done. **Standards** (and **targets**) specify a desired level of performance. Here are some examples you might have encountered.

- **Manufacturing standards** such as units of raw material per unit produced
- **Cost standards**. These convert physical standards into a money measurement by the application of standard prices. For example, the standard labour cost of making product X might be 4 hours at £5 per hour = £20
- **Capital standards**. These establish some form of standard for capital invested (eg the ratio of current assets to current liabilities) or a desired share price
- **Revenue targets**. These measure expected performance in terms of revenue earned (such as turnover per square metre of shelf space in a supermarket)
- **Deadlines for programme completion**. Performance might be measured in terms of actual completion dates for parts of a project compared against a budgeted programme duration
- The **achievement of stated goals** (eg meeting profit objective)
- **Intangible standards**. Intangible standards might relate to employee motivation, quality of service, customer goodwill, corporate image, product image etc. It is possible to measure some of these by attitude surveys, market research and so on

2.3 Stages in the control cycle

Control depends upon the issue, receipt and processing of **information**. The basic control process has six steps.

Step 1. **Making a plan and/or set standards:** deciding what to do and identifying the desired results. Without plans there can be no control.

Step 2. **Recording** the plan formally or informally, in writing or by other means, statistically or descriptively. The plan should incorporate standards of efficiency or targets of performance.

Step 3. **Carrying out** the plan, or having it carried out by subordinates recording what happens and measuring actual results achieved.

Step 4. **Obtaining** actual results and comparing them with the plan. This is sometimes referred to as feedback.

Step 5. **Evaluating** the comparison, and deciding whether further action is necessary the ensure the plan is achieved.

Step 6. Where **corrective action** is necessary, this should be implemented.

2.4 The control system

We introduced control in the context of planning and standard setting in Chapter 5.

Control system

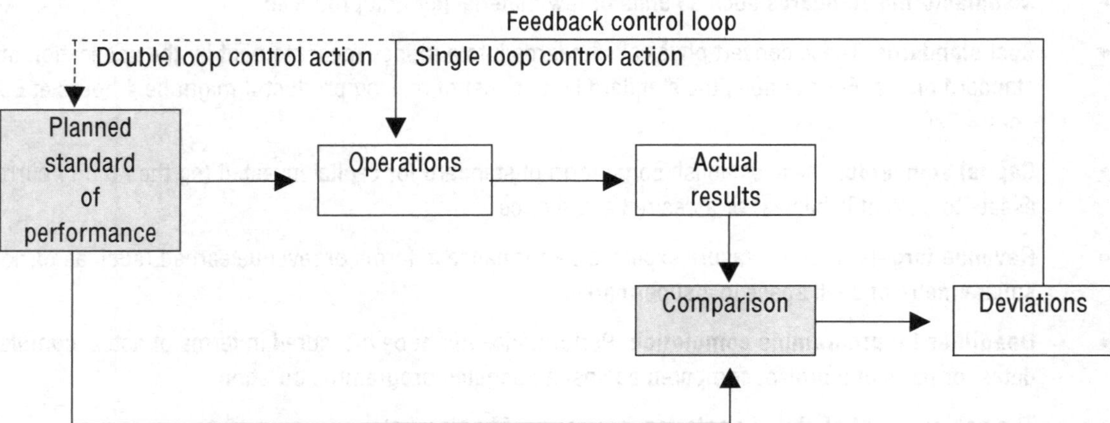

Under this system, the results of operations are **compared** with the standard of performance set in the plan. Deviations from plan are measured and form a basis for control action which aims to bring operations back into line with the plan. It may be necessary to change the plan if it proves over– or under-ambitious.

Control is in terms of what was **planned** and what has been **achieved**.

Feedback occurs when the results (outputs) of a system are used to control it, by adjusting the input or behaviour of the system. Businesses use feedback information to control their performance but environmental factors matter too.

It may be the case, especially with uncontrollable factors, that tinkering with inputs and processes may not be enough. The plan itself may have to change and so a comparison of actual results against the existing plan might not be enough.

- **Single loop feedback** results in the system's behaviour being altered to meet the plan.
- **Double loop feedback** can result in changes to the plan itself.

2.5 External influences

Organisations use a combination of controls.

- If sales figures appear worse then expected the organisation may automatically devote more resources to improving them. This is control from within the organisation.
- For example, the required standards for reporting financial information to shareholders are set by an external body. This is an control imposed from the outside.

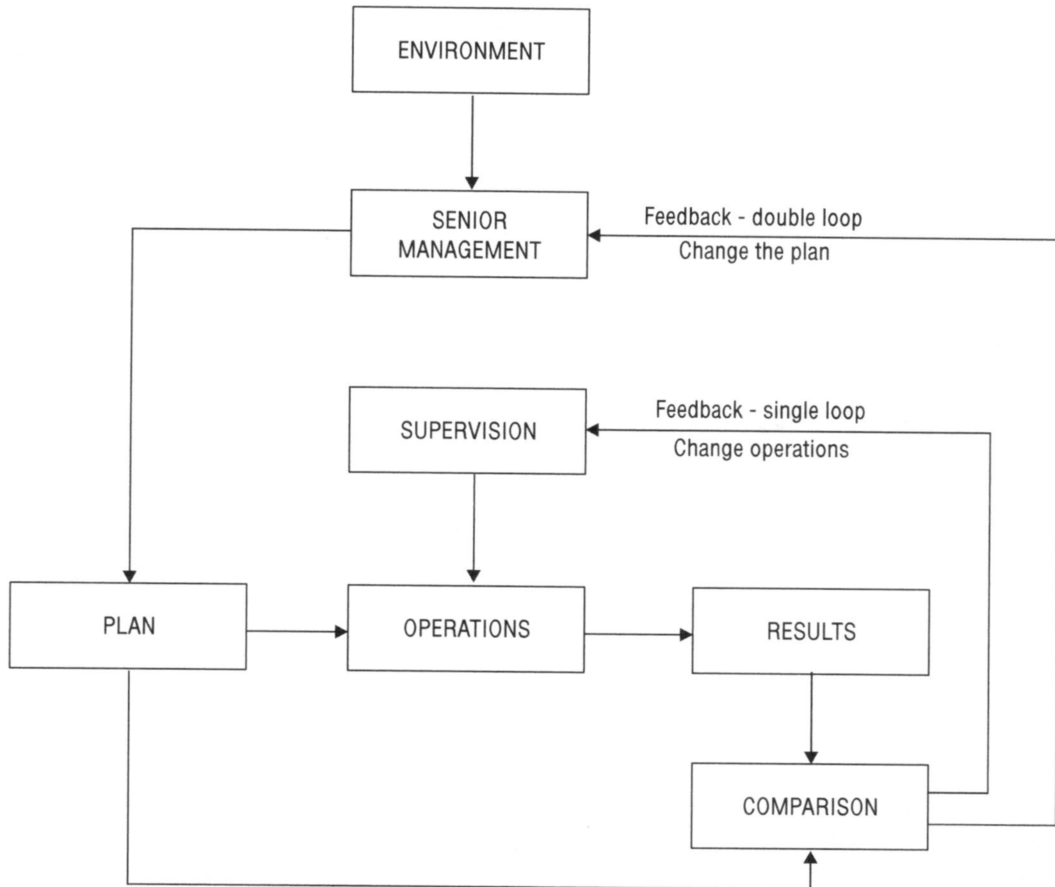

Example

We now relate the **control system** to a practical example, such as **monthly budgetary control variance reports.**

Step 1. **Standard costs** and a **master budget** are prepared for the year. Management organises the resources of the business (inputs) so as to achieve the budget targets.

Step 2. At the end of each month, **actual results** (output, sales, costs, revenues etc) are reported back to management. The reports are the measured output of the control system, and the process of sending them to the managers responsible provides the feedback loop.

Step 3. Managers **compare actual results against the plan** and where necessary, take corrective action to adjust the workings of the system, probably by amending the inputs to the system.

Differences from planned information may result from a number of factors.

(a) **Controllable factors**, such as high labour turnover resulting from bad management. This should lead to control action.

(b) **Uncontrollable factors**, such as changes in the weather affecting production (eg of agricultural crops), a sudden rise in raw material prices. It may be necessary for higher management to amend the organisation's plans.

Note that not all output is measured. **Unmeasured output** might include the **morale** and **motivation** of staff, the number of labour hours wasted as idle time or the volume of complaints received about a particular product or service.

2.6 Budgetary control system

A **budgetary control system** may incorporate these principles.

(a) The **master budget** might have to be changed if it is realised that actual sales volumes will be radically different from those budgeted (eg as a result of a new competitor).

(b) There will be **environmental influences** (eg government legislation about safety standards) affecting both inputs to the system and also how the budget is established or amended.

2.7 Feedforward control

Control delay. A timelag may occur between the actual results and the corrective action. However these results might have been anticipated. **Feedforward control** uses anticipated or **forecast results**, and compares them with the plan. **Corrective action** is thus taken **in advance**, before it is too late to do anything effective. Control is exercised **before** the results, rather than after.

Activity 8.1

Task

Note the factors you might have to consider when designing a control system.

3 Types of control

The control model outlined above is ideal for controlling financial performance which can be measured easily. However, many control issues are not so **easily** measured, even though control theory can still be applied.

In **service industries** that the cost of attracting a new customer exceeds the cost of keeping existing customers satisfied: repeat business, rather than new business, is the origin of success. The factors that lead to repeat business are often intangible, such as **staff courtesy**. How do you control these factors?

(a) Regular **staff appraisal** is an example, as is a simple reprimand for rudeness, but that only occurs **after** the event.

(b) You can possibly apply a **feedforward control** system. Although you cannot **predict** when a member of staff is going to be rude, you can **train** staff in stress management, so they can control their **own** behaviour.

A wider concept of control is therefore needed to include staff controlling their own performance.

3.1 Control strategies

There are three main **design choices** in the structure of a management control system. These will vary from department to department, depending on what is being controlled.

These design choices can be implemented in four **control strategies**.

Types of control	Comments
Personal centralised control	• Centralised decision-making • Personal leadership; direct supervision • Often a feature of small owner-managed companies
Bureaucratic control	• Based on **rules** and **procedures**, budgets and budgetary control • Features as much programmed decision-taking as possible. The amount of individual discretion is limited. For example, customers over thirty days late in payment are **always** sent a letter. • Control is based on the principles of scientific management (see Chapter 5) – specialisation of work, simplification of work methods, and standardisation of procedures
Output control	Systems of **responsibility accounting** are operated so that authority over operations and responsibility for output are delegated to operational managers. In other words **control is exercised over results**.
Cultural control	Management promote a culture under which all employees develop a strong personal identification with the goals of the organisation and take responsibility for their own performance.

Activity 8.2

Sally Keene works for a large department store, as a manager.

(a) At the beginning of each year she is given a yearly plan, divided into twelve months. This is based on the previous year's performance and some allowance is made for anticipated economic conditions. Every three months she sends her views as to the next quarter to senior management, who give her a new plan in the light of changing conditions.

(b) She monitors sales revenue per square foot, and sales per employee. Employees who do not meet the necessary sales targets are at first counselled and then if performance does not improve they are dismissed. Sally is not unreasonable. She sets what she believes are realistic targets.

(c) She believes there is a good team spirit in the sales force, however, and that employees, whose commission is partly based on the sales revenue earned by the store as a **whole**, discourage slackers in their ranks.

(d) Every day, cash taking in tills are totalled and reconciled.

Task

Identify the kind of control, control system or control information you can identify in the cases above. Make any other comments you feel appropriate.

3.2 Control over employee behaviour

Two types of control strategies are related to employees.

- **Behaviour control** deals with the behaviour of individual employees. In other words, control is exercised over the **procedures**, to ensure they are correctly executed.
- **Output control** is where management attention is focused on **results**, more than the way these results were achieved.

Example

An example of **behaviour control** is that exercised by audit managers over junior audit staff. Audit procedures have to be carried out **in the right way** for the information to be of any use. This is because audit procedures are investigative: and to ensure that the investigations are done in the **right** way, so that the information is reliable for the audit manager or partner to come to an opinion, control must be **exercised over how the work is done**. The output of the audit (whether or not to qualify the accounts) comes at the end: junior staff are not assessed as to whether they reach favourable opinions or not.

3.3 Good control systems

3.3.1 Characteristics of a good control system

Characteristic	Comments
Acceptable	Achieving the organisation's goals depends on the efforts of the members. The control system's methods must therefore be acceptable to them.
Appropriate	Controls should be tailored to the capabilities of individual managers.
Accessible	Controls should not be too sophisticated, using techniques of measurement and analysis which only a statistical or accounting expert might understand.
Action oriented	A control system must prompt management into taking corrective action.
Adaptable	Controls should continue to be workable even when events show that original plans are un-achievable (and should therefore be changed) perhaps due to unforeseen circumstances which arise.
Affordable	Controls should be economical and worth their cost in terms of the benefits obtained.

3.3.2 The need for good control information

A good control system should generate good information. The characteristics are listed below.

Characteristic	Comments
Accuracy	Inaccurate control information will either misdirect the people that need the information and make them overlook matters requiring control action, or else it will make them take incorrect and inappropriate control decisions.
Timeliness	To avoid control delay and encourage prompt control action. Information for control should therefore ideally be reported at the earliest opportunity.
Clarity	The person receiving a control report will understand what the report is telling him.
Comprehensiveness	Unless there is a complete picture of events, the inadequate and insufficient information might be used to make an inappropriate control decision.
Cost effectiveness	Resources should not be wasted on collecting information which is of little use.
Relevance	**Information** should **be relevant**. For example, the supervisor of department A should normally receive control information about the performance of department A only.
Objective information	Subjective measurements (for instance on the morale of staff) might be disbelieved by the manager or supervisor receiving the report.
Draw attention to critical success factors	These are points about performance that require special attention because they are judged **critical to the success of operations**.

The activity below shows some links between corporate control over performance and the integrity of accounting data (and the controls that support it).

Activity 8.3

U Ltd carries out its business in an industry where it is customary to settle invoices after 30 days. It is one of the objectives of the company to minimise outstanding debtors. To achieve this, the credit control department has been set a target that 'no more than 25% of accounts receivable should be outstanding for more than 30 days'. Each individual credit clerk has the same target. The credit clerks' pay is performance-related.

Andrew, one of the credit clerks, has worked very enthusiastically persuading customers that prompt payment will enable U Ltd to provide an even better service. As a result, many of the accounts for which he is responsible have paid promptly.

Just before the end of this accounting period, the accounts in Andrew's section of the sales ledger were outstanding in the sum of £100,000, of which £25,000 exceeded the 30-day limit. He then received notification of further cheques of £20,000 from customers paying within the normal payment period. This meant that only £80,000 was outstanding, making the percentage overdue £25,000/£80,000 = 31.25%, ie well outside the target.

To avoid missing his own target and embarrassing the department, Andrew decided not to record the cheques for £20,000 for a few days, until the next accounting period. No one would know because the mail was so irregular, and the cash book and banking systems functioned independently of the credit control department. He would then have a good start towards his target for the next period.

Tasks

(a) Discuss the basis on which the targets are set for the credit control department, with particular reference to Andrew's behaviour.

(b) How else could the performance of the credit control department be measured?

(c) Decide whether you consider Andrew to be guilty of fraud, and justify your decision.

4 Internal controls and internal checks

4.1 Internal control systems and internal controls

'An **internal control system** is 'the whole system of controls, financial and otherwise, established by the management in order to carry on the business of the enterprise in an orderly and efficient manner, ensure adherence to management policies, safeguard the assets and secure as far as possible the completeness and accuracy of the records. The individual components of an internal control system are known as controls or internal controls'. (Auditing guideline: *Internal controls)*.

This definition of **internal control** should draw your attention to several matters which you should keep clear in your mind.

(a) **Internal control** refers to **control by management** – that is, controls applied from within the organisation itself.

(b) A system of internal control **extends beyond matters that relate to accounting** and the work of the finance and accounting department of an organisation. It embraces all types of controls implemented by management – such as controls over late attendance by employees and control over operator efficiency levels.

4.2 Types of internal control

There are two types of internal control.

(a) **Administrative controls**. These consist of the plan of organisation and all methods and procedures that are concerned mainly with operational efficiency and adherence to management policies. These controls will emphasise statistical analysis, time and motion study, performance reports, quality control, employee training programmes and so on.

(b) **Accounting controls**. These consist of all **methods** and **procedures** that are concerned with the safeguarding of assets and the reliability of financial records. Such controls will include systems of authorisation and approval, separation of duties concerned with asset custody, physical controls over assets and internal auditing.

A list of the range of internal controls which may exist in an organisation is given in the appendix to the Auditing Guideline *Internal controls.*

There are eight types of control listed. One way of remembering them is to use the mnemonic **SPAM SOAP**.

- **S**egregation of duties
- **P**hysical
- **A**uthorisation and approval
- **M**anagement
- **S**upervision
- **O**rganisation
- **A**rithmetical and accounting
- **P**ersonnel

4.2.1 Segregation of duties

Clear **job descriptions** should segregate **execution** from **control** tasks. One of the prime means of control is the separation of those responsibilities or duties which would, if combined, **enable one individual to record and process a complete transaction.**

Segregation of duties reduces the risk of intentional manipulation or error and increases the element of checking. Some functions should be separated whenever possible.

- Authorisation
- Execution
- Custody
- Recording
- Systems development and daily operations.

Example

A classic example of segregation of duties, which both internal and external auditors look for, concerns the receipt, **recording and banking of cash**. It is not a good idea for the person who **opens the post** to be the person responsible for **recording that the cash has arrived**. It is even poorer practice for that person to be responsible for **taking the cash to the bank**. If these duties are not segregated, there is always the *chance* that the person will simply pocket the cash, and nobody would be any the wiser. More about this when we cover fraud.

4.2.2 Physical controls

Procedures and security measures are needed to ensure that access to **assets** is limited to authorised personnel. Such controls include locks, safes, entry codes and so on.

4.2.3 Authorisation and approval

The Guideline states that 'all transactions should require authorisation or approval by an appropriate responsible person. The limits for these authorisations should be specified.'

Example

A company might make a regulation that the head of a particular department may authorise revenue expenditure up to £500, but that for anything more expensive he must seek the approval of a director. Such authorisation limits will vary from company to company: £500 could be quite a large amount for a small company, but seem insignificant to a big one.

4.2.4 Management controls

Management controls are exercised by management outside the day-to-day routine of the system.

- Overall supervisory controls
- Review of management accounts and comparison with budgets
- Internal audit function
- Special review procedures

4.2.5 Supervisory controls

'Any system of internal control should include the **supervision** by responsible officials of day-to-day transactions and the recording thereof.'

4.2.6 Organisation as a control

Enterprises should have a plan of their organisation, defining and allocating responsibilities and identifying lines of reporting for all aspects of the enterprise's operations, including the controls. The delegation of authority and responsibility should be clearly specified.

Example

An employee in a company may work for two managers, say a brand manager (who is responsible for the marketing and profitability of one particular product) and a production manager who supervises the production of all products. As you know, a company which is organised in this overlapping fashion is said to have a matrix organisation. The point here is that all the employee's actions must be supervised by one or other of the two managers.

4.2.7 Arithmetical and accounting controls

These controls within the recording function which check that the transactions to be recorded and processed have **been authorised**, that they are all **included** and that they are **correctly recorded** and **accurately processed**.

- Checking the arithmetical accuracy of the records
- The maintenance and checking of totals
- Reconciliations
- Control accounts
- Trial balances
- Accounting for documents

Accounting controls (and many administrative controls) depend on the accounting system of the organisation, and the information and reports produced by the system.

4.2.8 Personnel controls

Personnel controls are 'procedures to ensure that personnel have capabilities commensurate with their responsibilities', since 'the proper functioning of any system depends on the competence and integrity of those operating it. The qualifications, selection and training as well as the innate personal characteristics of the personnel involved are important features to be considered in setting up any control system.'

Example

A company accountant should be suitably qualified. Nowadays, **qualified** tends to mean someone who possesses a professional qualification of some sort, but it is important to remember that others are still able to do a job because of work experience – they are **qualified** through that experience.

4.3 The internal control system

A company will select internal controls from the SPAM SOAP list above and incorporate them into its organisation. Which controls it selects depends on the particular circumstances of the company, but the range of internal controls it ends up with is called the company's **internal control system**.

An organisation may not possess all of the SPAM SOAP internal controls – or indeed may not be able to implement all of them. For example, a very small organisation may have insufficient staff to be able to organise a desirable level of segregation of duties.

If controls are absent, managers should be aware of the risk. It is then the responsibility of management to decide whether the risk is acceptable, or whether the missing control should be instituted.

4.4 Internal checks

Internal controls should not be confused with **internal checks**, which have a more restricted definition.

Internal checks are defined as: 'the checks on the day-to-day transactions which operate continuously as part of the routine system whereby **the work of one person is proved independently or is complementary to the work of another**, the object being the prevention or early detection of errors and fraud; it includes matters such as the delegation and allocation of authority and the division of work, the method of recording transactions and the use of independently ascertained totals against which a large number of individual items can be proved.'

Internal checks are an important feature of the day-to-day control of financial transactions and the accounting system. **Arithmetical** internal checks include pre-lists, post-lists and control totals.

- A **pre-list** is a list that is drawn up before any processing takes place.
- A **post-list** is a list that is drawn up during or after processing.
- A **control total** is a total of any sort used for control purposes by comparing it with another total that ought to be the same.

A pre-list total is a control total, so that for example, when cash is received by post and a pre-list prepared and the receipts are recorded individually in the cash book, and a total of amounts entered in the cash book is obtained by adding up the individual entries, the control total obtained from the cash book can be compared with, and should agree with, the pre-list control total. Control totals, as you should already be aware, are frequently used within computer processing.

4.4.1 Aims of internal checks

- **Segregate tasks**, so that the responsibility for particular actions, or for defaults or omissions, can be traced to an individual person.
- **Create and preserve** the records that act as confirmation of physical facts and accounting entries.
- **Break down routine procedures** into separate steps or stages, so as to facilitate an even flow of work and avoid bottlenecks.

- **Reduce the possibility of fraud and error**. The aim should be to **prevent** fraud and error rather than to be able to **detect** it after it has happened. Efficient internal checks make extensive fraud virtually impossible, except by means of collusion between two or more people (and even then, the fraud will come to light eventually if there is job rotation and staff are periodically moved from one task to another).

Internal checks, importantly, imply a **division of work**, so that the work of one person is either **proved independently** or else is complementary to the work of another person

Activity 8.4

The Geton Company specialises in providing cleaning services. It is currently undertaking an expansion programme, much of which is achieved by supplying services previously carried out by employees of client organisations. In many cases these same employees are then recruited by Geton to work on the contracts using the improved procedures developed through its specialisation in this type of work.

For each large contract, or a number of small contracts in the same location, a supervisor is appointed to oversee the activities of the employees and to provide basic control data for hours worked, materials issued, use of equipment and so on. Invoices are prepared centrally as are wages. These are paid weekly in arrears via BACS. Each supervisor has a van in which the materials are kept and replenished from a central store. Equipment is normally kept at the purchasing organisation.

As a senior accounts assistant with Geton you have been asked to oversee the clerical activities associated with the work of the supervisors.

Tasks

(a) Outline and explain the basic data you would expect to be completed by the supervisor.
(b) Explain what **checks** you would apply to confirm the correctness of the data provided.

4.5 Characteristics of a good internal control system

Feature	Comment
A clearly defined organisation structure	• **Different operations must be separated** into appropriate divisions and sub-divisions. • People must **be appointed to assume responsibility** for each division. • **Clear lines of responsibility** must exist between divisions and levels. • There must be overall **co-ordination of the company's activities**.
Adequate internal checks	• **Separation of duties** for **authorising** a transaction, **custody** of the assets obtained by means of the transaction and **recording** the transaction. • **'Proof measures'** such as control totals, pre-lists and bank reconciliations should be used.
Acknowledgement of work done	Persons who carry out a particular job should acknowledge their work by means of signatures, initials, rubber stamps and so on.
Protective devices for **physical security**	Safes, locks, passwords etc.
Formal documents	**These should acknowledge the transfer of responsibility for goods.** When goods are received, a goods received note should acknowledge receipt by the storekeeper.
Pre-review	The authorisation of a transaction (for example a cash payment, or the purchase of an asset) should not be given by the person responsible without first checking that all the proper procedures have been carried out.
Authorisation	A clear **system for authorising transactions** within specified spending limits.
Post-review	Completed transactions should be reviewed after they have happened; for example, monthly statements of account from suppliers should be checked against the purchase ledger accounts of those suppliers.
Custody and **re-ordering** procedures	• Funds and property of the company should be kept under **proper custody**. Access to assets (either direct or by documentation) should be **limited to authorised personnel**. • Expenditure should only be incurred **after** authorisation and all expenditures are properly accounted for. • All revenue must be properly accounted for and received in due course.
People	People should have the capabilities and qualifications necessary to carry out their responsibilities properly.
Systems	An **internal audit** department should be able to verify that the control system is working and to review the system to ensure that it is still appropriate.

Activity 8.5

It is quite possible that you have had some experience of working in an accounts department, processing transactions, running off reports and so on. Occasionally things go wrong, and there are mistakes generated by the system.

Task

Identify some errors you have encountered – something which was wrong and which you had to correct at a later stage.

4.6 Limitations on the effectiveness of internal controls

Not only must a control system include sufficient controls, but also these **controls must be applied properly and honestly**. If people are dishonest, especially in collusion with each other, then internal controls can be avoided.

- Internal controls depending on **segregation of duties can be avoided by the collusion** of two or more people responsible for those duties.
- **Authorisation controls can be abused** by the person empowered to authorise the activities.
- **Management can often override the controls they have set up themselves.**

Activity 8.6

Jones and Jones Limited is a firm of electrical contractors. The Directors, George and his sister Alice, are responsible for estimating, tendering and contracting for jobs and for the supervision of the workforce. The firm does not have an accounts department; responsibility for the accounts is shared among its office staff.

John keeps records of all purchases and expenses. He also makes out cheques for the directors' signatures and records them in the cash book.

Joyce maintains records of jobs done. She sends out invoices and statements, looks after the sales ledger, records receipts in the cash book and prepares a monthly balance which she does not reconcile with the bank.

Betty calculates the wages, draws an appropriate amount of money from the bank, makes them up and distributes them among the firm's employees. She is also responsible for petty cash for which she periodically draws £100 from the bank.

You are required to produce a **report** to the directors in which you advise them on what you see as weaknesses in the internal control of the firm's accounts and recommend ways of securing effective control of the accounts.

5 Internal audit and internal control

5.1 Internal audit

Internal audit has been defined as:

'An independent appraisal activity established within an organisation as a service to it. It is a control which functions by examining and evaluating the adequacy and effectiveness of other controls.

'Originally concerned with the financial records, the investigative techniques developed are now applied to the analysis of the effectiveness of all parts of an entity's operations and management

The work of internal audit is distinct from the external audit which is carried out for the benefit of shareholders only and examines published accounts. Internal audit is part of the internal control system.

5.2 The features of internal audit

From these definitions the two main features of internal audit emerge.

(a) **Independence:** although an internal audit department is part of an organisation, it should be independent of the line management whose sphere of authority it may audit.

(b) **Appraisal:** internal audit is concerned with the appraisal of work done by other people in the organisation, and internal auditors should not carry out any of that work themselves. The appraisal of operations provides a service to management.

5.3 Types of audit

Internal audit is a management control, as it is a tool used to ensure that other internal controls are working satisfactorily. An internal audit department may be asked by management to look into any aspect of the organisation.

Three types are considered further in the table below.

Operational audits can be concerned with **any sphere** of a company's activities. Their prime objective is the monitoring of management's performance at every level, to ensure optimal functioning according to pre-determined criteria. They concentrate on the outputs of the system, and the efficiency of the organisation. They are also known as **'management'**, **'efficiency'** or **'value for money'** audits

A **systems audit** is based on a testing and evaluation of the **internal controls** within an organisation so that those controls may be relied on to ensure that resources are being managed effectively and information provided accurately. Two types of tests are used.

- **Compliance tests** seek evidence that the internal controls are being applied as prescribed. The auditor will be interested in a variety of processing errors when performing compliance tests.
  - At the wrong time
  - Incompleteness
  - Omission
  - Error (for example, advance payments from customers being credited to sales)
  - Fraud

- **Substantive tests** substantiate the entries in the figures in accounts. They are used to discover **errors and omissions**.

The key importance of the two types of test is that **if the compliance tests reveal that internal controls are working satisfactorily, then the amount of substantive testing can be reduced**, and the internal auditor can concentrate the audit effort on those areas where controls do not exist or are not working satisfactorily.

Example

Suppose a department within a company processes travel claims which are eventually paid and recorded on the general ledger.

(a) When conducting **compliance tests**, the internal auditor is **looking at the controls** in the travel claim section to see if they are working properly. This is not the same as looking at the travel claims themselves. For example, one of the internal controls might be that a clerk checks the addition on the travel claim and initials a box to say that he has done so. If he fails to perform this arithmetic check, then there has been a control failure – regardless of whether the travel claim had, in fact, been added up correctly or incorrectly.

(b) When conducting **substantive tests**, the internal auditor is examining figures which he has extracted directly from the company's financial records. For this sort of test, the auditor is concerned only with establishing whether or not the figure in the ledger is correct. He or she is not concerned as to how it got there.

A transactions or probity audit aims to detect fraud and uses only substantive tests.

5.4 Accountability

Ideally, the internal auditor should be directly responsible to the highest executive level in the organisation, preferably to the audit committee of the Board of Directors. There are three main reasons for this requirement.

- The auditor needs access to all parts of the organisation.
- The auditor should be set free to comment on the performance of management.
- The auditor's report may need to be actioned at the highest level to ensure its effective implementation.

In practice, however, the internal auditor is often responsible to the head of the finance function.

5.5 Independence

Given an acceptable line of responsibility and clear terms of authority, it is vital that the internal auditor **is and is seen to be independent**. Independence for the internal auditor is established by three things.

- The responsibility structure
- The auditor's mandatory authority
- The auditor's own approach

Internal audit requires a highly professional approach which is objective, detached and honest. Independence is a fundamental concept of auditing and this applies just as much to the internal auditor as to the external auditor. The

internal auditor should not install new procedures or systems, neither should he engage in any activity which he would normally appraise, as this might compromise his independence.

Activity 8.7

The Midas Mail Order Company operates a central warehouse from which all merchandise is distributed by post or carrier to the company's 10,000 customers. An outline description of the sales and cash collection system is set out below.

Sales and cash collection system

Stage		*Department/staff responsible*	*Documentation*
(1)	Customer orders merchandise (Orders by phone or through the postal system)	Sales dept Sales assistants	Multiple copy order form (with date, quantities, price marked on them) Copies 1-3 sent to warehouse. Copy 4 sent to accounts dept. Copy 5 retained in sales dept
(2)	Merchandise requested from stock rooms by despatch clerks	Storekeepers	Copies 1-3 handed to storekeepers. Forms marked as merchandise taken from stock. (Note. If merchandise is out of stock the storekeepers retain copies 1-3 until stockroom is re-stocked). Copies 1-2 handed to despatch clerks. Copy 3 retained by store-keepers.
(3)	Merchandise despatched	Despatch bay Despatch clerks	Copy 2 marked when goods despatched and sent to accounts department
(4)	Customers invoiced	Accounts dept: sales ledger clerks	2-copy invoice prepared from invoiced details on copy 2 of order form received from despatch bay Copy 1 of invoice sent to customer. Copy 2 retained by accounts dept and posted to sales ledger
(5)	Cash received (as cheques, bank giro credit, or cash)	Accounts dept: cashier	2-copy cash receipt list Copy 1 of cash receipt list retained by cashier Copy 2 passed to sales ledger clerk

Tasks

(a) State four objectives of an internal control system.

(b) For the Midas Mail Order Company list any four major controls which you would expect to find in the operation of the accounting system described above and explain the objective of each of these controls.

(c) For each of the four controls identified above, describe briefly two tests which you would expect an internal auditor to carry out to determine whether the control was operating satisfactorily.

Key learning points

- ☑ There are various types of control in an organisation.
- ☑ Control in an organisation is needed to ensure that standards of performance are adhered to, by monitoring actual performance against standard and taking action.
- ☑ Control has very wide implications for accountants, who produce information but who are also responsible for safeguarding the assets of the business.
- ☑ Sometimes the plans or standards have to be amended. The control action itself is not enough.
- ☑ Accountants deal with procedural controls to safeguard the assets of the organisation and in the integrity of the information.
- ☑ The main **internal controls** that an organisation may adopt are those covered by the SPAM SOAP mnemonic.
- ☑ **Internal checks** are part of the internal controls in an accounting system: they are designed to check that everything that should be recorded is recorded, that any errors come to light and that assets and liabilities genuinely exist and are recorded at the correct amount.
- ☑ **Internal audit** is itself an internal control whose function is to assess the adequacy of other internal controls. The main types of audit are systems audits, transactions audits and value for money audits.

Quick quiz

1 List the steps in control.

2 What is feedback?

3 List four strategies for control.

4 List features of a good control system.

5 What is an internal control system?

6 Distinguish between administrative controls and accounting controls.

7 What is the well-known mnemonic for the eight types of internal control listed in the Auditing Guideline *Internal Controls*, and what does it stand for?

8 The person who authorises a transaction should ideally be separate from the person who executes it. Give an example of this and state what other functions should be kept separate

9 What is the purpose of arithmetical and accounting controls? Give some examples.

10 What is an internal check?

11 Briefly describe five characteristics of a good internal control system.

12 Are internal controls foolproof? If not, why not?

13 What is internal audit?

14 Distinguish between internal audit, internal control and internal check.

Answers to quick quiz

1 Make a plan. Record the plan. Carry out the plan. Compare results with plan. Evaluate comparison. Take corrective action.

2 Outputs of a system that are used to control it

3 Personal, bureaucratic, output, cultural control

4 Acceptable, appropriate, accessible, action-oriented, adaptable, affordable

5 An internal control system is 'the whole system of controls, financial and otherwise, established by the management in order to carry on the business of the enterprise in an orderly and efficient manner, ensure adherence to management policies, safeguard the assets and secure as far as possible the completeness and accuracy of the records. The individual components of an internal control system are known as controls or internal controls'. (Auditing Guideline: *Internal controls)*. The overall **system** of internal control consists of a number of individual controls known as internal controls.

6 **Administrative** controls consist of the plan of organisation and methods and procedures that are concerned with operational efficiency and adherence to management policies. Examples are time and motion study, performance reports, quality control, and employee training programmes. **Accounting** controls consist of methods and procedures that are concerned with, and relate directly to, safeguarding of assets and the reliability of financial

records. Examples are systems of authorisation and approval, separation of duties concerned with asset custody, physical controls over assets and internal auditing.

7 The eight types of control listed in the Auditing Guideline can be remembered using the mnemonic SPAM SOAP.

- Segregation of duties
- Physical controls
- Authorisation and approval controls
- Management controls, such as internal audit or review of management accounts
- Supervision
- Organisation (that is, the formal structure of authority and responsibility)
- Arithmetical and accounting controls
- Personnel controls

8 An example would be the authorisation for the payment of a supplier's invoice and the drawing up and signing of the cheque. Other functions that should be kept separate are the custody of assets (for example cheque books), and the recording of transactions (writing up the payment in the cash book and purchase ledger). The Auditing Guideline also gives the example, in the case of a computer-based accounting system, of systems development and daily operations.

9 Accounting and arithmetical controls check that the transactions to be recorded and processed have been **authorised**, that they are all **included** and that they are **correctly** recorded and **accurately** processed. Here are some examples.

- Checking the arithmetical accuracy of the records
- The maintenance and checking of totals
- Reconciliations
- Control accounts
- Trial balances
- Accounting for documents

10 Internal checks are: 'the checks on the day-to-day transactions which operate continuously as part of the routine system whereby **the work of one person is proved independently or is complementary to the work of another**, the object being the prevention or early detection of errors and fraud'. Control totals and pre-lists are examples of them.

11 **Characteristics of good internal control**

(i) A clearly defined organisation structure

(ii) Adequate internal checks

(iii) Acknowledgement of work done

(iv) Protective devices for physical security

(v) The use of formal documents to acknowledge the transfer of responsibility for goods

(vi) Pre-review of transactions

(vii) A clearly defined system for authorising transactions within specified spending limits

(viii) Post-review*:* completed transactions should be reviewed after they have happened.

(ix) Authorisation, custody and re-ordering procedures over the funds, property and expenditure of the organisation

(x) Personnel should be adequately trained, and there should be appropriate remuneration, welfare, promotion and appointment schemes (adequate 'hygiene' and 'motivation', in Herzberg's terms). There should also be adequate supervision by responsible officials and management

(xi) An internal audit department should be able to verify that the control system is working and to review the system to ensure that it is still appropriate for (changing) current circumstances.

12 Internal controls have to be applied properly and honestly in order to work.

13 Internal audit is a form of control which has been defined as 'An independent appraisal activity established within an organisation ... which functions by examining and evaluating the adequacy and effectiveness of other controls'. It can be applied to the analysis of the effectiveness of all parts of an organisation's operations and management.

14 Internal **controls** embrace **all** controls (both financial and non-financial) established by management to ensure efficiency and adherence to management policies, properly safeguarded assets and complete and accurate records. Internal **checks** are specific types of internal controls in an accounting system, and are procedures designed to ensure complete and correct recording of transactions and other accounting information, and the discovery of errors or irregularities in processing accounting information. Internal **audit** is a part of the internal control system acting as a 'watchdog' over the other internal controls.

Activity checklist

This checklist shows which performance criteria, range statement or knowledge and understanding point is covered by each activity in this chapter. Tick off each activity as you complete it.

Activity

8.1	☐	This activity deals with Knowledge & Understanding point 11: How the accounting systems of an organisation are affected by its organisational structure, its Management Information Systems, its administrative systems and procedures and the nature of its business transactions (Elements 10.1 & 10.2)
8.2	☐	This activity deals with Knowledge & Understanding point 11: How the accounting systems of an organisation are affected by its organisational structure, its Management Information Systems, its administrative systems and procedures and the nature of its business transactions (Elements 10.1 & 10.2)
8.3	☐	This activity deals with Performance Criterion 10.2.A: Identify weaknesses and potential for improvements to the accounting system and consider their impact on the operation of the organisation and Range Statement: potential for errors
8.4	☐	This activity deals with Performance Criteria 10.2.D: Make recommendations to the appropriate person in a clear, easily understood format and 10.2.F: Update the system in accordance with changes that affect the ways the system should operate and check that your update is producing the required results and Range Statement: potential for errors
8.5	☐	This activity deals with Range Statement: potential for errors
8.6	☐	This activity deals with Performance Criteria 10.2.A: Identify weaknesses and potential for improvements to the accounting system and consider their impact on the operation of the organisation and 10.2 E: Ensure recommendations are supported by a clear rationale which includes an explanation of any assumption made and 10.2 F: Update the system in accordance with changes that affect the ways the system should operate and check that your update is producing the required results
8.7	☐	This activity deals with Knowledge & Understanding point 11: How the accounting systems of an organisation are affected by its organisational structure, its Management Information Systems, its administrative systems and procedures and the nature of its business transactions (Elements 10.1 & 10.2) and Performance Criterion 10.2.D: Make recommendations to the appropriate person in a clear, easily understood format

chapter 9

Fraud and its implications

Contents

Performance criteria

10.2.A Identify weaknesses and potential for improvements to the accounting system and consider their impact on the operation of the organisation

10.2.B Identify potential areas of fraud arising from control avoidance within the accounting system and grade the risk

10.2 D Make recommendations to the appropriate person in a clear, easily understood format

10.2.E Ensure recommendations are supported by a clear rationale which includes an explanation of any assumption made

10.2.F Update the system in accordance with changes that affect the way the system should operate and check that your data is producing the required results.

Range statement

Weaknesses:

- Potential for errors
- Exposure to possible fraud

Knowledge and understanding

2 Common types of fraud (Element 10.2)

3 The implications of fraud (Element 10.2)

7 Methods of detecting fraud within accounting systems (Element 10.2)

1 Introduction

Fraud had a high profile in the previous standards, and has had a high profile in the media recently. Your report in the project may need to be alert to fraud as an issue.

Every business is unique in its own way and offers different opportunities for fraud to be committed. You need to be able to think about a situation and identify for yourself areas and ways in which frauds could be occurring.

When trying to identify areas of potential fraud, it is sometimes easiest to consider the company on a department by department basis. Think about the functions of each department and the ways in which staff could abuse the systems. However it is quite possible that opportunities for fraud could be caused by poor co-ordination between departments.

Controls should exist to try to prevent fraud from ever occurring at all. However, to manage the risk of fraud effectively, it is equally important to recognise that controls must also be devised to ensure that if fraud is happening, it will be detected.

2 What is fraud?

No precise legal definition of fraud exists. However, **fraud** may be generally defined as 'deprivation by deceit'. In a corporate context, fraud can fall into one of two main categories.

	Comment
Removal of funds or assets from a business	The most obvious example of (a) above is outright **theft**, either of cash or of other assets. However, this form of fraud also encompasses more subtle measures, such as overstatement of claims, 'creation' of liabilities, undisclosed creation of credit and the manipulation of the company's relationships with suppliers or customers.
Intentional misrepresentation of the financial position of the business	This includes the **omission or misrecording of the company's accounting records.**

3 Implications of fraud

Whilst it is clear that fraud is bad for business, the precise ways in which the firm is affected depends on the type of fraud being carried on. All businesses, without exception, face the **risk** of **fraud** and the directors' responsibility is to manage that risk. It is naïve to ignore the possibility.

3.1 Removal of funds or assets from a business

Immediate financial implications

Profits are lower than they should be. The business has less cash or fewer assets, and therefore the net asset position is weakened. Returns to shareholders are likely to fall as a result.

Long term effects on company performance

The reduction in working capital makes it more difficult for the company to operate effectively. In the most serious cases, fraud can ultimately result in the collapse of an otherwise successful business, such as Barings.

3.2 Intentional misrepresentation of the financial position of the business

Financial statements do not give a true and fair view of the financial situation of the business. Results may be either artificially enhanced or, less frequently, under-reported.

It is also possible that managers in charge of a particular **division** can artificially enhance their division's results, thereby deceiving senior management.

Activity 9.1

Task

Note reasons why someone might want to:

(a) Artificially enhance the results
(b) Under-report the results

If results are overstated...

(a) A company may **distribute too much** of its profits to shareholders.

(b) **Retained profits will be lower than believed**, leading to potential shortfalls in working capital. This makes the day-to-day activities more difficult to perform effectively. This type of fraud can sometimes explain why a firm may be experiencing going concern difficulties whilst apparently reporting healthy profits.

(c) **Incorrect decisions will be made**, based on inaccurate knowledge of available resources. The effects of fraudulent activities can also affect **stakeholders** if the financial statements upon which they rely are misrepresentations of the truth.

- **Investors** making decisions based on inaccurate information will find their expected returns deviating substantially from actual returns.
- **Suppliers** will extend credit without knowing the financial position of the company.

If results are understated...

(a) Returns to investors may be reduced unnecessarily.

(b) If the company is quoted on the stock exchange, the share price might fall.

(c) Access to loan finance may be restricted if assets are understated.

(d) The **bad publicity** can damage the business by affecting the public perception.

Legal consequences. Finally, fraudsters open themselves up to the possibility of arrest. Depending on the scale and seriousness of the offence some may even find themselves facing a prison sentence.

4 Types of fraud

To recap, fraud in business organisations tends to fall into one of two categories – removal of funds or assets or intentional misrepresentation of the financial position of the business. Let us consider some practical examples within each category.

4.1 Removal of funds or assets from a business

4.1.1 Theft of cash

Employees with access to cash may be tempted to steal it. A prime example is theft from petty cash. Small amounts taken at intervals may easily go unnoticed.

Retail businesses offer another common example. Cashiers may not ring up all the sales on the cash register and merely pocket the amount not recorded.

4.1.2 Theft of stock

Similarly, employees may pilfer items of stock. The most trivial example of this is employees taking office stationery, although of course larger items may be taken also.

These examples are of unsophisticated types of fraud, which generally go undetected because of their immateriality. On the whole, such fraud will tend to be too insignificant to have any serious impact on results or long-term performance.

4.1.3 Payroll fraud

Employees within or outside the payroll department can perpetrate payroll fraud.

- Employees external to the department can falsify their timesheets, for example by claiming overtime for hours which they did not really work.
- Members of the payroll department may have the opportunity deliberately to miscalculate selected payslips, either by applying an inflated rate of pay or by altering the hours to which the rate is applied.
- Alternatively, a fictitious member of staff can be added to the payroll list. The fraudster sets up a bank account in the bogus name and collects the extra cash himself. This is most feasible in a large organisation with high numbers of personnel, where management is not personally acquainted with every employee.

4.1.4 Teeming and lading

This is one of the best known methods of fraud in the sales ledger area. Basically, **teeming and lading** is the theft of cash or cheque receipts. Setting subsequent receipts, not necessarily from the same debtor, against the outstanding debt conceals the theft. This process can continue until the fraudster repays the amount or, more likely, leaves the firm or is discovered.

4.1.5 Fictitious customers

This is a more elaborate method of stealing stock. Bogus orders are set up, and goods are despatched on credit. The 'customer' then fails to pay for the goods and the cost is eventually written off as a bad debt. For this type of fraud to work, the employee must have responsibility for taking goods orders as well as the authority to approve a new customer for credit.

4.1.6 Collusion with customers

Employees may collude with customers to defraud the business by manipulating prices or the quality or quantity of goods despatched.

(a) For example, a sales manager or director could **reduce the price** charged to a customer in return for a cut of the saving. Alternatively, the employee could write off a debt or issue a credit note in return for a financial reward.

(b) Another act of collusion might be for the employee to **suppress invoices** or under-record quantities of despatched goods on delivery notes. Again, the customer would probably provide the employee with a financial incentive for doing this.

In all these situations, both the employee and the customer benefit at the firm's expense.

4.1.7 Bogus supply of goods or services

This typically involves senior staff who falsely invoice the firm for goods or services that were never supplied. One example would be the supply of consultancy services. To enhance authenticity, in many cases the individual involved will set up a personal company that invoices the business for its services. This type of fraud can be quite difficult to prove.

4.1.8 Paying for goods not received

Staff may collude with suppliers, who issue invoices for larger quantities of goods than were actually delivered. The additional payments made by the company are split between the two parties.

4.1.9 Meeting budgets/target performance measures

Management teams will readily agree that setting budgets and goals is an essential part of planning and an important ingredient for success. However, such targets can disguise frauds. In some cases, knowing that results are unlikely to be questioned once targets have been met, employees and/or management siphon off and pocket any profits in excess of the target.

4.1.10 Manipulation of bank reconciliations and cash books

Often the simplest techniques can hide the biggest frauds. We saw earlier how simple a technique teeming and lading is for concealing a theft. Similarly, other simple measures such as incorrect descriptions of items and use of compensating debits and credits to make a reconciliation work frequently ensure that fraudulent activities go undetected. For example, an entry in the cash book with the narrative *missing cheques* may be all that is needed to ensure that stolen cheques do not appear in the bank reconciliation as a reconciling item.

4.1.11 Misuse of pension funds or other assets

This type of fraud has received a high profile in recent years, not least in the Maxwell case. Ailing companies may raid the pension fund and steal assets to use as collateral in obtaining loan finance. Alternatively, company assets may be transferred to the fund at significant over-valuations.

4.1.12 Disposal of assets to employees

It may be possible for an employee to arrange to buy a company asset (eg a car) for personal use. In this situation, there may be scope to manipulate the book value of the asset so that the employee pays below market value for it. For example, this could be achieved by over-depreciating the relevant asset.

4.2 Intentional misrepresentation of the financial position of the business

Here we consider examples in which the intention is to overstate profits. Note, however, that by reversing the logic we can also use them as examples of methods by which staff may deliberately understate profits. You should perform this exercise yourself.

4.2.1 Over-valuation of stock

Stock is a particularly attractive area for management wishing to inflate net assets artificially. There is a whole range of ways in which stock may be incorrectly valued for accounts purposes.

- Stock records may be manipulated, particularly by deliberate miscounting at stock counts.
- Deliveries to customers may be omitted from the books.
- Returns to suppliers may not be recorded.
- Obsolete stock may not be written off but rather held at cost on the balance sheet.

4.2.2 Bad debt policy may not be enforced

Aged debtors who are obviously not going to pay should be written off. However, by not enforcing this policy management can avoid the negative effects it would have on profits and net assets.

4.2.3 Fictitious sales

These can be channelled through the accounts in a number of ways.

- Generation of false invoices
- Overcharging customers for goods or services
- Selling goods to friends with the promise of buying them back at a later date

4.2.4 Manipulation of year end events

Cut off dates provide management with opportunities for window dressing the financial statements. Sales made just before year end can be deliberately over-invoiced and credit notes issued with an apology at the start of the new year. This will enhance turnover and profit during the year just ended. Conversely, delaying the recording of pre-year-end purchases of goods not yet delivered can achieve the same objective.

4.2.5 Understating expenses

Clearly, failure to record all expenses accurately will inflate the reported profit figure.

4.2.6 Manipulation of depreciation figures

As an expense that does not have any cash flow effect, depreciation figures may be easily tampered with. Applying incorrect rates or inconsistent policies in order to understate depreciation will result in a higher profit and a higher net book value, giving a more favourable impression of financial health.

4.3 Computer fraud

Organisations are becoming increasingly dependent on computers for operational systems as well as accounting and management information. With this dependency comes an increased **exposure** to fraud. The computer is frequently the vehicle through which fraudulent activities are carried out.

4.4 Problems particularly associated with computers

	Comments
Computer hackers	The possibility of unknown persons trying to hack into the systems increases the potential for fraud against which the firm must protect itself.
Lack of training within the management team	Many people have an inherent lack of understanding of how computer systems work. Senior management can often be the least computer literate. They may also be the most reluctant to receive training, preferring to delegate tasks to assistants. Without management realising it, junior staff can secure access to vast amounts of financial information and find ways to alter it.
Identifying the risks	Most firms do not have the resources to keep up to date with the pace of development of computer technology. This makes it ever more difficult to check that all major loopholes in controls are closed, even if management are computer literate.
Need for ease of access and flexible systems	In most cases, a firm uses computers in order to simplify and speed up operations. To meet these objectives, there is frequently a need for ease of access and flexible systems. However, implementing strict controls can sometimes suppress these features.

4.5 Types of computer fraud

Three main types of computer fraud exist. They relate directly to the key stages in computer processing.

Input
↓
Data processing/program-related
↓
Output

Activity 9.2

Task

Note examples of input-related fraud, program-related fraud and output-related fraud.

Use the earlier examples from Activity 9.1 and think about the ways in which computers can be used to carry out those fraudulent activities

Activity 9.3

Smiths Ltd is a small, family-run manufacturing firm that makes office furniture. The directors, Stuart and his sister Michelle, share responsibility for running the business, although Stuart concentrates on trying to bring in new business while Michelle takes a more active role in day-to-day management.

John runs the purchasing department. Martha, who has just recently been recruited to the firm, looks after the cash book and is responsible for performing monthly bank reconciliations.

John keeps records of all purchases and related expenses as well as looking after creditor accounts. When an invoice comes in, he checks the details against the purchase ledger details. If he is satisfied that the invoice is correct, he draws up a cheque for Michelle to sign. He also supervises Martha's work.

All accounting systems are computerised. The firm employs one staff member, Craig, in an IT capacity. Craig has full control of the computer network, with access to all programs and reporting systems.

Task

Produce a report to the directors in which you advise them on ways in which the firm is exposed to the risk of fraud.

5 Prevention and detection of fraud

Hindsight is a wonderful thing. Journalists reporting high profile frauds frequently raise the question of why nobody noticed earlier that something was wrong. They ask why the warning signs that should have signalled that all was not well were missed somehow. The answer is usually that there were **insufficient internal** controls in place.

A primary aim of any system of internal controls should be to prevent fraud. However, the very nature of fraud means that people will find ways to get around existing systems.

In a **limited company** or **plc**, it is the **responsibility of the directors** to prevent and detect fraud. They should do three things.

- Ensure that the activities of the entity are conducted honestly and that its assets are safeguarded.
- Establish **arrangements to deter fraudulent or other dishonest conduct** and to detect any that occurs.
- Ensure that, to the best of their knowledge and belief, financial information, whether used internally or for financial reporting, is reliable.

6 Assessing and grading risk

The starting point for any management team wanting to set up **internal controls** to prevent and detect fraud must be an assessment of the extent to which the firm is exposed to the **risk of fraud**.

What follows is a guideline of how such a task might be approached. The best approach is to consider separately the extent to which **external** and **internal** factors may present a risk of fraud.

6.1 External factors

Step 1. First, consider the market as a whole. The general environment in which the business operates may exhibit factors that increase the risk of fraud. For instance, the trend to de-layer may reduce the degree of supervision exercised in many organisations, perhaps without putting anything in its place.

Step 2. Next, narrow the focus a little and consider whether the industry in which the firm operates is particularly exposed to certain types of fraud. For example, the building industry may be particularly prone to the risk of theft of raw materials, the travel industry may face risks due to the extensive use of agents and intermediaries, the retail industry must be vigilant to the abuse of credit cards and so on.

Activity 9.4

Task

Note some examples of such general external factors that might influence the degree of risk that a company is exposed to.

6.2 Internal factors

Having considered the big picture, the next step is to apply the same logic at a company level. Focus on the general and specific risks in the firm itself.

Be alert to circumstances that might increase the **risk profile** of a company. The following factors can cause risks.

- Changed operating environment
- New personnel
- New or upgraded management information systems restructuring
- Rapid growth in operations
- New technology
- New products
- Corporate
- New overseas

6.3 Fraud risk management

The CIMA undertook a study of fraud risk management and published its findings in 2001. It says that '**risks** are the opportunities and dangers associated with uncertain future events. **Risk management** is the process of understanding the nature of such future events and, where they represent threats, making positive plans to counter them'.

6.4 The risk management cycle

This is an 'interactive process of identifying risks, assessing their impact, and prioritising actions to control and reduce risks.'

Steps to take

1. Establish a **risk management group** (RMG) and set goals eg what level of risk is acceptable?
2. Identify **risk areas**
3. Understand and assess the **scale** of risk (see Paragraphs 7.5 and 7.6)
4. Develop a **risk management strategy** eg small risks might be ignored
5. **Implement the strategy** and allocate responsibilities
6. Implement (and monitor) **controls**

6.5 Grading the risk

In your review of the accounting system and its internal controls, some aspects of it may be more serious than others. You need to grade the risk in two ways.

- Likelihood of occurring (probability).Is it very difficult to perpetrate?
- Impact if it did occur (impact). Would the fraud have a serious impact? The financial impact should be considered along with commercial sensitivities eg company reputation.

Type of fraud	How it might occur	Likelihood of occurrence High/moderate/low	Impact High/medium/low
Theft of cash	Thief can steal from reception	Medium: the drawer is not locked	Low: only petty cash
and so on			

The risk assessment displayed above could be enhanced by assessing the **controls** over petty cash, leading to a view of the **net likely impact** and recommendations for actions. For example, a high probability risk area with a high impact, over which the controls appear to be low, will have a high net impact and action ought to be a priority.

6.6 The Ernst and Young model

Fraud risk reviews should be carried out by people with in-depth knowledge of the business and markets and knowledge and experience of fraud. Risks should be classified by reference to the possible type of offence, and the potential perpetrator (not just third parties!). This matrix was developed by Ernst and Young.

Department area	Risk	Management/ employees	Third parties	Collusion
Fixed assets	Over-ordering eg computer equipment	Buyers		Purchase ledger clerk; recipient of goods
Expense claims	Overstating vouchers filled out for inflated amounts	Claimant		
Sales	Reducing the price charged and sharing the saving	Sales manager		Sales manager and customer

7 Common indicators of fraud

A number of factors tend to crop up time and time again as issues that might indicate potential fraud. Attention should be drawn to them if any of these factors come to light when assessing external and internal risks.

7.1 Business risks

An alert management team will always be aware of the industry or business environment in which the organisation operates.

7.1.1 Profit levels/margins deviating significantly from the industry norm

As a rule of thumb, if things seem too good to be true, then they generally are. If any of the following happen, alarm bells should start ringing.

- The company suddenly starts to exhibit profits far above those achieved by other firms in the same industry.
- Turnover rises rapidly but costs do not rise in line.
- Demand for a particular product increases significantly.
- Investors seem to find the firm unusually attractive.

Such patterns can indicate problems such as the manipulation of accounting records, collusion with existing customers or the creation of fictitious customers.

Similarly, results showing that the organisation is under-performing relative to competitors may be an indication of theft, collusion with suppliers or deliberate errors in the accounting records.

7.1.2 Market opinion

If the market has a low opinion of the firm, this might indicate something about the company's products, its people or its way of doing business.

7.1.3 Complex structures

- Organisations with complex group structures, including numerous domestic and overseas subsidiaries and branches, may be more susceptible to fraud.
- The sheer size of the group can offer plenty of opportunities to 'lose' transactions or to hide things in intercompany accounts.
- Furthermore, vast staff numbers contribute to a certain degree of employee anonymity, making it easier to conceal fraudulent activities.

7.2 Personnel risks

Fraud is not usually an easy thing to hide. A person's behaviour often gives clues to the fact that they are engaging in fraud. Some of the most common indicators are listed below.

7.2.1 Secretive behaviour

A High Court judge once described secrecy as 'the badge of fraud'. If an individual starts behaving in a more secretive way than is generally considered normal, then there may be cause for concern.

7.2.2 Expensive lifestyles

A well-known indicator of fraud is a life-style beyond an individual's earnings. A recent case involved an Inspector of Taxes who started driving expensive sport cars, taking lavish holidays and so forth. It was later discovered that he was being paid by a wealthy businessman in return for assisting him to evade tax. Life-styles of work colleagues may not always be apparent but fraudsters often cannot resist the temptation to flaunt their new-found wealth.

7.2.3 Long hours or untaken holidays

Workaholics and staff who do not take their full holiday entitlement may be trying to prevent a temporary replacement from uncovering a fraud. Also, staff who insist that certain tasks be left for them to complete upon their return from holiday might do so because they have something to hide.

7.2.4 Dominant personality

Some fraudsters were able to get away with it for so long because they were dominant personalities in very senior positions. The prime example is Robert Maxwell. Junior staff members are often loath to question the decisions or actions of an aggressive manager or director. A forceful personality may be sufficient, therefore, to ensure that a fraud remains undetected, at least for a considerable period of time.

7.2.5 Autocratic management style

In some organisations a sole manager or director has exclusive control over a significant part of the business. This can provide ample scope for fraud, particularly when the situation is compounded by little, if any, independent review of those activities by anyone else at a senior level.

7.2.6 Lack of segregation of duties

Employees occasionally have more than one area of responsibility, particularly in small businesses where staff numbers are low. This can make it easy for the employee to conduct and conceal fraudulent actions. For example, if the employee who prepares the payslips were also the person who authorises the payments, payroll fraud would be relatively simple to put into practice.

7.2.7 Low staff morale

One motive for fraud is resentment towards the firm. Staff may start defrauding the firm because they feel that they are not rewarded sufficiently for their work or because they were passed over for a promotion that they believed they deserved. Alternatively, low staff morale may lead indirectly to fraud, insofar as employees fail to take pride in their work and start to cut corners. This can lead to the breakdown of internal controls, yielding opportunities for fraud.

8 Internal controls and fraud

Controls must be developed in a structured manner, taking account of the whole spectrum of risk and focusing on the key risks identified in each area of the business.

We looked at internal controls generally in Chapter 8. Let us think about appropriate controls that could be introduced to combat fraud. The paragraph below gives you a flavour of the means by which management can fight fraud.

8.1 Physical controls

Basic as it seems, physical security is an important tool in preventing fraud. Keeping tangible assets under lock and key makes it difficult for staff to access them and can go a long way towards discouraging theft.

8.2 Segregation of duties

Staff who have responsibility for a range of tasks have more scope for committing and concealing fraud. Therefore the obvious way to control the risk is to segregate duties.

If an employee's duties do not extend beyond one domain, it will be more difficult for an employee to conceal a fraud. It is more likely that it will be picked up at the next stage in the process.

So, for example, the employee responsible for recording sales orders should not be the same person responsible for maintaining stock records. This would make it more difficult to falsify sales records, as a discrepancy between sales figures and stock balances would show up. For the same reason, it makes it more difficult to amend stock records.

Segregating responsibility for packaging goods for delivery from either of the recording tasks **would also help** to minimise the risk of theft and increase the likelihood of detection.

8.3 Authorisation policies

Requiring written authorisation by a senior is a good preventative tool. It increases accountability and also makes it harder to conceal a fraudulent transaction.

8.4 Customer signatures

Requiring customers to inspect and sign for receipt of goods or services ensures that they cannot claim that the delivery did not match their order.

It also provides confirmation that the delivery staff actually did their job and that what was delivered corresponded to what was recorded.

8.5 Using words rather than numbers

Insist that all quantities be written out in full. It is much more difficult to change text than to alter a figure. This is particularly useful in the payroll department. For example it is very easy to change, say, '1.5' to look like '15' but it is very difficult to change 'one and a half' to look like 'fifteen'.

8.6 Documentation

Separate documents should be used to record sales order, despatch, delivery and invoice details. A simple matching exercise will then pick up any discrepancies between them and lead to detection of any alterations.

8.7 Sequential numbering

Numbering order forms, delivery dockets or invoices makes it extremely simple to spot if something is missing.

8.8 Dates

Writing the date on to forms and invoices assists in cut-off testing. For example, if a delivery docket is dated pre-year end but the sale is recorded post-year end it is possible that results are being manipulated.

8.9 Standard procedures

Standard procedures should be defined clearly for normal business operations and should be known to all staff. For example:

- Independent checks should be made on the existence of new customers.
- Credit should not be given to a new customer until his/her credit history has been investigated.
- All payments should be authorised by a senior member of staff.
- Wages/payslips must be collected in person.

Any deviations from these norms should become quite visible.

8.10 Holidays

As we have said, fraud is difficult to conceal. Enforcing holiday policy by insisting that all staff take their full holiday entitlement is therefore a crucial internal control. A two-week absence is frequently sufficient time for a fraud to come to light.

However, it is equally important to ensure that adequate cover is arranged in good time.

8.11 Recruitment policies

Personnel policies play a vital part in developing the corporate culture and deterring fraud. Something as obvious as checking the information and references provided by applicants may reduce the risk of appointing dishonest staff.

8.12 Controls against computer fraud

Any situation involving the use of computers opens up a whole new set of risks. Controls must be specifically tailored to deal with these additional risks.

Activity 9.5

Task

Note possible **controls** which management could use to combat the specific computer risks identified in the previous chapter.

(a) Input-related fraud
(b) Program-related fraud
(c) Output-related fraud

Activity 9.6

[**Note** This case study is a continuation of the scenario set out in Activity 9.3.]

Due to the small number of staff employed by Smiths Ltd, there is little segregation of duties. This automatically enhances exposure to risk of fraud.

Martha is responsible for both the cash book and bank reconciliations. This makes it easy for her to conceal theft or to manipulate accounting records.

John keeps the records of all purchases and expenses but he is also responsible for confirming that invoice details agree to purchase ledger details and for maintaining creditor accounts. He therefore has ample opportunity to manipulate accounting records, such as turnover figures. He is also responsible for drawing up the cheques for Michelle to sign. This means he could easily steal from the firm by drawing up cheques for fictitious creditors.

Craig has sole control of all computer systems. He has unlimited access to files and is in a unique position to carry numerous types of fraud. The firm essentially relies on nothing more than trust to ensure that he does not engage in any fraudulent activities.

As Stuart (one of the two directors) focuses almost entirely on bringing in new business, he has little time to spend on the supervision of day-to-day activities. The bulk of this work falls on Michelle (the second director). The sheer weight of her responsibilities means that in many cases there is little independent review or supervision of work.

Overall, the firm suffers from a high level of exposure to risk. You are asked to write a report to the directors suggesting a system of internal controls that could be introduced to prevent and detect incidences of fraud.

Key learning points

☑ The purpose of this chapter has been to outline in broad terms different types of fraud and their implications for businesses.

☑ Fraud may be generally defined as '**deprivation by deceit**'.

☑ In a corporate context, fraud can fall into one of two main categories:

– Removal of funds or assets from a business; and/or

– Intentional misrepresentation of the financial position of the business

☑ **Computers** are frequently used as a means of carrying out fraudulent activities.

☑ The three main types of computer fraud are **input-related, program-related and output-related** fraud.

☑ It is the responsibility of the directors to take such steps as are reasonably open to them to **prevent and detect fraud**.

☑ The key to devising successful internal controls is to **identify the risks** clearly first. If the risks are not known, they cannot be managed effectively.

☑ A number of factors tend to crop up time and time again as issues that might indicate potential fraud situations. These can be categorised under **business and personnel risks.**

☑ **Controls must be developed in a structured manner**, taking account of the whole spectrum of risk and focusing on the key risks identified in each area of the business.

Quick quiz

1 What is the key to devising successful internal controls?

2 What is the first step in assessing the risks faced by an organisation?

3 List five common indicators of fraud

4 In what manner should controls be developed?

5 List five examples of internal controls (not computer-related).

6 What is fraud?

7 What are the two main types of fraud from a corporate perspective?

8 Give two consequences of each type.

9 Give three examples of each type.

10 Why do computers increase the risk of fraud?

11 What are the three main types of computer fraud?

Answers to quick quiz

1 The key to devising successful internal controls is to identify the risks clearly first.

2 The first step is to consider separately the extent to which external and internal factors may present a risk.

3 Common indicators of fraud include trends that start to deviate from the industry norms, complex changes to business structures, secretive behaviour and evidence of an expensive lifestyle not commensurate with earnings.

4 Controls must be developed in a structured manner, taking account of the whole spectrum of risk and focusing on the key risks identified in each area of business.

5 Examples include physical controls, segregation of duties, authorisation policies, using words rather than numbers and enforcing holiday policy.

6 Fraud may generally be defined as 'deprivation by deceit'.

7 The two types of corporate fraud are:

(a) Removal of funds or assets from a business and
(b) Intentional misrepresentation of the financial position of the business.

8 Consequences of 7(a) include lower profits and a reduction in working capital. Consequences of 7(b) include incorrect decision-making by management or by investors and fluctuations in share price.

9 Examples of 7(a) include theft of cash or other assets, payroll fraud and teeming and lading. Examples of 7(b) include overvaluation of stock, failure to adhere to bad debt or depreciation policy and manipulation of year-end events.

10 Computers tend to increase exposure to fraud because they are used to commit fraud.

11 The three main types of computer fraud are input-related, program-related and output-related fraud.

Activity checklist

This checklist shows which performance criteria, range statement or knowledge and understanding point is covered by each activity in this chapter. Tick off each activity as you complete it.

Activity		
9.1	☐	This activity deals with Knowledge & Understanding point 2: Common types of fraud (Element 10.2) and Performance Criterion 10.2.B: Identify potential areas of fraud arising from control avoidance within the accounting system and grade the risk
9.2	☐	This activity deals with Knowledge & Understanding points 2: Common types of fraud (Element 10.2) and 7: Methods of detecting fraud within accounting systems (Element 10.2) and Range statement: exposure to possible fraud
9.3	☐	This activity deals with Knowledge & Understanding point 7: Methods of detecting fraud within accounting systems (Element 10.2) and Performance Criteria 10.2.B: Identify potential areas of fraud arising from control avoidance within the accounting system and grade the risk and 10.2.D: Make recommendations to the appropriate person in a clear, easily understood format.
9.4	☐	This activity deals with Knowledge & Understanding points 2: Common types of fraud (Element 10.2) and 3: The implications of fraud (Element 10.2)
9.5	☐	This activity deals with Performance Criterion 10.2.D Make recommendations to the appropriate person in a clear, easily understood format.
9.6	☐	This activity deals with Performance Criterion 10.2.F: Update the system in accordance with changes that affect the way the system should operate and check that your update is producing the required results.

chapter 10

Monitoring and improving the system

Contents

Performance criteria

10.2.A Identify weaknesses and potential for improvements to the accounting system and consider their impact on the operation of the organisation

10.2.C Review methods of operating regularly in respect of their cost-effectiveness, reliability and speed

10.2.D Make recommendations to the appropriate person in a clear, easily understood format

10.2.E Ensure recommendations are supported by a clear rationale which includes an explanation of any assumption made

Range statement

Accounting system:

- Manual
- Computerised

Recommendations:

- Oral
- Written

Changes affecting systems:

- External regulations
- Organisational policies and procedures

Knowledge and understanding

6 Methods of measuring cost-effectiveness (Element 10.2)

1 Introduction

This last chapter, before we touch on the project proper, deals with ways of improving the system according to a number of frameworks and approaches. We mention quality, at the outset. This is specifically referred to in the standards.

In general, you can look at three issues.

(1) What the system/department is trying to achieve
(2) How well it achieves what it sets out to do: can it be more efficient and effective
(3) Risks of error, misstatement or fraud

New methods might involve changes in planning and control systems, a new departmental structure, changing the equipment (such as telephones and computer terminals, and the size and number of filing cabinets); recommending computerisation of some activities; or changing methods of working or documents used. In all such plans, the supervisor in the relevant sections will be involved – at least in the implementation of the recommendations. In your project, you might have to **make** recommendations.

2 Quality and benchmarks

2.1 Looking at quality

One overall framework is to look at the **quality** of the system.

Quality is 'fitness for use': how good is a product/service at satisfying the customer's needs.

- Quality is something that requires *care* on the part of the provider.
- Quality is largely subjective – it is in the eye of the *beholder*, the customer.

The **management** of quality is an aspect of control and involves advance planning.

Step 1. Establish standards of quality for a product or service. External quality assurance includes ISO 9000.

Step 2. Establish procedures and methods to ensure that these required standards of quality are met.

Step 3. Monitor actual quality.

Step 4. Take control action when actual quality falls below standard.

Example

An accounts department may have a standard that 95% of invoices are despatched to customers within three days of the goods being delivered, and that 100% will be sent within three days. Procedures would have to be established for ensuring that these standards could be met (attending to such matters as goods received notes). Actual performance could be monitored, perhaps by sampling delivery dates and invoice dates. If the quality standard is not being achieved, the management of the department should take control action (employ more staff or change systems).

2.2 Principles of quality

Some basic principles of quality are outlined below.

(a) Preventing mistakes is less costly in the long run than fixing them after they have happened. The aim should therefore be to **get things right first time**.

(b) **Continuous improvement**. It is always possible to improve and so the aim should be to 'get it more right next time'. A '**continuous improvement cycle**' can achieve this.

Step 1. Describe

Having identified an area for improvement it must be determined exactly what the problem is, when it started, who is affected by it, and what its effects are in terms of cost, dissatisfied customers and so on.

Step 2. Analyse

This has two sub-steps.

(i) Identify potential causes of the problem.
(ii) Collect data to verify which is the root cause.

Step 3. **Correct**. This means identifying the best solution to the root cause, implementing it, and measuring its effects to make sure that it has produced the expected improvement.

Step 4. **Prevent**. Only permanent solutions lead to continuous improvement. This step identifies what needs to be done to prevent recurrence of the problem, perhaps by redesigning other parts of the process to complement the new, improved method of dealing with the original problem.

2.3 Internal customers

Any unit of the organisation whose task contributes to the task **of other units can be** regarded as a **supplier of services**. The **receiving units are thus customers of that unit**.

The concept of **customer choice** operates within the organisation. If an internal service unit fails to provide the right service at the right time and cost, it cannot expect customer loyalty: it is in **competition** with other internal and external providers of the service.

The service unit's objective thus becomes the efficient **identification and satisfaction of customer needs** – as much within the organisation as outside it. This has the effect of integrating the objectives of service and customer units throughout the organisation.

The internal customers of the accounting function are:

- **Line management**, who need accounting information to help them do their jobs
- **Senior management** and **shareholders**, who need information to assess how well jobs are being done
- **Employees**, who also need information to do their jobs, and who are almost equivalent to external customers for some accounting services like payroll.

Activity 10.1

Eleanor Ferguson is the head of a management accounts department in her organisation. Her department supplies accounting data and other management information to other departments, as well as to customers.

Eleanor was perturbed to receive a memorandum from George Henderson, a manager in a department which uses the services of Eleanor's department regularly.

The following is an extract from George's memorandum:

'..... It seems to me that the changes which you are making take no account of our information needs as users.

'Whilst I can appreciate that these changes will assist you by containing your costs I would have expected, as a major and regular user of your services, to have been consulted prior to their implementation, since their introduction has had the predictable effect of limiting my ability both to cut my own costs and to enhance the service to my customers.

'I'm told that it would now be too disruptive and costly for you to meet my requirement for this year, and that rewriting your computer programme in time for next year may prove difficult.

'Furthermore, I do not take kindly to being told by letter by your staff that I should 'get my priorities right' and understand that the interests of the organisation and of the organisation's customers must come before those of my department. I do, after all, use your services in connection with managing one of the organisation's most high-profile and important customers.'

Eleanor's low-key investigation has established that George's memorandum is substantively correct.

Tasks

(a) Discuss the issues which George's memorandum raises for Eleanor.
(b) How would you advise her to deal with these issues?

2.4 Benchmarking

Benchmarking is a process of comparing an activity carried out by one department with the same or similar activity carried out by another department (or organisation). the comparison may give useful data for potential improvement.

Some system improvements can be suggested from the process.

Example

An article in *Management Accounting* (April 1997) by Ian Malcolm describes benchmarking applied to purchase/sales order processing.

	Best	*Worst*
Accounts payable		
Number of purchase invoices processed per full-time equivalent (FTE) accounts payable member of staff per annum	50,000	3,000
Accounts receivable		
Number of remittances processed per FTE remittance-processing staff per annum	750,000	12,000

The article then goes on to describe the **different processes** in which key billing tasks are divided. Clearly, automating some processes enhances efficiency, but also accuracy is important.

Accounts payable (A/P) – process options chart

Process tasks *Invoice type*	*Receive and sort post*	*Register*	*Authorise*	*Match with order or GRN*	*Code*	*Approve*	*Pay against terms*	*Advise payment*
EDI invoice	Not required	Auto or manual	Auto or manual	Auto or manual	Auto or manual	Auto or manual	Auto or manual	Auto or manual
Self-billed invoice	Not required	Auto	auto	Not required	Auto or manual	Auto or manual	Auto or manual	Auto or manual
Paper invoice	Manual	Manual	Manual	Auto or manual	Auto or manual	Auto or manual	Auto or manual	Auto or manual
Purchase card	Summary statement and file of receipts	Optional for statement	Pre-determined	Match statement with receipts		Not required*	Auto	Not required
Cheque or cash paid by service/product recipient	Maintain file of receipts	Summary level only	Pre-determined	Not required	Manual	Not required	Not required	Not required

*Sample audits are a necessary control to replace the payment-approval process in these cases

Clearly, process failures have to be investigated.

2.5 Quality assurance (ISO 9000)

In Chapter 5 we covered Quality Standards as a type of plan that influences how an organisation documents its procedures. We mention it again here as quality assurance can lead to wholesale changes in systems and can form part of your recommendations.

3 Efficiency and work study

Some definitions

- **Effectiveness** means achieving the desired objective.
- **Economy** means operating at minimum cost.
- **Efficiency** means getting the most output for a given level of input.

One means of raising the efficiency of an operating unit is to study what is being done at present and re-organise the work where it is beneficial to do so: in short by work study.

3.1 Work study

There are two main aspects of work study.

- **Method study**: the systematic recording and critical examination of existing and proposed ways of doing work as a means of developing and applying easier and more effective methods, and reducing costs.
- **Work measurement**: the application of techniques designed to establish the time for a qualified worker to carry out a specified job at a specified level of performance.

Method study is therefore concerned with how work should be done, and work measurement with how long it should take.

Work study is of value for five reasons.

- Tangible results are produced quickly.
- No large capital outlay is required.
- It is, in its basic form, simple and readily grasped in outline, by all.
- The facts it produces can be used to increase efficiency throughout the organisation.
- There is no work to which it cannot be applied; in office work it is called Organisation and Methods study (O&M).

You can use these techniques to see how efficient the office is. For example: you could reduce the number of forms people have to fill in to process a transaction; customers can be asked to order goods on line. Alternatively, increasing efficiency does not have to be a 'high tech' exercise: it could mean simply improving a filing system.

3.2 Organisation and methods

3.2.1 Objectives of Organisation and Methods (O and M) study

(a) Determine the way in which work should be organised and what methods should be adopted for jobs.

(b) Review and improve existing methods, so that effort, time, materials and machinery will be used to greater advantage.

The study is sometimes carried out by **specialists**, but in some organisations, **supervisors** might do it themselves to analyse the work done in their section.

O&M attempts to increase the efficiency of an organisation by improving procedures, methods and systems, communication and controls, and organisation structure. The principal aim of O&M may therefore be described as the **elimination of waste**. This includes waste of time, human effort and skills, equipment and supplies, space, and money. Eliminating waste will increase productivity, reduce administrative costs and improve staff morale and satisfaction.

3.2.2 Types of problems which an O&M investigation is likely to be concerned

(a) **Getting a job done more efficiently** and so more cheaply

(b) **Rationalising work** – questioning whether work needs to be done at all, or whether it can at least be done *more simply* and with less effort; alternatively trying to establish whether better use can be made of existing idle time, by spreading employees' work loads more evenly over their working time

The aim of O&M is not to ***add*** **new systems** to old ones, but to **simplify systems** and their relation to each other, to cope with new demands. If an aspect of a system or organisation structure is unnecessary, or even necessary but over-complicated, it is **wasteful of resources**.

4 Analysing work

4.1 Step 1. Collecting data

The full investigation starts with **research of the existing system**.

Sources of data

- Existing records, including organisation charts and manuals, job descriptions and specifications, procedure manuals
- Observation of procedures, forms and control systems in action
- Discussion with managers, supervisors and employees
- Questionnaires

4.2 Step 2. Recording data

Data will then be recorded to show:

- **What** is done in the course of an operation – what steps are accomplished?
- **Why** it is done – does each step contribute to the efficiency and effectiveness of the operation?
- **How** it is done – what work methods, procedures and equipment are used?
- **Where** it is done – how much movement is involved?
- **Who** does it – what department/individual? who is responsible?
- **When** it is done – what is an operation's place in a sequence? what timescales are involved?

The recording of data may take various forms.

- It may start with a **procedure narrative**. This is a narrative statement of the steps involved in a procedure, detailing the name, duties and actions of each person.
- **Charts** are also commonly used in O&M, as they can show at a glance what is going on in a system and where faults are occurring. However, the preparation of such charts is a rather specialised activity, so we will not cover it any further.

Narrative notes have the advantage of being simple to record but are awkward to change. The purpose of the notes is to describe and explain the system, at the same time making any comments or criticisms which will help to demonstrate an intelligent understanding of the system.

- What functions are performed and by whom?
- What documents are used?
- Where do the documents originate and what is their destination?
- What sequence are retained documents filed in?
- What books are kept and where?

4.3 Step 3. Examination and development

Once collected, data will be analysed in order to reach conclusions.

- How **efficiently** the system creates, moves and stores documents and utilises available personnel and resources of time, space, equipment, materials and services.
- How **effective** the system is, for example whether budgets, quality standards and deadlines are adhered to.
- Whether **the organisational structure** as a whole is an effective framework for operations.

The activities in a process can be subjected to an interrogation which follows a fixed pattern. They are tested by asking five sets of questions.

Issue	Comment
Purpose	What is being done? Why is it being done? What *else* can be done? What *should* be done?
Place	Where is it being done? Why there? Where *else* could it be done? Where *should* it be done?
Sequence	When is it done? Why then? When *else* could it be done? When *should* it be done?
Person	Who does it? Why that person? Who *else* might do it? Who *should* do it?
Means	How is it done? Why that way? How *else* could it be done? How *should* it be done?

These questions are asked **in the above order**. If the 'purpose' is not worthwhile, for example, all other questions are pointless. If the means were questioned first, a great deal of effort could be spent in analysing and improving a method which is later found to serve no useful purpose. Be aware that some apparently purposeless activities take place for their value as **internal controls**.

4.4 Step 4. Make recommendations

Once faults have been examined, recommendations can be drawn up, suggesting revisions to organisational structure or procedures. These might involve the achievement of one or all of the aims of O & M mentioned above.

- Reorganise **office layout**, to smooth the path of workflow or increase productivity through worker morale
- **Re-allocate duties** (centralising a function, distributing work loads)
- **Computerise** routine procedures
- **Redesign or eliminate forms** (for example using carbonised document sets and the like to cut down on rewriting and movement)
- **Establish procedures** (with manuals and schedules as appropriate) or revising them
- **Improve control mechanisms** to cut down errors in or abuse of the system
- **Reduce staff** (on the basis of natural wastage if possible)
- **Change IT configuration** or requirement

4.5 Step 5. Implementing recommendations

Once the study itself has been made, its recommendations have to be dealt with. Implementing your recommendations is an important part of the project.

4.5.1 Recommendations must be considered by and sold to the staff concerned

Outline plans, and later detailed schedules of how changes will affect the department should be looked over and discussed, and perhaps given a dummy run demonstration.

Staff should be allowed to air their worries, criticisms and opinions: they will, after all, be called upon to work with the new procedures. It should be recognised, however, that staff will be resistant to change, especially if existing practices are long established.

4.5.2 Recommendations must be planned, scheduled, authorised and implemented

Procedure manuals might be written as a guide to action, a role which could also be filled by procedure and process flow charts.

Test runs of the new system, in parallel with the existing arrangements, should ensure that objectives of the change will in fact be met, and will give staff time to adjust; staff will have to be trained in the use of new methods and equipment.

4.5.3 Recommendations should also be followed up and maintained

O&M staff will help deal with any problems that appear in the new system, or any difficulties encountered by staff.

Once the system is operating smoothly, results should be measured for comparison against former methods, and might thereafter be audited regularly to ensure continuing effectiveness and efficiency.

Example

We will now analyse one aspect of the improvement process, using forms and input screens as an example.

Principles of form design

	Comment
Forms should be **easy to *read* and to *use***	• Wording of instructions and requirements should be clear and concise. • Adequate space should be provided for entries. • Layout should enable information and identification to be easily found. • Title of the form (Invoice, Delivery Note) and name of the organisation should be prominent; different sections should be separated, marked and in logical order.
Size	Forms should not be too small and cramped (for use, and attractiveness), but size should take into account mailing and filing requirements.
Paper and print quality	They should be considered in relation to the handling the form is likely to receive.
The **number of operations**	These should be reduced as far as possible: document sets with selective carbon backing or the equivalent could be used instead of writing details in quadruplicate or photocopying. In this way, a single design and input of data can be adapted for many purposes.
Colour coding of copies	They may be convenient in any set of forms, and if copies of a master form act variously (for example as order, confirmation, goods received, invoice and so on) they should be clearly identified.

Forms in use should be reviewed to ensure:

- Their contents are still needed.
- They are still used in practice.
- All their elements are still relevant.
- They are not duplicating the work of other forms.
- No changes in practice need to be added.

If it becomes necessary to change forms, or design new forms for revised systems, a simple procedure should be followed.

- Inform staff
- Withdraw old forms from circulation
- Issue all new forms from a central store
- Keep a register of form designs now in use

Similar considerations apply to the design **of computer input screens and computer output.**

(a) The design will partly be determined by the system but some applications allow reasonable flexibility of layout.

(b) The design of computer output may be something you can experiment with, particularly as many applications offer shading, different fonts and a variety of formats.

Activity 10.2

The Smith and Otis Company manufactures small items of brass giftware. Over recent years there has been a continuing expansion in sales, both home and overseas, with the consequent increase in the activities in all departments. This has led to ever increasing demands for information such as sales reports, manufacturing costs, departmental expenses and wages analyses. Because of the pace of the expansion and the continuing pressure on staff, all the reports have been drawn up in haste with no attempt at even standardising the sizes of forms.

The company has now entered a period of consolidation and there is a full establishment of staff. The Managing Director has asked the Chief Accountant to look at all the various aspects of reporting within the organisation. She has also suggested to the Chief Accountant that you, as the first accounting technician appointed by the company, should be involved in the initial investigations into this problem.

You have been asked to investigate the Cost Office and the Work Study Department in the first instance. It has been established already that the cost office prepares 38 reports, which with the differing levels of circulation are received by 120 recipients. The corresponding figures for the Work Study Department are 10 reports and 23 recipients. (Recipients who have more than one report from a department have been recorded for each report they receive.)

(a) Outline the steps you would take in this initial investigation.

(b) Prepare the draft of an informal report you would make to the chief accountant commenting on the problem after you have completed your initial investigation. You may make up (or draw from experience) any further information you wish.

5 Improving work

5.1 Work measurement

'Work measurement' is carried out in order to set standards for:

(a) The quantity of work produced by a group or a person (output)
(b) The quality of work produced (number of errors in relation to output)
(c) The time spent on work produced

The setting of standards and recording of actual results for evaluation should not be made in a vacuum: however interesting the resulting information may be, it will not be worth its cost in time, effort and money if it is not *applied* for the benefit of the organisation. Measurement must have specific (useful) objectives, such as:

- Comparing results from a present system with an intended alternative
- Finding out why costs are rising or productivity falling
- Identifying errors and their overall effects
- Identifying bottlenecks and idle time (man and machine) which could be more efficiently organised
- Evaluating the worth of a particular employee or post (for wage setting)

5.1.1 Types of job

Not all types of work can be easily measured in terms of 'output' (jobs completed). **Clerical work measurement** is difficult in this respect.

Routine or repetitive jobs in production, or in the office, and most jobs involving machine operation and output will be easier to set standards for and measure. For example how many orders are processed per hour, how many ledger entries made or pages typed, how many envelopes franked, copies made, documents filed.

Meetings, telephone calls, planning, research, non-routine or non-repetitive and thinking tasks will be **harder to evaluate**: what is their value to the organisation relative to the time they take? Measuring the overall time taken in these activities (which will have to be the way they are evaluated) may be hard, because the office rarely allows pure and uninterrupted execution of a piece of work (the phone goes, unscheduled tasks or visitors arrive, decisions have to be made).

It is not easy to determine an accurate time that someone spends planning and reviewing work, or managing or 'handling' people. How much of the non-productive time is constructively spent in this way, and how much is simply wasted? Should time thinking about the problem on the train on the way home be taken into account?

Even routine tasks will vary greatly as to time taken and resources used. A particularly difficult draft to type up, for example, or a telephone call from a particularly demanding customer may not be readily quantified.

5.1.2 Standard times

Work measurement techniques are intended to reveal the work content of a task, or quite simply the means for establishing the time to carry out work.

In order to express the amount of work that can be produced by a given number of personnel or equipment, some common scale of measurement is needed. Standard time provides this, but only in situations where work is of a repetitive and fairly predictable nature.

Standard times are most accurately set by observation of the activity and the application of an assessment of its difficulty (a **rating**). This is a specialist task. However, other, simpler methods may be used by the supervisor to produce time estimates which are good enough for making improvements.

Standard performance is the rate of output which qualified workers will naturally achieve without over-exertion as an average over the working day or shift, provided they adhere to the specified method and provided that they are motivated to apply themselves to their work (British Standards definition).

What this means is that there is an optimum rate of work and one would expect the standard time for a job to be the total time taken by a qualified worker under sensible, normal conditions.

The standard of output should be that of a competent person working under normal conditions. Several techniques might be used to establish this standard, with varying degrees of accuracy. For your project you might be able to use one of the following:

- Personal observation and time recordings
- Estimates
- Time sheets and diaries
- Time and motion study

There is also guesswork, of course. When work is non-routine or unpredictable, guessing the time needed to complete jobs might be the only thing work planners can do. Guesswork should be based on the opinion of a person with a good knowledge of the work likely to be involved, such as a section supervisor.

5.1.3 Estimates

(a) **Estimates** may be **made by employees**. They will be familiar with their own tasks and how long they take, but they might not be entirely objective, giving a shorter standard time to 'look good' or a longer one because they know they will have to live up to it later.

(b) **Supervisors** might also give estimates, if they are sufficiently experienced, closely involved and aware of exactly how subordinates' time is spent.

5.1.4 Time and diary sheets

Time and diary sheets are a more precise way of keeping track of the allocation and duration of tasks, provided that they are conscientiously maintained and truthful. Sheets are filled in on a daily or weekly basis and summarised for each individual or group to show amounts of time actually spent on various activities. This is particularly useful for activities which cannot be measured in output terms, only in 'time spent' such as answering phones, dealing with visitors, or running errands.

When estimating how long work should take, take into account factors that may not have appeared in the figures. **Allowances** will have to be made for the following.

Allowance	Comment
Rest and relaxation	No-one can work at 100% speed without a break: energy and concentration will flag (and so will effectiveness) if a rest period is not allowed. VDU operators, for example, are advised by European standards to have a 10 minute break in every hour.
Refreshment	Tea or coffee breaks and lunch breaks are similarly essential to employee satisfaction and continuing effectiveness.
Fluctuating performance	Trainees, temporary staff and new employees will probably work more slowly and less efficiently than established staff who know the routines and environment. Each employee's performance will also fluctuate according to time of day, pressure of work and physical and emotional state.
Contingencies	Standard times usually incorporate an allowance for contingencies such as machine breakdowns.

When comparing performance with target, also consider:

(a) **The variable nature of work**. Even routine and measurable tasks like typing (where lines per hour is the simplest measurement) may be held up by a variety of problems.

- Difficult work, such as tabulations and calculations
- Standard of written drafts or dictation making it difficult to recognise words
- Intervening tasks (having to consult files) and interruptions

(b) **The variable nature of work flow**. There is no point reprimanding an employee for low productivity (compared to standard) if (s)he was not given a 'standard' amount of work to do, in other words a full day's steady work load.

5.2 Activity analysis

Activity analysis calculates the **proportion of time** spent by a member of staff on each of his or her various tasks. Here is an example.

ACTIVITY ANALYSIS

Job title: **Office junior**

Department: **Office Services**

Activity	*Hours per week*
Filing	8
Typing	16
Inward mail	2
Outward mail	4
Switchboard/reception	5
	35

By **combining individual analyses** in tabulated form, an overall picture of division of **work in the department can be obtained**. This may reveal anomalies such as a shorthand typist spending a large proportion of time on less demanding tasks like copy-typing, or a general drain on office staff from a particular task such as duplicating, in which case alternative methods (or delegation of the function to outside services) might be considered.

5.3 How can quality be maintained and improved?

Standards for quality control will depend on the circumstances of each activity and the organisation or section in which it takes place. They may be formally incorporated in a ISO 9000 system.

People are bound to make mistakes, but some errors will be more costly than others.

	Comments
Time	An error may mean re-doing a job (say re-typing a contract) or other delays (waiting for a reply to a letter which was wrongly addressed, dealing with customer complaints).
Money	Loss of time will mean a drop in productivity, which will increase overhead costs for each 'unit' produced. The organisation may also lose money through calculation or copying errors on invoices or statements or the cost of running a large complaints department.
Image	No customer or supplier will be impressed by ill-presented correspondence, inaccurate transaction details to chase up, mis-spelt names, faulty products, late deliveries, or 'mix-ups' of any sort, no matter how apologetic the company is.

However, achieving 100% accuracy is also time-consuming and costly. An employee may have to spend too much time on **ensuring** complete accuracy and even more time will be spent on **checking** that he has done so.

5.3.1 Methods of checking

You can check some or all of the output of a system.

- **100% checking** – this is time-consuming and expensive, so it would only be used for important work.
- **Partial checking** – only important parts of a task are checked, or parts which are prone to error (checking for common mistakes) or are otherwise under suspicion.
- **Random sampling** – frequent checks of random pieces of work, which should turn up areas prone to error or inaccuracy.

Where errors are discovered, there may be a **root cause** which will continue to produce errors if not identified and dealt with.

- The worker himself if he is badly organised or trained, inexperienced, tired or just inattentive.
- The fault might be traced back to **managers and supervisors**: ill-planned recruitment, unreasonable expectations, lack of clear instruction, bad morale or badly designed systems and forms.
- **Office environment** also affects performance. Temperature, lighting, noise, humidity, easy availability of facilities like filing space and photocopying and the appropriateness of furniture and décor can all influence both attitudes and achievement.

6 Cost

Work should be carried out to the standard required to meet the section's objectives but at the lowest cost commensurate with this aim. In other words, the work should be **cost effective**.

Control	Comment
Expenditures	When staff have the authority to spend money (for example on supplies) they should avoid unnecessary spending.
Resources and productivity	Costs can get out of hand because of poor productivity or because other resources are used carelessly or wastefully – for example, time is wasted because of disorganisation and double-handling, heating is left running unnecessarily, vehicles are used so infrequently that a carrier would be cheaper.

In the first analysis, cost control for a supervisor means that staff are properly supervised, and all work procedures are carried out as they should be. Good supervision should ensure that costs are kept under control as a matter of course, and that the section contributes more to the organisation's revenues than it incurs in costs.

6.1 Budgetary control and standard costs

Cost control activities are closely associated with budgeting. Supervisors may be involved in a variety of tasks.

- Preparing the budget (sometimes)
- Reviewing the regular budgetary control report, showing budgeted performance levels and costs, actual performance levels and costs, and the differences between them (variances)
- Investigating the cause of any significant variances, and taking action to rectify any problems that are identified
- Explaining any control actions

6.2 Costs of the accounts department

- **Wages of permanent staff;** this is the biggest cost, especially when overtime is taken into account.
- **Wages of temporary staff**
- **Costs of equipment and software**
- **Stationery**
- **Overheads** such as heating, lighting and rent: there may be a management charge for cost allocation purposes.

As a supervisor, you are rarely free to spend as you wish, and the accounts department budget will normally be determined at the beginning of the year. You should thus try to schedule work to avoid unnecessary overtime or weekend working and to avoid the unnecessary use of temporary staff.

6.3 Cost reduction

Cost reduction is the task of reducing the current or planned level of costs. For example, if a procedure currently has a cost of £10 per unit, cost control might be concerned with ensuring that actual costs do not exceed £10, whereas a cost reduction programme might be concerned with reducing the cost to £9 per unit.

Cost reduction programmes are planned campaigns to cut expenditure; they should preferably be continuous, long-term campaigns, so that short-term cost reductions are not soon reversed and forgotten.

Again, in your project, you may think of ideas to reduce the cost of your department's operations. Some of these can be quite simple – such as centralised buying. Other cost reduction programmes do require some investment. Relatively simple measures, such as ensuring all lights are switched off after office hours, can save money.

You can also save time and money by organising work more efficiently, for example by getting key suppliers to invoice once a month.

6.3.1 Difficulties with cost reduction programmes

(a) **Resistance by employees** to the pressure to reduce costs, sometimes because the nature and purpose of the campaign have not been properly explained to them, and they feel threatened by the change; sometimes because they genuinely *are* threatened.

(b) They may be **limited to a small area of the business** (eg to one department) with the result that costs are reduced in one cost centre only to reappear as an extra cost in another cost centre.

(c) Cost reduction campaigns are often a **rushed, desperate measure** instead of a carefully organised, well-thought-out exercise.

6.3.2 How supervisors can help in cost reduction programmes

(a) **Ideas**. Many of the best ideas for particular cost reductions might come from a supervisor and his or her staff

(b) **Implementing**. Any cost-reducing measures must be put into effect by the supervisors.

6.3.3 Guidelines

	Comments
Beware of compromising quality	A reduction in quality may be justifiable in order to save cost. For instance, internal reports might be produced on cheap paper and stapled rather than bound; this would hardly affect their usefulness. However, there is no point in reducing processing costs by, say, 10% if the resulting documents are riddled with errors.
Identify any constraints on opportunities for cost reduction	For example, if the organisation decides that there must be no redundancies as a result of cost reductions, and every employee must be guaranteed security for his or her job, this constraint must be recognised, otherwise you might end up recommending job cuts as the best approach to reducing costs.
Concentrate on areas of high expenditure	They are more likely to produce savings potential.
Committed costs are fixed in the short term	They are immune from immediate cost reduction measures.

6.3.4 Areas to consider for cost reductions

- **Reducing personnel** levels
- **Deferring expenditure** on new equipment and continuing to use existing equipment. This cuts the planned costs of interest and depreciation
- Using **cheaper supplies** or buying in bulk to obtain discounts
- **Stricter rules about how resources are used** or money spent (at a very simple level, for example, making sure that lights are switched off, or heating equipment not kept on longer than necessary)

- **Changing operations to make them cheaper** (for example, paying employees by BACS rather than by cheques or in cash)
- **Training staff** so that they work more efficiently
- **Rationalisation measures**. Where organisations grow, especially by means of mergers and takeovers, there is a tendency for work to be duplicated in different parts of the organisation. The elimination of unnecessary duplication and the concentration of resources is a form of rationalisation

Savings in direct labour costs will inevitably be a focus of attention for a cost reduction programme. The ideal solution for management might be to achieve the same output levels with a smaller workforce, but there may be problems.

- Reductions in labour costs might involve more capital expenditure on labour-saving machinery;
- The costs of redundancy payments to sacked employees might be high.
- Surviving staff members' morale may be adversely affected.

In any proposal for improvement or change, you must estimate the resources you need and cost them as best you can.

7 SWOT and 'PEST'

You may need to get an overview of an accounting system in your section. The techniques below are **mentioned specifically in the assessor's guidance for this unit**.

7.1 'PEST' and accounting systems

PEST stands for Political, Economic, Social and Technological factors that affect a system. This includes external factors such as new technology, new legislation and new Financial Reporting Standards. Economic and social factors also affect the accounting system. Economic factors affect the level of demand for a company's products and hence the number of transactions that must be processed. Economic factors also affect the availability of resources to invest in new machinery, and wage rates. Social factors affect the organisation, for example equal opportunities policies, and **flexible working arrangements**.

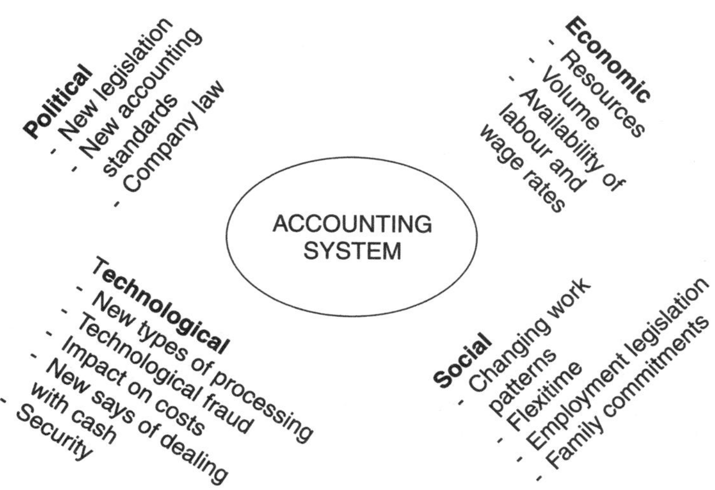

In the UK, employees with children have the right to ask employers to consider seriously requests for flexible working conditions. (Employers can refuse these requests, but have to justify the refusal according to a number of criteria.)

Within the company, you could develop a 'mini' PEST. Political factors could include the status of the accounts department. Economic factors should include the profitability of the company and the resources it can devote to the department. Social factors could include the work force of the department. Technological factors will include information technology.

7.2 SWOT

SWOT – standing for strengths, weaknesses, opportunities and threats – is a handy technique for grouping your findings relevant to an accounting system. Generally, strengths and weaknesses are internal, opportunities and threats are external. They can be of High, Medium or Low importance.

Examples	Strengths	Importance H/N/L	Weaknesses	Importance H/M/L
• Design of controls • Implementation • Computer systems • Staff ability • Integrity • Resources				
Opportunities and threats	**Opportunities**		**Threats**	
• Increasing workload can lead to pressure to cut corners • new technology provides opportunities to speed things up • There is a threat of fraud				

This is a general outline. It is a useful model for gathering the data together in one place helping you to prioritise the key issues. Obviously weaknesses or threats with a 'high' importance level need to be tackled seriously.

Activity 10.3

You have done some initial investigation about an accounting system, and have made some brief notes as follows. These are itemised below. Plot these into a SWOT grid and identify whether they are of high, medium or low importance. Some items might be both an opportunity and a threat.

Item

1 You maintain data on a set of Excel spreadsheets, which you use to develop several reports. Recently, you have noticed that the formulae are incorrect and that incorrect information has been sent to management.

2 You read in the local newspaper that salaries are a lot higher in your area than the salaries your staff currently receive.

3 Bank reconciliations are done every week.

4 The cashier does the bank reconciliations.

5 The stock control system and sales order processing systems use different coding systems.

6 The company invests heavily in training all its staff, and is officially an 'Investor in People'.

Key learning points

- ☑ **Quality** focuses on the **needs of customers**. For the accounting function many of these are internal customers.
- ☑ One means of raising the efficiency of an accounts section is by **work study** – analysing how things are done and how they can be done better, and finding ways of measuring work.
- ☑ **Method study** (or O & M) aims to eliminate waste of time, effort, skills, equipment, supplies, space and money.
- ☑ **Data may be collected** in the form of notes, flow process charts, procedure flow charts, document flow charts and so on. It must then be analysed to see where improvements can be made.
- ☑ **Forms** are used extensively in accounts departments. They should be carefully designed, regularly reviewed and carefully controlled.
- ☑ **Measurement of clerical work** procedures is **not always easy**. A supervisor can apply some of the ideas of O & M by estimating target times for simple operations and analysing staff activity.
- ☑ **Quality control** methods include 100% checking, partial checking and random sampling.
- ☑ **Accounting departments** should operate **cost-effectively** just like any other part of the business. The supervisor is likely to be involved in cost control and may sometimes be required to implement cost reduction measures.
- ☑ **SWOT** (strengths, weaknesses, opportunities and threats) is a useful framework for analysing a system, with a view to suggesting improvements.
- ☑ **PEST** is another model that categorises the environment of a system.

Quick quiz

1 Explain how quality can be managed.

2 What are the implications of the internal customer concept, and who are the accounting function's internal customers?

3 What are the two main aspects of the study of work?

4 What types of problems is an Organisation and Method (O & M) study likely to be concerned with?

5 Why is it a good idea to eliminate waste?

6 What sources of data will be used in an (O & M) study?

7 What will this data show?

8 What are the five sets of questions that should be asked when analysing data about work?

9 What are the principles of form design?

10 How hard or easy is it to measure office work?

11 What is the drawback of time sheets?

12 Suggest three methods of checking work.

13 How might a budgetary control system affect a section supervisor?

14 What are the major difficulties with cost reduction programmes?

15 If you were told to reduce costs in your section what areas of spending would you concentrate on?

Answers to quick quiz

1 The management of quality involves four activities.

(a) Establishing standards of quality for a product or service

(b) Establishing procedures and methods which ought to ensure that these required standards of quality are met in a suitably high proportion of cases

(c) Monitoring actual quality

(d) Taking control action when actual quality falls below standard

2 The internal customer concept has several implications.

(a) Any unit of the organisation whose task contributes to the task of other units can be regarded as a supplier of services. The receiving units are thus **customers** of that unit.

(b) The concept of **customer choice** operates within the organisation as well as outside. If an internal service unit fails to provide the right service at the right time and cost, it cannot expect customer loyalty: it is in **competition** with other internal and external providers of the service.

(c) The service unit's objective thus becomes the efficient and effective **identification** and **satisfaction of customer needs** – whether within the organisation or outside it.

The internal customers of the accounting function include **line management**, who need accounting information to help them do their jobs (they may prefer to generate their own information if they get poor service from accounts); **senior management** and **shareholders**, who need information to assess how well jobs are being done; and **employees**, who also need information to do their jobs, and who are almost equivalent to external customers for some accounting services like payroll (which could be contracted out).

3 The two main aspects of **work study** are **method study**, which is concerned with how work should be done, and **work measurement**, which is concerned with how long it should take.

4 A typical O & M investigation is likely to be concerned with three things.

(a) Getting a job done more efficiently

(b) Questioning whether work needs to be done at all, or whether it can at least be done more simply and with less effort

(c) Trying to establish whether better use can be made of existing idle time, by spreading employees' work loads more evenly over their working time.

5 Eliminating waste (particularly wasted effort) increases productivity, reduces administrative costs and improves staff morale and satisfaction. It brings about these benefits by, for example, cutting out unnecessary operations and streamlining remaining ones, using staff and equipment to the full, and using office space effectively.

6 Data for an (O & M) study may be drawn from four sources.

(a) Organisation charts and manuals, job descriptions and specifications, procedure manuals
(b) Observation of procedures, forms and control systems in action
(c) Discussions with managers, supervisors and employees
(d) Questionnaires

7 The data will show **what** is done, **why** it is done, **how** it is done, **where** it is done, **who** does it, and **when** it is done.

8 Data about a process or method can be analysed by asking five sets of questions. These fall into a clear pattern.

Purpose	**Place**	**Sequence**	**Person**	**Means**
What is being done?	Where is it being done?	When is it done?	Who does it?	How is it done?
Why is it being done?	Why there?	Why then?	Why that person?	Why that way?
What else can be done?	Where else could it be done?	When else could it be done?	Who else might do it?	How else could it be done?
What should be done?	Where should it be done?	When should it be done?	Who should do it?	How should it be done?

9 The principles of form design are as follows.

(a) Forms should be easy to **read** and to **use**, with clear and concise wording, adequate space for entries, and user-friendly layout (both for the person completing the form and the person who deals with it).

(b) Forms should not be too small and cramped (for use, and attractiveness), but size should take into account mailing and filing requirements.

(c) Paper and print quality should be considered in relation to the handling the form is likely to receive: for example the machines or writing implements that will be used, whether the form needs to last, or whether it will be read by somebody important.

(d) The number of operations involved in filling forms should be reduced as far as possible: document sets with selective carbon backing or the equivalent could be used instead of writing details in quadruplicate or photocopying. In this way, a single design and input of data can be adapted for many purposes.

(e) Colour coding of copies may be convenient in any set, and if copies of a master form act variously (for example as order, confirmation, goods received, invoice and so on) they should be clearly identified.

10 Routine or repetitive jobs in the office are fairly easy to set standards for and measure (how many orders are processed per hour, how many pages typed, and so on). Much office work falls into this category.

Non-routine or thinking tasks will be harder to measure, because the office rarely allows uninterrupted execution of a piece of work. It is not easy to determine an accurate time that someone spends planning and reviewing work, or managing or handling people Even routine tasks may vary greatly as to time taken and resources used.

11 Time sheets rely on the individuals completing them to do so conscientiously and truthfully.

12 **Methods of work checking**

(a) 100% checking, which is time-consuming and expensive, and so should only be used for important work

(b) Partial checking, where only important parts of a task are checked, or parts which are prone to error or otherwise under suspicion

(c) Random sampling should turn up areas prone to error or inaccuracy.

13 A supervisor should ideally be involved in the preparation of the budget for his section, although he might instead be given budget targets and standard performance levels that have been set by someone else. A regular budgetary control report will be given to the supervisor, showing budgeted performance levels and costs, actual performance levels and costs, and the differences between them (variances). The supervisor will be required to investigate the cause of any significant variances, and to take action to rectify any problems that are identified, and that are within his ability to control. The supervisor might be required to explain to his superior any control actions he has taken, because his superior will be responsible for the costs incurred by all the sections below him.

14 **Major difficulties with cost reduction programmes**

(a) Resistance by employees to the pressure to reduce costs, sometimes because the programme has not been properly explained to them and they feel threatened by the change, or sometimes because they genuinely *are* threatened.

(b) The programme may be limited to a small area of the business with the result that costs are reduced in one cost centre only to reappear as an extra cost in another cost centre.

(c) Cost reduction campaigns are often introduced as a rushed, desperate measure instead of a carefully organised, well-thought-out exercise.

15 To make the best use of time, the investigation should concentrate on the areas most likely to produce savings: high-cost areas rather than low-cost areas, and areas of discretionary expenditure rather than costs that are already committed and cannot be avoided, at least in the short term. Some obvious areas to consider for cost reductions are: reducing manpower levels; deferring expenditure on new equipment and continuing to use existing equipment; using cheaper supplies or buying in bulk to obtain discounts; and 'rationalisation' measures to eliminate unnecessary duplication.

Activity checklist

This checklist shows which performance criteria, range statement or knowledge and understanding point is covered by each activity in this chapter. Tick off each activity as you complete it.

Activity		
10.1	☐	This activity deals with Performance Criteria 10.2.C: Review methods of operating regularly in respect of their cost-effectiveness, reliability and speed and 10.2.D: Make recommendations to the appropriate person in a clear, easily understood format and 10.2.E: Ensure recommendations are supported by a clear rationale which includes an explanation of any assumption made.
10.2	☐	This activity deals with Performance Criteria 10.2.C: Review methods of operating regularly in respect of their cost-effectiveness, reliability and speed, 10.2.D: Make recommendations to the appropriate person in a clear, easily understood format and 10.2.E: Ensure recommendations are supported by a clear rationale which includes an explanation of any assumption made.
10.3	☐	This activity deals with Performance Criteria 10.2.C: Review methods of operating regularly in respect of their cost-effectiveness, reliability and speed, 10.2.D: Make recommendations to the appropriate person in a clear, easily understood format and 10.2.E: Ensure recommendations are supported by a clear rationale which includes an explanation of any assumption made.

PART D

Answers to Activities

Answers to activities

Chapter 1

Answer 1.1

(a) Four classifications are: by type of activity, by size, according to whether it is profit orientated or non profit orientated, and according to legal status and ownership.

(b) Size can be measured in terms of number of staff, number of branches, geographical spread, financial characteristics, number of customers served, and in comparison with competitors.

Answer 1.2

For an accounts department:

Mission: 'Our mission is to ensure that the business's financial transactions are recorded and processed completely, accurately and securely and that relevant information is given to management.'

Long-term objective: 'Computerise the sales ledger'.

Short-term objective: 'Do that bank reconciliation by lunchtime!'

Answer 1.3

The group has identified three major functions of their business (sales, repairs and quality control) and two main product areas (guitars and drums). They might decide to structure the business in the following ways.

(a) Have one general manager (whose responsibilities may include quality control) and three operatives who share the sales and repair tasks.

(b) Divide tasks by function: have one person in charge of sales, one quality controller and two repairers (perhaps one for drums and one for guitars).

(c) Divide tasks by product: have a two-man drums team (who share sales/repair/control tasks between them) and a similar guitars team.

Since there are only four individuals, each (we assume) capable of performing any of the functions for either of the products, they may decide to have a looser social arrangement. They may prefer to discuss who is going to do what, as and when jobs come in. A larger organisation would not have this luxury.

Answer 1.4

Tutorial note. There are a variety of ways in which the organisation could be structured. This is only one suggestion. It is possible that the purchasing and stock control functions would be under much closer supervision of the accounts department. Nor do we know how the separate manufacturing operations will be organised. The three different products could still be organised in different manufacturing departments.

(a) Organisation chart

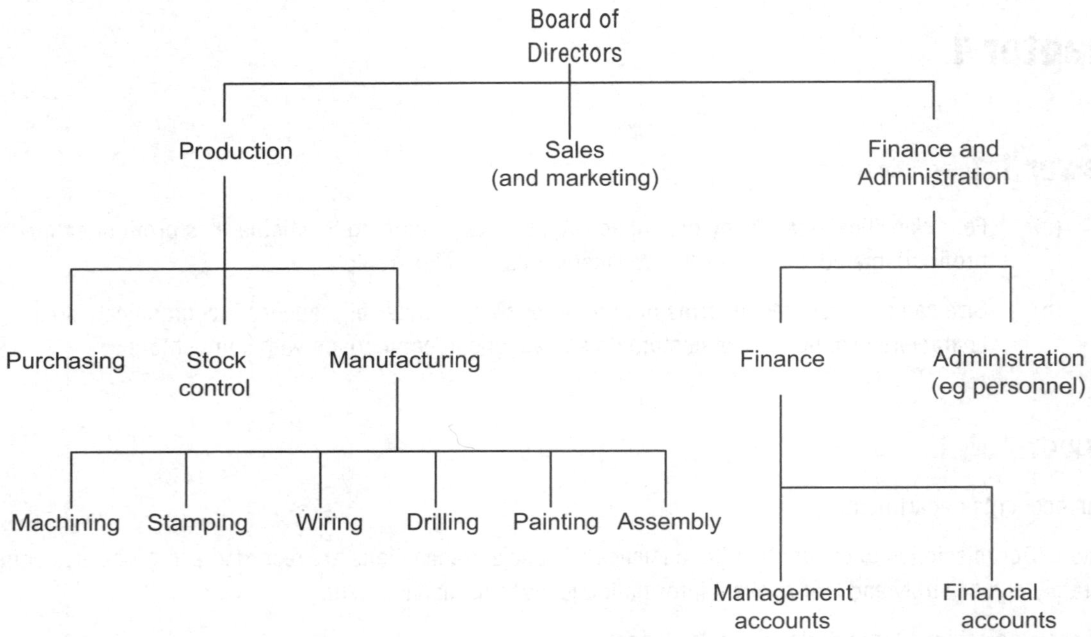

(b) Many of the reasons for changing organisation structure are those which are disadvantages of product organisation structures in any circumstances.

Principal disadvantages of product organisation structures are as follows.

(i) Duplication of functions such as sales order administration, accounting, personnel and other administrative functions. This leads to higher costs.

(ii) Loss of other economies of scale in production and administration.

(iii) If selling and marketing are decentralised, there can be a loss of opportunities for cross-selling different products to the same market.

(iv) Conflict between different products in the market place.

In the case of Q plc, it appears that the product organisation structure was the result of the company's geographical split into three locations. Where this is the case, a product structure might make some sense, to ensure that time is not wasted on paper work going to and from a head office. However, given that Q plc is to relocate to a single site, the geographical imperative leading to a product departmentation structure no longer holds.

The advantages of moving to a functional structure for Q plc are as follows.

(i) More efficient use of resources: for example, the accounts department is likely to be in one place, and so staff time can be used more efficiently.

(ii) The pooling of administrative resources may lead to better management information systems, as there could be a more efficient division of labour.

(iii) On the production side, manufacturing planning can be enhanced, as production can be switched between different machines if production flows are uneven. There would be fewer bottlenecks.

(iv) In purchasing, it may be possible to take advantage of quantity discounts on raw materials, if this is a centralised function for each of the three products.

(v) Centralisation in one spot could make decision-making easier as all of the relevant personnel are on site, and management can react immediately to problems and opportunities.

(c) Implications for the accounting function.

The accounts department was slit up and organised on a divisional basis. the different divisional sections may have operated in different ways, with their own systems and procedures, and these are likely to be standardised.

Answer 1.5

(a) One of the main purposes of a commercial organisation is to make profits for its owners. Other objectives may include survival, growth and cash flow. Subsidiary to the main objective of making profits, there are aims such as improved quality of a product or service, the satisfaction of the customer and/or the consumer, and gaining a share of the market. Non-profit-making organisations, especially government-run organisations, may have the purpose of providing a service of a certain standard rather than making a profit.

(b) 'Missions' are objectives formulated at the top of the organisation hierarchy and are long-term in nature.

(c) Where there is a hierarchy of objectives, the objectives of the total organisation will be reinterpreted as objectives of each division; the objectives of each division will in turn be reinterpreted as objectives of each department within the division; and the objectives of each department will in turn be reinterpreted as objectives for each work group within the department.

(d) The organisation brings in resources (inputs) from the environment, processes the resources, and produces outputs to the environment – finished goods, services, satisfied customers, trained employees and so on. The organisation has to take account of various interest groups in the environment, including customers, the government, the general public, suppliers, shareholders and employees. The environment provides opportunities which the organisation can exploit and threats which the organisation must respond to in order to survive.

Answer 1.6

Although not directly involved in every function, you are still involved in the organisation's critical relationships.

- Customers: offering/refusing credit; chasing payment; accurately processing sales orders and remittance advices.
- Suppliers: paying on time.
- The government: dealing with tax authorities and making statistical returns.

Chapter 2

Answer 2.1

In a functional system, all the accounts staff work together, reporting to the finance director. The accounts department is likely to record information:

- by function (all the costs for a department will be collected in one place)
- by convenience, for example, running only one payroll rather than subdividing it by divisions.

Answer 2.2

User departments may influence the **content** (**what** gets reported) and the **format** (how it looks). User departments may focus on key data or ratios, so you may provide the detail in the appendices.

Answer 2.3

Briefing notes

(a) **Organisation of flexitime**

Flexitime systems enable employees to work at times of their own choosing within guidelines to ensure that the office is adequately staffed at all times). Here is an example.

(i) Staff might be required to work, on average, a thirty-five hour week (excluding lunch hours) over a four week period (subject, of course, to holidays).

(ii) The office opens at 8am and closes at 6pm (ie it is open for 10 hours a day). The office is open Mondays to Fridays.

(iii) The latest time staff can arrive is 10am. The earliest they can leave is 4pm.

(iv) Lunch will be taken between 12 noon and 2pm.

(v) Staff have to take at least half an hour for lunch.

(vi) Staff must have no more than 14 hours owing to them at a particular time and must use it up when this limit is reached. Staff must *owe* no more than seven hours.

(b) **Control systems over flexitime**

(i) Records should be kept of the hours actually worked and the use and/or abuse of the flexitime system. A signing in book or a clocking on system may be a means of ensuring that the procedures are adhered to. This would be used for three things.

- To record arrival time
- To record the timing and duration of the lunch break
- To record departure time

(ii) The clock or signing in book would be input to a system which ensured that the other flexitime rules were adhered to.

(iii) To ensure that there is an adequate number of staff in the office at all times, an employee who wishes to take time off in lieu of flexitime must agree with the supervisor in advance when this is to be taken.

(iv) Flexitime decisions must be taken with the interests of other employees as well in mind, so that the 8am to 10am period is covered as is the 4pm to 6pm period.

(v) The supervisor must be prepared to distinguish between flexitime hours built up and genuine overtime which should be authorised and paid accordingly.

(vi) The supervisor might care to check the signing in book, if this is used, and to check that staff's actual attendance is in conformance with their records.

(vii) The supervisor must be prepared to take disciplinary action in the case of any abuse of flexitime. This might include requiring the employee to attend at normal office hours (eg from 9am to 5pm) thereby withdrawing the flexitime privilege.

(c) **Communicating the proposals to staff**

Introducing flexitime is a significant change in working practices.

The firm's managers should discuss the proposals with staff or their representatives. It is unlikely that any scheme suggested will be immediately acceptable to all parties. Wide-ranging discussion will identify problems and options.

Once the proposal has been discussed and agreed by management and employees' representatives, the final details will be communicated to staff. Then a vote can be taken, if this is necessary.

There are a variety of communication media which could be used for the initial proposal requesting comments and the final details of the agreement.

- Staff newsletter
- Noticeboards
- Staff meetings
- Union newsletter
- Individual letter sent to each member of staff

It is probable that the first stage of the communications process (where an outline is suggested and comments are requested) would use staff or union newsletter and noticeboards. However, when the details of the scheme have to be explained, a staff meeting would be best to answer any questions people have. A formal description of the details of the scheme will be sent as a matter of course to each member of staff.

Answer 2.4

(a) We are not told the precise arrangements made by TAA for sales and distribution: there may be particular information requirements of the managers at the different locations, in which case the cost and management accounting functions at least may need to remain decentralised, or a skeleton accounting staff may be retained on site for day to day collection and processing of accounting data.

In general terms, however, centralisation would have advantages.

(i) The accounting function would be moving into a new and more suitable accommodation.

(ii) Specialist staff and equipment (such as computers) will be used more extensively and therefore more economically, and with less duplication of effort.

(iii) Procedures and information formats could be standardised.

(iv) Staff and equipment can be used more flexibly to cope with fluctuating work loads.

(v) A greater degree of supervision, consultation and communication within the function is facilitated.

On the other hand, there may be disadvantages.

(i) The operations to which the accounting information relates are geographically dispersed. There may be delays in the collection and provision of data from and to diverse locations, with some loss of control by factory managers.

(ii) Centralisation and standardisation may overlook the conditions and characteristics peculiar to different factories and local areas, and the information provided to them may not be appropriate to their needs.

(iii) Staff *not* centralised to the new Head Office may resent being overlooked, or losing a measure of their responsibility. Directives from Head Office may be regarded with suspicion.

No conclusion as to the best course of action for TAA can be reached without further information about the business and its products, its structure and organisation. Centralisation, however, is capable of bringing substantial benefits to the group, if it is carefully planned and handled.

(b) **Guidelines for location and layout of space**

(i) **Location**. In determining the best layout to facilitate work flow, attention should be given to the matters below.

(1) The proximity of people and sections who regularly work together, such as cashiers and ledger clerks

(2) The proximity of supervisors and their subordinates, for the sake of communication and control

(3) The accessibility of people whose services and/or advice are required by the section as a whole (such as secretarial support staff)

(4) Particular requirements dictated by the activities and equipment used (for example floor strength and power sources for computers and natural light for offices)

(ii) **Layout**. Decisions will have to be made about potential staff growth, and the availability and cost of a number of options in terms of decor, furniture and type of layout. The most popular modern option in space planning is the open plan office, which facilitates workflow, equipment sharing and flexible arrangements. The layout should satisfy a number of requirements.

(1) Economical use of space, in terms of flexible arrangements of furniture and equipment, economies on heating and lighting (for example by not having separate offices) and sharing of equipment

(2) Efficient work flow, that is, movement of people and documents and communication without unnecessary expense of time and effort

(3) Ease of supervision: where control is necessary, supervisors should be able to oversee subordinates' work and be available to give guidance.

(4) Respect for status: if the culture of the department attaches importance to the status symbol of private offices for managers, these should be provided, or morale may suffer.

(5) Provision for security: the cashier's office and the computer room would need security measures with restrictions on entry. Activities such as payroll should also be in private offices, rather than in the general open plan area.

(6) Safety of the occupants: gangways and fire exits must be kept clear and furniture should be arranged to avoid knocks and falls and to facilitate exit.

Answer 2.5

Your advertisement should have included the following essential data: who is offering the job; what the job is; what the salary is; whether there are any other benefits; what qualifications are needed; what the job consists of; whether there are career prospects; how to apply for the job.

(a)

BROOKSIDE RETAIL SERVICES

ASSISTANT ACCOUNTANT

£XX, 000

Brookside Retail Services, a fast-growing company based in Leeds, needs an Assistant Accountant to join its large accounts department and to be responsible for maintaining the company's computerised nominal ledger records and for the preparation of interim and published accounts.

The successful applicant will be a qualified accounting technician with previous experience of working with computerised financial accounting systems. Experience in the supervision of staff would be an advantage.

Career prospects for a hard-working and well-motivated accountant are outstanding and conditions of employment are all that could be expected from a successful company.

For further information about the job and for an application form, please telephone or write to

John Smith
Personnel Manager
Brookside Retail Services
(Address)
(Telephone number)

The most appropriate media to advertise the job vacancy should be those which are most likely to reach the target audience of qualified accounting technicians, probably in the Leeds area only.

Two media would seem to be most suitable:

(i) An advertisement in *Accounting Technician*, the magazine of the AAT. This magazine is sent to accounting technicians throughout the country. An advertisement in another professional accountancy magazine such as *Accountancy Age* might also be considered appropriate.

(ii) An advertisement in one or more local newspapers in the Leeds area, which will be read by local residents, including accounting technicians

(b) The following information might be expected to be included in the job description.

Job title: Assistant accountant

Department: Accounts department

Job summary

The job holder is responsible for the preparation of the company's interim and published accounts and for the maintenance of the computerised nominal ledger records from which these accounts are compiled.

The computer system consists of a multi-user system of [type of computer] using [type of software].

(i) **Main duties**

(1) To maintain up-to-date nominal ledger records on the computerised nominal ledger system
(2) To provide for the security of the nominal ledger accounts by maintaining suitable back-up files

(3) To supervise the work of the three data input clerks who input data to the nominal ledger system
(4) To provide the management accountant with data for the budgetary control system
(5) To assist the senior accountant in the preparation of the interim and published accounts

(ii) **Responsible for**

(1) The section budget for the nominal ledger section of the accounts department

(2) Three data input clerks in the nominal ledger section

(3) Liasing with the computer sales agency which provides software and hardware for the computer system

(iii) **Co-operative relationships**

To co-operate with the management accountant for budgetary control

(iv) **Reporting to**

Senior accountant

(v) **Experience required for the job**

(1) Working experience with financial accounting microcomputer systems.
(2) Professional qualification as an accounting technician.

Prepared by: J. Smith, Senior Accountant

Agreed by: W Brown, Chief Accountant

Date:

Answer 2.6

(a) **OFFICE MANUAL**

Task: Receipts of cash and cheques and payment into the bank
Frequency: Daily
Staff responsible: Senior Accounting Assistant
Supervisor: Senior Accounting Officer

Daily receipt of cheques

(i) Attend at post room at 0900 and in early afternoon following the arrival of the second post. Open post under supervision of the Deputy Company Secretary. Separate out and inspect all cheques for correctness. Where necessary restrictively cross cheques using rubber stamp.

(ii) Place cheques in a secure case and carry to the accounts office.

(iii) Using analysis paper, prepare a list of all cheques received, including date, customer name, customer reference and the amount. Total the list. Where details are not clear, the cheque should be noted on a separate exception list for subsequent checking. Include on the list items brought forward from previous day's exception list.

(iv) Total the amounts on the cheques and agree the total with the total on the list.

(v) When completed, the list should be photocopied and a copy supplied to the sales ledger accounting section. The top copy should be filed in the loose-leaf cash diary folder.

(vi) Items on the exception list should be checked with the sales ledger section and retained for the following day's list.

(vii) Prepare cheques for banking.

Cash receipts

(i) Count money and agree to copy statement or invoice provided by the customer. If no copy statement or invoice is provided, check details with the sales ledger section. Note customer account number and invoice number.

(ii) Issue a numbered receipt for the agreed amount, entering the statement or invoice reference and the amount. Different receipt books are used on consecutive days.

(iii) Retain money in the Cash Sales box in the safe until banking is carried out.

(iv) Each day just before the close of business, pass the receipt book to the sales ledger section for writing up in the appropriate accounts, and collect the other receipt book which is to be placed in the safe.

Banking

(i) On request, a member of the security section will attend at the office each afternoon (times to be varied) for collection of the package to be taken to the bank. If cash in excess of £500 is to be carried, two carriers should be requested.

(ii) Details of each cheque and cash should be entered on paying-in slips and the total agreed with the total on the cash diary list.

(iii) Details of cash paid in should be agreed with the cash receipt book.

(iv) Any cash received after the banking procedures commence will be retained for banking on the following day.

(b) The following control activities are important in dealing with **petty cash procedures**.

(i) Physical security should be ensured by keeping petty cash in a separate locked box which is kept in a strong locked cupboard or safe.

(ii) Numbered vouchers from voucher booklets will be issued by the petty cash clerk.

(iii) A list of authorised signatories, showing specimens of their signatures and relevant authority limits should be kept by the petty cash clerk.

(iv) Payments should only be made against properly authorised numbered vouchers, which should also be signed by the employee receiving the cash.

(v) Petty cash payments should be recorded regularly (at least daily) in an analysis book.

(vi) The analysis book should be balanced off and agreed with the amount of cash in the box frequently, and not less than once weekly.

Chapter 3

Answer 3.1

1 = controlling; 2 = planning; 3 = commanding; 4 = co-ordinating; 5 = organising

Answer 3.2

Your answer may well be that the cinema manager takes on all of Mintzberg's roles, although **figurehead** and **negotiator** play a very minor part in his day.

Answer 3.3

(a) You are asked to draw upon your experience and observation of what supervisors actually do and from this draw conclusions about what their roles are. Mintzberg's list in paragraph 2.2 might get you thinking.

(b) Dawn should be told that in her present job as supervisor she is not expected to act in all these roles at once, but that some of them are to be found within her scope as a supervisor.

(i) Liaison – Dawn's section communicates with the organisation as a whole through her, and it is part of her job to ensure that the assistance which her section requires is obtained from the organisation.

(ii) Leader – she seems to be performing well in her role as leader of the section – the increase in output appears to be linked with her new duties, which must mean that she is motivating her team.

(iii) Disturbance handler and resource allocator – these two roles include most of the work of supervision.

Activity 3.4

This is essentially a reflective exercise. It may take you some time as you will have to analyse your own work, and reflect on the tasks that make up your job.

Answer 3.5

You may have your own views on examples managers could set. Some managers provide an aspirational model: showing junior staff that it is possible for them to achieve success. A manager may also model the roles of popular leaders, a person who combines work and life, a person who does not panic in a crises, a person who is developing skills and so on. Others provide a model of ethical behaviour in business situations.

Answer 3.6

You probably felt as we did that none of the qualities listed were unimportant. You probably had similar priorities to ours, as follows.

1 = b, c, e, g, j.   2 = a, d, f, h, i.

However, priorities might change if the qualities were considered in relation to a particular role, and some might, in fact, be quite unimportant.

Answer 3.7

Now consider what your answer says about **you** and the culture of your organisation.

Answer 3.8

Keep this in mind as you cover the next section. this will enable you to assess how **you** are motivated: bear in mind that other people may be motivated in different ways.

Answer 3.9

Maslow's categories for the listed circumstances are as follows.

(a) Esteem needs
(b) Social needs
(c) Self-actualisation needs
(d) Physiological needs
(e) Physiological and safety needs initially; esteem needs above in a certain income level
(f) Social needs or self-actualisation needs
(g) Esteem needs

Answer 3.10

(a) Job satisfaction could be improved in the following ways.

(i) It appears that each employee performs a single task and this is likely to lead to monotony, poor concentration and frustration. Allowing employees to swap jobs after a period of time would add variety to each employee's work and make the department as a whole more flexible.

(ii) Harriet could attempt to widen jobs by increasing the number of operations in which the job holder is involved. This lengthens the time-cycle of repeated operations and thus reduces monotony.

(iii) Harriet could attempt to build greater responsibility, breadth and challenge of work into a job. At present it seems that work is conducted according to a rule book: allowing the employee greater freedom to decide how the job should be done will encourage innovation and give employees more sense of responsibility.

(iv) Communication between employees is not encouraged and this may mean that one part of the department does not know what the other is doing. This, in turn, is likely to lead to misunderstandings and errors and cause a general sense of failure. The ban on conversations should therefore be relaxed and communication about work could be encouraged.

(v) Teamwork is a further possibility, growing naturally out of the changes outlined above. If these are implemented there is likely to be more overlap between the individual employee's work. If a group has collective responsibility for the whole group's output they will be more inclined to put in the required effort (for the sake of the group) and take an interest in the work of the department as a whole.

(vi) Participation in decisions that affect their jobs may help the employees to feel that they have some control over what they are expected to do and encourage commitment to the work.

(b) Problems in changing the design of such jobs may be as follows.

(i) Opposition from other departments. If the present working conditions are typical of the organisation, then changes in one part of it may cause resentment elsewhere.

(ii) The relative abilities of staff. Rotating jobs, for example, may not be possible if different jobs require different abilities.

(iii) The timescale of the changes. Some of the changes proposed would require the staff to learn new skills and this will take time and slow down the work of the department as a whole.

(iv) The nature of the work. The work itself may not lend itself to some of the changes proposed. Swapping jobs round, for example, may confuse the people whom the department serves, who may be used to dealing with a particular person. Sharing responsibilities may reduce control over certain areas where duties have been segregated deliberately so that different employees check each other's work.

Answer 3.11

For your ideal team, you might have listed: a person with originality and ideas; a 'get up and go' type, with energy and enthusiasm; a logical thinker who can be sensible about the ideas put forward; a plodder who will be happy to do the routine leg-work; and a leader who can organise the others and help them reach agreement on ideas.

Answer 3.12

Categorising the behaviour of group members in the situations described results in the following: (a) storming, (b) performing, (c) forming, (d) norming.

Answer 3.13

(a) Belbin's picture of the most effective character-mix in a team involves eight necessary roles which should ideally be balanced and evenly spread in the team.

In the situation described we can see several of these roles being played out by the people concerned.

Co-ordinator	Neville
Shaper	Olivia
Plant	Peter
Resource investigator	Rosalinde
Implementer	Quentin
Team worker	Sheila

Prior to the resignation of Olivia the group was clearly at the *performing* stage in Tuckman's terms (see below) but has now reverted to forming and storming. A particular problem is the conflict between Peter and Rosalinde, both of whom seem to want to take on the 'shaper' role formerly occupied by Olivia.

(b) Four stages in the development of a group are: forming, storming, norming and performing. Briefly, the first stage is the coming together of the group, the second a phase of conflicts, the third a settling down period and the fourth the point where the group can execute its task unhindered by the problems of growth and development.

Assuming that these theories apply, the group clearly faces an unsettled period. Neville has a number of options for dealing with this.

(i) He can simply allow the development to continue without interference. The problem with this is that it may take time and the group will be underperforming until its development is complete.

(ii) He can encourage the group to develop more quickly. For example, either Peter or Rosalinde should be formally appointed to Olivia's former role. This will end the bickering between them and establish a clear hierarchy, to the benefit of the whole group. The unlucky candidate may leave as a result, but it may be possible to find a satisfactory compromise. However, he can allow some of the others to find their own roles.

(iii) Neville himself should get more involved in the day to day work of the group for a time. This will serve two purposes.

(1) He will be able to establish a new leadership style more appropriate to the needs of his new group (a contingency approach to leadership).

(2) He will gain a fuller understanding of the present abilities and desires of old group members and become acquainted with those of the new members. This will help him to reassess roles and responsibilities.

Answer 3.14

(a) Two main issues immediately present themselves. Firstly, the management styles of Ruth and her predecessor are very different. This might be a problem for the team, and for Ruth. Secondly, the people she is to manage are members of quite a closely integrated team.

Both these factors could cause potential difficulties as Ruth and the team get used to each other.

Management style

Ruth uses a **tells** style, in the terminology adopted by the Ashridge studies. Basically, the manager makes the decisions and issues instructions to subordinates who carry them out. Its strength is that it facilitates quick decisions, and there are defined lines of responsibility. Communication is generally one-way, so subordinates might have valuable information which is being ignored.

The team, on the other hand, have been used to something quite different. Subordinates have been given little direction and allowed to establish their own objectives and make their own decisions.

Ruth does not really know the ropes, and so she will be forced, in some cases, to rely on her team's technical expertise. This she might find uncomfortable, as she is not naturally a team player. Moreover, Ruth will be forced to delegate in periods when she is faced with higher demands from her family (eg in school holidays). Motivating the team on a personal level is important in peak periods and when complex problems must be solved.

Both the job and her own personal circumstances will force Ruth to moderate her natural leadership style.

(b) Ruth is probably aware of her own natural managerial style. She should be made aware that the team's previous manager took a rather different approach, and there are occasions where team maintenance and consideration is important.

Ruth should endeavour to be consistent. This does not mean that she should not be flexible when the circumstances demand it. Nor does it mean that she cannot alter her style over time. It would be best for her to start off with a consistent style: a basis on which to build, as it were.

The team can also be expected to adjust its expectations of a manager in due course, so it will be a process of learning and change for them as well.

Chapter 4

Answer 4.1

Disadvantages to the individual of not having an appraisal system include:

- The individual is not aware of progress or shortcomings, is unable to judge whether s/he would be considered for promotion, is unable to identify or correct weaknesses by training and there is a lack of communication with the manager.

Answer 4.2

You might have identified such things as:

(a) Numerical ability applicable to accounts staff, say, more than to customer contact staff
(b) Ability to drive safely, essential for transport workers – not for desk-bound ones
(c) Report-writing (not applicable to manual labour, say)

Answer 4.3

(a) Overall assessment of the blandest kind
(b) This is a grading system, based on a guided assessment
(c) Results orientated scheme

Answer 4.4

In your project an improvement to a system could be built around the appraisal system. The appraisal could tackle identified weaknesses.

Answer 4.5

(a) **Steve's problems**

(i) **Pauline's feelings**

Pauline makes a connection between performance and reward. She feels she has worked hard and that this should be recognised in financial terms. Steve, on the other hand, is under pressure to keep costs under control.

Pauline, however, does make a crude assumption that effort equals performance. She is highly motivated at the moment, but her performance is not outstanding. Her performance is only satisfactory in her changed job, and therefore it would not be appropriate to tell her otherwise.

Steve is thus faced with a dilemma. If she is not rewarded, it is likely that she will make less effort to perform well. Steve will suffer, as the rationalised department depends on her continual hard work.

Another factor is fairness. Pauline cannot expect special treatment, when compared to other workers, who may have made an equal effort. Over-rewarding average performance, despite the effort, might demotivate other staff who will accuse Steve of favouritism.

(ii) **The organisation's systems**

It is clear that Steve is having to negotiate the requirements and failings of 3 different systems here.

(1) The budgetary control system, restricting pay rises
(2) The appraisal system, which contributes to pay rises
(3) The remuneration system, by which pay rises are awarded

Finally, Pauline's job is very different from what it was when she first started.

The source of the problem is the failure to recognise that Pauline is now doing a different job. Her job should have been re-evaluated. If this were the case, Steve could assess her reward on the basis of the performance in this re-evaluated job. She would have higher pay, commensurate with her enhanced responsibilities, but not an unfairly favourable grading.

However, Steve realises that the appraisal system is the one over which he has most direct control. He is in a position to reward her effort, but her performance in the new job is not exceptional. Yet her enhanced responsibilities need to be recognised somehow, although Steve, under pressure from the budgetary control system, may not be able to reward it financially.

There is little Steve can do about the budgetary factors, apart from stating to Pauline that everybody is in the same boat. There might be non-financial rewards that he can offer her. Pauline might like to have her own separate office space, for example, if it were available, or Steve might be able to offer her increased annual leave or a unique job title.

Pauline might also resent waiting for the outcome of a job re-evaluation exercise, as, from her point of view, that is the organisation's problem, not hers.

(b) **What Steve should do**

Steve has a choice either to overrate Pauline, according to the appraisal system, in recognition of her efforts rather than her performance in the changed job, or, alternatively, to try and negotiate a job re-evaluation first, with the risk that Pauline will become demotivated.

Steve needs to consider the effects of an unfairly favourable appraisal grading on the other staff. There are good reasons to believe that, while it might let him off the hook immediately, it would have bad long term repercussions, as it would send the wrong signals to Pauline about her current performance. Next year, for example, if her performance had not improved, he would have to downgrade her.

He will have to try and persuade Pauline of the complexities of the situation.

Steve can promise Pauline that the job will be re-evaluated. This might be a long term objective. He can promise Pauline that he will be supportive in the re-evaluation exercise, and involve her in any input to it.

Steve can also suggest new targets for Pauline to achieve in her changed job, to give her something to aim for. This might still motivate her, providing Steve can explain to her the slightly difficult situation he is in.

He might give her formal recognition of her status, and allow her more autonomy in planning her work, if she is sufficiently competent.

Obviously he cannot guarantee the result of the job evaluation system, but he can make some effort to solve the problem.

Answer 4.6

Nothing. There would be no momentum.

Answer 4.7

Few employers throw you in at the deep end – it is far too risky for them! Instead, you might have been given induction training to get acclimatised to the organisation, and you might have been introduced slowly to the job. Ideally, your employer would have planned a programme of tasks of steadily greater complexity and responsibility to allow you to grow into your role(s).

Answer 4.8

You should have started with two issues in mind: the role itself, and the employee. Your should also bear in mind that the new employee will inevitably learn lots of other things, not just the job.

Answer 4.9

Training methods for the various workers indicated are as follows.

(a) Worker on a new machine: on-the-job training, coaching

(b) Accounts clerk working for professional qualification: external course – evening class or day-release

(c) Supervisors wishing to benefit from participative management and democratic leadership: internal or external course. However, it is important that monitoring and evaluation takes place to ensure that the results of the course are subsequently applied in practice.

(d) New staff: induction training

Answer 4.10

Depending on your answer you will learn most effectively in particular given situations. For example, the theorist will learn best from lectures and books, whereas the activist will get most from practical activities.

Chapter 5

Answer 5.1

A strategy is to exploit the art movie market segment. A programme is the build-up of the distribution system. A policy is home delivery. The £5 charge is an aspect of the budget.

Activity 5.2

(a) The procedures manual might contain the following sections.

(i) **Introduction**. This section would set the scene by outlining the history of the business, the nature of its products and the location of branches together with relevant telephone numbers. Organisation charts including the names of managers and supervisory staff could also be included in this section.

(ii) **Summary of accounting procedures**. This will list all of the accounting procedures which are to be carried out or supervised by mini-market managers together with due dates for completion of procedures.

1 There will be the daily routines, such as paying in cash receipts, as well as weekly and monthly procedures.

2 Details of how cash is to be handled will be provided, including instructions on how often to remove money from tills for safekeeping and what security measures are to be taken. Procedures covering the recording of stock movements in the mini-markets would also be included.

3 Notes on policies on return of goods would be included, as well as ordering procedures, including authority limits applying to managers.

(iii) **Forms**. This section will explain the purpose of the various forms and how they are completed. Sample forms – blank or completed, as appropriate – will be provided. For example, for routines covering cash receipts there will be a form completed daily, analysing cash receipts and cheque receipts and splitting these among separate sales categories.

Forms for weekly wage routines will include time sheets and individual staff records. Weekly summary sheets would show staff attendance records, holidays and other absences, overtime worked and so on.

(b) **Layout and presentation**

(i) **Professionalism**. The manual should have a professional appearance, with a clear, concise and easily followed layout. Typeface, paper type and binders should be chosen with care.

(ii) **Updating**. If the manual is contained in a loose-leaf binder, updating can easily be achieved by exchanging existing pages with updated pages. There should be included within the binder a schedule for recording when updates have been made, so that a user of the manual will be easily able to tell how up-to-date it is.

(iii) **Intranet**. The manual can be kept permanently up to date on the group intranet.

(c) There will be several advantages for the control of the business as a result of introducing such a manual.

(i) The manual will be easy for managers to refer to instead of consulting the head office, thus saving administration time at head office.

(ii) Errors may be avoided because setting out procedures clearly in a manual will improve manager's overall knowledge of procedures.

(iii) The process of documenting the system at the time the manual is compiled may encourage a rethinking of some aspects of the control of the business.

(iv) Staff may feel happier and more motivated if their responsibilities are set out clearly in a manual.

(v) The manual may provide useful training material for new managers, or may serve as retraining material for existing managers.

(vi) The standardisation of procedures in the manual should help to ensure that different individuals do not develop and use their own versions of procedures. If there is no central reference manual, there may be a tendency for people to invent procedures on an *ad hoc* basis, as the need arises. In an organisation such as this, which is made up of units which should be relatively homogeneous, variations in procedures may simply cause confusion or misunderstanding.

Activity 5.3

The plan in Section 4 is an example of how planning techniques can be used. But any plan requires the specification of desired outcomes and results.

Answer 5.4

The 'good of the company' is a subjective concept. The union would not take the view that because of the company's failure to meet its targets (note that the company is still in profit) the workers' pay should be cut. Clearly the Managing Director and Finance Director have not considered the extent to which this would have to be 'sold' to the workforce, who might regard this idea as an abuse by management of the workers' generally co-operative attitudes.

Chapter 6

Answer 6.1

The underlying problem is that responsibility (for the management of accounts) has been delegated without authority (to hire a temp and to obtain information from the payroll dept).

Answer 6.2

(a) The problem appears to be that the new supervisor is taking too much of the department's work on to herself. While she is overworked, her subordinates are apparently not being stretched and as a result motivation and morale are poor. The supervisor herself is unhappy with the position and there is a danger that declining job satisfaction will lead to inefficiencies and eventually staff resignations.

(b) There could be a number of causes contributing to the problem.

(i) The supervisor may have been badly selected; she may not have the ability required for a supervisory job.

(ii) Alternatively she may just be unaware of what is involved in a supervisor's role. She may not have realised that much of the task consists of managing subordinates; she is not required to shoulder all the detailed technical work herself.

(iii) There may be personality problems involved. The supervisor regards her clerks as incompetent and this attitude may arise simply from an inability to get on with them socially. (Another possibility is that her staff actually are incompetent.)

(iv) The supervisor does much of the department's work herself. This may be because she does not understand the kind of tasks which can be delegated and the way in which delegation of authority can improve the motivation and job satisfaction of subordinates.

As manager you have already gone some way towards identifying the actual causes of the problem. You have spoken to some of the subordinates concerned and also to the supervisor. You could supplement this by a review of personnel records to discover how her career has progressed and what training she has received (if any) in the duties of a supervisor. You may then be in a position to determine which of the possible causes of the problems are operating in this case.

Answer 6.3

(a) The following points might be raised by members of other departments.

- 'Accounting reports are often produced too late for us to use for decision-making. What is the point in telling us what has gone wrong when it is too late for us to put it right?'
- 'We often get a lot of accounting information which is of no use to us. We cannot be expected to spend a lot of time sorting through lengthy reports to find what is relevant to our department.'
- 'The information which concerns my work is all sent to my senior manager, who then passes it on to me. It is really of no use to my senior manager, so why send it to him?'
- 'I get daily computer reports on labour variances, which I simply put in the bin. What I need is weekly and monthly summaries.'
- 'Accounting information is often compiled without any explanation or commentary.'
- 'I do not understand a lot of the terms used in reports which I receive. For example, I do not know what "DCF return" means, and it has never been explained to me.'
- 'The accounts department sends out information late in July and August. They say that it is because of staff holidays.'
- 'The accountants seem to put their own interpretation on data, even when they do not have the authority to do so.'
- 'It is very difficult to make anything of cost information, because the cost categories keep changing.'

(b) A number of areas may be identified in which the accounting departments may consider taking action in response to the points raised by other departments. First of all, it is useful to identify the qualities of good accounting information. Accounting information should be:

- Relevant to its recipients
- Understandable by the recipients
- Reliably accurate
- Complete for its particular purpose
- Objectively presented
- Comparable with related information (eg relating to other periods or sections, as appropriate)
- On time

The possible points raised by other departments identified in (a) above can each be associated with one or more of the above qualities of good information. The following areas may be addressed to improve the quality of accounting information.

(i) **Staff training**. Training of accounting staff providing information, whether oral or written, could be extended to include communication skills training specifically.

(ii) **Morale of accounting staff**. If accounting staff feel that they are always on the receiving end of criticism, morale may have been adversely affected, and staff may lack the motivation to try to make improvements. This is really a matter to be considered by accounts department management.

(iii) **Briefing of recipients.** Recipients of accounting information should be fully briefed on the interpretation and use of the information. Briefing may be in written form, such as manuals and explanatory notes, or through seminars and meetings.

(iv) **Presentation**. Presentation of information may be an area for improvement, ideally following research of the views of information users. Presentation may be improved by technical innovations, such as the use of colour in reports.

(v) **Quality control**. Information should be subject to checking and review by appropriately qualified staff before being released. However, it should be borne in mind that it may be better to be approximately right and on time than precisely right too late.

(vi) **Timeliness of reporting**. As implied in the above point about quality control, information becomes of less value the later it is delivered. The timeliness of reporting may be investigated by monitoring the publication dates of reports over a test period.

(vii) **User feedback**. It may be useful to provide on an on-going basis channels of communication by means of which information users can feed back comments on their needs to information providers.

Answer 6.4

Here are some suggestions.

(a) What are the deadlines for jobs A to D?

(b) Are any of them late already?

(c) Do any of them depend on the office being tidy or filing being done? This should be done before the job(s) in question if so.

(d) Does Usha need help or training before any of the jobs can be tackled?

(e) Is she waiting for others to finish their work before she can start work on certain jobs?

(f) Is there a queue for resources that Usha will need, such as computer time or the assistance of more junior staff?

(g) What are the consequences of jobs not being finished? They could include lost income, disgruntled customers and holding up other people's work.

Activity 6.5

Did you find that you were surprised by the complexity of what you ended up producing? Did you end up with lots of 'sub tasks' that needed to be done? Only by finding out exactly what needs to be done can you plan for it realistically.

Answer 6.6

Andrew's informal advisor might make the following suggestions.

(a) Andrew obviously has too much work – since he has to take so much home – despite his ability and willingness to delegate effectively. Something has to go. The first step for Andrew would be to keep a detailed time diary, which might highlight areas on which he is spending sizeable portions of time, or the frequency of interruptions during the day for various reasons. Superfluous activity and drains on Andrew's time might then be identified.

(b) Andrew devotes 'considerable time' to the solution of his team's work problems and deals with them 'as they arise'. Although he is justifiably satisfied that his relationship with his team is good, and although it seems he has achieved that through his ever-open door policy, it is one aspect of his job that should be looked at. It may be possible for him to appoint (and perhaps coach if necessary) a member of the team to be supervisor, so that at least the routine work problems can be dealt with by someone else. Alternatively, he could schedule surgery hours: only problems of an urgent nature would be brought to him as they arise. He could still maintain good relationships by making sure that he talks to his team where opportunities do arise to do so and so on.

(c) Andrew's own work is making sizeable inroads on his family life. This may be a question of poor time management or inefficient performance by Andrew, in which case he needs guidance on two things.

   (i) **Job management**. Andrew must assess his job and his own capabilities to perform it. Ideally, this would be done as part of a formal appraisal by Andrew's boss.

(ii) **Time management**. Andrew should be encouraged to identify objectives and the key tasks that are most relevant to achieving them, and to weed out desirable but unnecessary drains on his time. He should be advised to prioritise and schedule his tasks, and to stick to a schedule as far as possible.

(d) Another reason for Andrew spending too long on his work may, however, be that too much is expected from him. The fact that he is seeking informal guidance because he 'feels he is not performing as well as he should' indicates that he has not sat down formally with his boss to appraise his performance and participate in formulating his targets and standards.

The most important suggestion and the most fraught with potential difficulties, is that Andrew should request an interview with his boss. He should stress the following.

(i) The volume of work is large. (If Andrew can show his boss the measures he has taken to improve his time management – as suggested above – he will be in a stronger position.) It may be that the boss is delegating too much work to Andrew, or that he demands excellence because he doesn't realise the volume is so great.

(ii) The performance standard of excellence are unrealistic in this context. They seem to have been set by the boss without Andrew's participation, and they are qualitative rather than quantitative: excellence has obviously conjured up a target of perfection in Andrew's conscientious mind. What is required is a set of specific, quantifiable and realistic objectives, as a basis for Andrew's efforts and as a standard against which his performance can be more objectively measured.

Chapter 7

Answer 7.1

Problems

The personnel in Samdip's department have been reduced from 10 to 6 at the busiest time of the year. Although the absence due to honeymoon should have been known about and planned for long in advance the other absences are quite unexpected. The section is clearly going to have problems in getting its work done.

Solutions

A variety of measures are possible.

(a) **Clarify the situation**. Find out exactly how long the injured staff will be away. Clarify the leaving date of the person who has resigned and take immediate steps to recruit a permanent replacement. If the leaver is going to work for a competitor, and has access to sensitive information, it may not be practicable for the leaver to work his or her notice.

(b) **Samdip** will probably have to get more involved in the day-to-day work of the section.

(c) It may be possible to **borrow** suitable staff from other parts of the organisation.

(d) **Recruit temporary staff**. This may be possible if the knowledge required to do the work of the section is not particularly specialised. However it is an expensive option.

(e) **Work overtime**. The section is down to almost half of its normal numbers so the amount of overtime involved would be considerable – perhaps unacceptable.

(f) **Renegotiate deadlines**. Whether this is possible depends on the type of work involved.

(g) **Establish clear priorities**. Possibly there are tasks which are good practice but not essential to get the job done: these could be neglected to free up time for essential tasks.

(h) Taking a longer term perspective, Samdip should **monitor** the way in which the section copes with the crisis carefully, since this will provide valuable evidence either to justify the current 10 person manning level of the section or to identify ways in which the size of the section could be permanently reduced.

Answer 7.2

Recovery plan

Aim

To maintain a normal level of service and also to clear the processing backlog caused by the disruption as quickly as possible.

Action

The three options in order of preference are as follows.

(a) Temporarily transfer appropriately skilled staff from other sections to help clear the backlog

(b) Overtime working: approximately 21 hours should be required if no order processing is done on the day of the disruption

(c) Employ temporary staff

Note. Given equal pressures on other sections, option (b) is the most likely to be implemented. Staff should clearly understand that it is in their own best interests as well as the company's that the backlog is cleared as soon as possible.

Answer 7.3

(a) Does your firm have anti-virus software? Did the information systems department give you clear instructions? If a machine was infected, what happened?

(b) You would **not** open the e-mail under any circumstances. You should contact your information systems department immediately, as they may have been notified of the problem, by relevant anti-virus companies. In some circumstances you would 'double delete' the e-mail (by deleting it from your inbox' (**and** then from your 'deleted items folder').

Chapter 8

Answer 8.1

Here are some ideas.

(a) How should output be measured, and in what ways should it be reported?

(b) What is the importance of environmental factors?

(c) What inputs should be regarded as controllable, and which of these would be worth attempting to control (the cost of one part of a control system might exceed the value of the benefits arising from its implementation).

(d) Who is responsible for exercising control, and how?

Answer 8.2

This shows the many different types of control system in any one environment

(a) This shows the operation of double loop feedback and some open loop input. The plan has to be altered. There is also some feedforward control in the form of Sally's views on the next quarter.

(b) This was a closed single loop system. Counselling is control action to improve the individual's performance. Dismissal is control action too, if the employee is replaced by someone who performs better, thus raising the performance of the department as a whole.

(c) This is an example of cultural control, perhaps.

(d) This is a bureaucratic control based on a procedure.

Answer to 8.3

(a) (i) The target is badly designed, as **it leads to behaviour directly opposed to the company's objectives**. Just before the end of the accounting period, Andrew's outstanding debtors were £100,000 of which 25% exceeded thirty days. By posting the £20,000 Andrew's total outstanding receivables would be £80,000; whilst the amount outstanding over 30 days remains the same (£25,000) in percentage terms it has risen from 25% to 31.25%, and Andrew's pay will suffer. This is a very important aspect of management control of people. Human beings will put their efforts into what benefits themselves. This means that the control system must try to measure what is good for the organisation very precisely. The aims of the organisation, the targets set and the objectives of the workpeople need to be identical. If not, **poor decision making** like Andrew's will result.

(ii) The 25% figure on accounts outstanding seems questionable. U's customer base probably includes **small**, **medium** and **large firms** who may have lodged small, medium and large orders respectively. Should there be 25% of **key account** (large orders) outstanding at any one time, U Ltd is likely to experience **severe** cash flow problems.

(iii) The debtors do not seem to be analysed any further (eg into 30 days, 60 days, 90 days overdue etc). Once the 25% target has been met, there is no incentive to collect the remainder.

(iv) Wider company objectives have not been incorporated into Andrew's work. The **purpose** of the target does not seem to have been explained to him. If it had, he may not have delayed banking the cheque; but it is still wrong that performance measures should reward dysfunctional behaviour.

(v) Other aspects of Andrew's performance could be rewarded.

(b) Credit control is often measured in terms of debtor days which looks at the magnitude of outstanding debt in the light of turnover achieved. Simply measuring debtors would be misleading as the value would be bound to change if turnover went up or down. Debtor days would also be affected by any change in credit policy and this would have to be taken into account when assessing performance.

(c) Was Andrew guilty of fraud?

Here is an example of information being manipulated to make results look better than they are. Andrew seeks to benefit – in performance related pay – from deceitfully manipulating accounting data. By misallocating transactions to the wrong periods Andrew stands to gain a performance bonus, to which he is not entitled. There are good grounds for disciplinary action at the very least.

This example shows the link between

- Control and performance against plan (performance targets)
- Internal controls over accounting data (how performance is measured)

Answer 8.4

(a) **Basic data to be completed by the supervisor**

(1) **Materials usage**. This will be determined by records of the use of van materials by job, materials drawn from central store to replenish the van and so forth. To assess usage the quantity and type of materials in stock at the beginning and the end of the week may need to be recorded, unless a running total is kept. Although the supervisor keeps the van topped up, it is not certain whether there is a minimum level kept in the van.

(2) **Van expenses**. It is a relatively simple matter to record the miles run on company business. Supervisors will need to keep receipts for amounts paid for petrol and oil, to enable reimbursement. Alternatively, a company charge card might be used.

(3) **Hours worked**. For each employee, the employee's name, grade if appropriate, hours at basic rate, and hours at overtime rates, type or category of work (if the company analyses its time in this way) should be recorded.

(b) **Checks to ensure data accuracy**

Geton can take a variety of approaches. They could require a great deal of documentation to ensure that errors do not arise. They could have a roaming inspection department to check on compliance with recording procedures. Other controls include the following.

(i) **Materials usage**

- Comparison between different jobs for reasonableness
- Van stock counts
- Reconciliation of van stock counts with recorded usage
- Materials usage could be part of the budget

(ii) **Van expenses**

(1) The company will not pay for private mileage so the mileage recorded must be reasonable. Van mileages can be checked. Supervisors might be required to log journeys and to produce all garage receipts, including those for cleaning the van.

(2) A mileage budget could be established to check for the reasonableness of any claims. Again, mileage on a job can be compared with other similar jobs.

(iii) **Work done**

(1) A budget can be set for each job. Actual hours worked can be compared to it: the difference may be perfectly reasonable but the supervisor will have to explain any significant variance. On occasions, a member of the inspection team can carry out further checks.

(2) The job to be done should be specified and the job specification might arise out of the contract itself. One of the supervisor's jobs will be to ensure that the work is done as required. In addition, an inspection team may visit the site now and then to ensure that standards are adhered to. Clients can also be sent questionnaires asking them about their satisfaction with the service.

Answer 8.5

Here are some possible ideas.

	Comment
Transposition error	The simplest of all: two digits are swapped.
Coding error and posting	The wrong account codes are used to process a transaction: this could have serious consequences if posted to the wrong account, for example in the sales ledger.
Completeness error	Not all transactions relevant to an item are posted: a supplier might send a statement with invoices that you have not seen.
Input error	The wrong data might be input (eg wrong tax rates for wages and salaries)
Double counting	The same transaction is processed twice, by accident.
Valuation errors	Are assets and liabilities listed at the correct values? Have external auditors asked you to correct the stock valuation for obsolete items.
Cut-off errors	Two aspects of the same transaction are not reflected in the same period. This is a particular problem if you do not have the benefit of an integrate system. For example, if you are preparing month-end accounts on a spreadsheet, and the firm maintains separate systems for stock control and creditors, the stock control system may record the receipt of stock on one day, but the invoice may not get posted to the purchase ledger the next day. And so on. If you do deal with external (or internal) auditors, it might be a good idea to ask them what they are looking for.

Answer 8.6

Date: **30 June 200X**
To: **George and Alice Jones, Directors, Jones and Jones Limited**
From: **Accounting Technician**
Subject: **Internal control**

You have asked me to advise on weaknesses in the internal control of your firm's accounts and to recommend ways in which effective control may be secured. My report has been based upon discussing the established work practices with the staff of Jones and Jones Limited and observing these work practices in operation. I have also reviewed the company's books.

Findings

Three members of your office staff, John, Joyce and Betty, are responsible for maintaining the accounting records. Unfortunately little attention has been paid to internal control, with the result that there are virtually no internal checking procedures and any discrepancy which arose (either deliberately or accidentally) would almost certainly escape detection.

(a) John keeps the record of all purchases and expenses but also makes out cheques for the directors to sign and records these payments in the cash book. He is thus in a prime position either to pay fictitious expenses or to pay twice against the same invoice without either transaction being queried.

(b) Joyce is responsible for recording all work done but also for receiving payment and for credit control. If she fails to invoice a customer, or to record a cash receipt, this would not be picked up.

(c) Betty could steal from the firm simply by drawing more money than she needs from the firm's bank account and altering the wage records to hide what she had done. She could also overpay members of staff without this being detected.

The fact that no fraud appears to have taken place so far is attributable entirely to the honesty of your staff who are being given every opportunity to steal from your firm, should they wish. The errors I discovered in the accounts were all small ones, but they had not been spotted previously and could have been very much larger. In short, your internal control system requires a radical overhaul if it is to be effective.

Recommendations

The changes outlined below are designed to ensure that the tasks of preparing and handling initial documents (such as sales invoices and suppliers' invoices), preparing records and handling cash are reallocated, as far as possible, between different employees and to introduce a proper internal checking procedure. However, I recognise that prior consultation with your office staff will be necessary if these improvements are to be implemented successfully.

(a) **Expenses and purchases**

John can continue to be responsible for maintaining trade creditor records. However, Joyce should check all suppliers' invoices against purchase orders before they are given to John for recording. The responsibility for preparing cheques should fall to Betty, who would draw cheques against suppliers' invoices passed to her by John. As directors, you should ensure that invoice(s) and cheque match before you sign each cheque.

(b) **Debtor balances**

Joyce should retain her present function of maintaining the sales ledger. However, the responsibility for initiating sales invoices should pass to John and the responsibility for receiving cash should pass to Betty. This is not ideal, though it is probably the best arrangement which can be achieved given the very small numbers of staff.

(c) **Cash payments and receipts**

Betty should be responsible for maintaining the cash book, recording both amounts paid and received. She would also be required to handle cheques received from debtors. The cash book must be reconciled with the bank statements. Preferably, this would be done by someone other than Betty. Joyce would be the most appropriate candidate for this task.

For petty cash payments, an imprest system would be appropriate. John or Joyce could pay claims as they were submitted, recording them in a petty cash book. This would be submitted to Betty when reimbursement was required.

(d) **Wages**

Wages represent a substantial expense item for the business. The procedures for calculating, checking and paying wages should be as secure as possible. Betty could calculate the wages due using the

employee time records. Her figures could be checked by John, who would then record them in the wages book. It might be worthwhile to consider paying all employees by cheque, which would avoid some of the security problems associated with paying wages in cash. Wages cheques made out to individual employees could be submitted to yourselves for signature, along with the wages book. Alternatively, a single wages cheque could be presented. After signature by yourselves, this would be taken to the bank by Joyce and Betty, who would make up the wages ready for paying out by you.

(e) **General supervision**

To ensure that these arrangements are working properly, you should regularly inspect the accounting records yourselves to ensure that the operations of the business are being recorded in a timely and accurate manner.

Answer 8.7

(a) **Four objectives of an internal control system**

(i) To enable management to carry on the business of the enterprise in an orderly and efficient manner

(ii) To satisfy management that their policies are being adhered to

(iii) To ensure that the assets of the company are safeguarded

(iv) To ensure, as far as possible, that the enterprise maintains complete and accurate records

(b) **Four major controls**

(i) **Control over customers' creditworthiness**. Before any order is accepted for further processing, established procedures should be followed in order to check the creditworthiness of that customer. For new customers procedures should exist for obtaining appropriate references before any credit is extended. For all existing customers there should be established credit limits and before an order is processed the sales assistants should check to see that the value of the current order will not cause the debtor's balance to rise above their agreed credit limit.

The objective of such procedures is to try to avoid the company supplying goods to debtors who are unlikely to be able to pay for them. In this way the losses suffered by the company as a result of bad debts should be minimal.

(ii) **Control over the recording of sales and debtors**. The most significant document in the system is the multiple order form. These forms should be sequentially pre-numbered and controls should exist over the supplies of unused forms and also to ensure that all order forms completed can be traced through the various stages of processing and agreed to the other documents raised and the various entries made in the accounting records.

The main objective here will be to check the completeness of the company's recording procedures in relation to the income which it has earned and the assets which it holds in the form of debtors.

(iii) **Control over the issue of stocks and the despatch of goods**. Control procedures here should be such that goods are not issued from stores until a valid order form has been received and the fact

of that issue is recorded both on the order form (copies 1-3) and in the stock records maintained by the store-keepers.

The objectives here are to see that no goods are released from stock without appropriate authority and that a record of stock movements is maintained.

(iv) Control over the invoicing of customers. The main control requirement here will be to use sequentially pre-numbered invoices with checks being carried out to control the completeness of the sequence. Checks should also be conducted to ensure that all invoices are matched with the appropriate order form (Copy 2) to confirm that invoices have been raised in respect of all completed orders.

The major concern here will be to ensure that no goods are despatched to customers without an invoice subsequently being raised.

(v) (**Tutorial note**. The question merely required four controls to be considered, but for the sake of completeness, each of the five main stages in processing as indicated by the question are considered here.)

Control over monies received. There should be controls to ensure that there is an adequate segregation of duties between those members of staff responsible for the updating of the sales records in respect of monies received and those dealing with the receipt, recording and banking of monies. There should also be a regular independent review of aged debtor balances together with an overall reconciliation of the debtors' ledger control account with the total of outstanding debts on individual customer accounts.

The objectives here are to ensure that proper controls exist with regard to the complete and accurate recording of monies received, safe custody of the asset cash and the effectiveness of credit control procedures.

(c) Appropriate tests in relation to each of the controls identified in (b) above would be as follows.

(i) **Controls over customers' creditworthiness**

(1) For a sample of new accounts opened during the period check to see that suitable references were obtained before the company supplied any goods on credit terms and that the credit limit set was properly authorised and of a reasonable amount.

(2) For a sample of customers' orders check to see that at the time they were accepted, their invoice value would not have been such as to cause the balance on that customers' account to go above their agreed credit limit.

(ii) **Controls over the recording of sales and debtors**

(1) On a sample basis check the completeness of the sequence of order forms and also that unused stocks of order forms are securely stored.

(2) For a sample of order forms raised during the period ensure that they can be traced through the system such that there is either evidence that the order was cancelled or that a valid invoice was subsequently raised.

(iii) **Control over the issue of stocks and the despatch of goods**

(1) For a sample of entries in the stock records check to ensure that a valid order form exists for all issues recorded as having been made.

(2) Attend the stockrooms to observe the procedures and check that goods are not issued unless a valid order form has been received and that the appropriate entries are made in the stock records and on the order form at the time of issue.

(iv) **Control over the invoicing of customers**

(1) On a sample basis check the completeness of the sequence of invoices raised and also that the unused stocks of invoice forms are securely stored.

(2) For a sample of invoices raised during the period ensure that they have been properly matched with the appropriate order form (copy 2).

Chapter 9

Answer 9.1

(a) Reasons for overstating profits and/or net assets

- To ensure achievement on paper, may have to meet targets in order to secure a promotion, bonuses or remuneration may be linked to performance
- Trying to conceal another form of fraud, such as theft
- Need a healthy balance sheet to convince bank to give loan finance
- Ailing company may be trying to entice equity investors

(b) Reasons for understating profits and/or net assets

- To facilitate a private purchase of an asset from the business at less than market value
- To defraud the Inland Revenue by reducing taxable profits or gains
- Trying to force the share price down so that shares can be bought below market value by friends or relatives

Answer 9.2

Input-related fraud

- Creation of input
- Amendment of input
- Deletion of input
- Duplication of input
- Abuse of access privileges

Program-related fraud

- Unauthorised program changes
- Abuse of access privileges
- Unauthorised access to data manipulation utilities

Output-related fraud

- Suppression or destruction of output
- Creation of fictitious output
- Improper amendment of computer output prior to transmission
- Theft of output

Answer 9.3

Report: exposure to fraud

Date: 30 June 200X
To: Stuart and Michelle Smith, Directors, Smiths Ltd
From: Accounting Technician
Subject: Risk of fraud

You have asked me to advise on ways in which Smiths Ltd is exposed to the risk of fraud. My report has been based on discussions with you both about the established work practices and on a review of the company's books.

Findings

Due to the small number of staff employed by the firm, there is little segregation of duties. This automatically enhances exposure to risk of fraud.

(a) Martha is responsible for both the cash book and bank reconciliations. This makes it easy for her to conceal theft or to manipulate accounting records. Simple measures such as the use of compensating debits and credits to make the reconciliation work or incorrect narratives facilitate such frauds.

(b) John keeps the records of all purchases and expenses but yet he is also responsible for confirming that invoice details agree to purchase ledger details and for maintaining creditor accounts. He therefore has ample opportunity to manipulate accounting records, such as turnover figures. He is also responsible for drawing up the cheques for Michelle to sign. This means he could easily steal from the firm by drawing up cheques for fictitious creditors.

(c) Craig has sole control of all computer systems. He has unlimited access to files and is in a unique position to carry numerous types of fraud. The firm essentially relies on nothing more than trust to ensure that he does not engage in any fraudulent activities.

(d) As Stuart focuses almost entirely on bringing in new business, he has little time to spend on the supervision of day-to-day activities. The bulk of this work falls on Michelle. The sheer weight of her responsibilities means that in many cases there is little independent review or supervision of her work.

Overall, the firm suffers from a high level of exposure to risk. In order to manage that risk effectively, a system of internal controls should be introduced to prevent and detect incidences of fraud.

Answer 9.4

You might have thought of some of the following.

- Technological developments
- New legislation or regulations
- Economic or political changes
- Increased competition
- Changing customer needs

Answer 9.5

Possible controls include the following.

(a) **Input-related fraud**

- Segregation of duties in user areas and between users and IT staff.
- Independent reconciliations.
- Authorisation of changes to standing data.
- Access controls over data files, such as password protection.
- Periodic listing and review of standing data.

(b) **Program-related fraud**

- Authorisation and testing of program changes
- Restricting access to system libraries containing live programs
- Using special utility programs to compare changed versions of programs to original versions to make sure that only authorised amendments have been made
- Reducing dependence on key systems staff

(c) **Output-related fraud**

- Segregation of duties in user areas
- Independent reconciliations
- Good custodial controls over sensitive print-outs
- Strong access controls

Answer 9.6

Report: Internal controls to prevent and detect fraud

Date: 30 June 200X
To: Stuart and Michelle Smith, Directors, Smiths Ltd
From: Accounting Technician
Subject: Internal controls

You have asked me to suggest some internal controls that could be introduced to reduce the extent to which the firm is exposed to the risk of fraud. My recommendations include the following measures.

Potential internal controls

(a) **Reallocation of work**

It may be worth training Martha so that she could take over control of the creditor accounts from John. Martha should check invoice details against the purchase ledgers maintained by John. Responsibility for drawing up cheques could also be passed to her. John could take over the running of the cashbook instead. This would separate out responsibility for related accounting functions somewhat.

(b) **Independent review and supervision**

As staff numbers are limited and it is not possible to segregate duties as much as you would wish, I would suggest that you recruit one more employee to act as an assistant director. This would take some of the pressure off Michelle and would ensure facilitate better supervision and review of work. As director, Michelle should ensure that cheques are matched to invoices before she signs them.

(c) **Reduction of dependence on Craig**

Computer fraud is very prevalent and steps should be taken to reduce dependence on just one person. Apart from the risk of fraud, other problems could arise, eg if Craig fell ill and was off work for any length of time.

It may be worth considering subscribing to a software helpdesk. Most software suppliers offer this type of service. Staff could also be trained to bring their skills up to a particular level of competence so that they can deal with more things themselves.

(d) **Authorisation policies**

Policies should be introduced requiring your authorisation before any program changes or changes to standing data can be made. Reports could be generated on a regular basis summarising changes that have been made over the relevant time period.

There are numerous controls that could be implemented to assist in the prevention and detection of fraud. The cost of introducing such controls must be weighed up against the perceived risk from fraud arising out of not having them in place.

Chapter 10

Answer 10.1

(a) **The issues for Eleanor raised by the memorandum.**

(i) Interdepartmental communication seems to be poor, as evidenced by George's memo. Clearly, he had not been consulted. Furthermore, what communication that does exist between the departments has been contaminated by the noise arising from George's off-hand treatment by one of Eleanor's staff. This has given the issue unpleasant personal overtones.

If George is as important a user as he says he is, then Eleanor should, as a matter of routine, have consulted him about any changes.

(ii) Lack of systems thinking. Clearly, staff in both departments have a difficulty in seeing exactly how their activities relate to the wider whole or even to the immediate users of their services. Eleanor's staff perhaps were unaware of the role of George's department, but they also seem unaware of the importance of their own.

(iii) Lack of internal 'marketing orientation'. Eleanor's staff talk about giving value to customers, but they do not appear to relate to their **internal customer**, who is George.

(iv) High level conflict between systems. It would appear that the instructions given to Eleanor to contain her costs were developed without any real thought as to the implication of the cutbacks for operations. This indicates that perhaps there is poor co-ordination at higher level, with budgets set simply on departmental lines, leading to conflicts between budgeting and marketing systems.

(v) Is George more angry about being unable to cut his own costs, or being unable to enhance the service? It may be that he is under budgetary pressures too, and hopes that Eleanor will take the blame for his failure to cut costs in other ways.

Other problems relate to the way in which the specific issue was handled.

(i) Eleanor's staff did not reply in an appropriate way to George. She needs to discover why the personal relationships between the staff member and George deteriorated to the extent that they resulted in such a brusque letter.

(ii) Eleanor should have known about the potential problem in advance. Her staff should have told her. Perhaps she has delegated too much of her job, and allowed subordinates too much unmonitored autonomy. Eleanor herself had not considered the wider implications of the changes she had authorised.

(iii) She needs to encourage an internal customer approach amongst her staff.

(b) **What Eleanor should do**

We know that George has a genuine case, as Eleanor has already conducted an investigation.

(i) George should be contacted immediately.

(ii) Eleanor should apologise to George for the rather cavalier way in which he has been treated.

(iii) She should endeavour to rectify the situation, winning extra resources from senior management if necessary, with the active co-operation of George. However, if resources of time, personnel and money are limited then she might have to reorder the priorities of her department, and perhaps defer some less critical projects. This might mean that other departments will have to be inconvenienced.

(iv) Some of her staff should be sent on customer care programmes – directed of course, to improving their relationships with internal customers.

(v) She must remember to include George's needs in her plans for next year.

Answer 10.2

(a) Firstly, ensure that all of the departments concerned have been informed of the investigation, and of its purpose. The most appropriate way of doing this would probably be for a memorandum to be sent to departmental supervisors from the chief accountant. The memorandum would explain that the investigation had been requested by the managing director.

The memorandum would explain that the investigation is to examine the reports and forms used within the organisation. The next stage would be to build up information on all of the reports and forms used in each department. This information would be gathered by visiting and interviewing supervisors and other departmental staff.

Samples of each form and report should be collected and details recorded.

- The purpose of forms
- Recipients of forms
- Sources of data
- Methods of processing the forms
- Time taken to prepare
- Frequency of preparation
- Processing of forms

It may transpire that because of particular problems or considerations highlighted by departmental staff visited, additional information should be added to the list of information to be compiled.

The departments to which the reports and forms are circulated could then be approached, and the following questions asked.

- What is your view of the purpose of this form?
- How much of the information which it contains do you use, and how do you use it?
- Do you receive the information at the frequency required?
- Is the information supplied in the correct format?
- Does the form duplicate information which you also receive from elsewhere?
- What is your overall opinion of the value of the form?

Having completed the process of gathering information, it will be appropriate:

- to make an initial assessment of the extent of any problems revealed;
- to formulate some recommendations about how to copy out a full investigation; and
- to draft an informal report to the Chief Accountant based on the above.

(b) **MEMORANDUM**

To: The Chief Accountant
From: A B C Technician
Subject: Reporting within the organisation
Date: 4 February 200X

I have now completed my initial investigations of reporting within the organisation along the lines discussed by Ms Green and yourself. My investigation involved a survey of forms and reports produced by the costing office and the work study department. A schedule of the forms and reports issued by these two departments is attached, together with samples of each form, at Appendix A.

I received full co-operation from the staff members concerned in carrying out my investigation. My initial findings can be summarised under the following headings.

(i) **Use and frequency of information in forms and reports**

Recipients of forms were asked how the information of the form or report was used by them. The results of canvassing are summarised in the table below.

	Cost office	*Work study dept*
Documents circulated	38	10
Number of recipients	120	23
Recipients' comments		
Useful	15	7
Some use	60	10
Very limited use	30	3
No information used	15	3
Total	120	23
Reports too frequent	25	2
Report frequency satisfactory	71	14
Reports not frequent enough	24	7
Total	120	23

(ii) **Format of the forms**

Some of the forms which are prepared manually take some time to complete because of the need to enter codes manually on sheets.

More explanatory information setting out how forms should be completed could usefully be included on the face of the forms. Many members of staff found some of the forms difficult to complete without consulting other staff or referring to manuals.

(iii) **Presentation**

There is currently no standardisation of layout in the forms, nor are standard sizes of paper used for forms. Various different types of code are used to identify particular forms. Some forms which are identified by different codes include very similar information. In particular, forms 01 and G3 produced by the cost office are so similar that no recipients understood why two forms were generated rather than just one. Colour coding of forms may be a useful means of differentiating types of form.

Recommendations

The findings highlight the need for a rethink of the design, presentation and circulation of forms and reports within the organisation. I suggest that the following points merit further consideration.

(i) The development of a consistent policy throughout the organisation covering forms and reports. A policy of consistency in layout and in the size of forms and reports will greatly streamline the processes of preparing, copying and filing of the documents.

(ii) Extension of the survey to all departments. The pilot survey carried out has indicated the general need for revision of the current forms and reports. The pilot survey provides sufficient information to formulate proposals for revision of the forms and reports in the two departments examined. However, considerably more time would be necessary to extend the survey to all departments.

(iii) Evaluation of savings arising from the exercise. This evaluation will, I believe, demonstrate the value of extending the survey to all departments.

(iv) A formal means of control over all forms and reports in the organisation. This will ensure that the standardisation of forms and reports used is maintained in the future.

Answer 10.3

Strengths	H/M/L	Weaknesses	H/M/L
3 Regular bank reconciliations	H	1 Excel formula incorrect	M
6 Staff training	M	4 Cashier does bank reconciliations	H
		5 Stock/sales order processing	H
Opportunities	**H/M/L**	**Threats**	**H/M/L**
		2 Low salaries	L

Item

1 A weakness – because the wrong information is being sent and the software is not robust enough. (There is an opportunity to make it better with an Access database.)

2 A threat, as the staff could move on: an opportunity could exist as you could offer flexible working.

3 Bank reconciliations are a good control.

4 Risk of fraud.

5 A weakness, if data produced by each system is incompatible with the other.

6 A strength, as it will help staff to do a better job.

PART E

The project and the report

chapter 11

Starting your project

Contents

1 The project: What you have to do

1.1 The project in outline

The project is quite unlike anything else you do for AAT. It requires you to do some research, to be decisive in making recommendations and to write a report of up to 4,000 words (realistically, no less than 3,000).

Report writing is an important part of business life, involving analysis, research and considering 'the bigger picture'. By writing a report you can show:

- Understanding of an accounting system and its controls
- Evidence of your competence in this unit (performance criteria, range statements and knowledge and understanding)
- Evidence of your communication skills.

4,000 words may seem a lot, but you may already have had experience of writing reports, for example through continuous assessment at school or reports at work.

1.2 The project and being deemed 'competent' in Unit 10

To be deemed competent in Unit 10, you must show evidence that you have covered all the performance criteria.

- Ideally, most will be covered in the report.
- If there are any gaps, you will attend a question and answer session with your assessor. Your assessor will ask you questions on the topics you have not covered, and will write down the answers.

1.3 Approaching the project

There are three different ways of approaching the project.

	Comment
Using your own experience as a manager	You have the expertise and can report on your own workplace and your experience as a **manager**. This can often involve responsibility for staff, scheduling and so on **What if you run and operate an entire accounts department single-handed?** This should not be a problem. You will still have experience of dealing with other people and other parts of your organisation. This is all part of management.
You work in an accounts department but do not have a management or supervisory role	**What if you are not the supervisor or manager of your section?** You can't report on your own experience as a manager, but you **can** report on your workplace, by observing how management is done. You are **managed** by someone and you know how the things that your manager thinks and does impinge upon your work and that of your colleagues. You may well often think: 'If I were in charge, I'd do it this way, not that way.' Thus your project will simply be a statement of things you think about all the time. It would be great if you could put all your good ideas into practice but you will probably be limited in what you can do if you are not in charge. You can at least consider **how** your ideas could be implemented.
You work in a non-traditional role or not in an accounts department	You can still do a report on your workplace, and it does not matter what your job title is. Even so, the **report needs to be based on an accounting environment**.
You do not work	Your colleges, for example, may have contact with local employers who would be willing to help. You may also have experience of: • Recent employment (in the **last two years**) • Work placements • Voluntary organisations (eg you could join a club or charity) • A college department (eg canteen, library) • Family work experiences • Other AAT members, perhaps contacted via your local AAT branch
You cannot get any relevant work experience	You will be able to use the **AAT's simulation** if you really need to. This simulation is meant for people who have no workplace evidence to draw upon. An example, Delmar Electronics, is given at the end of the text. If you use the AAT's simulation, you still have to produce a 4,000 page report. Note that you will have to obtain the actual simulation from your college (which obtains it from AAT). You **cannot** use Delmar Electronics as the basis of your project.

1.4 The skills you need

A number of skills are useful in the project.

Type of skill	In the workplace	In the project
Planning	Any sequence of tasks involves a plan.	• You will have to identify what your project is to cover. • You will have to identify the tasks you need to do to fulfil the objective (what you must research and analyse). It is best to prepare a formal assessment plan, which can be reviewed and updated regularly.
Research	• You may have to investigate a variance. • You may have to research the skills needed for the department. • You may have to research new software.	You may have to hunt for relevant data about a topic for review. For example if you are doing something on financial controls you may have to research how they operate and then document them.
Analysis	You may need to spend some time calculating data and manipulating it to find the reason for something.	Analysis can cover many activities, not just calculation.
Report writing	You might have to write reports to your manager at various times. Many of these might be in a standard format.	You must write a 4,000 word report. This could be more wide ranging than the sort of reports you do at work. You **can** use the official style of report used by your organisation – not a memo, but a formal report written to a senior manager.
Oral communication	As a manager, you talk to people all the time!	Oral communication for the purpose of finding out information for the project. You may also have to answer questions on material not covered in the report.
Time management Evidence that you have planned and managed your time for the project will count as evidence that you have satisfied the Performance Criteria.	You probably work to deadlines and have to juggle a number of tasks – preparation of accounts data, dealing with queries and interruptions, and so on.	Your project will need to be submitted by a certain time. You will have to work back from your delivery date, and be realistic in your allocation of time to tasks. This project has to be managed over a long period. It is not routine work, so you will be faced with a learning curve. You need to create time for the project.

2 The project topic and project plan

2.1 Getting started

The diagram on the next page shows the stages in project report preparation. The initial question, 'What do I want to know?', may derive from the following considerations

- What is the system in your accounting section?
- How has it been or might it be modified or improved?
- Are there training and other people management issues that ought to be addressed?

At this point in time you are at that daunting stage where you have up to 4,000 words to produce and nothing but a blank sheet of paper in front of you. How can you begin to describe something as complicated as an accounting system? What improvements could you possibly suggest?

2.2 Basic steps in a project

A project usually starts with a problem or a question. It involves the following framework.

Step 1. Identify what you must cover
Step 2. Generate a plan
Step 3. Gather data
Step 4. Analyse the data
Step 5. Draw conclusions
Step 6. Develop and justify recommendations
Step 7. Write up report

Pay attention to these steps. They will help you to make progress.

Stages in report preparation

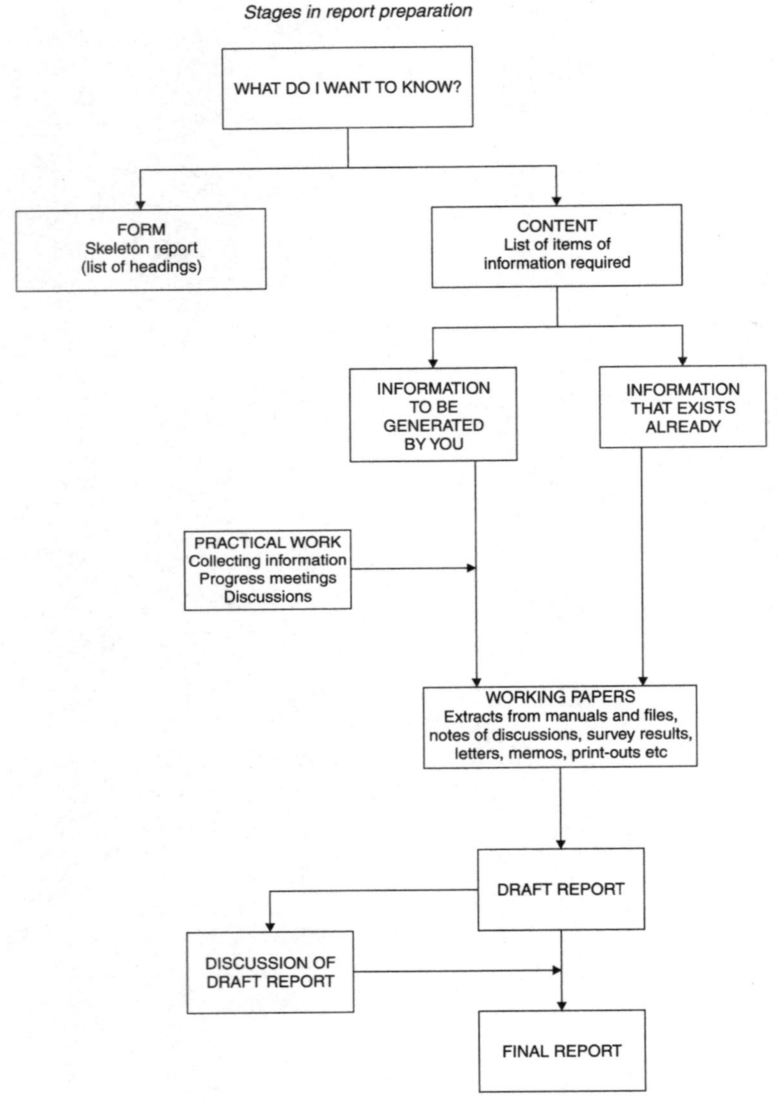

2.3 Step 1: What your report must cover

Here is some indicative **guidance** from the AAT.

Unit 10.1

The project should include evidence that the student has planned and undertaken:

1 Work routines to meet organisational time schedules and to make the best use of both human and physical resources (Performance Criteria A). Planning and scheduling the project for completion to standard and on time will also provide evidence towards Performance Criteria A. The content of the project can also assist with this Performance Criteria, with for example the student ensuring that resources such as computer time and staff time are used efficiently.

2 The systematic review of staff competencies and training needs, together with details of the training actually arranged (Performance Criteria B).

3 Contingency planning, in collaboration with management, for possible emergencies (eg computer system not being fully functional, staff absences, and changes in work patterns and demands) (Performance Criteria C).

4 The clear communication of work methods and schedules to colleagues so that they have understand what is expected of them (Performance Criteria D).

5 The monitoring of work activities sufficiently closely against quality standards to ensure they are being met (Performance Criteria E).

6 The co-ordination of work activities effectively against workplans and contingency plan (Performance Criteria F).

7 The encouragement of colleagues to report promptly issues beyond their authority and expertise, and resolved these where possible (Performance Criteria G); and that

8 Otherwise, he/she has referred such issues to the appropriate person to resolve them (Performance Criteria H).

Unit 10.2

The project should include evidence that the student has planned and undertaken.

9 A situation analysis of the accounting system under scrutiny (eg a SWOT analysis), which will generate evidence towards performance criteria Performance Criteria A and B.

10 Evidence of resulting recommendations made to the appropriate people in a clear understandable format and supported by a clear rationale will generate evidence towards Performance Criteria D and E. All assumptions made should be clearly listed.

11 Research into any potential areas of fraud within their accounting system (eg teeming and lading, fictitious employees or suppliers) and into appropriate fraud risk standard swill generate evidence for Performance Criteria B. Students are advised to use some form of matrix approach toward grading the various elements of risk.

12 A regular review of methods of operating, providing evidence for Performance Criteria C.

13 Updates to the system which, where appropriate, have been made in accordance with both internal factors (eg changes in the organisational structure, responses to customer surveys) and external factors (eg change in company law, VAT rates, FRSs) that require such updates to be made. This evidences Performance Criteria F – SWOT and PEST analyses respectively would be useful here.

Any of the above evidence that does not sit naturally within the project should be included as additional evidence in the appendices to it. As indicated earlier, a project which does not cover all of these will be supplemented by documented assessor questioning.

Use this list of criteria below to make sure you have covered then in your project.

Performance Criteria checklist

	Unit 10.1 Co-ordinate work activities within the accounting environment	Have you covered this?
A	Plan work activities to make the optimum use of resources and to ensure that work is completed within agreed timescales.	________
B	Review the competence of individual undertaking work activities and arrange the necessary training.	________
C	Prepare, in collaboration with management, contingency plans to meet possible emergencies.	________
D	Communicate work methods and schedules to colleagues in ways that help them to understand what is expected of them.	________
E	Monitor work activities sufficiently closely to ensure that quality standards are being met.	________
F	Co-ordinate work activities effectively and in accordance with work plans and contingency plans	________
G	Encourage colleagues to report to you promptly any problems and queries that are beyond their authority or expertise to resolve, and resolve these where they are within your authority and expertise.	________
H	Refer problems and queries to the appropriate person where resolution is beyond your authority or expertise.	________

	Element 10.2 Identify opportunities for improving the effectiveness of an accounting system	
A	Identify weaknesses and potential for improvements to the accounting system and consider their impact on the operation of the organisation	________
B	Identify potential areas of fraud arising from control avoidance within the accounting system and grade the risk.	________
C	Review methods of operating regularly in respect of their cost-effectiveness, reliability and speed.	________
D	Make recommendations to the appropriate person in a clear, easily understood format.	________
E	Ensure recommendations are supported by a clear rationale which include and explanation of any assumption made.	________
F	Update the system in accordance with changes that affect the ways the system should operate and check that your update is producing the required results.	________

2.4 Step 2. Develop a project idea and choosing a topic

Your organisation and your project	You will need to consider how the system/section you have chosen fits in. You will need to consider the size of the organisation, what type of organisation it is and the role of the department (key personnel, relationship with other departments). You might include a diagram or organisation chart.
Improving the system and your department	Here you can look a planning, schedules, checks and controls, training, productivity and contingency plans. It sometimes helps to look at something that has gone wrong in the past: critical incidents. Complete a **SWOT** analysis. (For example, is there a risk of fraud?)
Gather data	How you plan to go about gathering data. You need to be systematic and you need to document your conclusions.
Recommendations and implementation	This is an important issue. If you make recommendations, this will involve considering how they can be implemented. • Staffing • Controls • Changes You will have to consider how your proposal might be implemented. If it was implemented, was it successful?

Choosing a topic

Your choice of topic is likely to be affected by the size of the organisation in which you work. If you work in a very small organisation then some topics (such as delegation or team-building) may not be so familiar to you in practice. Ideally you should choose an area which is specifically **accounting** or directly **relates to an accounting system**.

It should be a 'real' information processing routine which is currently your experience or has been previously. Having practical experience will make it easier to complete the project and expand on its contents.

Here are some suggestions for generating ideas.

(a) Ask your college for a list of successful project topics.

(b) Look at your own workplace. What could you improve? Describe the systems and processes as they stand and consider any improvements to be made. Your emphasis will be on methods of upgrading its effectiveness and efficiency, and any relevant management issues.

(c) Ask your line manager. He or she might have some ideas.

(d) Identify one or more of the conventional accounting sections such as payroll, purchase ledger, sales ledger, costing

Here are some suggestions for getting ideas.

(a) Go back to the material in Chapters 1 to 10. Not all of the material will be relevant to your current circumstances, but it is very likely that something will strike a chord and set you thinking. Analyse all the components of your accounting system at work.

(b) Glance through the remainder of this Text, without actually tackling any of the tasks.

(c) Most importantly, talk to your **employer**, who may (especially in a larger organisation) have many good ideas about problems that need to be researched and tackled and may be just waiting for the opportunity to get them investigated. Look at some reports at work.

(d) Look at AAT's sample simulation for ideas.

2.5 Project feasibility checklist

Once you have selected a topic to cover, will you be able, in practice, to complete the project? You need to be able to assess its feasibility. Look at the checklist below.

Factor	How feasible?
Your employer Is your employer happy with the project chosen? If 'yes', fine. If not, ask how you can deal with your employer's objections. A few minor changes might be enough. Alternatively, you might have to consider another project.	
Can you collect valid evidence? Spend some time deciding **what** sort of information you expect to find, **where** you are most likely to find it, and whether you have enough **time** to acquire it. **Does the data you will need already exist, or will it need to be generated?** The former (secondary data) requires less time to compile, while the latter (primary data) has the benefit of originality. **Will access to existing data be a problem?** For example, confidential corporate information may be difficult to obtain. **If you need to generate data, is this practical?** This is not just a question of the time required, but also whether it will be generated in the appropriate quality and quantity.	
Confidentiality? **Can you reproduce it**? You must ask your employer's permission to reproduce original documents. Practically all information about your organisation could be considered to be sensitive, so be *very* careful about this. You may be able to change the names of people mentioned in the report. Any personal information about people (eg about salaries) is likely to be very confidential.)	
Opportunity While a number of possible topics might interest you, some areas are likely to be more accessible than others. Partly, this will be related to costs and resources, but also it is dependent on the approval of superiors and the co-operation of others.	
Time Finding enough time to collect data and compile a final report is always a challenge. • It will be worthwhile to prepare a time **schedule** and **action plan**. • Are some tasks dependent on other people, whose time pressures may be even greater than your own? **A rough guide to time** • 1/3 of the time will be spent investigating the project • 1/3 collecting data • 1/3 writing it up Don't delay starting work on your project!	
Technical skills The success of a project will be increased if the topic selected makes use of your own expertise, skills and knowledge. However, a project may provide an opportunity for you to extend your skills.	
Size and scope Don't' be too ambitious.	
You! Does this topic interest and motivate you?	

3 Gathering data

3.1 Information

The information requirements for any project are specific to that project, so it is very difficult to be specific about the sort of data and its sources that would be appropriate for your chosen area. Some topics will rely more on existing information, perhaps from within your own organisation, while other areas will require you to generate your own data, perhaps using some form of survey. There are two types of data source.

3.1.1 Primary source

A **primary source** is as close as you can get to the origin of an item of information: the eyewitness to an event, the place in question, the document under scrutiny. 'Tapping' the primary source requires initiative and time. You must do four things.

- Identify the right person to talk to, the right document to see and place to visit
- Find them
- Ask the right questions, so that you obtain the right answers
- Clearly document your questions and answers

3.1.2 Secondary source

A **secondary source** provides second hand information: examples are company files and records, procedural manuals, brochures, accounting reports, books, articles, verbal or written reports by someone else.

3.1.3 Trusting the source

In some situations, a secondary source might be satisfactory and possibly the only convenient means of obtaining an item of information – but you must be able to trust the accuracy and integrity of the source. It may be preferable to seek a primary source if any of the circumstances below apply.

(a) If the matter under investigation is of particular importance, and any extra expense of time and money can be justified

(b) If you have reason to suspect that the secondary sources are unreliable

(c) If a sensitive personal matter is involved, in which case the individual concerned should be interviewed.

3.1.4 Checklist

The following chapters of this part of the Text contain a wide variety of information-gathering exercises. These are written with a close eye on what the AAT have suggested a report is likely to contain, but there are bound to be some tasks that are not appropriate for your chosen topic. Equally your chosen topic will require you to gather and analyse data in ways other than those we suggest.

3.1.5 Analysing data

Analysing data is not as difficult as it sounds. It is usually a matter of looking at what you have and drawing common sense conclusions from it. If there is any maths involved, it is usually quite simple.

Example: Gathering and analysing data

You are the senior in a small section of an accountancy firm that prepares year-end accounts for a variety of small traders.

On Monday morning at 9.30am you dish out three jobs to Paul, Jyoti and Mandy. You instruct them that their first task is to perform a bank reconciliation and that when this is complete they should come and show you immediately. Office hours are 9am to 5.30pm with one hour for lunch.

You are interested in improving efficiency in your section so you keep a careful note of the work involved and the time taken. The results are as follows.

	Bank statement pages	*Reconciliation completed*	
Paul	17	Monday	5pm
Jyoti	58	Tuesday	3pm
Mandy	47	Tuesday	12am

Who is the most efficient, Paul, Jyoti or Mandy? What other information would you like to have to help you judge?

Solution

All you need to do to analyse the data is to apply some simple maths. Because each bank statement is of a different length, the times cannot be compared directly. However, they can be made comparable by calculating a measure such as pages per hour. Another option would be minutes per page.

	Hours	*Pages*	*Pages per hour*	*Ranking*
Paul	6.5	17	2.62	3
Jyoti	12	58	4.83	1
Mandy	10	47	4.70	2

On this evidence, Jyoti and Mandy are about equally efficient and Paul is quite significantly less so. However, account needs to be taken of a number of other factors, including the following.

- Were there interruptions for any of the three staff?
- Were the cashbooks for each client equally well prepared?
- Do all three staff have the same level of experience and training?
- Were Paul's reconciliations more demanding or detailed?

4 Suggesting improvements and implementing them

4.1 Improvements already in place

You may have **already** made considerable improvements to the way your section is managed, and you may want these improvements to be the subject of your report. This will make things easier in some ways – it will provide you with a very clear focus from the outset – but bear in mind that after the event it may not be possible to collect the information you might need to compare the old way with the new way.

4.2 New improvements

If you know what improvements you are going to suggest, collect information now on the current situation to compare with the situation after you have made your changes.

There is, of course, no need for your improvements to have been **fully achieved** by the time you write your report. They could be in progress at the time you prepare your final report or they could be just about to be implemented.

What if your plans for improvement fail? Or more senior managers will not agree to them? Again this need not be a problem: such things are not always within your control. Lessons will have been learned for the future, so emphasise this aspect.

4.3 What if you are worried about being critical of your employer (or of fellow employees)?

There may be some things that you would like to say, and perhaps should say, that cannot be said without making things difficult for you or your section. Tact and diplomacy will always help.

- Avoid being negative – be constructive.
- Identify the problem, but then propose a positive solution to it.
- Remember that most people have good reasons for behaving in a particular way. There may be difficulties in the work that you do not fully understand.

If you have nothing but criticism, ask yourself whether you are being entirely objective.

4.4 What next?

If you cannot think of any improvements what should you do?

(a) Improvements can be **small scale and incremental**. Don't be afraid of stating the obvious. For example, it might have occurred to you, or some of your colleagues that you take too long over Excel spreadsheets: **training is an improvement**.

(b) Ask for ideas from your colleagues: 'What can be done to make it better?'

4.5 A suggested approach

Step 1. Start collecting information for your final report. To help with this and to provide a framework, whichever of the tasks in the following chapters are appropriate to you.

Step 2. You will soon start to have ideas about other tasks that you could usefully perform, other information that it would be useful to collect, other ways of analysing the information and so on. We don't know anything about *your* organisation or your job so there is a limit to the suggestions that we can make.

Step 3. Before you start writing the first draft of your report, read the chapter on writing up your report and the sample reports. Read them critically and think how they could be better.

Step 4. Draw judiciously upon the information you have collected and write up the first draft of your report. Apply what you learnt in Step 3 in your approach to your own report.

Step 5. Keep working on your report until you are fully satisfied with it. Let others read it and listen to their criticism.

It will be necessary for you to amass quite a volume of notes and documents. Equip yourself with a lever-arch binder and a set of divider cards. This will be your **project file** and will help you keep everything tidy.

4.6 What if you cannot implement your changes?

If you cannot implement your changes, the relevant performance criteria will be covered by documented assessor questioning.

Consider **why** you cannot implement the changes. Perhaps the impact is too serious. When making changes, consider:

- Who will be affected? How will they react? For example, some members of staff may have to change what they do. This can affect their job description, their pay and their relationships with others.
- How disruptive will the change be?
- What will be the cost in time and other expenses? Your recommendations may require more staff. Can the firm afford this?

chapter 12

Your organisation, your department and your section

Contents

BPP note

From this chapter onwards, the activities form part of your project, so we do **not** provide answers.

1 Introduction

This chapter asks you to look at your organisation and section in outline. More detail will follow in later chapters. It is the **first stage** of the information gathering process. You need to keep the **overall** role of the department in mind. Go back to Chapters 1 and 2 if you need some revision.

2 Background

Activity 12.1

Obtain a copy of your organisation's most recent annual report and accounts. These are public documents and often contain useful information.

Record the following information about your organisation.

	Overall	**Your subsidiary (if applicable)**
Name		
Main activity or activities, services and products		
Industry sector (If applicable)		
Legal status (eg public company, charity)		

Even if you are using the most recent annual report and accounts of your organisation there could still have been significant changes in the business since they were published. Make sure that you are using up to date information. The accounts will also provide information for other tasks in this chapter, so keep them to hand.

Activity 12.2

Obtain copies of any current brochures or leaflets about your organisation's activities. Consider which are relevant background information to the work that you do and include them in your project file.

Other possible sources of information about the work of your organisation include its advertisements and newspaper and magazine articles. Keep an eye out for these in case of potential relevance to your project.

Documents collected

____
____
____
____
____
____

Activity 12.3

If your organisation has a mission statement, or similar document setting out its overall objectives obtain a copy for inclusion in your project file.

If possible, summarise the main objective of your organisation here

____
____
____
____

3 Environment

Activity 12.4

Prepare a description of your organisation's commercial environment.

Who are its owners or main shareholders?	
If a listed company, on what stock markets are its shares quoted?	
Who are its main suppliers?	
Who are its main customers?	
Who are its main competitors?	

Activity 12.5

(a) Consider briefly **political and legal** factors influencing your department and the demands placed on it. We will cover this in more detail in Chapter 13.

(b) What economic factors influence the work of the department (eg availability of resources, VAT returns and the impact of changes in sales revenues).

(c) Consider whether **social or ethical issues** have any impact on your section's work. For example, is it difficult to recruit staff with the appropriate skills in the local catchment area. Do you work for a building firm and have to deal with payments to subcontractors?

(d) Consider whether the **technology** used by other parts of your organisation has any impact on the accounts department. Make notes of any factors that significantly affect your work.

3.1 Organisation size and structure

Activity 12.6

Obtain or draw an **organisation chart** for your organisation as a **whole**.

(a) If you work for a very large company this may simply show a holding company at the top and a family tree of subsidiaries. (You ought, in theory, to be able to work out 'who owns who' from the most recent annual report and accounts, but it is not always so simple in practice, and be aware that things may have changed since these were published. If this task causes you problems, ask for the help of a more senior person in the accounts department.)

(b) Highlight your own subsidiary of the organisation on this chart.

(c) Obtain or draw an organisation chart for your subsidiary, if applicable, or for your organisation as a whole if it is a single entity. Chapter 1 of this Text gives examples of the different ways organisations may be structured.

(d) Highlight your own part of the organisation on this chart.

Activity 12.7

(a) Note down the size of your organisation in as many ways as possible. The annual accounts may be useful here.

	Overall	*Your subsidiary (if applicable)*
Number of staff	______________	______________
Number of branches/offices	______________	______________
Geographical spread	______________	______________
Annual sales (£)	______________	______________
Annual sales (units)	______________	______________
Annual profit(£)	______________	______________
Number of customers	______________	______________
Market share (%)	______________	______________
Other sources of income	______________	______________
	______________	______________
	______________	______________
	______________	______________
	______________	______________
	______________	______________

(b) Which measure(s) noted above give(s) the best idea of the size of your organisation?

Activity 12.8

Obtain or draw an organisation chart of your **department** that shows its division into different sections. Highlight your section.

Activity 12.9

Obtain or draw an organisation chart depicting the **structure of your section**.

4 Your section: activities

Activity 12.10

Unless one already exists, prepare a mission statement for your **section** and discuss it with your manager. Your mission statement should be as brief as possible, but it should include a brief and readable explanation of the following matters.

(a) The **purpose** or **objective** of the section: for example 'to safeguard the organisation's assets and secure as far as possible the completeness and accuracy of the records', to borrow the language of an Auditing Guideline.

(b) The **strategy** it adopts, for example, aiming to minimise errors. How, in outline, does it go about achieving its purpose?

(c) The **values** it holds, for example, honesty. These should link to the purpose of the section and be in line with the values of the organisation as a whole.

(d) The **behaviour standards** expected, for example, dealing promptly and courteously with all enquiries (there may be some overlap with (c) here).

If a mission statement for your section already exists, obtain a copy for inclusion in your project file. First, though, assess how satisfactory you think it is by comparing it with the items discussed above.

Activity 12.11

As briefly as possible, describe the main **activities** of your section of the accounts department and how often the activities are carried out (daily, weekly, monthly etc).

Main activities

___

___

___

___

___

5 Your section: performance targets

Activity 12.12

What service or quality systems affect the operations of your section?	
Has your employer or department participated in a Quality Assurance scheme such as ISO 9000?	
If so, note down the principal record keeping requirements as they affect your section.	
Note who is responsible and how up-to-date the records are.	
How are errors and unusual circumstances dealt with?	

Activity 12.13

Note down the performance or service standards which the department is expected to adhere to. (For example, answer 95% of enquiries within 24 hours.)

Note down how these are monitored and controlled.

Who reports on adherence to quality and service standards and targets?

6 Your section: overall control environment

Activity 12.14

We covered controls in Chapter 8. In outline, what use does your section make of the following types of controls (high, medium, low)?

	High	Medium	Low
Segregation of duties			
Physical controls			
Authorisation approval			
Management controls			
Supervision			
Organisation (formal, structured)			
Arithmetical and accounting			
Personnel			

Activity 12.15

Briefly describe your organisation's approach to managing risk of fraud.

Does the organisation actively identify risk areas? If yes, how?	
Does it assess and understand the state of risk, being high/medium/low?	
Has the organisation developed a risk management strategy?	
Is the strategy implemented?	
Are controls monitored for effectiveness?	
Is there a group of people in the organisation with overall responsibility for looking at risk?	

7 Your section: people and jobs

Activity 12.16

Note down the names and job titles of each person in your section, starting with yourself.

If there are no formal job titles, you may wish to think up some for ease of reference when you come to write your report (you may know who Jane, is and how her job differs from Pete's, but the reader of your report could easily forget and get confused).

Whether or not there are formal titles it would probably be illuminating to get your staff to tell you what they think their job titles should be.

Name	*Job title*

Activity 12.17

Obtain or prepare outline job descriptions for each member of your section.

It may be useful from a management point of view to ask your staff to prepare their own job descriptions. This will also save you some work, but bear in mind the pitfalls of this approach. At the very least you will have to check them and perhaps amend them after discussion with staff members.

The following is a possible outline for job descriptions. The **duties** part is the most important. Do not go into every detail, but be sure to include all the main duties.

A word of warning: you'll need your manager's permission to obtain job descriptions if they have been prepared already, and you should **discuss the matter with your manager** if you are to prepare job descriptions yourself.

JOB DESCRIPTION

1 Job title: Accounts Assistant

2 Department: Payroll – Production Staff

3 Responsible to: Supervisor, Production Staff Payroll

4 Age range: over 18 (no upper limit)

5 Supervises work of: N/A

6 Has regular co-operative contact with: Production department supervisors and clerical staff; fellow accounts assistants

7 Main duties/responsibilities: Calculating wages due to production staff and statutory and other deductions. Analysing labour costs for management information purposes

8 Location: Head office, accounts department

9 Employment conditions: Salary: £18,000 per annum
Hours: 9 am – 5 pm (1 hour for lunch)
Holidays: 4 weeks per annum

Prepared by: Sue James, Production Staff Payroll Supervisor **Date**: 20 November 20XX

8 Other sections and departments

Activity 12.18

Referring to the organisation charts that you have already drawn, identify which other **sections** of the accounts **department** and other departments of the organisation your department deals with.

Mark them 'I' (Input) if they are mainly a source of information and 'O' (output) if they mainly receive information from you. Mark 'I/O' if there is a two-way exchange of information.

Other sections		*Other departments*	

Activity 12.19

How often does your section have dealings with the other parts of the organisation noted above? List them in order of frequency (for example, 'constantly', 'once daily', 'once weekly', 'once monthly', 'less regularly').

Activity 12.20

Regarding those other parts of the accounts department and the organisation as a whole that you deal with **most often**, do you know what the full range of their activities are? This information may be set out in an organisation manual, or you may have to go and talk to people in that part of the organisation to find out.

(a) Complete the boxes for those that are **sources** of information for your section.

How do they come to have the information?	
What processing do they have to do to obtain the information?	
Who else do they have to provide information to ?	
What else do they do?	
When are their busiest times?	
If they delay in getting data to you, how are you affected?	

(b) Do likewise for those who mainly **receive** information from your section.

Why do they need the information and what do they do with it?	
Is their work delayed if you are late in providing the information?	
Does your delay have a knock-on effect on tasks they perform for yet other parts of the organisation?	
What else do they do?	
When are their busiest times?	

Activity 12.21

Control over resources is spread in different departments in the organisation. Note the resources used by your department, and the other departments that must be contacted for such resources to be obtained.

Type of resources	*Department providing or authorising resources*

9 Other departments: service agreements

Activity 12.22

Does your section have **formal agreements** with other departments as to the provision of information? What agreements are these?

Activity 12.23

Do you and do all of your staff understand the internal customer concept? To drive it home see if you can answer the following questions. We shall repeat this task in the session on performance, but it is worth starting to think about the issues now.

The point of these questions is to make you realise that the different parts of an organisation are each others' customers.

(a) Assuming no difference in the costs, could your section's work be done by, say, an outside firm of accountants?

(b) Assuming they had the resources, could other departments or sections do your section's work? (For example, could the personnel department handle payroll, or the marketing department handle bad debts, and so on?)

(c) Do you think employees would rather take up pay queries with the personnel department or the accounts department?

(d) Do you think a production department would be more inclined or less inclined to take note of and make use of cost information that it generated for itself?

(e) Do you sometimes wish that you didn't have to deal with a certain department (or a certain person within it) and that you could go elsewhere to get what you need?

(f) Do you sometimes bypass formal channels at work and get information from those who properly understand why you want it and when you need it?

(g) Can you name one **unique** skill or piece of expertise that your section possesses?

10 Your organisation and your section: overall

Activity 12.24

Review your notes so far, and note down any strengths, weaknesses, opportunities and threats arising out of the work of the section. Note whether they are of high, medium and low importance.

Strength	H/M/L	Weakness	H/M/L
Opportunity	H/M/L	Threat	H/M/L

Activity 12.25

Note down what you might do to deal with the weaknesses and threats, especially those of high importance.

chapter 13

Regulations in your organisation and section

Contents

1 Introduction

This chapter acknowledges the changing regulatory environment in relation to the work of the section.

2 External regulations relevant to accounting

Activity 13.1

UK accounting standards

If your section's work has any connection with the information contained in your company's financial accounts then many of the current accounting standards are potentially relevant to your work, but some are probably more important to you than others. For example you will need to know about FRS 11 if your section is responsible for maintaining the organisation's fixed asset records, or about SSAP 9 if it is involved in costing and stock valuation.

Below is a list of UK standards in force at the date of writing. Some are too advanced for AAT studies but they are included for completeness. Tick off those which are currently relevant to your work and state briefly why.

UK accounting standards

	Title		Why relevant to your job?
FRS 1	Cash flow statements (revised 10/96)		
FRS 2	Accounting for subsidiary undertakings		
FRS 3	Reporting financial performance		
FRS 4	Capital instruments		
FRS 5	Reporting the substance of transactions		
FRS 6	Acquisitions and mergers		
FRS 7	Fair values in acquisition accounting		
FRS 8	Related party disclosures		
FRS 9	Associates and joint ventures		
FRS 10	Goodwill and intangible assets		
FRS 11	Impairment of fixed assets and goodwill		
FRS 12	Provisions, contingent liabilities and contingent assets		
FRS 13	Derivatives and other financial instruments disclosures		
FRS 14	Earnings per share		
FRS 15	Tangible fixed assets		
FRS 16	Current tax		

	Title	Why relevant to your job?
FRS 17	Retirement benefits	
FRS 18	Accounting policies	
FRS 19	Deferred tax	
FRSSE	Smaller entities	
SSAP 4	Accounting for government grants	
SSAP 5	Accounting for value added tax	
SSAP 9	Stocks and long-term contracts	
SSAP 13	Accounting for research and development	
SSAP 17	Accounting for post balance sheet events	
SSAP 19	Accounting for investment properties	
SSAP 20	Foreign currency translation	
SSAP 21	Accounting for leases/HP contracts	
SSAP 25	Segmental reporting	

There are also **Exposure drafts** in operation. These describe proposed changes in UK financial reporting standards, for industry comment.

Finally, international accounting standards are being adopted. See Activity 13.2 below.

Activity 13.2

International accounting standards and the convergence project

In 2005, all countries in the European Union must adopt international accounting standards for the purpose of financial reporting. In the UK, it is planned that UK standards should, as far as possible, converge before this time. The adoption of international accounting standards, however, could have a major impact on some departments before this, if comparative figures have to be produced from 2005.

Note down the preparations, if any, that your section is making for the adoption of international accounting standards. Do you consider enough is being done?

Activity 13.3

Legislation of some kind is likely to have an impact on the work of your section. At what intervals or at what times of year do the following occur in your organisation? You should note down the specific dates wherever possible (for example 'quarterly VAT returns, due on 31 July, 31 October, 31 January and 30 April') but you will probably have to be general in some cases.

You may want to make a separate, more detailed list for your section if you work somewhere like payroll that has to report extensively to government bodies.

	Interval	*Date(s)*
End of financial year	________	________
Final audit	________	________
Interim audit(s)	________	________
Reporting to government bodies:		
• Companies House	________	________
• Inland Revenue	________	________
• DSS	________	________
• Customs and Excise (VAT returns)	________	________
• DTI	________	________
Other (specify)	________	________
	________	________
	________	________
	________	________

Activity 13.4

Other external parties may also have a significant impact on the work of your section. Conduct a similar exercise to task 13.3 for any of the following that apply. By 'reports' we simply mean any information that is supplied to somebody outside the organisation, whatever its format. Again if there are cases where you think it may be helpful to make a more detailed list for your section, by all means do so.

	Interval	*Date(s)*
Reports to banks/other lenders		
Information required by landlords		
Reports to the Stock Exchange		
Reports to insurance companies		
Reports to pensions administrators		
Reports to trade bodies, such as the Chamber of Commerce		
Reports to employees' groups such as trade unions and social clubs		
BS EN ISO 9000 (quality systems) compliance information		
Information exchanged with competitors		
Information required by major customers		
Information required by major suppliers		
Pressure group activities		
Other (specify)		

Activity 13.5

If any of the external parties that you have identified as having an impact on your work require information to be submitted in a prescribed format, it would be useful to include an example in your project file and a copy of (or extract from) their instructions as to how information should be set out.

Whether or not there is a prescribed format, an example of the information submitted would also be a useful addition to your file. You may have to bear in mind the need for confidentiality. A compromise would be to prepare an example with Xs in place of any figures and with names blocked out or disguised.

3 Other external regulations

Other government regulations affect the work of your department and section.

Activity 13.6

As far as you are aware what steps are taken to ensure your department complies with health and safety regulations? For example, there are government regulations on the use of VDU equipment

Activity 13.7

Does your organisation have an equal opportunities policy? Does your department implement this policy?

4 Internal regulations

Activity 13.8

If possible, obtain the current budget for your section and include it in your project file. The more detailed this is, the better, so if you can prepare a document that goes into more detail than the official budget, then do so. (For example there may only be a budget for the accounts department as a whole.) But remember to get permission to use it.

(a) If your section is to stay within budget, what is the maximum amount per month that can be spent on staff salaries? ____________________

(b) What does the sum identified in (a) represent in terms of number of staff? ____________________

(c) What does the sum identified in (a) represent in terms of normal hours worked? ____________________

(d) Wages and salaries is almost certain to be the largest item of expenditure for your section. What item of expenditure is the next largest? ____________________

Activity 13.9

(a) Make a note of any formal manuals issued by your organisation that affect the work of your department. Some examples are given below, but these things tend to have different names wherever you work.

	Name in your organisation	**Pages relevant to your section**
General conditions of work (eg hours, time off)		
Staff regulations (eg behaviour, dress)		
Procedures manual: dealing with the public		
Procedures: dealing with other departments		
Procedures: technical matters		
Procedures: detailed operational matters		
Other (specify)		

(b) If possible include copies of those parts of the above documents that are particularly relevant to your section's work in your project file. If the document in question is very lengthy you may have to be very choosy about what you do and do not copy: hence the page references in the table above.

Activity 13.10

Identify what you think are the most important regulations affecting operational matters in your section. Pick no more than five.

(a) In what way (if any) does each regulation chosen contribute to the achievement of the objective(s) of your section? (You should have identified the objective(s) in the previous session, as part of your mission statement.)

(b) Do the regulations chosen actually achieve their purpose? How are they enforced?

Activity 13.11

Make a list of reports that you, your staff, or your section as a whole are expected to prepare for your own use, for more senior managers and for people in other parts of the organisation, and the intervals at which these are required. A few examples are given, but this list should be specific to your section.

Example	Interval	Date(s)
Aged debtors listing	__________	__________
Stock levels	__________	__________
Variance reports	__________	__________
Timesheets	__________	__________
Reports produced by your section		
	__________	__________
	__________	__________
	__________	__________
	__________	__________
	__________	__________

Your project file should contain a copy of (or an extract from) each of these reports.

Activity 13.12

If you have completed all of the tasks above you should be in a position to draw up a fairly comprehensive planner for your section's year showing all the important deadlines and the extent to which your annual workload is dictated by the demands of others.

If you don't already have such a planner on the wall of your offices it would be a good idea to obtain one.

chapter 14

Operations and procedures in your section

Contents

1 Introduction

This chapter deals specifically with different sections of the accounts department. Obviously there is no **need** to perform the tasks on the purchases cycle if you work in a sales ledger section and so on. (On the other hand, if you think it might be useful to do them and you have access to the information there is no reason why you shouldn't do so.) You may find that none of the sections of this session fully covers the work of your part of the accounts department, in which case you may prefer to tackle tasks from several sections of this session, as appropriate.

(a) Throughout we suggest you use the control model identified earlier, as a handy checklist.
(b) You should also consider whether there is a risk of fraud.

Identifying a 'risk' arising out of weak internal controls does not mean that people are dishonest, but that the control environment is not strong enough. Go back to Chapter 9 to review the types of fraud that can be perpetrated.

2 Purchases cycle

Read the whole of this section on the purchases cycle before starting any of the tasks, because you might be able to do several different tasks at the same time.

Activity 14.1

Here is a typical purchases cycle. Fill in details for your organisation as appropriate.

	Who is involved?	How is this done?	When is this done?	Who authorises this?
1 The need to purchase an item is identified.				
2 This need is communicated to the person or department responsible for ordering goods.				
3 A supplier of the goods is identified				
4 The goods are ordered.				
5 The goods are received.				

	Who is involved?	How is this done?	When is this done?	Who authorises this?
6 The goods are checked before storage to make sure that the right quantity, type and quality of goods have been received.				
7 Any discrepancies between what was ordered and what is received (as identified in 6) are recorded.				
8 This information is communicated to whoever liaises with suppliers.				
9 The supplier is informed of any discrepancies and credit is claimed and/or a fresh order is placed.				
10 An invoice is received from the supplier.				
11 The invoice is checked against records of goods received to ensure that it is valid.				
12 The invoice is entered in the organisation's records.				
13 A statement is received from the supplier.				
14 The statement is agreed to your organisation's records.				
15 A decision is made as to how much to pay the supplier (for example paying all outstanding invoices or only those that have become due, according to the supplier's terms of trade).				

	Who is involved?	How is this done?	When is this done?	Who authorises this?
16 Payment is made.				
17 The payment is recorded in the organisation's records.				
Other steps specific to your organisation				
18				
19				
20				

Activity 14.2

You have probably found that the list in 14.1 above includes as separate items tasks that are done by the same person, or that the tasks are done in a different order, or that some are not done at all, or that there are extra tasks involved. Prepare a new list, based on the information you have recorded above, that is tailored to and properly describes the purchases cycle in your organisation.

Activity 14.3

Here is a list of documents and records that might typically be used in a purchasing section. Identify those that are used in your organisation, and obtain a copy of each if possible (you will probably have to photocopy a representative page or two of large records like ledgers). For multipart documents identify the number of copies (for example, a goods received note may consist of a white copy kept in the stores department and a green copy sent to accounts). This will help you with tasks 14.4 and 14.5.

Document checklist

Standard name		**Name in your organisation**	**Parts**
Purchase requisitions	☐	______	______
Purchase order forms	☐	______	______
Suppliers' price lists/catalogues	☐	______	______
Goods received notes	☐	______	______
Suppliers' delivery notes	☐	______	______
Goods inspection notes	☐	______	______
Goods returned notes	☐	______	______
Suppliers' invoices	☐	______	______
Suppliers' statements	☐	______	______
Suppliers' remittance advices	☐	______	______
Suppliers' credit notes	☐	______	______
Purchase day book	☐	______	______
Purchase ledger	☐	______	______
Nominal ledger	☐	______	______
Cheque requisitions	☐	______	______
Other documents and records	☐	______	______
	☐	______	______

Activity 14.4

Typical procedures in a purchasing section would include checking supplier's invoices against the details recorded on goods received notes and checking suppliers' statements against the details recorded in their accounts in the purchase ledger. Make notes detailing all the **checking procedures** that are carried out in your section.

Identify strengths and weaknesses on the list below.

Type of control	Strengths	Weaknesses
Segregation of duties		
Physical controls		
Authorisation and approval		
Management controls		
Supervision		
Organisation		
Arithmetical and accounting		
Personnel		

3 Sales cycle

Read the whole of this section on the sales cycle before starting any of the tasks, because you might be able to do several different tasks at the same time.

Activity 14.5

Here is a typical sales cycle. Fill in details for your organisation as appropriate.

	Who is involved?	How is this done?	When is this done?	Who authorises this?
1 A customer places an order				
2 This is passed to the person or department responsible for processing orders				

		Who is involved?	How is this done?	When is this done?	Who authorises this?
3	The order is checked to ensure that the goods are available				
4	The customer is checked to ensure that he/she is creditworthy, and entitled to any discount claimed				
5	The order is passed to the person or department responsible for delivering goods				
6	A despatch note is prepared and the goods are despatched				
7	An invoice is prepared and processed				
8	Claims for errors, short deliveries, or defects are received and checked				
9	Any discrepancies between what was ordered and what was despatched (as identified in 6) are recorded				
10	Credit notes are sent out if necessary				
11	Statements are prepared and despatched				
12	Payment is made and cash or cheques are banked				

	Who is involved?	How is this done?	When is this done?	Who authorises this?
13 Discounts taken are validated				
14 The payment is recorded in the organisation's records				
15 Overdue debts are pursued				
16 Bad debts are identified				
Other steps specific to your organisation				
17				
18				
19				
20				

Activity 14.6

You have probably found that the list in 14.5 above includes as separate items tasks that are done by the same person, or that the tasks are done in a different order, or that some are not done at all, or that there are extra tasks involved. Prepare a new list, based on the information you have recorded above, that is tailored to and properly describes the sales cycle in your section.

Activity 14.7

Here is a list of documents and records that might typically be used in a sales section. Identify those that are used in your organisation, and obtain a copy of each (you will probably have to photocopy a representative page or two of large records like ledgers). For multipart documents identify the number of copies (for example, an invoice may consist of a white copy sent to the customer, a yellow copy kept in accounts and a green copy sent to the despatch bay). This will help you with task 14.8.

Document checklist

Standard name		**Name in your organisation**	**Parts**
Sales order forms	☐		
Price lists/catalogues	☐		
Terms of trade notices	☐		
Despatch notes	☐		
Proof of delivery	☐		
Invoices	☐		
Credit notes	☐		
Statements	☐		
Remittance advices	☐		
Sales day book	☐		
Sales ledger	☐		
Nominal ledger	☐		
Cash received records	☐		
Other documents and records			
	☐		
	☐		
	☐		
	☐		

Activity 14.8

Typical procedures in a sales section would include checking despatch notes to ensure that all goods have been invoiced and checking payments received against the details recorded in customers' accounts in the sales ledger. Make notes detailing all the checking procedures that are carried out in your section. Think about SPAM SOAP and internal controls, as for purchases above.

Identify strengths and weaknesses on the list below.

Type of control	Strengths	Weaknesses
Segregation of duties		
Physical controls		
Authorisation and approval		
Management controls		
Supervision		
Organisation		
Arithmetical and accounting		
Personnel		

Do you consider that the control environment places the organisation at risk of fraud?

What improvements would you make?

4 Payroll cycle

Read the whole of this section on the payroll cycle before starting any of the tasks, because you might be able to do several different tasks at the same time.

Activity 14.9

Here is a typical payroll cycle. Fill in details for your organisation as appropriate.

	Who is involved?	How is this done?	When is this done?	Who authorises this?
1 Details to ensure the wages and salaries due to employees are collected (for example clock cards, personnel records)				
2 These are passed to the person or department responsible for processing payroll				
3 The details are checked to ensure completeness and identify unusual items like starters and leavers				
4 Unusual items are processed first (new employee records, new rates of pay, inputting overtime due, SSP, SMP and so on)				
5 Gross pay and deductions are calculated and entered into employee records				
6 Payslips are prepared for each employee				
7 A summary of total gross pay, PAYE, NICs and so on is prepared				
8 Arrangements are made for the payment of net pay (by cash or bank transfer)				
9 The figures are entered into the financial records				

	Who is involved?	How is this done?	When is this done?	Who authorises this?
10 Monthly returns are prepared for submission to government bodies				
11 Payments are made to the Inland Revenue, the DSS, and any other collectors of deductions				
12 Annual returns are submitted to the Inland Revenue				
Other steps specific to your organisation				
13				
14				
15				
16				

Activity 14.10

You have probably found that the list in 14.9 above includes as separate items tasks that are done by the same person, or that the tasks are done in a different order, or that some are not done at all, or that there are extra tasks involved. Prepare a new list, based on the information you have recorded above, that is tailored to and properly describes the payroll cycle in your section.

Activity 14.11

Here is a list of documents and records that might typically be used in a payroll section. Identify those that are used in your organisation, and obtain a copy of each (you will probably have to photocopy a representative page or two of large records like ledgers). For multipart documents identify the number of copies (for example, a payslip may consist of a white copy sent to the employee and a yellow copy kept in accounts). This will help you with task 14.12.

Document checklist

		Name in your organisation	**Parts**
Clock cards	☐	__________	____
Timesheets	☐	__________	____
Other attendance records	☐	__________	____
Piecework records	☐	__________	____
Sickness records	☐	__________	____
Holiday records	☐	__________	____
Lists of personnel	☐	__________	____
Lists of rates of pay	☐	__________	____
Personnel cards or files	☐	__________	____
Payslips	☐	__________	____
Note and coin analyses	☐	__________	____
Cheque requisitions	☐	__________	____
BACS documentation	☐	__________	____
Pension contribution records	☐	__________	____
SAYE records	☐	__________	____
Employee loan records	☐	__________	____
Payroll summary	☐	__________	____
Nominal ledger accounts	☐	__________	____
Inland revenue/DSS forms			____
All?	☐	__________	____
Selected forms only?	☐	__________	____
Other documents and records			
	☐	__________	____
	☐	__________	____
	☐	__________	____

Activity 14.12

Typical procedures in a payroll section would include checking that overtime is properly authorised, validating holiday pay entitlement, or reconciling payroll and costing records. Make notes detailing all the checking procedures that are carried out in your section.

Think about SPAM SOAP and internal controls as for purchases above.

Do you consider that the control environment places the organisation at risk of fraud?

Type of control	Strengths	Weaknesses
Segregation of duties		
Physical controls		
Authorisation and approval		
Management controls		
Supervision		
Organisation		
Arithmetical and accounting		
Personnel		

Do you consider that the control environment places the organisation at risk of fraud?

What improvements could you make?

5 Cash cycle

Read the whole of this section on the cash cycle before starting any of the tasks, because you might be able to do several different tasks at the same time.

Activity 14.13

Here is a typical cash cycle. Fill in details for your organisation as appropriate.

	Who is involved?	How is this done?	When is this done?	Who authorises this?
1 Requisitions for payments are received from other parts of the organisation				
2 If a cheque is required the cheque is made out. If cash is needed it is taken from the petty cash box				
3 Cheques are signed by the authorised signatories				
4 Cheques are sent to the payee				
5 Cash or cheques are received either directly or through the post				
6 Receipts are recorded on cash received sheets or in a cash diary				
7 The receipts are banked as soon as possible.				
8 Payments and receipts are entered into the cash book with appropriate analysis				
9 Postings are made to the ledgers.				
10 Bank reconciliations are performed at regular intervals				
11 Regular contact is maintained with the bank to check on the current balance				

	Who is involved?	How is this done?	When is this done?	Who authorises this?
12 Spare cash is placed on the money market				
13 Interest received is recorded				
Other steps specific to your organisation				
14				
15				
16				
17				
18				

Activity 14.14

You have probably found that the list in 4.13 above includes as separate items tasks that are done by the same person, or that the tasks are done in a different order, or that some are not done at all, or that there are extra tasks involved. Prepare a new list, based on the information you have recorded above, that is tailored to and properly describes the cash cycle in your section.

Activity 14.15

Here is a list of documents and records that might typically be used in a cash section. Identify those that are used in your organisation, and obtain a copy of each (you will probably have to photocopy a representative page or two of large records like ledgers). For multipart documents identify the number of copies (for example, a remittance advice may consist of a white copy for retention by the customer and a blue copy to be sent with the payment). This will help you with task 4.16.

Document checklist

Standard name		**Name in your organisation**	**Parts**
Cheque requisitions	☐		
Petty cash slips	☐		
Cheques	☐		
Credit card vouchers	☐		
Standing order mandates	☐		
Remittance advices	☐		
Paying-in slips	☐		
Bank statements	☐		
Credit card statements	☐		
Cash received sheets	☐		
Cash diary	☐		
Cash book	☐		
Petty cash book	☐		
Posting documents	☐		
List of nominal ledger codes	☐		
Ledgers	☐		
Other documents and records			
	☐		
	☐		
	☐		
	☐		

Activity 14.16

Typical procedures in a cash section include checking that cheque requisitions are properly authorised, checking that the paying-in book is properly stamped, or doing bank reconciliations. Make notes detailing all the checking procedures that are carried out in your section.

Think about SPAM SOAP and internal controls as for purchases above.

Identify the strengths and weaknesses on the list below.

Type of control	Strengths	Weaknesses
Segregation of duties		
Physical controls		
Authorisation and approval		
Management controls		
Supervision		
Organisation		
Arithmetical and accounting		
Personnel		

Do you consider that the control environment places the organisation at risk of fraud?

What improvements could you make?

6 Cost and management accounting sections

Read the whole of this section on cost and management accounting sections before starting any of the tasks, because you might be able to do several different tasks at the same time.

Activity 14.17

It is extremely difficult to set out a typical operating cycle for cost and management accounting work because it varies so much from organisation to organisation. Here we describe the operation of a traditional standard costing system, since research suggests that these are still fairly widespread. However, you may find it more appropriate to prepare your own, completely different, list, just using the column headings shown below.

	Who is involved?	How is this done?	When is this done?	Who authorises this?
1 Standards are set and targets issued, probably in the form of budgets				
2 Production takes place (or services are delivered) and information is collected about activities and usage of resources				
3 This information is coded up, analysed and costed				
4 Variances are calculated				
5 Statements of variances are drawn up				
6 The statements are scrutinised to distinguish significant and insignificant differences, identify trends				
7 Statements are sent to managers with comments as required				
8 Managers take corrective action, or perhaps provide further information to be used as a basis for modifying the standard				

	Who is involved?	How is this done?	When is this done?	Who authorises this?
Other steps specific to your organisation				
9				
10				
11				
12				

Activity 14.18

If you used the list in 14.17 above you probably found that it includes as separate items tasks that are done by the same person, or that the tasks are done in a different order, or that some are not done at all, or that there are extra tasks involved. Prepare a new list, based on the information you have recorded above, that is tailored to and properly describes the operations of your section.

Activity 14.19

Here are a few examples of documents and records that might typically be used in a cost and management accounting section. (Unlike other sections, in this case a full list would be almost endless, so we have left you plenty of blank space to fill in your own section's documents.) Identify those that are used in your organisation, and obtain a copy of each (you will probably have to photocopy a representative page or two of large records like ledgers). For multipart documents identify the number of copies (for example, a materials requisition may consist of a white copy kept in the stores department and a green copy sent to the purchasing department). This will help you with task 14.20.

Document checklist

Standard name		Name in your organisation	Parts
Unit cost card	☐		
Bill of materials	☐		
Explosion records	☐		
Materials requisition note	☐		
Materials returned note	☐		
Bin cards	☐		
Stores ledger cards	☐		
Time sheets/clock cards	☐		
Job cards	☐		
Variance reports	☐		
Budget statements	☐		
Other documents and records			
	☐		
	☐		
	☐		
	☐		
	☐		
	☐		
	☐		
	☐		
	☐		
	☐		
	☐		
	☐		
	☐		
	☐		

Activity 14.20

Typical procedures in a cost and management accounting section might include checking that the quantities of materials requisitioned is consistent with the quantities likely to have been used, or that standards are up to date, or that costs were properly coded and allocated. Make notes detailing all the checking procedures that are carried out in your section.

Think about SPAM SOAP and internal controls as for purchasing.

Identify the strengths and weaknesses on the list below.

Type of control	Strengths	Weaknesses
Segregation of duties		
Physical controls		
Authorisation and approval		
Management controls		
Supervision		
Organisation		
Arithmetical and accounting		
Personnel		

7 Your section overall

Activity 14.21

Note down the strengths, weaknesses, opportunities and threats raised by this chapter. Do you consider that the control environment places the organisation at **risk of fraud**? What improvements could you make? Grade them as high, medium or low in seriousness.

Strength	H/M/L	Weakness	H/M/L
Opportunity	H/M/L	Threat	H/M/L

Activity 14.22

Note down any risks – as described in earlier chapters – to which your department is subject.

Activity 14.23

How would you deal with the weaknesses and threats especially those of high importance?

chapter 15

Performance in your section

Contents

1 Introduction

This chapter concentrates on the **effectiveness** of the section, in contrast to Chapter 14 which dealt mainly with the control environment and fraud.

2 Targets and productivity

Activity 15.1

If your organisation measures the performance of your department how does it do so? A few suggestions are given below. Write out the targets that your section is currently expected to achieve for any that apply (or include any formal written notification of targets in your project file).

Costs ______________________________

Income ______________________________

Productivity ______________________________

Training ______________________________

Quicker cash collection ______________________________

Fewer complaints ______________________________

Others ______________________________

Activity 15.2

It should be possible to get a fairly accurate idea of the workload of your section. See if you can find out the answers to the questions below. This task concerns the last complete financial year in your organisation. The next task asks you to find out the same information for the current year to date, so you might find it more efficient to do both at the same time. Task 15.4 covers possible seasonal factors: again you might be able to do this at the same time, if it applies. We suggest that you read all three before getting started.

(a) How many documents were processed by your section in the last complete financial year? Find the answer for **each type** of document processed. Assuming there is a single sequence, a sales ledger section, for example, should be able to find the number of the first and last invoice issued during the year and subtract the one from the other. If absolute precision is difficult (for example, if you are not sure whether some documents were cancelled and reissued), don't worry too much about this: get as accurate a number as you can.

(b) What is the normal working week and hours for your section (eg five days, Monday to Friday, 9 to 5 with one hour for lunch (or 7 hours per day per person))?

(c) Including holidays, how many days were worked by your section in total in the last complete financial year (eg five people times five days times 52 weeks)?

(d) How many days holiday were taken (eg five people times 20 days plus five times public holidays)? Don't include weekends (or other non-working days in the normal week): you have already excluded these in (ii).

(e) How many hours overtime were worked by your section in the last complete financial year? Your colleagues in the payroll section should be able to help you out here.

(f) From your answers to questions (ii) to (v) you should be able to calculate how many **productive** hours were worked by your section in the last complete financial year, and split your answer between normal hours and overtime hours.

(g) With the information that you have collected here and elsewhere you should be able to provide a number of statistics about the workload of your department last year. Here is a suggested format: you will have to tailor it to your section's circumstances.

	Document type (give name)					
Documents processed	*A*	*B*	*C*	*D*	*E*	*Total*
In the year						
Per month (12 Months)						
Per week (52 weeks)						
Per productive hour						
Per employee						
Per type A employee						
Per type B employee (etc)						

Activity 15.3

(a) Make a note of any significant differences in your section's capacity now as compared with last year (for example, whether you now have one less person in your section).

(b) Choose a suitable cut-off point (for example the end of last month) and carry out the tasks in Task (a) for the year to date. Your monthly figures will of course divide the annual total to date by the number of months to date, not by 12, and so on.

Activity 15.4

If, as a result of completing Tasks 15.2 and 15.3, you have found that there are significant differences between your section's current productivity and its productivity last year, what are the reasons for this?

(a) One factor that may be distorting the current year's figures is seasonality. Perhaps you have not had your busy season yet this year. If so, this is a good opportunity to plan ahead. Talk to your own boss and see whether the general view is that your section will be busier this year than last or otherwise. What is the likely volume of transactions during this period, and on the evidence above, does your section have the resources (in terms of people and time) to cope?

(b) You may feel that the figures are unrepresentative because they suggest that your workload is evenly spread throughout the year, or that your section is fully staffed throughout the year, when these implications are not true. If so you could also collect information for, say, your busiest month and your quietest month for each year, and compare these figures.

Activity 15.5

In the above tasks we talk in general terms about 'processing' documents, because this is basically what all accounting sections do.

It may be possible for you to analyse the processing done in your section in more detail. Processing an order, say, may involve an average of three minutes on the telephone, two minutes checking details, one minute inputting data, and two minutes printing out and filing.

The best way to find out information like this is to get the staff who actually do the job to keep a note of the time they spend on each activity, but you need a reasonable size of sample (perhaps from several different team members) to make sure that you have representative data, and even then you are relying on your staff's accuracy.

If you think that it would be worthwhile to collect this sort of information you must handle it sensitively: your staff will probably feel that you are checking up on them. Don't forget, also, that it will take a bit of extra time for them to record the information for you, so make allowances for this.

Activity 15.6

Don't restrict your enquiries to transaction processing. You could also try to analyse your section's productivity in terms of report preparation (number prepared, time taken), phone calls made and answered, number of letters received and replied to, average time between receipt and reply, and so on. You should have some sort of performance measurement for all the major activities of your section that you have identified in earlier sessions.

3 Planning issues

Activity 15.7

(a) What plans determine the work of the section? ______________________________

(b) Is there a daily/weekly/Monday routine? ______________________________

(c) Do staff know when the busy periods are likely to be? ______________________________

(d) How are work plans communicated to staff? ______________________________

- Verbally, eg weekly meetings
- Wall chart
- E-mail instruction
- Spreadsheet schedules
- Microsoft Outlook calendar, Lotus notes etc

Activity 15.8

Have there been failures to communicate important planning information? What improvements would you make?

Activity 15.9

Common methods of scheduling and sequencing a number of tasks are as follows. Note down their use in your department.

Method	Description
Arrival time	This is the first come, first served basis that you encounter all the time, in the bank, or whenever you ring somebody, for example.
Least slack time	Slack time is the total amount of time left until the task is due to be done less the processing time needed to complete the task. (If something is due in two days and will take one day to complete, the slack time is one day). Tasks are prioritised in order of slack time available.
Most nearly finished	This is not very scientific, but it recognises that great frustration can be caused by interrupting a job just before it is completed.
Shortest queue at next operation	For example, seeing that the typist is about to run out of work, you draft some letters before making the lengthy series of phone calls you are due to make.

____

Method	Description
Highest priority	Priorities are dictated by external factors. You may drop everything else to get something done for your organisation's most important customer, for example
Least changeover cost	For example if someone is about to go on holiday, you get them to finish off all the things that it will be difficult for someone else to take over.
Shortest task first	Then next shortest, and so on. This is not very scientific, but it gets lots of things out of the way quickly.
Longest job first	Followed by next longest, and so on. Again, this is not very scientific, but it gets the most daunting task out of the way rather than letting it hang about becoming ever more daunting.

Which of these do you usually use? Do you use a method not mentioned above? Have you tried any of the other methods? It may be worthwhile to try a different approach if this causes problems in your section.

Method	Description	Use in department

Activity 15.10

Loading is a term used for deciding how work should be allocated to people or machines/ equipment. The way this is done depends upon three factors.

- The precise skills needed to do the job, or the capacity of the machine
- The other work already allocated to people with the appropriate skills or equipment with the appropriate features
- The demand for commonly used facilities

Identify the specific factors in your section affecting work allocation – specialist skills, bottlenecks and so on.

Activity 15.11

Do you find that some people get given more than their fair share of the work? Why is this? Is this because other people are not properly trained?

Can you suggest improvements to reduce your dependency on these people?

4 Skills requirements and training

Activity 15.12

(a) How do you identify the training needs of the department or section?
(b) Is there a mapping of the work that is needed to be done to the skills and qualifications that people have?
(c) What type of training records are kept?

Activity 15.13

Looking at the workload of the department, how dependent are you on the work of key individuals?

Activity 15.14

What steps have been taken to ensure that you are not deprived of key skills in case of staff sickness, for example? (You could include procedures manual, having a 'backup' person who knows what to do and so on.)

Activity 15.15

Training is also a form of development for skill. How are your staff's training needs identified? If there is no formal system, you might like to pick, say, one weak aspect of each member's current performance and suggest how this could be improved with training. But remember you need to have regard to confidentiality.

Name	Current ability	Job requirement	Training need

Activity 15.16

Does your organisation have a formal **appraisal** system for individual performance? If so this may affect your work in two ways: your performance will be appraised by your boss and you may appraise the performance of your staff.

(a) How often are appraisals held, and when was your own last appraisal?

(b) What was agreed at your last appraisal? In other words what are your strengths and weaknesses and what specific areas have been highlighted as needing improvement? If they are not confidential you may like to include copies of appraisal reports in your project file.

(c) Is your pay dependent upon the results of the appraisal?

(d) On the basis of formal appraisals of the work of your staff, pick out one aspect of their work that they have agreed to try to improve and enter it below.

(e) Are appraisals followed up by training?

Name	Area for improvement

Activity 15.17

(a) What sort of **training** is provided for your section's staff? Fill in the table below. If your organisation produces booklets, leaflets or information sheets about the availability and nature of training you may wish to include these in your project file.

Type of training	Frequency	Brief details (eg who provides training, technical content)
Internal courses		
External courses		
On the job training		

(b) If you think that no training at all is available within your organisation, how do you and your staff find out about changes such as the following?

- New legislation that affects your work
- New accounting standards affecting your work
- Developments in your organisation's technology
- New procedures and policies

How do new staff find out about such matters as:

- The range of products and services the organisation offers
- The degree of formality that is adopted in dealing with superiors?

You may be taking too narrow a view of what constitutes 'training'. The vast majority of training in organisations is that provided or obtained informally: passing on experience by demonstration, good example or word of mouth, reading leaflets published by government departments, and so on.

5 Managing the team

Activity 15.18

Review Chapter 3 and then consider these questions.

(a) Describe your leadership style in terms of the Ashridge studies (tells, sells, consults, joins).
(b) Would you describe yourself as a task-centred manager or a people-centred manager?

Activity 15.19

Now ask a key colleague or a trusted member of your team to answer the question in 15.18 above. You are looking here for constructive feedback.

Activity 15.20

Have you encountered any problems in managing your section? Have you tried to diagnose the cause?

Activity 15.21

Chapter 3 of this Text discusses team work and the roles team members play.

Can you analyse your team in terms of team roles? Remember that some people may play more than one role. Don't automatically cast yourself in the role of Chairman just because you have seniority over the others.

Role	Description	Person(s) in your team
Chairman	Presides and co-ordinates; balanced, disciplined, good at working through others	
Shaper	Passionate about the task itself, a spur to action	
Plant	Intellectually dominant and imaginative; source of ideas and proposals	
Monitor-evaluator	Analytically (rather than creatively) intelligent; dissects ideas, spots flaws	
Resource-investigator	Popular, sociable, extrovert, relaxed source of new contacts	
Implementer	Practical organiser, turning ideas into tasks, scheduling, planning. Trustworthy and efficient; not a leader, but an administrator	
Team worker	Most concerned with team maintenance: supportive, understanding, diplomatic; contribution noticed only in absence	
Finisher	Chivvies the team to meet deadlines, attend to details; urgency and follow-through important, though not always popular	
Specialist	Joins the group to offer expert advice when needed	

Activity 15.22

Here are the characteristics of an effective work group. How many ticks can you give to your team?

Rate your teams effectiveness as high, medium or low.

	H	*M*	*L*
Low rate of labour turnover			
Low accident rate			
Low absenteeism			
High output and productivity			
Good quality of output			
Individual targets are achieved			
There are few stoppages and interruptions to work			
There is a high commitment to the achievement of targets and organisational goals			
There is a clear understanding of the group's work			
There is a clear understanding of the role of each person within the group			
There is trust between members and communication is free and open			
There is idea sharing			
The group is good at generating new ideas			
Group members try to help each other			
There is group problem solving which gets to the root causes of the work problem			
There is an active interest in work decisions			
Group members seek a united consensus of opinion			
The members of the group want to develop their abilities in their work			
The group is sufficiently motivated to be able to carry on working in the absence of its leader			

Activity 15.23

What does your team see as the major problems facing your section? You may be able to have a meeting and ask them what difficulties they expect to have to cope with, both on a day to day basis and over the longer term. You could encourage all those present to consider issues from one point of view at a time. For example, you could spend five minutes in which **everybody** discussed a problem purely from the point of view of the organisation, then five minutes discussing it from the point of view of how they personally felt about it, five minutes discussing the benefits of a proposed solution, five minutes discussing the risks, and so on. If the team members can focus their contributions to the discussion in this way a great deal of time can be saved.

6 Audit

Activity 15.24

(a) Is your organisation subject to an annual audit? If so it is possible that your section was commented upon in the external auditor's management letter, which points out areas of the business in which controls are weak and improvements can be made. Discuss this with your boss and try to get permission to include the external auditor's comments about your section in your project file.

(b) What efforts have been made to implement the external auditor's recommendations?

Activity 15.25

(a) Is an internal audit carried out on the work of your section (either regularly or as a one-off exercise in the fairly recent past)? If so, obtain a copy of any internal audit report and include it in your project file.

(b) What efforts have been made to implement the internal auditor's recommendations?

7 Quality standards

Activity 15.26

What do other parts of your organisation that you deal with think of the service you provide? You could devise a questionnaire to send to your main 'customers'. The payroll department, for example, could include a questionnaire like the one shown on the next page, in pay packets.

Activity 15.27

Do you and do all of your staff understand the internal customer concept? We asked this question earlier. Do you now have answers for the following questions?

(a) Assuming no difference in the costs, could your section's work be done by, say, an outside firm of accountants?

(b) Assuming they had the resources, could other departments or sections do your section's work? (For example, could the personnel department handle payroll, or the marketing department handle bad debts, and so on?)

(c) Do you think employees would rather take up pay queries with the personnel department or the accounts department?

(d) Do you think a production department would be more inclined or less inclined to take note of and make use of cost information that it generated for itself?

ABC LIMITED

Payroll Department

In keeping with the company's commitment to Total Quality we should like to know whether we are offering the type and standard of service that you require. Please take a few moments to complete and return this short questionnaire, so that we know where we are doing well and where there is room for improvement. We shall make every effort to meet your needs – if you will tell us what they are!

PART A – ALL EMPLOYEES

Please circle one number only
1= 'poor'; 5 = 'excellent'

1 How do you rank the payslips you receive from us?

Supplied on time?	1	2	3	4	5
Accuracy of information?	1	2	3	4	5
Ease of understanding?	1	2	3	4	5

2 Is there any other information that you would like to see appearing on your payslip? Please specify, if so.

3 How do you rank the pensions information we provide?

Supplied when needed?	1	2	3	4	5
Accuracy of information?	1	2	3	4	5
Ease of understanding?	1	2	3	4	5

4 Is there any other information that you would like to receive regularly about the company pension plan? Please specify.

5 How do you rank the payroll department in terms of dealing with your queries?

Courtesy (face to face)?	1	2	3	4	5
Telephone manner?	1	2	3	4	5
Written answers to queries?	1	2	3	4	5
Income tax/national insurance queries	1	2	3	4	5
Sick pay queries	1	2	3	4	5
Maternity pay queries	1	2	3	4	5
Pensions queries	1	2	3	4	5

6 Have you any other reason to be dissatisfied with the service provided by the payroll department? Please specify.

PART B – MANAGERS AND SUPERVISORS

7 If you are a manager or supervisor, have you ever requested information from the payroll department to help in the management of your department? Yes ☐ No ☐

8 If you have requested management information, were you satisfied with the information you received? Yes ☐ No ☐
If not, please explain why.

9 If you have not requested management information, did you know that we can readily supply and/or analyse information about such matters as rates of pay, departmental wages and salary costs, hours worked, overtime hours and costs? Yes ☐ No ☐

10 Is there any particular information that you would like to receive regularly from the payroll department? Please specify, or contact us direct.

There is no need to complete this section Name and employee number
if you would prefer not to do so Department

Thank you for taking the time to complete this questionnaire. Please return it via internal mail to:
Rachana Davidson, Payroll Department Supervisor, Room 101

(e) Do you sometimes wish that you didn't have to deal with a certain department (or a certain person within it) and that you could go elsewhere to get what you need? Do you think anybody feels this way about you and your section?

(f) Do you sometimes bypass formal channels at work and get information from those who properly understand why you want it and when you need it?

(g) Can you name one **unique** skill or piece of expertise that your section possesses?

As we have said, the point of these questions is to make sure that you realise that the different parts of an organisation are each others' customers. If your section's customers are unhappy with the service they receive then they may well be able to go elsewhere.

What have you done since first reading this task to make your customers happy?

8 Contingencies

Activity 15.28

(a) Have any of the following affected your section in the recent past? Write details alongside any ticks you make.

Computer problems

Damage due to fire, floods or explosions	☐
Computer viruses	☐
Software bugs	☐
Technical faults in the computer hardware	☐
Damage to telecommunications links	☐
Damage caused by unauthorised users	☐
Other (specify)	☐

Procedural difficulties

Data input errors	☐
Processing errors	☐
Other errors, due to uncertainty about treatment, or about how the system works	☐
Other (specify)	☐

Staff problems

Insufficient staff, due to sickness, maternity leave and so on	☐
The departure or temporary absence of key personnel	☐
Other (specify)	☐

Sudden changes in operating conditions

A sudden increase in transactions ☐

The bankruptcy of a major supplier or customer ☐

Radical cost-cutting measures ☐

A new senior management ☐

New accounting standards ☐

Large currency fluctuations or interest rate changes ☐

Political or social problems like riots or terrorist bombs, or public transport strikes ☐

Other (specify) ☐

Fraud

Stealing petty cash ☐

Payroll frauds ☐

Misappropriating cash receipts from customers ☐

Making payments to fictional suppliers ☐

Stealing of fixed assets ☐

Other (specify) ☐

(b) This is not an exhaustive list, just one to set you thinking about the sort of problems that can occur. If your section has dealt with some other kind of crisis or made some other kind of spectacular error in the recent past, be sure to note it down!

Activity 15.29

Did formal **contingency plans** exist for dealing with any of the incidents that you have identified above? Include a copy in your project file if the answer is yes.

Note that they may not be called contingency plans in your organisation: they may simply be paragraphs in the procedures manual.

Activity 15.30

In the course of your work for Unit 10, or otherwise, have you identified any risks for which no formal plan exists but which you feel should be prepared for in advance?

If so, draw up your own emergency plan and recovery plan, and get it approved by your manager. These are the matters that you should consider:

(a) Who will be in charge during the crisis and who will be responsible for doing what?

(b) What priorities should be given to tasks?

(c) What information needs to be available during and after the crisis? This should be gathered in advance.

(d) Whether all staff involved are aware of the potential problem and what they are supposed to do if it occurs. Effectively this means making sure that they have read the contingency plan, or have their own personalised instructions.

(e) Whether staff have been encouraged to be open about mistakes.

(f) Whether the plan works in practice.

Activity 15.31

The good thing about making mistakes and having problems to tackle is that you *learn* from the experience. What you learn is something that you are expected to describe in your report. You are also expected to be able to 'analyse the competences you display in dealing with critical incidents'.

Thus, for example, if a new recruit in your section had made a mess of a piece of work because he or she had been thrown in at the deep end, the lesson that you would have learnt would be that staff need to be adequately trained to perform their duties.

For any major incident that you have identified, set down the lessons that you and your section learned from it, and explain what competences you displayed in dealing with it.

Activity 15.32

All of the tasks in this section are continuing. There may be a critical incident just around the corner! Remember to keep notes of how you cope and what you learn.

9 Change

Activity 15.33

Make a list of **any** changes that have affected the work of your section in the recent past, or that are about to hit you (somebody leaving or joining, a new piece of equipment, **anything**).

Activity 15.34

(a) How did you, or how will you, help people in your section to cope with the changes noted in Activity 15.33?

(b) Have **attitudes** changed in keeping with the change in circumstances?

Activity 15.35

(a) How would you go about implementing a proposed change?
(b) Whose support would you need most of all?

Activity 15.36

Summarise strengths and weaknesses in the chapter so far.

	Strengths	*Weaknesses*
Workload		
Planning		
Skills and training		
Managing		
Audit		
Quality		
Contingencies		

What improvements could you make?

(For example, if you found there existed no contingency plan for staff absence, an improvement could be to prepare one.)

chapter 16

Writing your report

Contents

1 Introduction

This chapter is designed to show you how you can produce a good report so that you can:

- Clearly communicate work methods and schedules to all individuals in a way which assists their understanding
- Make recommendations to the appropriate people in a clear, easily-understood format
- Support your recommendations with clear explanations of any assumptions made

Fundamentals

Your research turns up raw materials. Writing and rewriting turns them into finished, usable products.

For the writing to proceed efficiently, a **logical structure** for the report is needed. When you begin writing-up you might want to consider the following points:

(a) Is the **purpose** of the report clearly defined from the outset?

(b) **Who** or what is the **target** of your report? The intended target of the report can influence the way data is handled or the recommendations made.

(c) Is there a wider **audience** for the report? The likely audience could influence the style in which the report needs to be written (for example use of technical jargon, diagrammatic presentation of information). Your report may well be a useful document for junior staff in your section, especially those new to the job.

(d) Are any **recommendations** made likely to be considered for action by the targeted audience? The answer to this is almost certainly 'yes', given that your manager at work, who will be expected to testify to the validity and usefulness of your project, is part of the targeted audience.

2 Structure and content of your report

You have to produce a formal report which should follow a coherent structure. We suggest a structure for you below: this is based on a proposed structure on AAT's website, but you need to be flexible.

Section of report	Comment
Covering page	Detailing how your report fulfils the Unit requirements and signed off by your employer and your assessor. • Include the sheet from your Student Record to indicate how the Performance Criteria have been covered • Ask your employer to sign off the report as being **your own work** and that the project reflects the actual processes in the company
Title and your name	• Title [of project not Unit 10!) • Submitted by [Your name] • AAT student membership number • Wording such as 'This report is submitted for assessment of competence in Unit 10 of the AAT Technician stage, Managing Systems and People in an Accounting Environment'.
Contents	This should indicate the sections of the report. Write this last.
Terms of reference	'What have I been asked to do?' Here you write the scope and purpose (objectives) of the report: what you have covered, what has not been covered.
Methodology	'How have I gone about it?' This will explain how your planned and prepared the report: the steps taken to make an investigation, collect data, put events in motion. Telephone calls or visits made, documents or computer files consulted, computations or analyses made and so on should be briefly described, with the names of other people involved.
Acknowledgements	People who have helped you in the process. This may also be included under the 'methodology' section.
Executive summary	This should give a brief summary of the findings and recommendations of the report. You will probably write this section last so that you can draw out the key points you have made in the body of the report.
Main content: Introductory background	A background description of the organisation. This can include: • What the organisation does • How long it has existed • Significant changes (eg getting a stock market listing, achieving Trust or Foundation status, in the case of NHS hospitals) • Major stakeholders • Location • Structure
Main content: the accounting function	You should describe the accounting function. • **People**. How many? • **Key staff**. Who are they? What do they do? What are they responsible for? • What is your position and **your role**? • You could include an organisation chart in the Appendix. • What is the relationship with other departments.

Section of report	Comment
Main content: evaluating the accounting function	An analysis of strengths, weaknesses, opportunities and threats (SWOT). As well as describing an area, you can identify it as a strength or weakness, which shows you understand its importance. You can cover issues such as: • Training • Work planning and other office processes • Risk: are risks identified, graded as high/medium/low? • Contingency plans (computer breakdown, staff absence) • Referral of issues to the right people • Software and technology • Staffing levels • Buying decisions and authorisation • Motivation • Controls • How errors are dealt with Show **what** was wrong, **how** it was identified and **how** resolved.
Recommendations including implementation issues and cost/benefit analysis	Strong, well-founded proposals for change will reflect a successful project and an impressive report. Avoid non-committal recommendations and try to present recommendations in a logical order, for example presenting recommendations for the short, medium and long term in sequence. For each recommendation state: • **What** is recommended • **Who** needs to act on the recommendation • **Cross-references** to the points in the report leading to the recommendation In addition, do a **cost/benefit analysis**: how much would it cost for each recommendation, eg new staff members, training, new equipment?
Fraud	Unless this is covered earlier, ensure that existing systems to prevent fraud are evaluated.
Conclusion	You could describe what has actually happened as a result of the changes.
WORD COUNT	
Appendices: these do not form part of the word count	To be included here are copies of any important supporting documentation. It may be necessary to include in an appendix any body of material that is too large or detailed for the findings section (for example computer analyses on meeting minutes). Your appendices are not included in your total word count. Typical appendices are: • Memos to management • Testimonials from employers related to specific performance criteria • Organisation charts • Minutes of meetings • Samples of documentation or spreadsheets

3 Planning your work

3.1 Structure your ideas

The advantage of having a clear structure is that your ideas and material are forced into some sort of order. If there is a great deal you want to say then order is essential, and a good way of achieving it is to produce a **report plan** at an early stage.

The best approach is to jot down all the things you want to say as a series of headings, with perhaps a little expansion of some points. Then look at them together and, by experiment if necessary, put them into a logical order by putting numbers against each. Only if you are very certain that your thoughts are logical and coherent should you omit putting them on paper as a plan – apart from any other reason, you are likely to forget vital material if you do not have a plan.

You might try writing 'network' notes to present your headings visually (see the diagram).

A network note

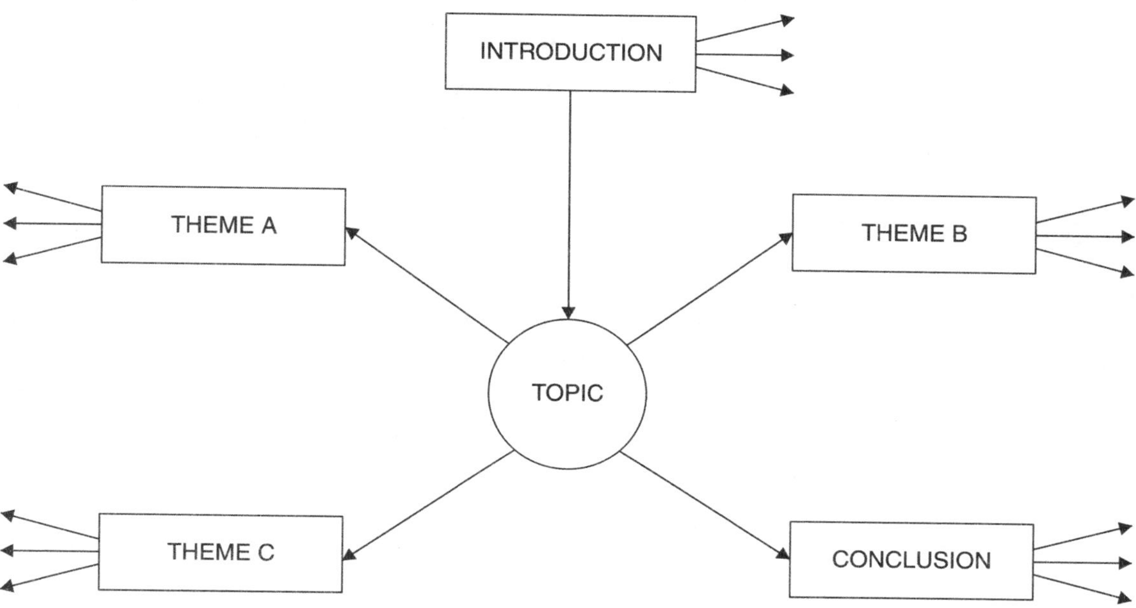

3.2 Key questions

	Comments
What is relevant to the user's requirements?	Some of the information you have collected or produced by analysis will go in the main body of the report. Other information will be included as appendices.
What is the information for?	Explanation, description? recommendation? instruction?
Do I need to follow a line of reasoning?	If so, what is the most logical way in which data can be broken down, grouped, and organised, to make my reasoning clear?
Do I need to include my own personal views?	If so, at what point: final recommendation, or throughout? What form should these take: recommendations or suggestions? interpretation? opinion? appraisal of options?
What can I do to make the report easier to read?	• Are there suitable section or sub-headings I can use to indicate effectively each stage of the information or argument? • Is the subject of the report too technical for the user? What vocabulary should I use to assist understanding? Will background or supporting information be helpful, perhaps in appendices to the report? • Do I have a clear introduction to ease the reader in to the subject, and a clear conclusion that will draw everything together?

3.3 Draft version

Once you have assembled your material and established your plan, it is time to write the report itself along the lines of the plan. Many people suffer from writer's block at this point and simply cannot get started, writing paragraph after paragraph of introduction and throwing each away. If you have this problem, try starting on the main body first, then go back to the introduction and end with the conclusion. Keep checking back to the Performance Criteria and fill in any gaps.

Here is some further advice from the AAT:

- Start early!
- Use diagrams and charts where you can
- Talk to other students about progress, and show your drafts to your tutor so that you can make sure that you are on the right lines
- Concentrate on the report's objectives, and cut out anything which is superfluous

4 Practical issues

4.1 Can I get help from other AAT students?

The report must be your own work. In other words, you must write (or, preferably, word process!) the report yourself.

However, you can **discuss** the reports with the other students in your group.

4.2 I'm using the AAT's simulation

Your centre will give you a copy of the AAT's simulation. You can take it home with you. It is not an 'exam' as such, but data for a project.

5 Layout and presentation

5.1 Organisation

The key is organisation: into sentences, into paragraphs, into chapters, into parts. A poorly organised report will be hard to read and it will be difficult for the reader to extract the value of the research you have done.

5.2 Layout

Various display techniques may be used to make the content of a report easy to identify and digest. For example, the relative importance of points should be signalled, each point may be referenced, and the body of text should be broken up to be easy on the eye. These aims may be achieved as follows:

Headings

S p a c e d o u t or **emboldened** CAPITALS may be used for the main title and for important headings, like sections of the report.

Underlining, *italics* or **bold** may be used for subheadings.

References

Each section or point in a formal report should have a code for easy identification and reference.

Use different
labelling for each type
of heading

Main section headings

I,II,III,IV,V and so on or A,B,C,D,E

Paragraphs

1,2,3,4,5

Points and subpoints

(a), (b), (c) and (i), (ii), (iii)

Alternatively a 'decimal' system may be used:

- 1 Section 1
- 1.1 Subsection 1
- 1.1.1 Point 1
- 1.1.2 Point 2
- 1.2 Subsection 2
- 1.2.1 Point 1
- 2 Section 2

Spacing

Intelligent use of spacing separates headings from the body of the text for easy scanning, and also makes a large block more attractive and digestible.

Consistency

When you have chosen your style of headings, references and so on, apply it consistently in your report.

5.3 Word processing

Your college may have some particular guidelines, but it is recommended that you use a word processor. It will be laborious and time consuming to hand write 4,000 words and maintain a consistent standard of neatness and layout.

If you have access to word-processing software and can use it effectively, by all means do so. Your college may be able to devise a standard template for things like cover pages, contents pages, page layout and so on: this could be used by all your fellow students and would save a lot of time. Remember to start each section on a new page.

Make sure that the final version is spell-checked by the computer. Some packages also have a grammar check, which you may find useful. However, you cannot **rely on** spell-checking software. (You still need to read the material for sense.)

As already mentioned, you may need to include graphs, charts or other diagrams where relevant. Be very neat when drawing them (they should be clearly labelled) and make sure you include all the visual material to which you refer. Spreadsheet software might be used for presenting tabular information, and most modern packages also have fairly sophisticated graphic capabilities.

5.4 Accuracy and unity

Accuracy is probably the most important requirement of any research project – not just in terms of the honest presentation of data, but also in giving the correct emphasis to the main themes – in order that an objective and useful report results.

Keeping within the terms of reference and only addressing the central issue at hand will **enhance the unity** of the report. Leave out material that is not really relevant and avoid discussions of marginal issues.

6 Style and language

There are certain stylistic requirements in the writing of reports, formal or informal.

6.1 Objectivity and impersonality

Even in a report designed to persuade as well as inform, subjective value judgements and emotions should be kept out as far as possible: the bias, if recognised, can undermine the credibility of the report and its recommendations.

(a) Emotional or otherwise loaded words should be avoided.

(b) In more formal reports, **impersonal constructions** should be used rather than 'I', 'we' and so on:

It became clear that...
Investigation revealed that...

(c) Colloquialisms and abbreviated forms should be avoided in formal written English: colloquial 'I've', 'don't' should be replaced by 'I have' and 'do not'. You should not use slang expressions like 'got cheesed off': say 'was irritated'.

6.2 Ease of understanding

(a) Avoid technical language and complex sentence structures for non-technical users.

(b) The material will have to be logically organised, especially if it is leading up to a conclusion or recommendation.

(c) Relevant themes should be signalled by appropriate headings, or highlighted for easy scanning.

(d) The layout of the report should display data clearly and attractively. Figures and diagrams should be used with discretion, and it might be helpful to highlight key figures which appear within large tables of numbers.

6.3 Precision

(a) Be as precise as possible and avoid vague generalisations. Note the important differences between 'a few', 'some', 'many' and 'most'.

(b) Recommendations should be specific and firm. 'I feel more could be done...' is too vague to be helpful. Say precisely what should be done: 'customers should receive a verbal explanation in layman's terms...'.

6.4 Good, clear English

The reason for having good, clear English is that is avoids ambiguity. That is the reason for what might appear to be 'petty' issues of house style. (**BPP note**. BPP publishes *Basic Maths and English for AAT students*: see order form at the back of this Text.)

7 Drafting and completing

7.1 Draft

Work on a draft first of all so as to produce a finished report. The draft will have given you confidence and shown you, perhaps, any flaws in your argument. The break will have allowed your brain to sort things out into a better order and more fluent style. All new ideas should be noted on the draft copy before you start afresh to write the final version.

Suppose you prepare an early draft of your report and find that you have already written far too much?

Our experience in preparing draft sample reports suggests that although it sounds like a lot, you may find the limit of 4,000 words rather restrictive. If you have this problem, and it is not simply because you have included large amounts of waffle (ask your tutor), we suggest that you allow original documents to speak for themselves wherever possible. Don't, for example, give a detailed description of the duties and career history of each member of your section if you have been able to collect original job descriptions and so forth which give the same information. You are entitled to expect your reader to read the information you have gone to the trouble to collect. If you need to refer to the detailed duties of individuals you should direct your reader, at the beginning of your discussion, to the relevant appendix in your report where full job descriptions will be found.

An advantage of using word processors is that they can do a rough word count.

7.2 Completing your project: a checklist

You will then write a final report.

A well-presented, professionally produced report attracts more positive attention than a scruffy set of papers. Also remember that the finishing touches – such as, proofing – nearly always take longer than you would expect.

Here are some things to keep in mind when your report has been written. Make sure that:

- It covers all Performance Criteria, Range Statements and Knowledge and Understanding
- The report is in the format of a report to management
- All of the stated objectives are covered
- The report is well laid out and easy to read, with a clear progression and reasoned analysis
- All appendices are cross referenced the body of the report
- Cross references to the Performance Criteria are included
- The diagrams and charts are appropriate
- The methodology is fully explained
- You have addressed the needs of the business (not your personal views)
- Spelling and grammar has been checked

8 Assessor questioning

8.1 What if I have not covered all the performance criteria?

You will be expected to go to an assessor interview. The assessor will ask questions covering the performance criteria that are not part of your report.

8.2 What if changes I recommend have not been implemented?

Your assessor will devote questions to the potential impact your recommendations might have had, if they were implemented. You might also want to consider the barriers to implementation.

chapter 17

Sample report

Contents

1 Your task

On the following pages you will find a **draft report** on an organisation's accounting system and the way its supervisor is managing it.

(a) Your first task is to read the report.

(b) Note down any points that you think should be made to its writer.

(c) Review them according to the Performance Criteria.

(d) We have only included the supporting documentation if it would be difficult for you to understand the report without it. Make a list of what other backing documentation you would find helpful.

This report is based on a real company, some details have been altered. All of the names and figures have also been changed to preserve confidentiality.

This report is not perfect. You are expected to review it critically and suggest improvements to format and content.

2 Sample report

REPORT INTO THE ACCOUNTING SYSTEM OF EATON MOTORS LIMITED

CONTENTS

REPORT

APPENDICES

1 Executive summary

(BPP note. This remains to be completed.)

2 Terms of reference

Investigate the accounting system and develop recommendations with a view to reducing the external cost of accounting and audit work, by demonstrating sound internal controls.

3 Business activities and commercial environment

3.1 Business activities

Eaton Motors Limited is a small family company established nearly 70 years ago by the present owners' father.

The company is in the motor trade, operating the largest General Motors dealership in the local area. Its main commercial activities are as follows.

(a) Selling fleets of new vehicles to local businesses
(b) Selling new vehicles to private buyers
(c) Dealing in second-hand vehicles
(d) Vehicle leasing and rental
(d) Selling parts for General Motors vehicles
(e) Servicing vehicles and bodywork

The company owns land adjacent to its main site and receives rental income from the petrol station located there. It also receives rental income from two cottages near to the main site and from a small hotel in Brighton.

Major bodywork repairs are conducted on a separate site, several miles from the main premises. About half of the company's new vehicle stocks are also kept on this site. So too are the parts needed for servicing vehicles not manufactured by General Motors.

3.2 Commercial environment

Shareholders

The company is owned by the Eaton family. Only Anthony Eaton, who owns a 50% share, is actively engaged in the running of the business: he is the Managing Director. The remaining shares are divided equally between his two sisters.

Other financial stakeholders

General Motors finance the company's unsold vehicle stocks and take an active interest in the running of the business as a condition for retaining the dealership. They also provide the software and hardware for all of the company's computer systems, including its main accounting systems

The company also has a (relatively small) overdraft facility with one of the high street banks for day-to-day working capital.

Suppliers

General Motors is, of course, the main supplier of vehicles and vehicle parts. The company also has reciprocal arrangements with other local dealerships for the supply of urgently needed GM parts and of parts needed for servicing vehicles not manufactured by General Motors.

Customers

The company supplies fleet vehicles to a number of local businesses. However none of these can be said to be a major customer. Most of the company's sales are to private individuals.

Competitors

As noted above, Eaton Motors is the largest GM dealership within a radius of about 20 miles. However, there are 3 smaller dealerships in the area and price competition in aspects of the business which are not dictated centrally by GM (principally services and body repairs) is fierce.

4 Organisation structure and size

4.1 Structure

The organisation structure is essentially product-based, as shown in the summary diagram below. A more detailed organisation chart is included as Appendix 1

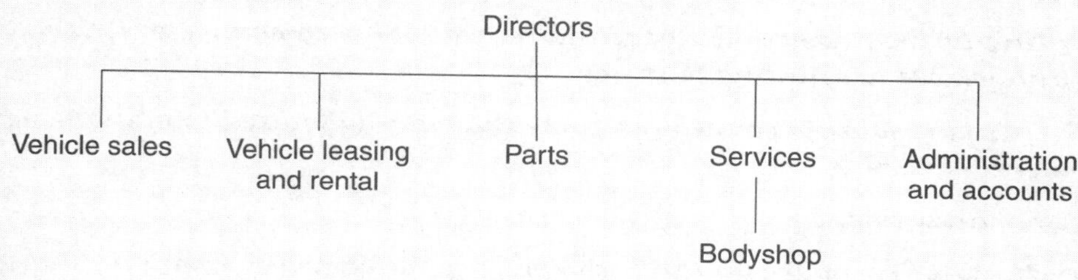

4.2 Number of employees

The company employs approximately 40 people (the numbers vary around this figure due to a fairly high turnover of junior mechanics).

4.3 Turnover

The annual turnover of the company in the year ended 31 December 2003 was around £15 million. The figure represents average sales of around 3 new vehicles per day plus a large volume of transactions in parts and services. Services is the most profitable area of the business. Further details of volume of transactions are given later in this report.

5 The accounting function

5.1 Structure

The accounting function of Eaton Motors Limited is staffed by seven people, divided into two sections. The larger section, called simply 'Accounts' within the organisation, consists of five people including as its supervisor the writer of this report. The 'Administration' section handles payroll and the fixed asset register as well as general office and business administration and personnel matters.

The structure is as shown in the diagram below.

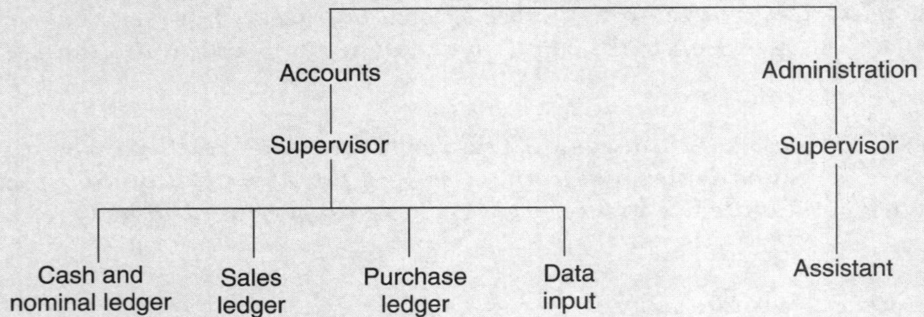

5.2 Role

The main tasks of the accounts section are as follows.

(a) Writing up the financial ledgers and records of the company, for financial and management accounting purposes

(b) Preparing regular accounting reports which are submitted to management and to General Motors

(c) Cash management

The company retains a firm of accountants who prepare the company's annual financial statements. This firm also acts as the company's auditors.

5.3 Relationship with other departments

The accounts section processes information received from all other parts of the organisation. It reports to the Managing Director on a regular basis, and is directly responsible to him. It also reports to departmental managers as required.

(a) Invoicing is done at the point of sale by the various product or service-based functions, but the sales ledger is maintained by the accounts section. Debt collection, where necessary, is a shared responsibility, depending upon the sensitivity of the debt in question.

(b) The bulk of the organisation's purchasing is done by the Parts department, although the Administration section is responsible for acquiring general supplies. The accounts section maintains the purchase ledger.

(c) Cash collection is mainly at point of sale. The post is opened by the vehicle showroom receptionist with a member of the accounts section in attendance.

5.4 Staff and responsibilities in the accounts section

Job descriptions for all members of the accounts section are included at Appendix 2. In outline the main responsibilities are divided as follows.

	Comment
Supervisor *Planning and scheduling* *Overseeing the day to day work of the section* *Scrutiny of daily and monthly transactions listings* *Nominal ledger review and journals* *Preparing reports for management* *Liaison with the bank/treasury management* *Liaison with the auditors* *Computer back-up procedures*	*I was appointed to the post of supervisor of the accounts section in November 2003, having previously worked as assistant supervisor of an accounts department of another company. I am aged 24 and am at the final stage of my studies to become an accounting technician.*
Cashier *Maintaining the manual cash books and petty cash books* *Bank reconciliations* *Sales ledger assistant* *Matching cash and debtors* *Coding up records of cash received for posting*	*Doris, the cashier, is aged 59 and has worked for the company for many years. She has a great deal of experience, but no formal accounting qualifications. She now works only three days a week, from Tuesday to Thursday.*
Sales ledger assessment *Maintaining sales ledger* *Liaison with sales departments on slow payers* *Issuing statements*	*Brenda, the sales ledger assistant is aged 45. She joined the company about two years ago, as her first job on returning to work after bringing up her family.*
Purchase ledger assistant *Maintaining purchase day book* *Coding and filing of invoices received* *Checking suppliers' statements* *Maintaining purchase ledger*	*Julia, the purchase ledger assistant is aged 34. She works part-time, from 10 till 3 each day, because she has a family of young children. She has recently returned from maternity leave. A temporary staff member, James, was hired to cover for her during her absence. He was with the firm for 6 months, during which time he took responsibility for all her roles. She formerly worked full-time on the sales desk of the Parts and Services department.*
Data input clerk *Posting transactions to the computer system* *Printing out daily and monthly transactions listings*	*Kathy, the data input clerk is aged 18 and has been with the organisation since leaving school. She has just started AAT studies.*

6 Problems encountered

A number of problems of varying degrees of magnitude came to light as a result of the visit of the external accountants and auditors, commencing in February 2004. Three examples of difficulties that were exposed at this time are given below.

6.1 Rental income: a communication problem

6.1.1 The problem

Rental income from the company's various properties had not been properly accounted for, and could not all be traced. This problem seems to have arisen because neither I, nor the previous accounts department supervisor (who was only in post for six months of 2003), were aware that the company owned the properties in question.

(a) Eaton Motors Limited acquired the properties on 1 January 2003. They had previously been the property of a separate company, also owned by the Eaton family, but were transferred to Eaton Motors because the sisters no longer wished to have direct responsibility for their management.

(b) Rent demands, which should have been issued quarterly for the petrol station and the hotel in Brighton, and monthly for the two cottages, were not issued at all after March 2003.

(c) This matter was mentioned in the auditor's management letter dated October 2003, but I was not shown a copy of this letter until February 2004.

(d) Some (but not all) of the tenants nevertheless continued to pay their rent. Rental income received was initially posted to a suspense account in the sales ledger.

(e) Some of the balance building up in the suspense account was mistakenly attributed to customers with similar names to tenants and netted off against the balance owing on their accounts.

6.1.2 The solution

This problem was resolved as follows.

(a) Kathy, the data input clerk, was allocated the responsibility of tracing money received from tenants during 2003 and 2004. It was relatively easy to trace the original receipt of the money, but proved more difficult to trace the subsequent postings.

(b) A schedule was drawn up showing rental income due and rental income paid. Demands for arrears of rent could then be issued. Clearly labelled rental income accounts were set up on the nominal ledger.

(c) Revised statements were prepared for customers whose accounts had wrongly been credited with rent payments. These were sent out with letters of apology for the error. Only one customer has refused to accept the situation.

(d) A meeting was held between the managing director, the auditors and myself. It was agreed that I should maintain closer contacts with the auditors in future, that I should receive copies of communications where relevant to my work, and that I should be regularly informed of matters decided by the senior management of the company, insofar as they affect the financial aspects of the business.

Lessons learnt

Aside from the obvious breakdown in communication, the main practical lesson to be learned from this episode is the need to enquire properly into any unusual transactions that occur at the earliest opportunity. Our computer system is capable of generating a wide variety of exception reports, and the daily reports that I review now draw attention to any items posted to suspense accounts. Most items are now cleared off suspense accounts within a few days.

6.2 Cash income: a training problem

The problem

A second problem concerned the maintenance of till accounts for the three cash tills in Parts and Services. The company has a rather unusual arrangement with a number of regular trade customers whereby urgently needed parts are supplied and invoiced to callers without payment, on the understanding that cash settlement will be made on the next visit. The system works in practice and encourages sales but was proving to be difficult from an administrative point of view because cash received was not being matched against debts incurred, as shown in the ledgers.

The result was that the three till accounts, which should in theory merely have had a balance of the till float (£100) at the end of the day in fact had balances of irregular sizes from day to day, each comprising several hundred unmatched debits and credits.

On investigation, and after discussion with General Motors accounts staff, this proved to be a training problem. Although copy invoices were retained in Parts and Services department until paid, the till staff had not been taught that when they accepted cash for one of these 'cash' sales made a few days ago they should also key in the appropriate invoice numbers. Likewise, Kathy, the accounts section data input clerk, had been wrongly taught to respond 'No' to the part of the cash input program that offers the option of matching and cancelling items.

How we dealt with the problem

This left the problem of existing unmatched receipts that had not been properly recorded by till staff. Although comprising literally hundreds of individual items the net shortfall came to less than £250 and it was decided that this amount was too small to justify the effort involved in attempting to match unmatched items. These were therefore cleared off the system. The problem has not occurred again now that proper procedures are being followed.

Although this matter was mentioned in the October 2002 management letter, I only became aware of it when it was drawn to my attention by the auditors in February 2004, because I had not been in the habit of examining detailed transaction listings for small balances. I now make a point of looking through all transaction listings at least once a week to ensure that all accounts are being properly maintained.

6.3 Collusion with a supplier: a fraud problem

The problem

This was the most serious problem that came to light. The auditors noticed after the year end stock count that there were discrepancies between balances in the purchases ledger and stock balances of parts needed for servicing vehicles not manufactured by General Motors. They were initially unable to reconcile the differences.

Testing revealed that details on the delivery dockets did not always match the purchase ledger details. It also revealed that all the discrepancies related to transactions with one particular external supplier.

Upon further investigation it transpired that James, the temp who covered for Julia for six months, had been colluding with a friend who worked in the accounts department at the suppliers. Together they had devised a system to defraud Eaton Motors Limited.

The way it worked was that James recorded a greater number of purchases than had been made in reality. His friend prepared false invoices on the supplier's headed paper. Therefore from an accounts point of view, our purchasing records agreed to the invoices received from the suppliers and payments were authorised. In the supplier's books, the friend recorded only the proportion of the payment that related to the actual parts supplied. He and James then split between them the excess payments made by Eaton Motors Limited.

The fraud did not come to light until the stock-take at the end of the year. A large part of the problem is that major bodywork repairs are conducted on a separate site several miles from the main premises. Deliveries are made to that location. Whilst the parts were physically checked against the details on the delivery docket, the delivery dockets were all filed and stored at that location. They were not checked against the purchase ledger details.

Another contributing factor was our recruitment policy in selecting James. Although we did ask for references to support his application, these were not followed up thoroughly. James provided two written references, which we accepted without further verification. We have now discovered that both of those references were false.

Action taken

To address the issues that facilitated the fraud, we have made a number of procedural changes. First, delivery dockets are now sent back to the main office and are checked against purchase ledger details rather than being filed and stored off-site. This has also led to better control over our records of damaged parts that we have had to return to suppliers.

We now perform quarterly rather than annual stock counts.

We have reviewed our recruitment policy and service contracts are no longer offered until we have confirmed the authenticity of references. This is done by means of either direct verbal or written communication with the named parties.

Although James had left the company by the time the fraud was discovered the matter has been reported to the police and we are taking legal action against him. We also reported the matter to the supplier in question. The employee at that firm has now been fired and legal action has been taken against him also. We believe that this will send the message out that we take this kind of offence very seriously and will not hold back in pressing criminal charges. We hope this will act as a deterrent to any other potential fraudsters.

7 Performance

7.1 Productivity

Normal man-hours per week within the accounts section presently amount to 146.

	Hours
Supervisor	35
Cashier	21
Sales ledger assistant	35
Purchase ledger assistant	20
Data input clerk	35
Total	146

This is adequate to cope with the section's current workload, even allowing for the seasonal nature of the new vehicle sales aspect of the business. In other words the section is slightly understretched for most of the year.

7.2 Future needs

Observation of and informal discussions with staff indicate that the following factors also need to be taken into account.

(a) Doris, the cashier, will reach 60 in the Autumn and has no interest in continuing work after that time. The section and the company as a whole will be deprived of a great deal of knowledge and experience. Although it is not formally part of her role, she takes care of many routine queries from other accounts staff and relieves the supervisor of much detailed day-to-day operational supervision.

(b) Brenda, the sales ledger assistant, is highly competent at her job, but has made it clear that she is not interested in taking on any further responsibility.

(c) Julia, the purchase ledger assistant, who presently works part-time, has indicated that she will be keen to work a full seven-hour day from September onwards.

(d) Kathy, the data input clerk, is not being challenged and is rarely fully occupied in her present job and yet she shows a great deal of promise.

(e) Brian Davis, who supervises the administration section, is also due to retire this year. No decision has yet been made as to what will happen to his various roles.

8 Recommendations in the light of impending changes

8.1 My role

The major task with which I was entrusted on joining the company was reducing the cost of accounting and audit work done by the company's external accountants. The ultimate aim is to present the auditors with:

(a) Firm evidence of strong internal controls, within the limits of the organisation's size

(b) A set of properly documented final accounts and supporting schedules, rather than merely a set of ledgers and a trial balance, as has previously been the case.

To this end I have identified the following matters that will need attention.

(a) *I need to continue to pursue my studies of accounting, and in particular to obtain broader and deeper knowledge of financial accounting and auditing. The company is sponsoring my present studies and has indicated its willingness to support further studies, perhaps with a view to obtaining the qualifications of one of the more senior accounting bodies, such as the ICAEW or CIMA.*

(b) *The staffing of the accounts section and the hours worked by the section need to be reviewed, to assess the impact of likely future changes as compared with the future needs of the section.*

(c) *The division of responsibilities for the various accounting or accounting-related activities carried out in the organisation needs to be reviewed. Control of information and information processing could be considered to be too widely spread.*

When Doris leaves a new junior will be taken on as data input clerk, freeing up Kathy for more challenging work. Kathy will initially be responsible for training the new recruit.

8.2 If Brian Davis is replaced

Assuming that Brian Davis is simply replaced by another person who will adopt the same role, the present two-part structure of the Administration and Accounts Department will remain unchanged. In this case, there are a number of options for the accounts section.

Option 1. My personal preference would be for Kathy to take on the role of cashier and also to take over some of my responsibility for the nominal ledger. She and I would jointly be responsible for preparing backing papers for final accounts preparation and for the auditors. This is simply because she is the best person for the job. The problem is that, because it is currently occupied by Doris, the cashier's post is viewed by other staff as the senior position within the section below that of supervisor, whereas Kathy is the most junior member.

Option 2. The second option is to give Julia the role identified for Kathy above and appoint Kathy as purchase ledger assistant. This has the disadvantage that it deprives the purchase ledger section of Julia's previous experience in the Parts and Services departments, with whom she is presently required to liaise a great deal. There is also the problem that running the purchase ledger is not a full time job.

8.3 If Brian Davis is not replaced

(a) *The accounting aspects of the work of the administration section could readily be subsumed within the accounts section, as could the responsibility for purchasing general supplies.*

(b) *However, a decision will have to be made as to who will take on his role as personnel manager. This is by no means a full-time role but informal discussions indicate that it is one that is valued by the company and by employees alike. It is unlikely that somebody under 30 would be perceived to have the experience and maturity to take on this post.*

Assuming that point (b) can be resolved, the consequences for the accounts section and the department as a whole will be as follows in terms of hours available per week.

	Hours	
	Currently worked	After retirements etc
Administration supervisor	35	-
Administration assistant	35	35
Accounts supervisor	35	35
Cashier	21	35
Sales ledger assistant	35	35
Purchase ledger assistant	20	35
Data input clerk	35	35
Total	216	210

Work would be reallocated as follows.

(a) The accounts supervisor would take on overall responsibility for payroll, with the assistance of the administration assistant and the data input clerk.

(b) The cashier function would be taken on by Kathy and to this would be added responsibility for the nominal ledger as indicated above.

(c) The sales ledger would continue to be operated by Brenda.

(d) Julia would retain her current role as purchase ledger assistant and would in addition take on overall responsibility for the fixed assets register, and for purchasing general supplies. She would be assisted by the administration assistant.

(e) The role of the new data input clerk would be similar to Kathy's current role, except that there would be the additional work of assisting with payroll.

(f) The role of the administration assistant would be basically unchanged. There would, however, be the opportunity to learn more about the work of the accounts section, and to help out as and when required.

It is hoped the impact of these changes in terms of staff motivation would be to create a more meaningful and challenging job for Kathy, whilst not undermining the position of Julia, who will have more responsibilities and also have a member of staff reporting to her. In terms of the aim of reducing the cost of accounting and audit work done by the company's external accountants, the changes would both bring more of the accounts work of the organisation as a whole under my scrutiny and control and also free up more of my time to devote to the financial accounting and internal auditing work that is required.

8.4 Medium term changes

One of the problems currently faced by the accounts section is its lack of flexibility. Individuals have clearly defined roles and complete tasks to perform, but there is little scope for learning. This limits the ability of the section to cope with absences for whatever reason (sickness, holidays and so forth) and will do so to a much greater extent in the future, when the highly experienced Doris is not around to keep things ticking over.

In the medium term, therefore, I should like to encourage a degree of job rotation, so that the three main roles in the accounts section - cashier, sales ledger assistant, and purchase ledger assistant - can each be performed by any member of the section.

Although there is a general view that job rotation is of limited value for motivational purposes, the aim in the case of the Eaton Motors accounts staff is to increase the flexibility of the section and to enhance internal control over each of the three main areas.

There is also scope for any or all of the team to learn about payroll, and I intend to encourage any offers of assistance that may be forthcoming in this area.

3,960 words

> *Tutorial note. Appendices are not shown except for one which is essential to your understanding of the report above. One of your tasks was to make a list of what supporting documents you would like to see. Did you remember to do this?*

Appendix 1: Organisation chart

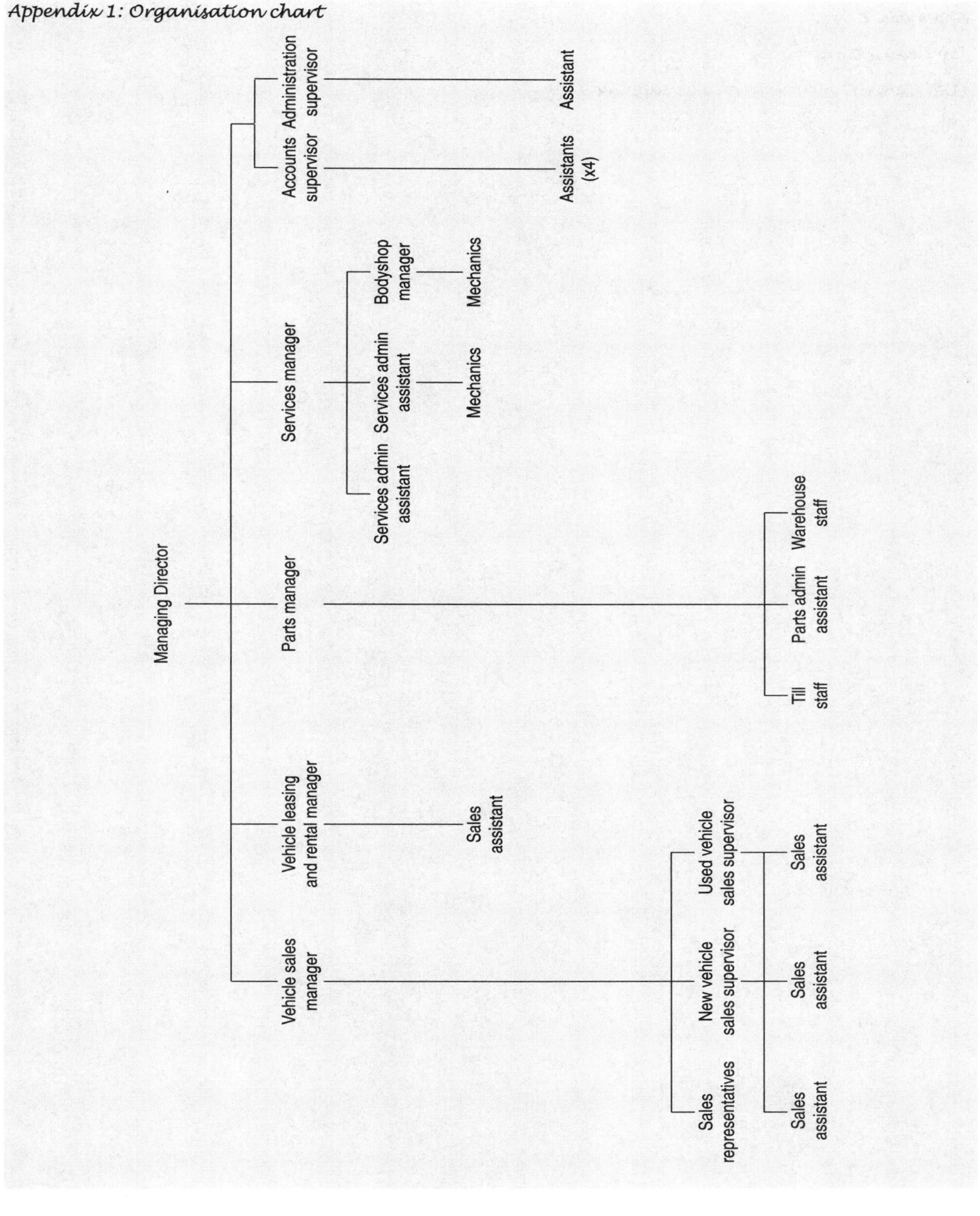

Appendix 2

Job descriptions

(BPP note. These remain to be supplied)

3 Comments on the report

3.1 Coverage of the performance criteria

We will now review the report for coverage of the performance criteria.

3.1.1 Element 10.1 Co-ordinate work activities within the accounting environment

In order to perform this element successfully you need to:

		BPP view: Is this covered?
A	Plan work activities to make the optimum use of resources and to ensure that work is completed within agreed timescales.	Not really
B	Review the competence of individuals undertaking work activities and arrange the necessary training.	Certainly considered
C	Prepare, in collaboration with management, contingency plans to meet possible emergencies.	Not clearly identified
D	Communicate work methods and schedules to colleagues in ways that help them to understand what is expected of them.	Not really
E	Monitor work activities sufficiently closely to ensure that quality standards are being met.	Yes, in places
F	Co-ordinate work activities effectively and in accordance with work plans and contingency plans	In places
G	Encourage colleagues to report to you promptly any problems and queries that are beyond their authority or expertise to resolve, and resolve these where they are within your authority and expertise.	No evidence either way
H	Refer problems and queries to the appropriate person where resolution is beyond your authority or expertise.	Implied but not clearly stated

3.1.2 Element 10.2 Identify opportunities for improving the effectiveness of an accounting system

		BPP view: Is this covered?
A	Identify weaknesses and potential for improvements to the accounting system and consider their impact on the operation of the organisation	No overall viewpoint
B	Identify potential areas of fraud arising from **control avoidance** within the accounting system and **grade the risk.**	No overall risk assessment
C	Review methods of operating regularly in respect of their cost-effectiveness, reliability and speed.	Yes
D	Make recommendations to the appropriate person in a clear, easily understood format.	Yes

		BPP view: Is this covered?
E	Ensure recommendations are supported by a clear rationale which include and explanation of any assumption made.	Yes
F	Update the system in accordance with changes that affect the ways the system should operate and check that your update is producing the required results.	Yes

In our view, this report is quite **unbalanced** when assessed against the Performance Criteria.

(a) There is a great deal about managing **people** but far less about important issues of internal control and risk assessment.

(b) Whilst we see problems have been dealt with, and certain sensible improvements are suggested, more could be done.

(c) Have the proposed changes in the short and long-term been discussed and agreed with more senior management?

3.2 Structure

The report needs a proper conclusion. It just stops in mid-air at present. With some adjustment, part 8 would be fine as a conclusion.

3.3 Comments on contents

The following are a few of the points you could have made. You may have many more.

Subsection 3.2. General Motors is mentioned several times at the beginning of the report as having a fairly significant impact on the accounting system, but this is never fully explained.

Subsection 4.3. Further details of volume of transactions are **not** given later in the report.

Subsection 5.1. The administration section is fairly important later on in the report, but it could almost be missed here. It needs a little more emphasis.

Subsection 5.3. The details of processing methods are very scanty indeed, and yet one of the problems described later (cash posting) seems to require quite detailed knowledge.

Subsection 5.4. The descriptions given are quite detailed. It is difficult to know whether this section is necessary if the author intends to include full job descriptions in the Appendix.

Subsection 6.2. It is quite hard to understand this explanation, although this may be because supporting documents are needed.

Subsection 7.1 and 7.2 and following. The analysis lacks precision here. It is not enough just to state that the weekly hours available are adequate to meet the current workload. What is the current workload? How slight is the understretch?

Subsection 8.1. We are never really told how the author intends to obtain 'firm evidence of strong internal controls'.

Subsection 8.3. It may be unfair to think so but there is a suggestion of bias in favour of Kathy over the other staff. Do others in the organisation share the author's opinion of her talents?

We are not told much about the culture of the section. Given the wide age range of its members this might be illuminating. It would be relevant to include a little more detail about the administration assistant. What does he or she think of the accounts section supervisor's plan to usurp his or her section? Why can he or she not do Brian Davis's job?

Subsection 8.4. There are no specific details of what is presently done when someone is absent from the section, although it is implied that the work is done by Doris.

Appendices

Further evidence that should be presented, as a bare minimum, is as follows.

Samples of any reports that have to be made to General Motors, and details of any rules they impose.

- Job descriptions, although these are flagged as going in the Appendix.
- Details showing how the misposted money was traced
- A copy of the schedule mentioned 8.1.2(b)
- A copy of the letter of apology 8.1.2(c)
- Minutes or some other written record of the meeting mentioned in 8.1.2(d)
- Copies of the exception reports 8.1.3
- An account print-out of the three till accounts showing the unmatched debits and credits
- Perhaps a procedures flow chart showing how the cash posting system works
- If possible, the auditor's management letter, or extracts from it
- Evidence of the section's workload
- Details of the exact timing of the various events mentioned in parts 7 and 8.

You may have many other ideas.

PART F

The AAT's Sample Simulation: Delmar Electronics

chapter 18

chapter 18

Sample simulation

Contents

1 Introduction

This chapter contains the AAT's Sample simulation. It is not a **live** simulation.

It is designed as an **example** of the type of simulation that AAT will produce for students who have no other means of preparing for Unit 10.

Chapter 19 contains an indicative report based on this simulation, but AAT will not issue such reports for the live simulation.

PLEASE NOTE

You cannot base your actual project on Delmar Electronics. You must use the AAT's own live simulation issued to you by your training provider.

AAT CASE STUDY: MANAGING SYSTEMS AND PEOPLE IN THE ACCOUNTING ENVIRONMENT

DELMAR ELECTRONICS LTD.

LES NIGHTINGALE

2/03

1

CONTENTS

This case study is designed for candidates to be able to use, in order to demonstrate their competence in managing systems and people in the accounting environment.

The performance criteria for this unit are set out on pages 2 to 3; the case study itself is set out on pages 4 to 21; and the candidate's briefing for writing their project is set out on pages 22 to 25.

PERFORMANCE CRITERIA FOR THIS UNIT

All performance criteria for this unit **must** be covered in the project report based on this case study, or by other documented evidence.

Element	PC Coverage
10.1	**Manage people within the accounting environment**
A	Plan work activities to make the optimum use of resources and to ensure that work is completed within agreed timescales.
B	Review the competence of individuals undertaking work activities and arrange the necessary training.
C	Prepare, in collaboration with management, contingency plans to meet possible emergencies.
D	Communicate work methods and schedules to colleagues in ways that help them understand what is expected of them.
E	Monitor work activities closely to ensure that quality standards are being met.

2

F Co-ordinate work activities effectively and in accordance with work plans and contingency plans.

G Encourage colleagues to report to you promptly any problems and queries that are beyond their authority or expertise to resolve, and resolve these where they are within your authority and expertise.

H Refer problems and queries to the appropriate person where resolution is beyond your authority or expertise.

10.2 Identify opportunities for improving the effectiveness of an accounting system

A Identify weaknesses and potential for improvement to the accounting system and consider their impact on the operation of the organisation.

B Identify potential areas of fraud arising from control avoidance within the accounting system and grade the risk.

C Review methods of operating regularly in respect of their cost-effectiveness, reliability and speed.

D Make recommendations to the appropriate person in a clear, easily understood format.

E Ensure recommendations are supported by a clear rationale which includes an explanation of any assumptions made.

F Update the system in accordance with changes that affect the way the system should operate and check that your update is producing the required results.

3

THE DEL CASE STUDY

THE COMPANY'S BACKGROUND AND MANAGEMENT

It is now April 2003.Your name is Tony Bush, and you are employed as an accounting systems technician with Delmar Electronics Limited (DEL).

The company was established six years ago by three colleagues, Richard West, Omar Sangha and John Bryce, who all knew each other well from working together in the electronics sector. Richard and Omar were both working at the time for Fort Technology Plc, a large quoted manufacturer of semi conductor testing equipment. Richard was the technical director and Omar a technical sales manager. John Bryce was employed as production manager in a similar electronics manufacturing company.

Four years ago Elaine Candler joined DEL as finance director, the fourth member of the board.

Their current positions in DEL are:

Richard West	**Managing Director**
Elaine Candler	**Finance Director**
Omar Sangha	**Sales Director**
John Bryce	**Production Director**

From their knowledge of the electronics business the company's founders believed there was a hole in the market for a high quality specialist range of semi-conductor test equipment. Using their combined expertise they were able to produce a convincing business plan. This enabled them from the outset to raise sufficient capital to launch DEL as a significant player in this particular sector.

Six years later the company has grown rapidly to a turnover of over £20 million, with net assets of over £3 million and with a workforce of over 200 employees. Details of DEL's accounts for the year to 31/3/02 are given in Appendix 1.

4

ACCOUNTING AND OTHER IT SYSTEMS

Most of the company's information systems have been in place for between 4-6 years and are in need of updating.

At present the principal systems are as follows:

- The main financial accounting system, including integrated general, purchase and sales ledgers. This operates in MSDOS and holds data in a non-relational database.
- A stand-alone full absorption costing system running on proprietary Wise software.
- A new integrated payroll and personnel database management system running in Windows 98, which was installed 3 months ago.
- A computer aided design/computer aided management (CAD/CAM) system, which is used for the design and control of the production of DEL products.

ACCOUNTING PERSONNEL

ELAINE CANDLER, BA, FCMA, FINANCE DIRECTOR

Elaine, aged 49, has overall responsibility for all accounting, finance, legal and IT issues. Elaine's primary responsibility is to manage the overall financial strategy of the business. Ensuring that capital investments are thoroughly appraised and in line with corporate strategy, that working capital levels are kept to a minimum, that the optimal mix of debt and equity funds DEL, and that its credit rating is maximized. In addition Elaine personally produces the annual company report, including its statutory accounts; deals with all banking and finance issues and fulfills the role of company secretary and handles all legal issues.

5

WILLIAM WHITELOW, AAT, COMPANY ACCOUNTANT

William, aged 59, has full day-by-day responsibility for the running of the DEL accounts department. He has been employed as company accountant since DEL was founded, and is AAT qualified. Originally William reported directly to the managing director, but since Elaine's appointment as finance director he has reported to her. William supervises the work of the accounting technicians and clerks running the transaction accounting systems i.e. the general ledger, purchase ledger, and sales ledger, together with the costing system and the payroll and personnel database management system. In addition, William personally produces the monthly management accounts, and approves all payments to suppliers.

The other five Accounts Department staff, which all report to William Whitelow, are:

SHARON EVANS, GENERAL LEDGER CLERK

Sharon, aged 26, is responsible for all data directly requiring input into the general ledger, and for producing the end of month trial balance. She is also responsible for maintaining the company's cashbook and its petty cash. Sharon has been in this job since she joined DEL three years ago, and has no accounting qualifications. Previously Sharon worked as a trainee personnel officer, but had to change job when her family moved area.

SUE MORAN, PURCHASE LEDGER CLERK

Sue, aged 36, is responsible for all data input into the purchase ledger, and for paying suppliers. Sue, who is William Whitelow's daughter, has been in this job for the past three years, and has foundation level AAT qualifications. Before working on the purchase ledger Sue spent the previous 18 months as the sales ledger clerk.

MOHAMED SINGH, SALES LEDGER CLERK AND CREDIT CONTROLLER

Mohamed, aged 27, is responsible for all data input into the sales ledger, and for the company's credit control. Mohamed has been in this job for the past

6

three years since joining DEL, from Withern Electronics Ltd., where he was the purchase ledger clerk. Mohamed currently has no accounting or credit control qualifications, but has expressed an interest in acquiring some.

DAVID BROWNE, COSTING TECHNICIAN

David, aged 47, is responsible for costing DEL's products. He has been in this job since the company was formed, and his only other previous employer was a furniture manufacturer, where he worked after leaving school until the firm closed just over six years ago. His final position there was as credit controller. David has no accounting qualifications, and has on several occasions expressed his reluctance to undertake any form of personal development or training.

RACHEL FREY, PAYROLL & PERSONNEL DATABASE CLERK

Rachel, aged 22, is responsible for running the monthly payroll (for salaried staff) and weekly payroll (for hourly paid staff), and issuing P45's, P60's and so on. She is also responsible for maintaining the personnel database. Rachel was recruited to do this job two months ago, when the previous clerk left. Rachel has no accounting qualifications, and joined the company straight from university, where she obtained a pass degree in history.
The software company who sold DEL the system gave Rachel three day's intensive training on the new payroll & personnel system.

The final member of the accounts team is you, **TONY BUSH, ACCOUNTING SYSTEMS TECHNICIAN.**

You report directly to Elaine Candler. You are aged 26, and are employed largely on reviewing accounting systems, plus any other project work that the finance director or company accountant may ask you to undertake. You have worked for DEL for the past two years and are hoping to complete your AAT qualifications this year. You have experience of working on both sales and general ledgers, but not at DEL.

7

BUSINESS & ACCOUNTING PRACTICES AND POLICIES

PURCHASES AND SUPPLIER PAYMENTS

The company buyer, George Stewart, is responsible for identifying and liaising with suppliers, and negotiating all contracts and prices with them. George has been in this position for the past four years.
The previous buyer had always followed a policy, set by the DEL board, of dealing with around 150 suppliers and playing one off against another in order to buy any materials or capital items at the lowest possible price available for that individual transaction. Three years ago, however, both George and William Whitelow had attended a seminar on "partnership sourcing", and had recommended to the board that a new policy of dealing with a much smaller number of suppliers on long-term contracts should be adopted. The board approved this change and DEL now operates with only around 30 regular suppliers, who are on two to three year contracts with annual price negotiations. The advantage of this policy to DEL is that it can get to know and understand 30 suppliers far better than it can 150, and can get the advantages of long-term stability in terms of product quality and prices.

Virtually all purchases are on 30-60 day credit terms. The purchase ledger clerk, Sue Moran, checks any new suppliers for financial stability.

All supplier invoices and goods received notes are sent initially to George Stewart, who is responsible for checking that the correct quantities have been received as ordered, and that the invoiced prices are correct.
George then passes the approved invoices to Sue Moran who enters them into the purchase ledger, and at the same time makes the appropriate general ledger postings. Every month the purchase ledger system produces an aged creditors listing which identifies those suppliers now due for payment. The company accountant, William Whitelow, is responsible for approving the actual payments to be made, but bearing in mind the company's cash position at the time. Suppliers are, in fact, nearly always paid on time.

Finally, the computer system produces the actual cheques, which are then signed both by William Whitelow and by one of the four directors. Usually this will be Elaine Candler, but when she is away on business, which is quite often the case, Richard West generally countersigns them. Increasingly

8

suppliers are paid by BACS, in which case the BACS payment authority is approved by William and then countersigned by one of the other directors. Neither the sales nor production directors are ever happy about countersigning all the individual cheques, because of the time involved, but are quite happy to put the one countersignature on the BACS payment authority form.

All company cheques are required to have two signatures, the authorised signatories being the four directors and the company accountant.

SALES AND CUSTOMER RECEIPTS

The company's sales force, led by Omar Sangha, are responsible for all dealings with existing customers and for identifying potential new ones. When a new customer is found, the company's policy is generally to trade with them on cash with an order basis of a three month trial period. The sales ledger clerk, Mohamed Singh, is responsible for credit checking these new customers, together with the relevant sales representative. This is to recommend a credit limit, which will apply after the three month trial period. All new credit limits and changes to existing limits are approved by the finance director, or in her absence by the managing director.

DEL has around 250 regular customers – 40 of whom account for 80% of the company's turnover.

The sales ledger clerk, Mohamed Singh, uses the goods dispatched listings as the trigger to produce sales invoices, which in accordance with Elaine Candler's instructions are sent out on a daily basis. All cheque payments received are sent to Mohamed who banks them also on a daily basis. Mohamed is responsible for all the postings to the sales ledger, and for the associated entries in the general ledger.

Sharon Evans produces a monthly bank reconciliation statement, which amongst other things reconciles the cashbook to the bank statement and the paying in book to the statement. The reconciliation is then checked by William Whitelow, who formally signs it off as being correct.

Mohamed produces a monthly aged debtors listing and all outstanding debtors more than one month overdue are reviewed with William Whitelow.

9

All outstanding debtors, more than three months overdue are reviewed both by Elaine Candler and by Omar Sangha.

PAYROLL AND PERSONNEL RECORDS

The company operates with two separate payrolls. Rachel Frey, the payroll & personnel database clerk runs the first every week to pay the hourly paid, largely the shop floor workers. Around 20% of these hourly paid employees are paid in cash, with the rest having payments made directly into their bank accounts via BACS. Those paid in cash collect their pay packets from Rachel's office every Friday, and those paid via BACS have their pay credited to their accounts on the same day. The second payroll is run three days before the last working day of each month to pay the monthly paid staff, which is either management, sales or office staff. All monthly paid employees are paid via BACS.

Once the two payrolls for the month have been finalised William Whitelow draws up manual cheques to the Inland Revenue in respect of income tax and NIC payments. William and one of the four directors sign these cheques.

As well as running the payroll, Rachel also maintains all the personnel records on the same integrated payroll and personnel database management system. This is DEL's newest system, having only been installed three months ago.

10

DIARY OF EVENTS WITHIN THE DEL ACCOUNTS DEPARTMENT OVER THE PAST TWELVE MONTHS

March/April 2002

31/3/2002: This was the company's financial year end. These months were, therefore, characterised by the usual peak in workload for any accounts department at this time of the year. In several areas specific problems in meeting the year end closure routines were experienced.

Mohamed Singh faced considerable problems this month. In his capacity as credit controller (with a brief to reduce year end debts outstanding) he was fully occupied chasing up debtors during the month. This prevented him from keeping up with his work in his other role as sales ledger clerk. By the end of the month Mohamed had only completed the postings for a small amount of the transaction entries affecting the sales ledger, and was working over 60 hours a week (with paid overtime) to try and catch up. Only Sue Moran was sufficiently experienced in operating the sales ledger to be able to provide any meaningful help, but this was however, severely limited because as usual at the year end Sue had enough work of her own to get through. Also she was three years out of practice in working in this area.

Sharon Evans also had great difficulties in meeting the required year end deadlines. During the year Sharon is usually extremely busy during the week of the month-end period, but has relatively little to do during the rest of the month. She knows that the year end period in particular is going to stretch her to the limit, and always tries to get well ahead with her work on direct general ledger postings, the cash book and petty cash so that she can concentrate on producing the trial balance. Since, however, both the sales ledger and the purchase ledger were closed off later than scheduled Sharon, in turn, was unable to complete balancing the trial balance until nearly two weeks after the set date.

The payroll system (that is the system in use at this time, which was subsequently replaced in early January 2003) had been causing problems for quite some time. David Watts, who was the payroll clerk at this time, reported problems caused by its extreme slow running during the month. As well as 31/03 being the company's financial year end, the UK tax year ends on 05/04. This makes this an extremely busy time for the payroll clerk,

11

since he was having to complete the normal payroll routines, he has also to ensure that the payroll closure ties in with DEL's internal year end timetable, and then produce the various forms and certificates required by the Inland revenue. Like Mohamed and Sharon, David was also behind schedule (in this case by four days) in terms of the DEL year end timetable.

These delays in finalising the transaction accounting meant that Elaine Candler, who always personally produces the statutory accounts, had to cancel or delay several important scheduled meetings with outside third parties in order to work full time on the statutory accounts. In particular, she and the managing director had to postpone a meeting with the company's bankers, which had been set to review the financial year 2001/2 accounts. This meeting was important because the company, in addition to renewing its annual overdraft facility was looking to raise a new £250,000 five year term loan to finance a replacement item of machinery.

The only element of light relief in the accounts department this month was a postcard from David Browne, costing technician, telling his colleagues that he was not really enjoying his annual skiing holiday because of the poor covering of snow this year. He did, however, report that the off piste activities were fine.

May 2002

In contrast to the traumas of the past two months, this was a fairly quiet and uneventful month.
Very little was seen of the finance director as she spent virtually the whole period off site, either with the company's auditors or in meetings with various banks.

William Whitelow largely concerned himself with reviewing outstanding supplier payments. As is normal practice at DEL, creditors are not generally paid the month before the full- year and half-year ends, but are then paid in the first two weeks of the following month. Since the company only operates with a relatively small number of suppliers, it is usually possible for Sue Moran, the purchase ledger clerk, to ring them and advise that their payments will be a few weeks late. Most suppliers accept that this tends to be standard business practice, and have no real problem with it. William,

12

however, felt that a full review of the purchase ledger, and in particular of outstanding balances, would be a useful supervisory exercise.
As a result of the problems in failing to meet the year end calendar, Tony Bush was instructed by Elaine Candler to undertake a work rescheduling and training review. Firstly, Tony was asked to carry out a systematic review of the competencies of the five members of the accounts department (excluding William Whitelow), to recommend what their training needs are and to advise Elaine of the type of training that should be provided. Secondly, he was to recommend ways of rescheduling the work of the department in order to make the best possible use of both the people working in it and of the systems operated by it.

June 2002

Elaine Candler announced to the staff that the five year term loan for the new machinery had now finally been agreed, but with a different bank than the company's regular bankers.

A major problem mid-month was a power cut, due to fallen electricity cables, which lasted for nearly two days. Although the company does have a standby generator this is only sufficient to power the whole of the factory and offices for up to four hours.

The normal practice in the accounts department is to back up all systems at the close of business each day. However since, the power failure occurred in the late afternoon, this meant that all that day's work on all the ledgers, the costing system and the payroll was lost. During the following day the accounts staff could do very little other than basic manual clerical work, and when it became clear that the power would not be restored until late evening the managing director took the decision to close the entire factory and offices for the rest of the day on health and safety grounds.

By the month end the accounts department had managed to effectively catch up their lost work by working a large number of extra hours, as paid overtime. It was generally felt by the staff that their being individually absent for a day or so was never a real problem, except at the year-end and half year-ends. This is because there is usually sufficient slack in the system to allow for this. However, their being all effectively unable to work for two

days did cause great difficulties because of the integrated nature of the transaction accounting system.

July 2002

Tony Bush reported back on the results of the work rescheduling and training review, and it was agreed that his recommendations would be implemented during the remainder of this financial year.

The old payroll system (that is in use at this time) has, as previously recorded been causing problems for quite some time. This month David Watts, the payroll clerk at this time, reported to Willam Whitelow that these regular problems of slow running and occasional crashes were continuing to get steadily worse as each month went by.

This system had been installed when the company and its accounts department were first set up, as a stand alone system running on spreadsheets on a PC. David Watts felt that, whilst this was alright for dealing with the 50 or so people employed at that time, it could no longer cope now that there were over 200 employees.

Since DEL does not have a personnel or HRM officer the personnel records are, by default, manually maintained by the payroll clerk. David and William both agreed that maintaining these manual personnel record cards for the steadily increasing number of employees was getting too overwhelming, and was causing David to duplicate work that he had already done for the payroll system.

August 2002

Tony Bush spent the first two weeks of this month sitting in with David Watts, with the two of them noting which problems occurred on the payroll system during which specific operations. At the end of this review both had reached the following conclusions. Firstly, that although the existing system could be updated and amended it would not make financial sense to do so, and it would be better to buy in a proprietary payroll software package. Secondly, it would make sense to acquire such a package that also integrated into it a personnel database that could to a large extent be maintained by the same entries as would need to be made for the payroll.

14

As usual, during August, there were problems caused by staff holidays. Although some aspects of the accounts department's work can be left for a couple of weeks, others, relating to the transaction accounting, always cause difficulties when they are not done on a day-by-day basis.
For example, no invoices were raised during the second and third weeks of the month because Mohamed Singh was on holiday.

September 2002

It was decided in principle by Elaine Candler that the company would invest in a new integrated payroll and personnel database software package. William Whitelow, David Watts and Tony Bush are to form a steering group to produce a detailed specification of exactly what DEL requires. Then they need to look at the available packages that meet this specification and finally make a cost recommendation to the finance director. Since Tony and David had already started looking at suitable packages it was expected that the three would be able to make a recommendation within the next month or so.

October 2002

Three members of the accounts department staff undertook some form of training this month. These were Sharon Evans, Sue Moran and Mohamed Singh. Training had also been organised for David Browne, but unfortunately David missed it due to being away sick on the relevant three days.

November 2002

The steering committee for the new integrated payroll and personnel database duly reported back, and the selected package was ordered with a scheduled installation date from the software company of the first week in January 2003.

December 2002

Richard West, the managing director, has spent three days this week on a CIMA Master Course on fraud. At the end of the course and on returning to DEL, Richard had his PA make copies of extracts from part of the course material. This is a paper entitled " Fraud Risk Management – A Guide to Good Practice", and extracts from this (Chapter 2 pages 5-9; and Chapter 5 pages 23-28) are included as Appendix 2 to this case study.

January 2003

The new integrated payroll and personnel database was installed on time, and David Watts was due to begin a training programme on it when he announced that he was resigning, having found a better paid position elsewhere. A temp, familiar with the new system, was brought in to cover the payroll whilst a replacement for David was found. All work on maintaining the personnel records was put on hold. William Whitelow undertook to dual run the old system for the next two months' payroll runs as an added test of the new system.

February 2003

David Watts left the company this month, and Rachel Frey, a 22 year old history graduate from Central Polytechnic University, replaced him. The software company who provided DEL with the new payroll and personnel database package provided Rachel with an in-house three day intensive training course on the system.

Product costing was unable to be undertaken for two weeks due to the absence due to sickness of David Browne, the costing technician. Normally David is able to plan his work well in advance to cover his work before going away on holiday etc., but this unexpected sick leave obviously prevented him from doing this. Unfortunately no other member of staff had the detailed knowledge of the company's products to be able to stand in for David.

16

March 2003

There were various problems with the new payroll system, and Rachel Frey is getting very worried about coping with the end of tax year P60's, P11D's and so on. In particular, the changes to NIC contribution levels, announced by the Chancellor of the Exchequer in last year's autumn statement, will require immediate updates to this part of the system.

During the month Tony Bush interviewed all members of the accounts department in order to formally report back to the finance director on the update from the work rescheduling and training review.

Appendix 3 contains the notes of a conversation from the meeting between Tony Bush and Mohamed Singh held on 31/3/2003.

17

APPENDIX 1

Summarised Profit & Loss Account and Balance Sheet for Delmar Electronics Ltd. for year to 31/3/02

Profit & Loss account for year ended 31/3/03

	2002 £000	2001 £000
Sales	20,152	18,564
Operating profit	1,364	1,226
Exceptional gain	327	-
Net interest payable	(560)	(617)
Currency exchange gain/ (loss)	(415)	(306)
Profit on ordinary activities before tax	716	303
Taxation on profit on ordinary activities	(167)	(68)
Profit on ordinary activities after tax	549	235
Dividends	(183)	(78)
Profit retained for the year	366	157

18

APPENDIX 2

Balance Sheet as at 31/3/03

	2002 £000	2001 £000
Fixed assets		
Intangible assets	312	264
Tangible assets	4,556	4,218
	4,868	4,482
Current assets		
Stocks	2,668	2,482
Debtors	5,846	4,127
Cash	361	103
	8,875	6,712
Creditors: amounts falling due within one year	(2,578)	(2,256)
Net current assets	6,297	4,456
Total assets less current liabilities	11,165	8,938
Creditors: amounts falling due after one year	(8,040)	(8,225)
Net assets	3,125	713

19

APPENDIX 3

Notes of a conversation from the meeting between Tony Bush and Mohamed Singh held on 31/3/2003.

Tony: Hello Mohamed. As you know I'm interviewing all staff in order to monitor how the changes are going from the work rescheduling and training review.

Mohamed: Erm… right…ok.

Tony: So how IS it going?

Mohamed: Tony, I've been wanting to talk with you anyway because I erm… I think we've got a major problem with the way that the purchasing system is being operated.

Tony: William is your line manager. Have you talked to him about this?

Mohamed: Erm well yes I would have done – but the thing is I think that whatever is going on he's well sort of involved in it. I'm also a bit nervous about bringing this up with Elaine – I don't want to make a complete fool of myself if I'm wrong. In any event, as you know, she's in hospital recovering from surgery this week..

Tony: This sounds rather serious, Mohamed. What do you mean?

Mohamed: You'll remember, of course, that a few months ago you were asked to advise on a work rescheduling and training review, and that – as part of this – Sue Moran and myself were trained to cover each others work…

Tony: Of course I remember….

Mohamed: Well the thing is whenever I do swap with or cover for Sue, and I've done this perhaps twenty times now, I've never seen any invoices or purchase orders or dealt with any paperwork at all for one of our suppliers – a company called Raymond Briggs Ltd. We've only got around 30 creditors and so it seems odd that this one never comes through on my days on the purchase ledger.

20

Tony: Go on….

Mohamed: Erm well…I've looked into the company's records on the purchase ledger, and it seems that we've dealt with them for the past 3 years, but apart from this there's very little information on the system. Far less than for most of our suppliers in fact.

I then went to see George Stewart about Briggs Ltd. and he immediately clammed up. The next morning I saw him in William Whitelow's office – which is also odd because in all the time I've worked here I can't recall seeing George in the accounts department at all.

Tony: Has this supplier ever been paid whilst you've been working on the purchase ledger?

Mohamed: I thought you might ask me that! The answer is no. I've checked back and every payment has been made while Sue Moran has been working on the purchase ledger.

Tony: Leave this with me – I'll get back to you on it later today.

21

CANDIDATE'S BRIEFING FOR A PROJECT REPORT BASED UPON THIS CASE STUDY.

Candidates who do not have the opportunity to undertake some form of work-based project are able to provide evidence of competence in this unit by writing a similar project report, but based on the material in this case study. The total length of the report should not exceed 4,000 words.

Specifically candidates should write a report, which demonstrates their underpinning knowledge and understanding of:

The Business environment

- External regulations affecting accounting practices (10.2)
- Common types of fraud (10.2)
- The implications of fraud (10.2)

Management techniques

- Methods of work planning and scheduling (10.1)
- Personal time management techniques (10.1)
- Methods of measuring cost-effectiveness (10.2)
- Methods of fraud detection within accounting systems (10.2)
- Techniques for influencing and negotiating with decision makers & resource holders (10.2)

Management principles and theory

- Principles of supervision and delegation (10.1)
- Principles of creating effective inter-personal relationships, team building and staff motivation (10.1)

The organisation

- The impact on an accounting system of organisational structure, Management Information Systems, administrative systems and procedures and the nature of its business transactions (10.1, 10.2)

22

- The organisation's business and its relationships with external stakeholders (10.1,10.2)
- The purpose, structure and organisation of the accounting system and its inter-relation with other internal functions (10.2)
- The control of resources by individuals within the organisation (10.1)

This can be demonstrated by writing a project report of up to 4,000 words, addressed to Elaine Candler - the finance director, which covers the following:

- **The co-ordination of work activities within DEL's accounting environment**

The candidate must demonstrate his/her ability to plan and co-ordinate DEL's accounts department's work activities effectively. Including setting and monitoring realistic objectives, targets and deadlines and managing people so that these can be met. In addition the candidate needs to show that he/she can develop contingency plans to deal with a range of problems that may detract from the organisation meeting these objectives, targets and deadlines.

- **Identification of opportunities to improve the effectiveness of DEL's accounting system**

The Candidate must demonstrate his/her ability to identify weaknesses in DEL's accounting system, and making recommendations to rectify these; to consider the impact that these would have on the organisation; to update the system to comply for example with legislative changes; and to subsequently check that the post-change output is now correct.

The project report should be both holistic and strategic in nature. That is, the candidate should report on each of the detailed areas listed below, and then bring these together in an integrated way so that the overall position can be seen. From this he/she should then identify perhaps 4-6 major issues, which are of strategic importance to DEL.

23

In detail the project should include:

- How the candidate would plan and monitor work routines to meet DEL's organisational time schedules and to make the best use of both their human and physical resources (PC A). Planning and scheduling this project report for completion to standard and on time will also provide evidence towards PC A.
- The systematic review of staff competencies and training needs, together with details of the training actually arranged (PC B).
- Contingency planning for possible emergencies, (e.g. computer system not being fully functional, staff absences, and changes in work patterns and demands) (PC C).
- How the candidate would communicate work methods and schedules to colleagues so that they have understood what is expected of them (PC D).
- How the candidate would monitor work activities closely against quality standards to ensure they are being met (PC E).
- How the candidate would co-ordinate work activities effectively against work plans and contingency plans (PC F).
- How the candidate would encourage colleagues to report promptly, issues beyond their authority and expertise. How he/she would resolve these where possible (PC G), or otherwise refer such issues to the appropriate person to resolve them (PC H).
- A situation analysis of the accounting system under scrutiny (e.g. a SWOT analysis), which will generate evidence towards performance criteria PCs A & B.
- Evidence of resulting recommendations made to the appropriate people in a clear understandable format and supported by a clear rationale. This will generate evidence towards PCs D & E. All assumptions made should be clearly listed.

24

- Evidence of research, pointing towards potential areas of fraud within DEL's accounting system (e.g. teeming and lading, fictitious employees or suppliers). Research into appropriate fraud risk standards, including the extracts provided in the case study, will generate evidence for PC B. Candidates are advised to use some form of matrix approach towards grading the various elements of risk.

- How the candidate would undertake a regular review of methods of operating, providing evidence for PC C.

- How the candidate would update the system in accordance with both internal factors (e.g. changes in the organisational structure, responses to customer surveys) and external factors (e.g. changes in company law, VAT rates, FRS's) that require such updates to be made. This provides evidence for PC F - SWOT and PEST analyses respectively would be useful here.

Any of the above evidence that does not sit naturally within the project report should be included as additional evidence in the appendices to it.
If the listed Performance Criteria and Underpinning Knowledge and Understanding have NOT been addressed sufficiently by the project content documented, then assessor questioning MUST be employed to address any gaps.

ALL Performance Criteria and Underpinning Knowledge and Understanding must be evidenced.

25

chapter 19

Report based on sample simulation

Contents

1 Introduction

This is a report based on the sample simulation in the previous chapter. We suggest you read the notes to assessors.

BPP's view is that your report will always be enhanced by numbered paragraphs. Here we will be dealing with content.

Pages 26 – 29 cover assessor briefings.

AAT CASE STUDY : MANAGING SYSTEMS AND PEOPLE IN THE ACCOUNTING ENVIRONMENT

DELMAR ELECTRONICS LTD.

NOTES FOR ASSESSORS AND INDICATIVE REPORT

LES NIGHTINGALE

26

2/03

PROJECT REPORT

DELMAR ELECTRONICS LTD.

NOTE TO ASSESSORS

The project report should be both holistic and strategic in nature. That is, the candidate should have reported on each of the detailed areas listed in the briefing notes for candidates. He/she should then bring these together in an integrated way so that the overall position can be seen. From this he/she should then identify perhaps four to six major issues, which are of strategic importance to DEL.

ASSESSMENT CRITERIA

This is a difficult paper to write both a case study and indicative solutions for. In some cases it is likely that candidates will produce valid alternative answers, perhaps from a completely different paradigmal perspective. Assessors should, therefore, look for underpinning knowledge, understanding of the key issues in the simulation and for reasonable method and process.

IT IS NOT THE AAT's INTENTION TO PRODUCE INDICATIVE SOLUTIONS FOR FUTURE CASE STUDIES. THESE HAVE BEEN PRODUCED FOR THIS INITIAL CASE STUDY ONLY TO GIVE ASSESSORS A BENCHMARK AGAINST WHICH TO ASSESS FUTURE PROJECTS.

27

PLANNING & MONITORING WORK ROUTINES

Here the key principle is that of separation of duties by some over-riding need (in this case the month end timetable) rather than by function (e.g. sales ledger work). Candidates could separate work by other well argued, valid means. Providing they demonstrate that their proposals optimise the use and time of the available personnel.

STAFF COMPETENCIES & TRAINING NEEDS REVIEW

The essential issue here is that before the review, all members of the accounts department can only work with their own individual part of the system, and also need to be trained so that they can work with at **least one** other part. The actual proposals as to who does what are fairly arbitrary, (based on employees' past experiences), and candidates will doubtless produce many other viable suggestions.

CONTINGENCY PLANNING

Candidates should be able to explain what is meant by contingency planning, and should be able to make some reasonable suggestions to cover **both** staff absences **and** computer system failure.

SITUATION ANALYSIS OF THE ACCOUNTING SYSTEM

Candidates at this level can be expected to produce a comprehensive, professional SWOT analysis. They should be able to conclude that in general the sales system works effectively, the payroll system needs some improvement and the purchases system is fundamentally weak. The detailed comments need not necessarily be as per those in the suggested solution.

The purchases and supplier payments systems and procedures **must** be identified as the weakest individual part. Candidates should be able to make recommendations, which relate to the purchase ledger system, ordering or receipt of goods.

28

POTENTIAL AREAS OF FRAUD

Candidates will probably be unfamiliar with the CIMA material. The aim of this part of the assessment is to give them the opportunity to apply their underpinning knowledge to a specific context. Assessors should expect that the weaker candidates, relying on route learning, are likely to experience difficulty here.

All candidates should be able to identify perhaps four areas at risk from fraud in the purchases and supplier payments system.

They should also be able to explain how these risks arise.

A reasonable attempt only is expected from using the risk analysis model. Look for process and understanding, rather than precise answers as per the indicative solution.

ENCOURAGING COLLEAGUES TO REPORT ISSUES & RESOLVING OR REFERRING THEM

This section of the standards is extremely difficult to assess (whether by work-based project or by case study simulation). Due to the subjectivity implicit in the performance criteria here, assessors should expect a variety of different approaches. Again, look for reasoned arguments and underpinning knowledge of the issues involved, rather than precise answers as per the indicative solution.

REVIEW OF METHODS OF OPERATING/ UPDATES TO THE SYSTEM & RESULTING RECOMMENDATIONS

Candidates can demonstrate their competence in these areas in a variety of ways by using the material in the case. One obvious way is to include in the report a recommendation to the board for a series of control checks that should be introduced over the purchase and supplier payments system.

29

<u>INDICATIVE REPORT EXTRACTS COVERING THE MAIN STATEGIC ISSUES FROM THE CASE STUDY</u>

To: Elaine Candler **From:** Tony Bush

<u>Training needs review identifying the competencies and training requirements of each of the five members of the accounts department.</u>

The starting point should be to establish what skills, knowledge and competencies DEL requires its accounts staff to have, and then decide whether these *can* be met internally or whether we need to recruit externally. I would suggest that the training required ensures that all members of staff become skilled and competent to operate at least two parts of the accounting system.

Considering each individual employee:

<u>Sharon Evans, General Ledger Clerk</u>
Sharon seems somewhat under-employed, in that other members of staff enter the sales and purchases figures into the GL – leaving Sharon only the direct entries (such as purchases of fixed assets) to make. In addition Sharon maintains the cashbook and petty cash and does the bank reconciliation's. The obvious area for Sharon to be trained in seems to be the payroll & personnel database. Since she has previously worked in HR she may well be interested and well suited to this work. This would also relieve the pressure on Rachel Frey, who is both a young and inexperienced member of staff but seems however to have a very heavy workload.

<u>Sue Moran, Purchase Ledger Clerk</u>
Since Sue is already familiar with DEL's sales ledger system, it would make sense from the company's point of view to give her refresher training in this area, so that she could cover for Mohamed Singh. Sue has started taking AAT qualifications, and to support her in this, DEL should also offer her training in a further new area of the accounts system – perhaps the GL or costing system.

30

Mohamed Singh, Sales Ledger Clerk and Credit Controller
Mohamed's previous job was as a purchase ledger clerk with another electronics company. Logically from DEL's point of view, he should be trained to operate the purchase ledger. Apart from the added flexibility, the accounts department may benefit from Mohamed being able to recommend changes to DEL purchase ledger practices, based on his experience at Withern Electronics Ltd.. Longer term, the company should seek to meet Mohamed's expressed interest in gaining either accounting or credit control qualifications.

David Browne, Costing Technician
From the information provided, David is the only employee who apparently has experience in costing the company's products. This places DEL in an exposed situation because, unlike maintaining the ledgers, costing requires detailed knowledge of the company's products. Another member of staff needs to be trained in this area as a matter of urgency. Based on David's previous background in credit control, it would be logical to train him in DEL's credit control procedures. David's reluctance to undertake training and development needs to be investigated and resolved.

Rachel Frey, Payroll & Personnel Database Clerk
As well as being the newest and youngest member of staff, Rachel is also working on by far the newest part of the system and therefore, the part most likely to experience problems. To cope with this she has only been given three days intensive training. Rachel should be given at least a further period of update training by the software company who sold DEL the system. Beyond this, her own development needs should be discussed with her and further training/development arranged.

31

Advice on how, after the training needs have been met, work activities could be rescheduled to optimise the use and time of the available accounts department personnel.

The fundamental aim of the training needs analysis was to multi-skill the accounts department staff. Previously they could each only effectively do their own specific job but after training they are able to undertake at least one other function. However, to maintain and develop their new skills, staff should have their work rescheduled so that they *regularly and as a matter of course* work in this other function, otherwise the training is likely to be forgotten.

The work of the department could be viewed and organised in several different ways. At present it is viewed as a series of disparate functional activities (sales ledger, payroll etc.). Another way of scheduling work would be to divide it into what needs to be done according to the month-end timetable and what does not. In the first category would fall activities such as closing the ledgers, extracting the trial balance and running the monthly payroll. In the second category would fall activities such as updating customer, supplier and personnel records and costing products.

As presently organised, the month-end routines severely affect some members of staff (such as Sharon Evans), whilst others (such as David Browne) are not really affected at all. This makes poor use of resources and time when considered from the viewpoint of the department as a whole.

An effective way, therefore, of rescheduling the workload would be by following the two principles:

- Staff all undertaking work in two areas.
- Activities being spread amongst staff in order to divide them between those crucial month-end routines and those, which are not.

Obviously these two principles may conflict at times and much more information would be needed to put this properly into practice. However, as an example David Browne (once trained in DEL's credit control practices) could leave most of his costing work to the final week of the month and chase up debtors. This would both allow Mohamed Singh to concentrate all his energies on the month-end sales ledger routines, and hopefully result in a lower figure of month-end debtors and higher cash at bank.

32

Explanation of the term "contingency planning", and a contingency plan, after the training needs review and work activity rescheduling has been implemented.

Contingency planning

Contingency planning involves assessing, and subsequently planning how best to manage, unplanned events, which may occur from time to time. In practical terms these are events where there is both a reasonable probability of them happening AND what the impact of them actually happening would be significant for the business. For example, the probability of an aircraft crashing directly on DEL's premises is not of a high order of probability and, although its effect on the business would be very significant, it would not normally be included in a contingency plan. This type of event is often covered by "shock event planning", and would be covered by risk transference, which usually means insurance. On the other hand, although there is a high probability that the accounts department might run out of paperclips the effect on the business of this happening would not be significant, so this event too would not form part of a contingency plan.

Staff absences

A contingency plan for staff absences is fairly straightforward since it largely emanates from the outcome of the training needs review and have the work rescheduling exercise.

Since all staff is now able to operate at least two parts of the accounting system, the absence of any one employee can be readily covered by his/her "shadow". For example, since both Sue Morgan and Mohamed Singh can run both the purchases and sales ledgers, Sue can, at least for a limited period, run both ledgers in Mohamed's absence, and vice versa.

Problems arise where more than one employee is absent at the same time and/or where an employee is absent near the month- end (or worse still half year or year end) period.

Where more than one employee is absent, or an employee is absent at a critical period end, it will be necessary either to utilise additional resource

33

from outside of the transaction accounting staff. Essentially, this means either:

- using myself, David Browne or even William Whitelow because the work that we do has, in general, less immediate impact on the business if it is left until later.
- using outside contract agency staff.

Failure of the company's computer system

In many ways this is far more difficult to plan for than staff absences because there is a larger number of events and variables, which could cause a failure of the computer system.

An effective contingency plan for the failure of computer systems needs to consider both a partial failure (affecting one part of the system only) and a total failure (affecting all parts of the system). A failure affecting more than one part of the system, but not the total system can probably for most practical purposes be considered to have the same implications as a total failure.

A partial failure could, for example, be caused by the failure of an individual element of the system such as the payroll & personnel database or the costing system being corrupted by a virus. Since these two systems are stand alone and not integrated with any other part of the system, the impact of this should be contained to those parts directly affected only.

A total failure could, for example, be caused by a computer virus destroying or corrupting all the files on the hard disk of the main integrated financial accounting system, or by a power cut.

All possible causes of a partial failure should, as far as possible, be identified and their probabilities and effects on the business assessed. For example, a failure of the costing system might cause the loss of a day or so's work by David Browne before the fault can be rectified. The cost of this can be estimated, and whilst waiting for the fault to be rectified David could be usefully employed elsewhere in the department. Those partial failures that meet the definition for inclusion in contingency planning given above should be formally planned for.

34

Costs of a total system failure are more difficult to estimate, but an attempt should be made in general terms to do so.

Once risks have been identified and assessed, the next step is to manage them. This could include any combination of the following contingencies:

- Of paramount importance is the regular back up of data and software, so that in the event of failure it is only the hardware, which needs to be supplied. If this is not undertaken the rest of the contingency plan, however good, is doomed to failure.
- Spreading computer facilities over more than one site or system, so that work can be transferred from the lost site or system. Since all DEL's systems stand alone apart from the main financial accounting system, this is the part of the system most in need of "distributed support".
- Subscribing to a facilities management service, which would allow DEL to buy into a shared standby computer service.

The effectiveness of DEL's business & accounting practices and policies

Our business & accounting practices and policies include purchases & supplier payments, sales & customer receipts, and payroll & personnel database administration. These are supported by the relevant parts of our accounting system, i.e. the general ledger, purchase ledger, sales ledger, credit control, costing, payroll & the personnel database. To identify which parts are good/satisfactory and which parts need improvement, I have prepared a SWOT analysis:

Strengths

Purchases & supplier payments:

- The company buyer, George Stewart, and the purchase ledger clerk are both experienced at their jobs, having been in these positions for four and three years respectively.
- The benefits of the "partnership sourcing" scheme, are the reduced admin. costs and long-term stability in terms of supplies, prices and quality.

35

Sales & customer receipts:

- Overall, this part of the system works very effectively.
- Again, the sales ledger clerk, Mohamed Singh, has three years experience at doing this job.
- The system for giving open credit, and increasing credit limits is effective. A three month trial period should be more than sufficient for DEL to both get familiar with the customer and to thoroughly credit check them. The involvement of the sales force in this process should result in useful market knowledge based information being available. Approval for credit limits and changes to them are made at the most senior level, by either the FD or MD.
- Sales invoices and cheques are both banked daily.
- Different people carry out the banking & account postings (Mohamed Singh) and the bank reconciliation (Sharon Evans).
- The aged debtors listing is used effectively with a two tier level of review, and with the involvement of the relevant directors at an appropriate time.

Payroll & personnel records:

- The use of BACS to pay all monthly employees and 80% of those paid hourly.
- The use of an integrated payroll and personnel database should lead to increased efficiency, as compared to two individual systems.

<u>**Weaknesses**</u>

Purchases & supplier payments:

This is by far the weakest part of the overall system, and is potentially open to fraud.

- Three employees control virtually the entire process (George Stewart, Sue Moran & William Whitelow). George & William were instrumental in introducing the present system, and George & Sue are father and daughter. The only third party checks against potential fraud are the final second signatures on the cheque or BACS run. Even these are rarely done

36

by the FD, but by one of the other directors, who will have little time to do any independent checks.

Sales & customer receipts:

None apparent.

Payroll & personnel records:

- The 20% of the hourly paid payroll paid in cash cause a disproportionate amount of work, cost and risk of theft.
- The payroll & personnel records clerk, Rachel Frey, is both new to the company and not properly trained on the system.
- The system itself is new, but does not seem to be being monitored for weaknesses or errors.

<u>Opportunities</u>

Purchases & supplier payments:

Since the present policy has been in place for three years, and the existing 30 suppliers are on two to three year contracts, there is now an opportunity to get NEW suppliers to tender for the next cycle of contracts. This would not necessarily increase the overall number of suppliers, but would allow fresh blood into the tendering system. It would also reduce the risk of fraud through collusion between an existing long-standing supplier and the buyer (plus the two other DEL employees involved).

Sales & customer receipts:

- The three month cash with order basis should be reviewed for any evidence that this is causing DEL to lose business. Is the policy applied across the board e.g. to plc's?
- 84% (210/240) of DEL's customers contribute only 20% of the profit. A pareto-type customer profitability analysis should be carried out to

37

identify any customers who are unprofitable or whether their profitability is too low for the support they require. An ABC system would help here.

Payroll & personnel records:

- The existing cash paid employees should be given an incentive to move to a BACS payment system, and all new employees should be automatically paid in this way.
- Rachel Frey needs more comprehensive training, as per task 1 above.
- Is the personnel database being used to its maximum extent. Given Rachel's lack of training and the fact that both she and the system are new, it is likely that only the key payroll aspects are being properly used.

Threats

Purchases & supplier payments:

- This part of the system is at threat from fraud. It would be possible for the company buyer to collude with one or more of DEL's long-standing suppliers to e.g. agree higher than arms length prices, or to sign off goods not actually received etc. The "back hander" from the supplier would then be shared with the two other DEL employees who control the system.
- Apart from fraud, there is a danger of complacency on the part of the suppliers, who may see themselves in a cosy relationship with DEL and feel able to creep up prices because of the lack of competition. These type of arrangements must be subject to regular audit by a senior member of DEL – probably Elaine Candler.

Sales & customer receipts:

None apparent.

Payroll & personnel records:

The cash payments to employees are at risk of theft.

38

The weakest individual part

From the SWOT analysis it is clear that the purchases and supplier payments system is by far the weakest individual part of the whole.
Detailed recommendations (two from the following) for its improvement include:

- The establishment of a Purchase Ledger Control account, maintained and periodically against the purchase ledger by another member of staff, probably the GL clerk.
- A better separation of duties between those employees who are receiving goods, maintaining the purchase ledger, authorising invoices, checking suppliers' statements to the purchase ledger account and running payment routines.
- Reviewing the financial stability checks currently carried out by Sue Moran. Perhaps the responsibilities could be rescheduled so that the sales ledger clerk can check out both potential customers AND suppliers.
- All cheques and BACS payments should be properly reviewed before they receive a director's second signature. Ideally the FD should undertake this, but in her absence another specified director who can make time available should deputise. An alternative would be for two directors (and not the company accountant) to sign off all payments to suppliers.

39

Potential for fraud in DEL's accounting system and procedures

Having read the extracts from the CIMA paper " Fraud Risk Management – A Guide to good Practice", I have used the Risk Management Cycle approach and Ernst & Young model to help do this.

Identification of the risks of fraud in the weakest individual part of DEL's accounting systems.

As identified earlier, the purchase and supplier payment system is the weakest element of our systems, and the potential for fraud has already been outlined in general terms.

A risk management group (RMG) should be established to review the risks, including those of fraud, in the purchase and supplier payments system. The board of directors needs to decide on the level of risk that DEL is prepared to accept. Once this has been done the RMG should understand and assess the scale of risks in this part of the system, prioritise these by the scale of their possible impact and probability of occurring, and then go onto develop a risk management strategy.

In considering the possible composition of this group, DEL should look for individuals with expertise in the company's systems and procedures, a basic knowledge of fraud, and the knowledge and authority to introduce changes to procedures and new controls. The obvious person to chair the RMG is the finance director, Elaine Candler. I would also recommend that myself, as accounting systems technician, and William Whitelow, company accountant, are part of the group. It would also be of benefit to have at least one non-finance/accounting individual on the group in order to provide a different perspective on the issues. One of the other directors or a manager from a different area would be appropriate.

40

Risk Analysis of potential fraud in the purchases and supplier payments system

Details of risk	Manage-ment	Employees	Third parties	Collusion
Scoping of contract		DEL buyer		Buyer & suppliers
Favourable contract terms & conditions		DEL buyer		Buyer & suppliers
Changing evaluation criteira		DEL buyer		Buyer & suppliers
Changing contract terms & conditions		DEL buyer		Co accountant
False invoices and authorisations		DEL buyer	Suppliers	PL clerk
Inflated pricing		DEL buyer	Suppliers	
Paying fictitious or controlled suppliers		DEL buyer		PL clerk Co accountant

How these risks arise

Scoping of the contract:
Contract specifications are written so as to favour one particular buyer, e.g. by specifying very tight and specific attributes, which only one supplier's product can meet.

Favourable contract terms & conditions:
The terms of the contract are altered in order to either exclude other companies from tendering or to accommodate the requirements of the favoured supplier.

41

Changing evaluation criteria:
The original criteria for deciding who gets a contract are subsequently changed, i.e. after all the tendering has been done, must ensure that the favoured supplier gains the contract.

Changing contract terms and conditions:
After the contract has been awarded to the favoured supplier, the terms and conditions are altered in his favour.

False invoices or authorisations:
The favoured supplier colludes with the buyer to produce invoices for goods not supplied. This would probably require the collusion of the purchase ledger clerk.

Inflated pricing:
The favoured supplier increases the prices of goods supplied, and the buyer approves these artificially inflated prices.

Paying fictitious or controlled suppliers:
The buyer produces false invoices from a fictitious supplier or one controlled by himself.

42

Assessment of their scale in terms of likelihood of occurrence and potential damage to the business.

Area of Risk	Probability	Impact	Controls	Net likely impact	Action
Scoping of Contract	High	High	Low	High	Priority
Favourable contract Terms & conditions	High	High	Low	High	Priority
Changing evaluation Criteria	High	High	Low	High	Priority
Changing contract Terms & conditions	High	Medium	Low	Medium	Second Order priority
False invoices and authorisations	Medium	High	Low	Medium	Second Order priority
Inflated Pricing	High	High	Low	High	Priority
Paying fictitious or controlled suppliers	Low	High	Low	Medium	Second Order priority

The company should be very concerned by the high net impact on the business arising from several areas at risk. A common element of this is the low level of controls across every area of this part of the system. The only reason that probabilities can be considered low or medium in two areas is the need for collusion between two or more DEL employees.

43

Encouraging colleagues to report issues and resolving or referring these

Referring to the notes of the conversation from a confidential meeting between myself and Mohamed Singh (see Appendix 3) and to the further extracts (Chap. 5 pages 23 – 28) from CIMA's fraud risk management paper.

What preliminary investigations and checks, if any, I would personally undertake in this matter:

Mohamed Singh has provided *prima facie* evidence of fraud only, i.e. based on first impressions there appears to be fraud or malpractice in the purchases & supplier payment procedures. This is not the same as *substantiated* evidence, which would only be provided by undertaking investigations and checks.

Before taking any further action myself, or referring the matter to higher management, it would be appropriate to undertake at least some preliminary investigations, as at the moment the only "evidence" is Mohamed's verbal statement. Furthermore, he himself has not been prepared to proactively "whistleblow", but has only raised the issue as part of a scheduled systems review interview. Finally, in the finance director's absence (through hospitalisation) and with the company accountant's possible involvement in the suspected fraud I am really the only individual with the skills and knowledge to at least start preliminary investigations.

That said, my investigations should be severely restricted to the minimum level needed to provide at least some hard evidence. Essentially, this means checking the system only, and not for both legal and practical reasons (i.e. alerting the suspects) and not getting involved with interviewing any other members of staff.

Preliminary investigations and checks would therefore, be restricted to *unobtrusively* finding out as much as possible about Raymond Briggs Ltd.. This would include:

- Interrogating the computer system in order to obtain a full record of the transaction history between DEL and Briggs. Details of all purchase orders, goods received notes; invoices, credit/debit notes and payments should be obtained.

44

- Obtaining a full credit check and, if possible, annual report for Briggs. Amongst other things this would reveal who its directors are and where its registered office is.

- If possible, obtaining copies of all the tendering documentation involving Briggs. This includes contract specifications, contract terms and conditions, the criteria for awarding the contract to this particular supplier, any post-contract being awarded changes to the contract; any subsequent changes to the original contract prices etc.

Whether I myself have the authority and expertise to take the matter further or whether I need to refer it to someone else:

As the accounting systems technician it is questionable whether or not I should personally undertake preliminary investigations and checks, or whether I should immediately refer the matter to more senior management. On balance, I believe that the right course of action has been to undertake limited preliminary checks. Once this has been done, I believe that I have reached the limit of my authority and expertise, and assuming there is some hard evidence, I will now refer the matter to higher management. The overriding point is that I have restricted my investigations to the minimum that it is reasonable for me, in my position, to undertake. Full investigations, including interviewing staff are the responsibility of a formal investigation team, the composition of which will be determined by the directors.

The most appropriate person to refer the matter to:

Although William Whitelow is Mohamed's supervisor, he is also one of the three employees who are *prima facie* implicated in the potential fraud. It would, therefore, not be appropriate to refer the matter to him. The obvious person to refer the matter to is the finance director, Elaine Candler, or in her absence the matter should be referred to the managing director, Richard West.

45

<u>Review of methods of operating/updates to the system and resulting recommendations</u>

I would recommend to the board that the following control checks should be introduced over the purchases and supplier payments system:

For purchase orders:

- All requisition notes for purchases should be authorised by the appropriate departmental manager.
- All purchase orders should be authorised by the buyer or the appropriate manager, and approval limits should be formally set.
- Beyond a certain level of expenditure, significant orders, such as for capital expenditure should be approved by the board.
- All orders should be made on official letter-headed purchase orders, and should show the supplier's name, the specification of the goods/services ordered and the agreed price.
- Purchase orders should be in multipart set format, with copies being retained to provide both an audit trail and a means of resolving queries.
- Re-order levels should, wherever possible, be set in advance and entered on the requisition note.

For receipt of purchased goods:

- All goods should be delivered to a designated goods inwards centre only.
- On arrival at the designated centre goods should be inspected to ensure that they meet the specifications on the supplier's delivery note. Once the quantities and condition of the goods have been agreed, a Goods Received Note (GRN) should be raised and signed by the goods inwards supervisor.

46

- The GRN should then be matched up with the purchase order. At this stage the delivery note, the quantity and quality of the physical goods and the purchase order will have been checked against each other and agreed. Suppliers will then be notified of under or over-deliveries.
- GRN's should be pre-printed with sequential numbers, and periodically checked for completeness by someone other than a goods inwards employee.

47

Index

See overleaf for information on other
BPP products and how to order

AAT Order

To BPP Professional Education, Aldine Place, London W12 8AW
Tel: 020 8740 2211. Fax: 020 8740 1184
E-mail: Publishing@bpp.com Web:www.bpp.com

Mr/Mrs/Ms (Full name)

Daytime delivery address

Postcode

Daytime Tel E-mail

FOUNDATION (£14.95 except as indicated)	5/04 Texts	5/04 Kits	Special offer	8/04 Passcards	Success CDs
Units 1 & 2 Receipts and Payments	☐	☐		Foundation	
Unit 3 Ledger Balances and Initial Trial Balance	☐ (Combined Text & Kit)		Foundation Sage Bookeeping and Excel Spreadsheets CD-ROM free if ordering all Foundation Text and Kits, including Units 21 and 22/23 ☐	£6.95 ☐	£14.95 ☐
Unit 4 Supplying Information for Mgmt Control	☐ (Combined Text & Kit)				
Unit 21 Working with Computers (£9.95)	☐				
Unit 22/23 Healthy Workplace/Personal Effectiveness (£9.95)	☐				
Sage and Excel for Foundation (Workbook with CD-ROM £9.95)	☐				
INTERMEDIATE (£9.95 except as indicated)					
Unit 5 Financial Records and Accounts	☐	☐		£5.95 ☐	£14.95 ☐
Unit 6/7 Costs and Reports (Combined Text £14.95)	☐			£5.95 ☐	
Unit 6 Costs and Revenues		☐			£14.95 ☐
Unit 7 Reports and Returns		☐			
TECHNICIAN (£9.95 except as indicated)					
Unit 8/9 Core Managing Performance and Controlling Resources	☐	☐		£5.95 ☐	£14.95 ☐
Spreadsheets for Technician (Workbook with CD-ROM)	☐				
Unit 10 Core Managing Systems and People (£14.95)	☐ (Combined Text & Kit)		Spreadsheets for Technicians CD-ROM free if take Unit 8/9 Text and Kit ☐		
Unit 11 Option Financial Statements (A/c Practice)	☐	☐		£5.95 ☐	£14.95 ☐
Unit 12 Option Financial Statements (Central Govnmt)	☐	☐			
Unit 15 Option Cash Management and Credit Control	☐	☐		£5.95 ☐	
Unit 17 Option Implementing Audit Procedures	☐	☐		£5.95 ☐	
Unit 18 Option Business Tax FA04 (8/04) (£14.95)	☐ (Combined Text & Kit)			£5.95 ☐	
Unit 19 Option Personal Tax FA04 (8/04) (£14.95)	☐ (Combined Text & Kit)			£5.95 ☐	
TECHNICIAN 2003 (£9.95)					
Unit 18 Option Business Tax FA03 (8/03 Text & Kit)	☐	☐			
Unit 19 Option Personal Tax FA03 (8/03 Text & Kit)	☐	☐			
SUBTOTAL	£	£	£	£	£

TOTAL FOR PRODUCTS £

POSTAGE & PACKING

Texts/Kits	First	Each extra	
UK	£3.00	£3.00	£
Europe*	£6.00	£4.00	£
Rest of world	£20.00	£10.00	£
Passcards			
UK	£2.00	£1.00	£
Europe*	£3.00	£2.00	£
Rest of world	£8.00	£8.00	£
Success CDs			
UK	£2.00	£1.00	£
Europe*	£3.00	£2.00	£
Rest of world	£8.00	£8.00	£

TOTAL FOR POSTAGE & PACKING £

(Max £12 Texts/Kits/Passcards - deliveries in UK)

Grand Total (Cheques to *BPP Professional Education*)

I enclose a cheque for (incl. Postage) £

Or charge to Access/Visa/Switch

Card Number CV2 No last 3 digits on signature strip

Expiry date Start Date

Issue Number (Switch Only)

Signature

We aim to deliver to all UK addresses inside 5 working days; a signature will be required. Orders to all EU addresses should be delivered within 6 working days. All other orders to overseas addresses should be delivered within 8 working days. * Europe includes the Republic of Ireland and the Channel Islands.

See overleaf for information on other
BPP products and how to order

AAT Order

To BPP Professional Education, Aldine Place, London W12 8AW
Tel: 020 8740 2211. Fax: 020 8740 1184
E-mail: Publishing@bpp.com Web:www.bpp.com

Mr/Mrs/Ms (Full name) ____

Daytime delivery address ____

Postcode ____

Daytime Tel ____ E-mail ____

OTHER MATERIAL FOR AAT STUDENTS	8/04 Texts	3/03 Text	3/04 Text
FOUNDATION (£5.95)			
Basic Maths and English	☐		
INTERMEDIATE (£5.95)			
Basic Bookkeeping (for students exempt from Foundation)	☐		
FOR ALL STUDENTS (£5.95)			
Building Your Portfolio (old standards)		☐	
Building Your Portfolio (new standards)	☐		
Basic Costing			☐

AAT PAYROLL	Finance Act 2004 8/04 December 2004 and June 2005 assessments	Special offer Take Text and Kit together	Finance Act 2003 9/03 June 2004 exams only	Special offer Take Text and Kit together
LEVEL 2 Text (£29.95)	☐	£44.95 ☐	☐	£44.95 ☐
LEVEL 2 Kit (£19.95)	☐		☐	
	For assessments in 2005		For assessments in 2004	
LEVEL 3 Text (£29.95)	☐	£44.95 ☐	☐	£44.95 ☐
LEVEL 3 Kit (£19.95)	☐		☐	
SUBTOTAL	£	£	£	£

TOTAL FOR PRODUCTS £

POSTAGE & PACKING

	First	Each extra	
Texts/Kits			
UK	£3.00	£3.00	£
Europe*	£6.00	£4.00	£
Rest of world	£20.00	£10.00	£
Passcards			
UK	£2.00	£1.00	£
Europe*	£3.00	£2.00	£
Rest of world	£8.00	£8.00	£
Tapes			
UK	£2.00	£1.00	£
Europe*	£3.00	£2.00	£
Rest of world	£8.00	£8.00	£

TOTAL FOR POSTAGE & PACKING £

(Max £12 Texts/Kits/Passcards - deliveries in UK)

Grand Total (Cheques to *BPP Professional Education*)

I enclose a cheque for (incl. Postage) £

Or charge to Access/Visa/Switch

Card Number ____ CV2 No ____ last 3 digits on signature strip

Expiry date ____ Start Date ____

Issue Number (Switch Only) ____

Signature ____

We aim to deliver to all UK addresses inside 5 working days; a signature will be required. Orders to all EU addresses should be delivered within 6 working days. All other orders to overseas addresses should be delivered within 8 working days. * Europe includes the Republic of Ireland and the Channel Islands.

Review Form & Free Prize Draw – Unit 10 Managing People and Systems(5/04)

All original review forms from the entire BPP range, completed with genuine comments, will be entered into one of two draws on 31 January 2005 and 31 July 2005. The names on the first four forms picked out on each occasion will be sent a cheque for £50.

Name: ______________________ **Address:** ______________________

____

____

How have you used this Interactive Text?
(Tick one box only)

☐ Home study (book only)

☐ On a course: college ______________________

☐ With 'correspondence' package

☐ Other ______________________

Why did you decide to purchase this Interactive Text? *(Tick one box only)*

☐ Have used BPP Texts in the past

☐ Recommendation by friend/colleague

☐ Recommendation by a lecturer at college

☐ Saw advertising

☐ Other ______________________

During the past six months do you recall seeing/receiving any of the following?
(Tick as many boxes as are relevant)

☐ Our advertisement in *Accounting Technician* magazine

☐ Our advertisement in *Pass*

☐ Our brochure with a letter through the post

Which (if any) aspects of our advertising do you find useful?
(Tick as many boxes as are relevant)

☐ Prices and publication dates of new editions

☐ Information on Interactive Text content

☐ Facility to order books off-the-page

☐ None of the above

Your ratings, comments and suggestions would be appreciated on the following areas

	Very useful	*Useful*	*Not useful*
Introduction	☐	☐	☐
Chapter contents lists	☐	☐	☐
Examples	☐	☐	☐
Activities and answers	☐	☐	☐
Key learning points	☐	☐	☐
Quick quizzes and answers	☐	☐	☐
Activity checklist	☐	☐	☐
Practice activities	☐	☐	☐
Full skills based assessments	☐	☐	☐
Full exam based assessments	☐	☐	☐
Lecturers' Resource Section			

Review Form & Free Prize Draw (continued)

	Excellent	*Good*	*Adequate*	*Poor*
Overall opinion of this Text	☐	☐	☐	☐

Do you intend to continue using BPP Interactive Texts/Assessment Kits? ☐ Yes ☐ No

The BPP author of this edition can be e-mailed at: janiceross@bpp.com

Please return this form to: Janice Ross, BPP Professional Education, FREEPOST, London, W12 8BR

Please note any further comments and suggestions/errors below

Free Prize Draw Rules

1 Closing date for 31 January 2005 draw is 31 December 2004. Closing date for 31 July 2005 draw is 30 JunOe 2005.

2 Restricted to entries with UK and Eire addresses only. BPP employees, their families and business associates are excluded.

3 No purchase necessary. Entry forms are available upon request from BPP Professional Education. No more than one entry per title, per person. Draw restricted to persons aged 16 and over.

4 Winners will be notified by post and receive their cheques not later than 6 weeks after the relevant draw date.

5 The decision of the promoter in all matters is final and binding. No correspondence will be entered into.